George Grove, Music and Victorian Culture

Also by Michael Musgrave

THE MUSIC OF BRAHMS

THE MUSICAL LIFE OF THE CRYSTAL PALACE

BRAHMS: A German Requiem

THE CAMBRIDGE COMPANION TO BRAHMS

A BRAHMS READER

George Grove, Music and Victorian Culture

Edited by

Michael Musgrave
Emeritus Professor of Music, Goldsmiths College, University of London and Visiting Research Fellow, Royal College of Music

palgrave
macmillan

Published by
PALGRAVE MACMILLAN
Houndmills, Basingstoke, Hampshire RG21 6XS and
175 Fifth Avenue, New York, N. Y. 10010
Companies and representatives throughout the world

PALGRAVE MACMILLAN is the global academic imprint of the Palgrave Macmillan division of St. Martin's Press, LLC and of Palgrave Macmillan Ltd. Macmillan® is a registered trademark in the United States, United Kingdom and other countries. Palgrave is a registered trademark in the European Union and other countries.

ISBN-13: 978–0–333–94804–0

This book is printed on paper suitable for recycling and made from fully managed and sustained forest sources.

A catalogue record for this book is available from the British Library.

Library of Congress Catalog Card Number: 2002028745

Contents

List of Plates

Preface and Acknowledgements

Perspectives change. At his death, George Grove (1820–1900) was a major public figure in the arts, but his achievements have long since been absorbed into the growing momentum of musical study: now he is known to the larger public only as founder of the *Dictionary of Music and Musicians*, where few of his numerous original entries remain. But with the inevitable reaction against the Victorian era now well past, the centenary of his death provided an appropriate moment to re-examine the scope of Grove's achievement, and not least the interconnection of its many strands: and to get closer to a complex and passionate man, who interacted particularly fruitfully with the world of his time.

The four parts of this book are built around the chronological pattern of Grove's life. The first is an introduction to its defining periods and themes, to his personality and drives, and contains illustrations of the scope of his life through extracts from his writings in different fields. The second presents him as a scholar, beginning with a crucial training in biblical research, then turning to the foundations of his expertise and special skills in musical research and criticism, and concluding with a view of the programme notes with which he is so widely associated, within the broader history of this emerging genre. Grove's life as editor at Macmillan is the subject of the third part; first, his all-embracing work as editor of *Macmillan's Magazine*, then the birth and completion of the *Dictionary of Music and Musicians* that grew from this connection – again with attention to its larger historical setting. Grove's work at the Royal College of Music is the topic of the fourth part: his role in creating it, not least the ever-present political dimension; his life as Director, with its daily practical challenges; and his legacy of documents and books to the institution he loved so much.

This book originated in the conference 'Grove's World' held at the Royal College of Music on 25 June 2000 to celebrate Grove's achievement and bring forward new research as the culmination of a month of activity, which included a centenary concert at the College on 25 May, and exhibitions mounted by the Department of Portraits and Performance History and the library of the College, and by Dr John Handford of Macmillan's Reference Division. The event could not have taken place without the help of many people. Thus thanks are due in the first place to the present Director, Dame Janet Ritterman, for making the resources of the College available, and for her constant support as well as participation; to Dr Paul Banks, Research Development Fellow at the RCM, who chaired the day's proceedings and, with Dr Peter Horton, led a large organizing team over many months; and to Ian Jacobs, then Head of the Reference Division at Macmillan, for making available financial support. The day concluded with a spirited Round Table 'Grove Today', and many thanks are due to its participants, beginning with the chairman, Dr Stanley Sadie, pioneering editor of *The New Grove* of 1980, and of its successor *The New Grove II*, Professor John Tyrrell, of the University of Wales at Cardiff, and Professor Simon McVeigh of Goldsmiths College, University of London.

I have to thank all my colleagues for their patience and helpful suggestions in the preparation of this book. The resources of the Royal College were of course central, and I thank the staff of the library, especially Celia Clarke and Peter Horton, for responding to endless queries and availing me of their expert knowledge of Grove materials; and likewise to Paul Collen and Oliver Davies of the Department of Portraits for their help with illustrations. A special word of thanks is due to Rosemary VanArsdel, Leanne Langley and David Wright for much helpful advice; at Macmillan Reference Division, now Palgrave Macmillan, my thanks are again due to Ian Jacobs for his support and interest at the outset in setting the project on a firm footing, and to Josie Dixon, then of Palgrave Macmillan for seeing it through to completion. Finally, I must express particular appreciation on behalf of myself and my contributors to Janey Fisher for her most sympathetic and painstaking editing of our text.

Kind acknowledgement is made to the following institutions and individuals for use of their resources and assistance: the John Murray Archive, and Mrs Virginia Murray, archivist; the Athenaeum and Sarah Dodgson, archivist; the Royal Society and Nicola Gray, librarian; the Royal Geographical Society, and Sarah Strong, archivist; the British Library and Elizabeth James; the Palestine Exploration Fund, Hynde Mews, London and its staff; the archive of the Commissioners for the Exhibition of 1851, and Valerie Phillips, archivist: Harry Scherman Library, Mannes College of Music, New York; Bobst Library of New York University; the New York Public Library at 42nd St and the Research Division; the Royal College of Music Library; the University of London Library; the Library of Congress, Washington DC; Professor Andrew D. Roberts; Professor Brian Trowell; Dr Stanley Sadie; Dr Michael Struck and Professor Cyril Ehrlich; Liza Musgrave.

Permission is acknowledged from the following libraries to reproduce materials in their collections: the Royal College of Music; the National Library of Wales; the Guildhall Library, Corporation of London; the RIBA Library Drawings Collection; the John Murray Archive; the Athenaeum. Any research on Grove must draw extensively on the work of Charles Larcom Graves, Grove's close friend and biographer (*The Life & Letters of Sir George Grove C.B.*, London, 1903), and also the biographer of his successor as Director of the College, C.H.H. Parry, and close colleague Alexander Macmillan. However, many of the sources Graves cites are no longer to be found. Every effort has been made to substantiate his facts through other sources, though this is often not possible: work in cataloguing the major collection of Grove materials at the Royal College still continues. Other collections, chiefly at the British Library, have been drawn on and are referred to as appropriate. Of modern work, Percy M. Young's *George Grove 1820–1900. A Biography* (London, 1980) put Grove's personal life and times as well as his achievements into much sharper psychological and cultural focus, drawing on many unpublished letters at the Royal College. This book is indebted to Dr Young's research and insights far beyond the pages in which his work is actually cited.

Michael Musgrave
New York

Notes on Contributors

Christina Bashford was Managing Editor of *The New Grove Dictionary of Opera* (1992) before taking up her current teaching post in the Music Department at Oxford Brookes University. She has written on the social history of chamber music, and on several aspects of nineteenth-century British concert life, including informed listening practices and aspects of musical reception. With Leanne Langley she edited *Music and British Culture, 1785–1914: Essays in Honour of Cyril Ehrlich* (2000). Christina is a contributor to *The New Grove Dictionary of Music and Musicians*, 2nd edn (2000) (hereinafter *New Grove II)*, and since 1997 has co-ordinated the Concert Life in Nineteenth-Century London Database, an inter-university research project.

Celia Clarke was for some years an assistant in various departments of the Royal College of Music. After retiring she has continued to work on the catalogue of the Library's holdings of Sir George Grove's letters and is currently also engaged on other aspects of Grove research.

Peter Horton read music at Magdalen College, Oxford, before embarking on a study of the music of Samuel Sebastian Wesley (D. Phil. 1983). His research has since centred on Wesley and includes an edition of his complete anthems for *Musica Britannica*, contributions to *Nineteenth-Century British Music Studies*, vols I & II and a recently completed book on Wesley's life and music. Other areas of interest include mid-nineteenth-century English song and stylistic links between English and continental composers of the same period. Since 1984 he has been on the staff of the Royal College of Music, latterly as Reference Librarian and Research Co-ordinator.

Leanne Langley is on the research staff of Goldsmiths College, University of London. With Simon McVeigh and Cyril Ehrlich she is currently studying London concert life from 1880 to 1914. She has taught music at the University of Notre Dame and the University of Southampton, and has written widely on the musical press, criticism and lexicography in Britain. Recently she co-edited *Music and British Culture, 1785–1914: Essays in Honour of Cyril Ehrlich*, with Christina Bashford. From 1984 to 1992 she worked in the Grove office, latterly as senior consulting editor of *The New Grove Dictionary of Opera*. She was also an advisory editor for *New Grove II*.

Michael Musgrave is Emeritus Professor of Music at Goldsmiths College, University of London, and lives in New York City. Originally trained as pianist and organist at the Royal College of Music, of which he is Visiting

Research Fellow, the focus of his scholarly work is German and English music of the nineteenth century, on which he has written, lectured and broadcast widely. His study *The Musical Life of the Crystal Palace* was published in 1995. Recent books on Brahms include *The Cambridge Companion to Brahms* (1997) and *A Brahms Reader* (2000). He is editing the Brahms Serenades, opp. 11 and 16, for the new Johannes Brahms *Gesamtausgabe*, and writing a biography of Schumann in the Cambridge Musical Lives series.

Janet Ritterman has been Director of the Royal College of Music in London since 1993 and received the damehood in 2002. She has worked as pianist and accompanist, and has specialized in the education and training of gifted musicians. Her research interests relate principally to European concert life, in particular the contribution of pianists; to the development of the conservatoire in the nineteenth and twentieth centuries, and to issues connected with instrumental pedagogy and historical performance practice. She is Chairman of the Federation of British Conservatoires, of the Advisory Board of Arts Research Ltd, and of the ABRSM Publishing Company, and a board member of English National Opera. She has contributed chapters to a monograph of Clara Schumann, published in 1996, and to *The Cambridge Companion to Chopin* (1992), and has given papers on learning, teaching and musical performance at national and international conferences.

Rosemary T. VanArsdel, Distinguished Professor of English, Emerita, University of Puget Sound, has most recently published *Florence Fenwick Miller: Victorian Feminist, Journalist, and Educator* (2001). She is co-editor, with J. Don Vann, of *Victorian Periodicals: a Guide to Research*, vols. I and II (1978, 1989); *Victorian Periodicals and Victorian Society* (1994); and *Periodicals of Queen Victoria's Empire* (1996). She is co-editor, with Gordon S. Haight, of *George Eliot: a Centenary Tribute* (1982). A founding member and past president (1981–83) of the Research Society for Victorian Periodicals, she served on the editorial boards of *The Wellesley Index to Victorian Periodicals, 1824–1900* (5 vols, 1966–89) and the *Union List of Victorian Serials in North American Libraries* (1985). She is the author of numerous articles on Victorian and Edwardian studies in scholarly journals in North America and the United Kingdom, and is a member of the editorial board of *Victorian Review*.

David Wright taught at Trinity College Music and Goldsmiths College, University of London. Followed by a period as Academic Registrar at Trinity, he moved to the Royal College of Music, where for four years he was Head of Postgraduate Programmes. He is currently engaged in a full-length study of concert life in London since the Second World War, on which subject he has contributed to *The New Grove II*. He has written a short history of Faber Music and many articles on twentieth-century music and composers for the *Listener*, the *Musical Times*, *Tempo* and *New Grove II*.

Percy M. Young is Honorary Senior Research Fellow in the Department of Music of Birmingham University. After a career in music education, he devoted himself to writing on music, musicological research, composition, and a range of other interests, and has lectured in many universities in Britain, Europe and the USA. His many community interests have included serving as a Woverhampton City Councillor and acting as the official historian of the Wolverhampton Wanderers Football Club. A prolific author whose first book appeared in 1939, Percy Young's work in English music has included studies of Handel, Elgar, including editions of his letters and writings, of Elgar's wife, Alice, of Ralph Vaughan Williams and Arthur Sullivan. He has a special interest in George Grove, having written his biography in 1980 and contributed the entries on the founder in *The New Grove* and *The New Grove II*.

Part 1

Grove's World

1
Themes of a Lifetime: the Many Interests of a Great Victorian

Michael Musgrave

Perspective

No one figure in later-nineteenth-century Britain is as worthy of the title Great Victorian of Music as Sir George Grove (1820–1900). He satisfied every criterion normally attributed to the age's outstanding figures: a wide range of interests and zest and energy in pursuing them; a devotion to great projects with a high sense of purpose and optimism; an assumed sense of the progress implicit in what he did, and the belief in a better future through education and self-improvement (as well as another side, where earnestness easily turned to melancholy, and even illness). Grove's wide achievements in music came not in spite of his lack of a professional career in the field, but essentially because of it. His life coincides with the great development of concert life in England, which gathered particular momentum in the 1850s, when he was entering his first mature professional years in London, and which had become totally transformed by the time of his death at the beginning of the new century. By comparison with the other arts with which it would today be naturally compared, for example, painting and sculpture, the status of public instrumental music in Grove's youth was low, and performance standards were often poor: most high-quality performances took place in private homes: the German orchestral repertory, soon to be the backbone of the emerging concert culture, was little known, because the world of musically well-educated individuals and thus audiences was small. Public status in music was attached to fashionable opera attended by the rich, or by oratorio attended by the affluent middle class. The steady emergence of great concert music to its later central position in musical performance is one of the most striking features of the period covered by Grove's life.[1]

Grove was a major figure in the communication of the new information that accompanied this change. But it is doubtful that he could have achieved what he did from inside the musical profession only. It was his capacity to influence events on the larger public stage that gave him his importance, and this arose from his wide experience in other disciplines and activities, his numerous contacts and access: no performing musician exerted comparable influence in this field. When Grove was elected to the Athenaeum – a club of artists and intellectuals – his *Dictionary of Music and Musicians* was yet to be produced and his musical notes for the Crystal Palace concerts were of peripheral interest to the men who were his peers: rather he was known as the Secretary of the Society of Arts (from 1908 the Royal Society), the Crystal Palace and, especially, as a biblical scholar and founder of the Palestine Exploration Fund: it was this background that counted. Thus the particular themes of Grove's life and circumstances are of immediate interest in surveying the expansion of musical culture within the larger public setting. They show how new initiatives came about. But Grove had remarkable gifts, which emerge in the following pages. As well as the Victorian professional virtues, he had personal qualities which identified him, and without which he would not have achieved what he did: kindness, genuine modesty, immense social skills partly springing from a real interest in people and their work. Grove had four phases of professional activity; as engineer, as institutional secretary, as editor, and as institutional director. That on which his fame chiefly rests, the *Dictionary*, was undertaken in a part-time capacity alongside other full-time editorial responsibilities. This chapter pursues the themes and connections through the four periods: youth and professional training, 1820–50 (to age 30); the secretarial phase at the Society of Arts and Crystal Palace, 1850–52, and 1852–73 respectively, to age 53; the editorial phase at Macmillan, from 1874–83, to age 62 (which overlaps with part-time advisory work for Macmillan and editorship of *Macmillan's Magazine* from 1868); finally, directorship of the RCM, 1882–94, and retirement, up to his death in the first year of the new century, 1894–1900.

Youth, education and a career in engineering, 1820–50

Considering that he was destined to play such a large role in the world of letters, Grove's choice of a career in engineering might at first seem unusual to the modern reader, not least by comparison with his contemporaries. His closest school – and lifelong – friend, George Granville Bradley, later Dean of Westminster, was educated at Oxford, as was a close fellow-spirit of later years, the critic, poet and educationalist Matthew Arnold, and such close friends as the Christian Socialist F.D. Maurice and Bradley's predecessor Dean A.P. Stanley. One can often sense that Grove would have preferred a university education, and especially one at Oxford. He speaks of himself and his younger brother Edmund as being sent from school 'too soon into the world' (at 15); and, though gratified with his honorary doctorate from Durham University in 1875, commented 'I wish it had been from Oxford'. He speaks of not being at Oxford during the 'great years of 1840–45...alas' (a reference to the high period of the Oxford Movement) when he might still have been a student from the age of 20.[2]

There are several indications why Grove did not follow this path. He is not recorded as being first-class academically at school: his younger brother Edmund did better. Equally, however, in light of his subsequent professional successes, it seems unlikely that he was ever really intellectually second-class (though a certain intellectual self-disparagement lingered on); rather, he seems a late developer, or someone preoccupied with his own thoughts and passions. One thing is certain: he was greatly influenced by the character of the teaching he received at school, which presented a career in technology as a very viable alternative to a higher education at the ancient universities since the (as yet) unreformed curriculum did not offer science. And the larger world itself now offered much more to someone with a practical and scientific bent (he was later described as a thoroughly 'modern' man) and may have made entry into the exciting and potentially lucrative world of science applied through engineering and industry more attractive to his parents and headmaster. Self-made men were an emerging breed.[3]

Grove's education took on a new significance in 1834 when, aged 14, he became a pupil at Clapham Grammar School under Charles Pritchard as headmaster. He had previously attended two other schools: as a weekly boarder from age 8 in 1828 at Elwell's School on Clapham Common, first run by one Mr Greaves; and then from 1832 as a pupil at Stockwell school, where Pritchard had previously taught; Pritchard had moved with the support of many parents to establish the new, progressive proprietorial school at Clapham. As the first head of Clapham Grammar School from 1834–62, he provided an exceptional education for his pupils. It offered a classical foundation but using new methods, plus science, which was not yet taught at public schools, which still focused on the classics. Grove was greatly impressed when he became one of 65 boys in the first intake of the new school. 'I had been at two other schools which were considered good in their class but with Pritchard the atmosphere was very different'. Grove especially enjoyed and excelled in the copying of maps of Palestine, and in the describing of imaginary travels, as well as the study of elementary science. Pritchard claimed that 'the main intention of early education should be the development of the habit of thinking, and the exhibition of the right mode of setting about it'; and in addition he insisted on the necessity of providing 'resources for the leisure hours of maturer life'. . . In translating from Latin and Greek, as Grove remembered, he urged his pupils to 'render the passages as well as construe them, and thus we felt that that they were about real transactions and people and reflected the same emotions as our own literature'. Grove wrote of Pritchard

> the master was younger and more sympathetic and full of wider knowledge than I had before dreamed of; also he had a great power of explanation and illustration and took constant interest in his boys. One or two things I had not met with before. They made a great impression on me. First the mathematics and the natural philosophy. These were taught in a practical and interesting way, and as connected with common life – not with the abstract world – which made them, always fresh. Some of his precepts and examples recur to me almost daily.'[4]

But Grove's stay at the school was to be short. By the end of 1835, aged 15½, 'already well grounded in the rudiments of science, natural history, and geography, with a fair knowledge of Latin and something more than a smattering of Greek', Grove was removed from Clapham and articled in January 1836 to Alexander Gordon, a civil engineer whose premises were at 22 Fluyder St, off Whitehall. Young observes that the fact that Grove was dispatched into technology shows the distinction between education at a proprietary school of progressive character and a public school. It seems that Pritchard's family connections with engineering may have been decisive and thus the school gave him an advantage. Grove walked the three miles to work. Gordon had worked for Thomas Telford, and was an expert on optical apparatus and transport, responsible in 1838 for the establishment of the Polytechnic Institution in London. So Grove found himself 'where the action was' in the modern world; in the building and design of railways, bridges and ships. Over the next three years many interesting perspectives opened to him, including a visit to Belgium with Gordon as the latter was negotiating a railway contract. Grove became a graduate of the Institute of Civil Engineers on 26 February 1839. Though his graduation certificate gives no details of his technical attainments, other than that he has satisfactory completed a course of study, Gordon's specialities indicate the technologies with which he would have been involved.[5]

Gordon represented the Glasgow-born engineer Robert Napier. Grove was seconded to him for two years at his Glasgow factory on the Broomielaw. Napier was the best engineer on the Clyde and one of the best in the world, building steamships to sail to the New World. It was a new world also for Grove, who later stressed how he got his hands dirty and had to rinse them before he read his papers and books in the evening. He worked in the pattern and fitting shops 'like a common mechanic', from which experience he later advised young people to be prepared to start at the bottom of any profession. On completion of his articles, his contract with Gordon took him further afield. Gordon was an authority on lighthouse design and construction, a vital technology in the fast-developing world of sea transport. Grove was sent to Jamaica in 1841 for the construction of the Morant Point lighthouse, a cast-iron structure which, built in parts in London, had to be erected on site with Grove as clerk of works and two labouring engineers who had attended the construction in London. As well as ensuring that the work was done on time and efficiently, Grove's main task was overseeing the itinerant workers. Almost immediately after returning to England towards the end of 1843, he was sent on a similar assignment, to oversee the building of the lighthouse at Gibbs Hill, Hamilton, Bermuda. Gordon had been called upon to advise on a project that had become controversial through bad planning and overspending. This was to last for almost three years until 1846. Grove had to deal not only with a labour force that had been conscripted mainly from able-bodied convicts on the island, but also from interference from the military, who had sent a lieutenant to act with Grove – Gordon having written a report indicating that the work was badly behind schedule, and should have taken only 12 months.[6]

On his return, Grove was drawn into the world of railways through his brother, now working for C.H. Wild, principal assistant to Robert Stephenson, 'especially entrusted with the laying out of stations' on the London and North Western Railway project. Grove now joined Stephenson's staff, working on a major new General Station at Chester.

> I was resident Engineer of the great station, and worked (as I have always done) like a tiger. That was in the year 1847–8. What an age ago, it's almost like looking back to the world before the flood. It was a warming time of my life – I was very good and religious. I had already done much in Jamaica and Bermuda – but that was nothing to what was to come after.

In the short term, the Chester work led directly to the construction of the Britannia Bridge over the Menai Straits at Bangor, another Stephenson project, initially completed in June 1849. Grove's position was that of assistant site engineer. As he later pointed out, he had a modest position in a major project. But he was obviously successful, because in September 1848, during the course of the project, Wild paid for his expenses for a trip to France with his brother Edmund.[7]

There was no music in any of these engineering jobs. But music had been an accompaniment to Grove's life since childhood (see Chapter 5). He recalled the musical side of his life in his 1880 address:

> I was articled to an engineer in London, even then I was fond of music and used to haunt every place where I could hear it or look at it and one of those places was Novello's music shop in Dean St, Soho, where, in a back room, there was a fine large case full of scores...The choir of [Westminster] Abbey was not in those days what it is now, but many an entrancing hour have I spent there in the winter months at afternoon service, with the dim candles below and the impenetrable gloom above, when I thought my heart must have come out of me with emotion and

> longing. I used to copy music in the British Museum with my friend William Pickering Stevens, and we sometimes finished the afternoon together at the Abbey.

Even when abroad, he took music and books with him, for use especially when he had time on his hands. In Chester, he became well known to the cathedral organist (as in Bangor) and introduced some little-known vocal music, including motets by Palestrina, to a singing class started by the organist.[8]

The Secretary 1850–73

Grove was not cut out to be an engineer for life. Though he had achieved much and he retained a wide interest in engineering projects, he had too many other interests to want to pursue engineering as a career. What would get him to where he wanted to go – a field more conducive to his skills and enthusiasms? He had clearly impressed his seniors on the Britannia Bridge project: he had played his part and written good reports. His modesty comes as he describes how it all happened.

> Looking back over the scattered course of my life, London, Scotland, West Indies, North Wales, London, again, the Society of Arts, the Crystal Palace, the Palestine Exploration Fund, it is curious now to see how many of the points in it have been determined by my friends. My whole London life and all that came out of it is due to three of them, now gone – Mr Robert Stephenson, Mr Brunel, Sir Charles Barry. I was then in 1848 in a subordinate engineering post, in Mr Edwin Clark's staff, on the Britannia Bridge, with no confidence in myself, and little chance of getting on. They used now and then to come down to watch the operations of the bridge, and these distinguished men used to notice me, and were as good as gold to me. They counselled me to go to London, and (there is no treason in saying so now) they forced me into the secretaryship of the Society of Arts, just then vacated by Mr Scott Russell.[9]

The Society of Arts and Crystal Palace positions were based on recognition of Grove's administrative skills, range of sympathies, grasp of issues, and capacity to deal with people. The new position simply increased the demands made on him in executing the directors' instructions, reporting, advising and interacting with people in a much more complex and many-sided environment. Grove was appointed probationary Secretary to the Society of Arts in February 1850 and succeeded John Scott Russell (who had been Secretary since 1846) as full Secretary in March. The position opened up new worlds of ideas and contacts. The energetic Henry Cole, now chairman of the

Society, had much work for the Secretary, and Grove became involved in leading public issues, such as how to set up enquiries into topics like the manufacture and supply of coal gas, the supply of water to London, the manufacture of sugar in the British colonies and the adulteration of food. Following Cole's commitment to free education, in 1852 the Society proposed to review the working of the Museums and Free Libraries Act as part of a serious attempt to lay the foundations for a broadly based adult and polytechnical educational provision, building on the Mechanics' Institutes and other such institutions; the organizing of lectures was essential to all these fields.[10]

Not least, Grove found himself involved in planning what was to be the biggest public event in history up to that time, the Great Exhibition of the Works of Industry of all Nations, which, following on earlier exhibitions, was planned to showcase modern design, with Britain at its centre and as its sponsor. It was chaired by Prince Albert with Henry Cole as Secretary, who was the driving force. In the Exhibition Grove records that his main role was to deal with ticket sales, which were made from the Society of Arts' house in the Adelphi, where Grove lived, and this is confirmed in the records. Over the period 20 February to 9 May, there is a series of letters concerning methods of entry, sale of tickets, and especially the arrangements regarding season tickets. But there were also issues concerning the problems of the exhibitors, including, for example, a long correspondence concerning the appointment of an arbitrator and legal costs relating to a contract.[11]

The Great Exhibition and the extraordinary building in which it was housed (Plate 7) did not need to have professional consequence for Grove. There had been great opposition to the location of the building, as well as to its modernistic character, and it was to be dismantled by law after the six months of the exhibition May–September 1851. Grove should have returned to his Society of Arts business. But the designer, Joseph Paxton, had created the Crystal Palace Company – grasping the popular name for the building – and raised money to rebuild on an impressive hill site at Penge Place, Sydenham, South London: the prefabricated structure had merely to be extended. Thus a job suddenly became available. Grove recalls:

> the Society of Arts originated the Great Exhibition of 1851 and from that naturally sprang the Crystal Palace. There again, two friends whom I made at the Society, Mr [Francis] Fuller [land agent] Mr Scott Russell, and I am glad to mention them, stepped in and gave me the secretaryship of the Crystal Palace in 1852.

In contrast to the Hyde Park Palace, the Crystal Palace at Sydenham was not a trade or industrial fair, but a permanent exhibition for leisured culture (Plate 8). The building was significantly bigger and less elegant than the Hyde Park structure; one-third of a mile long, of several storeys, with a huge nave the full length of the building flanked with courts, each illustrating a different period of history from ancient to modern, taken over and extended from the Hyde Park concept and with the addition of a Shakespeare house, a reading room, a chess room, and later a school of art and science, as well as constant visiting exhibits. Additionally, the new Palace had extensive grounds and wonderful gardens and fountains modelled on those of Versailles. The first heads of departments included such experts in their fields as the Middle Eastern scholars James Fergusson and Austin Layard, the illustrator George Scharf, and the architect Francis Penrose.[12]

The Crystal Palace became a focus for the major public issues of the day, a natural location for large meetings and public events. Grove in turn became even more of a focal figure there than in the less exposed position of a Society secretary, though dealing with many of the same issues. Two areas had most impact on him in light of his interests: social issues, especially the wider provision of schooling; and a host of religious issues bearing largely on the impact of science and of religious reforming movements on the Church of England. The promotion of educational issues became particularly associated with the group known as the Christian Socialists, of which the leading figures were Frederick Denison Maurice and Charles Kingsley. Grove's interest had first been aroused by a pamphlet sent to him whilst still in Jamaica. On settling in London he became closely associated with them for a while, first with Septimus Hansard, a curate in Marylebone (later rector of Bethnal Green), then with J.M. Ludlow, F.J. Furnivall and Thomas Hughes (also a Director of the Crystal Palace). Kingsley, vicar of a parish in Hampshire, was not as closely associated with the London circle. Grove was especially attracted to Maurice's wide outlook, personal culture and warmth, and was to name his first son after him. Maurice (1805–72) was a liberal-minded churchman who had been appointed Professor of English Literature at King's College, London, in 1840, and who focused his social commitment on the education of the working class. In 1853 he founded the first women's college in London, Queen's College, Harley St. But in 1853 he was dismissed from King's College for his socialist convictions. He then founded the Working Men's College in Red Lion Square in 1854 and became its principal; later he was appointed Professor of Moral Philosophy at Cambridge. Maurice's extensive writings influenced events, such as the removal of sanctions against the admission of dissenters to Oxford and Cambridge in 1854/1856. Grove had opposed Maurice's dismissal from King's; and Maurice supported Grove when the vexed issue of Sabbath Observance impinged directly upon Grove as Secretary of the Crystal Palace, since he supported the financial necessity of Sunday opening (the prohibition against which crucially affected the Palace's economics). Grove had been interested in the Mechanics' Institutes: Thomas Carlyle noted his support in replying to him in 1852 that 'surely if you can do anything to resuscitate the decayed vigour of the

Mechanics' Institutes it will be well done'. But Grove did not retain his interest. Ludlow later recalled that, though he gave a lecture on 'mechanical principles in common things', which he thought very good, 'for professional reasons he never became fully involved'. Grove seems never to have been politically involved: he could never get beyond a certain point in radical thought and reform, and as he got older, he retreated from the principles of liberalism. In general he opposed Gladstone, Irish Home Rule, and the Reform Bill of 1867. He was wary of extending the franchise and seems to have opposed female suffrage, all of which were sensed as a threat to the established order he increasingly treasured, though informally his views were more flexible.[13]

Grove's abiding interest in the Bible and the religion of the Church of England naturally came to the fore in this environment: the huge impact of social, economic and philosophical issues on the traditions and reform of the state church; the growth of nonconformity; and later the claims of Darwin and their implications. As a young man Grove had been attracted to the Oxford Movement and the ritualism of the High Church movement. But his new life in London subjected him to a much wider range of influences. On settling in Sydenham and as a committed member of the Church of England, he became an intimate member of the church community, his home the focus for socializing. The young curate of the parish church, St Bartholomew's, Sydenham, recalls the hospitality of Grove's house:

> there were distinguished people of all kinds, travellers connected with the Palestine Exploration, a musician or two, and friends who had come to dine after the afternoon's concert at the Crystal Palace. Everyone seemed to be cheerful and happy. There was no pretence about anything; no starch or stiffness. After dinner we all went out into the garden. We talked and smoked and had tea. There were endless stories and endless jokes, Sir George taking the lead, but just as good a listener as he was a talker, till at length came eleven o'clock – what might be described as 'closing time' on Saturday evenings at Lower Sydenham – when the Londoners had to leave to catch the 11–22 train to Victoria.

This was a tradition that would grow throughout his life, often including musical performance. He was constantly attracted to debate, but had to decide on the level of his commitment for time and pressure of interests. In 1869 he became a founder member of the Metaphysicial Society for the discussion of matters of belief in a scientific age, with an array of distinguished members. He had known Thomas Huxley from early on, and Charles Darwin was also a member. But Grove withdrew quickly. His ultimate view was that the worlds of science and religion were incompatible, though he looked forward to progressive thought in the Church of England and possessed it himself to a degree surprising in relation to other attitudes: 'I am always looking for a time when the modern scientific spirit shall invade it. It must come sooner or later. That, and the marriage of priests seem to me two things that must happen.' And in recommending a friend to get the *Bampton Lectures on Science and Religion* he comments that

> they are worth reading even if you don't agree with them. I am afraid [the lecturer] has not solved the difficulty, but I find [his views] very interesting and quite fair. The drawback is, no advocate of 'religion' – no 'believer' – knows science accurately enough to argue adequately, just as no scientific man is religious enough (by conviction, I mean) to appreciate the religious difficulty'.[14]

If Grove was not destined to follow science professionally, some of the scientific method became crucial to the other greatest preoccupation of his early years aside from music, the study of biblical lands and people. It was this that turned Grove from an educated lover of the scriptures into what Dean Stanley would assess by 1865 as 'the best Old Testament scholar he knew.' These interests found a focus at the Crystal Palace, where James Fergusson, who was the initiator of the so-called Assyrian Court of the Palace, had been General Manager since 1856. The future lexicographer of music needed only an opportunity to focus his biblical interests. It came through a chance word of Fergusson's that he should begin making lists of biblical places and persons. This dictionary-like work suddenly found an outlet through Grove's connection with Arthur Penrhyn Stanley, then Dean of Canterbury: George Bradley had introduced Grove to Stanley in 1853 or 1854. Stanley invited Grove to produce an appendix to his recent book *Sinai and Palestine*, an important travelogue of the Holy Land. Grove revised his Hebrew (learnt at school) and his German (self-taught) and did the work (for which Stanley insisted that he accept remuneration). Stanley indicates that he also did much proof checking, commenting that 'I ought never to write a book without a Grove or an Albert Way to correct references and proofs'. Stanley's personality and character, shared interests in the Holy Land and values had a powerful effect on Grove. He revered his personality, culture and kindness and he became a mentor similarly close as Maurice, especially when Stanley became Dean of Westminster in 1864. If Maurice was Grove's mentor in social matters then Stanley performed the same role in matters religious.[15]

Grove's connection with Stanley was to bring about an even more significant link in terms of his scholarly development. Stanley was in contact with Dr William Smith, who was seeking help in connection with his *Dictionary of the Bible*, for which Stanley recommended Grove. Smith (1813–93) was the doyen of lexicographers, having already produced the *Dictionary of Greek and Roman Antiquities* of 1842 and subsequent dictionaries of Greek and Roman biography, a *Dictionary of Christian*

Antiquaries, and a *Classical Atlas* (see Chapter 4); his *Dictionary of the Bible* would be followed by many other works. The *Dictionary of the Bible* was Smith's greatest work.

Grove's contribution was far bigger than indicated. A later critic observed that, despite later advances in biblical scholarship, Smith's book was almost a beginning of such work in England that deserves to be called scientific and comments that

> of this work Sir George Grove was the very soul. He began it by compiling a concordance of proper names in Bible and Apocrypha, he wrote most of the articles on obscure names in the first volume, corrected the proofs and revised the whole book. This would have been labour enough for most men. But besides all this, he wrote many articles of first-rate importance. Amid these I mention a long article of the geography of Palestine, till lately the best account which we had and still worth careful study, with two brilliant biographies of Elijah and Elisha.[16]

It took him seven years, from 1857 to 1863. Grove soon became deeply immersed in the work and worked late at it. In November 1858 and April 1859 he had to decline to write some articles for lack of time. 'I cannot go on any longer being torn to pieces as I am, even for the *Bible Dictionary*'. The work gave a huge opportunity for all Grove's interests to find a focus. The completion of the three-volume work by the end of 1863 drew warm praise from Smith for his work in his Preface, as well as praise in the press:

> there is however one writer to whom he owes a more special acknowledgement. Mr George Grove of Sydenham, besides contributing articles to which his initial is attached [Grove's contributions are signed 'G', as are his concert programme notes] has rendered the editor important assistance in writing the majority of the articles on the more obscure names in the first volume, in the correction of proofs and in the revision of the whole book.

Typically Grove regarded his work as humble and mechanical. But it gave him a huge reputation and the appetite for more work, both fulfilled – as with his involvement with the Palestine Exploration Fund – and not fulfilled, as with his 'Speakers Commentary' to the *Dictionary of the Bible*, planned in 1863.[17]

There did not need to be a vital change in Grove's musical life when he went to the Crystal Palace at Sydenham. There had not been any real musical life at Hyde Park and the plans for Sydenham were modest: a resident brass band, though quite big at 58 members, to perform inside and out – typical regimental band fare as had been performed at Hyde Park after the Great Exhibition ended. But Sydenham changed everything. It enabled Grove's developing interests to burst into bloom: it was the crucial link to the increasingly powerful role music was to play in the rest of his life. What changed everything was the arrival of August Manns and Grove's reaction to him: namely, Grove's spotting of ability and handling of a situation. The director of music at the Crystal Palace at its opening in 1854 was Heinrich Schallehn. He had heard Manns in Germany and appointed him assistant conductor, librarian and E flat clarinettist for the opening at Sydenham in June 1854. Schallehn then abused Manns by passing Manns's band arrangements off as his own; Manns complained and Schallehn sacked him. Manns went to the press. Grove was sympathetic because he admired Manns. He kept in communication and Schallehn was duly relieved of his responsibilities within the year, Manns being appointed as director. Manns then transformed his wind band into an orchestra and developed the Saturday Concerts with bold new repertoire and high standards. The Crystal Palace became the focus of developing orchestral music in Britain and was of international standard within the decade. The partnership with Manns, allied to Grove's own influence with the Directors of the Palace, gave him the opportunity to participate actively in developing his enthusiasms for modern music, building on his already considerable experience and study. An immediate focus was provided by the need for programme notes, a central preoccupation pursued later in this book (see Chapter 6).

The editor 1874–83

Apart from the music and its performance, Grove was naturally to tire of the administrative responsibilities of the Crystal Palace position over the years, and he applied for many other positions. 'I hope you will succeed in getting some employment which leaves you a little more leisure than you can get at the Crystal Palace' was the comment of Matthew Arnold in 1867 when Grove applied (unsuccessfully) for the post of librarian to the House of Commons, and others had looked out for him as well. He wanted something closer to his developing interests in the arts. Finally by the end of 1873 he was in a position to give his resignation to the Palace and assumed full responsibility for all Macmillan's literary editing, as well as editing *Macmillan's Magazine*. The relationship with Macmillan had come about by degrees. Grove had been the unofficial assistant to the first editor David Masson from 1859 when the magazine began. Grove had been connected with Alexander Macmillan through his friendships with the Christian Socialists including Maurice and Kingsley who were also close to Macmillan from 1868; Grove took over on a part-time salary, and in January 1874 with a full-time salary acknowledging his varied responsibilities for the firm (see Chapter 7, p.147). The agreement was for seven years. With the new contract, Macmillan assured him of £3,000 as editor of *Macmillan's Magazine*: £2,600 for 'managing the literary side of their business' and a guarantee of

£400 per annum in the event of profits from the sale of books or series of which he was editor or compiler not amounting to that sum in any one year'. The agreement was for seven years. But it was to last for nine.

As an editor, Grove had already gained much experience with John Murray on Smith's *Dictionary of the Bible*. The Macmillan connection offered him a huge opportunity to shift his orientation from administration into letters, and his great knowledge and sensitivity were used fruitfully. His great attraction from the publisher's point of view was his reliability: he worked endlessly and got copy in. In his first year he was able to receive contributions from F.D. Maurice, J. Scott Russell, J.R. Seeley (Professor of Modern History at Cambridge), Thomas Huxley (on the education of the working man), Matthew Arnold, Harriet Beecher Stowe, and George Eliot. It was an exciting time: world events included the political consequences of the Franco-Prussian War, which prompted suggestions of a United States of Europe, for example. But the work also challenged him. He needed tact when tough reviews were offered, as for example of the work of the prestigious historian James Anthony Froude; or in reaction to a challenging poem of Alfred, Lord Tennyson.[18]

The nature of his work for *Macmillan's Magazine* is discussed in Chapter 7. Here however, one can note the larger perspective in terms of Grove's personal growth. From the beginning, the work with Macmillan had given him the opportunity to go deeper into cultural issues stimulated by figures such as Maurice and Stanley, and the increasing stress in Grove's life on what emerges as his primary skill and drive: education and the qualities and values that ideally inhere within it, values that would characterize his period as Director of the Royal College of Music. Lying behind the practicalities of educational provision and reform, so often tied up with political ideology and expediency, lay a broader, more detached image of a spiritual quality articulated by many writers in different fields; for example, the three great figures who addressed the spiritual issues left by the Oxford Movement: Matthew Arnold in criticism, John Henry Newman in religion, and John Ruskin in art.

Grove was particularly drawn to the writings of Newman and Arnold, though they represented emphases at different parts of his life. Both promoted the ideal of the spiritually refined individual, based on an education resulting from a response to what they took to be the vulgarity and philistinism emerging from industrialization, the creation of rapid new wealth, a grasping new middle class and the philosophy of utility attached to it. They espoused a belief in knowledge as a whole: the parts of science as one unity, and acknowledgment of the distinction between education and instruction. At the personal level, they valued the qualities of gentleness, dispassionate evaluation and courteous bearing, in an era when social change had undermined the traditional assumptions about behaviour and personal character. Newman famously commented of the philosophy of utility that it 'has at least done its work... – it aimed low, but it has fulfilled its aim.' Grove first admired Newman's writings, especially the *Apologia Pro Vita Sua*, which Newman wrote in response to an exchange prompted by Kingsley's review of Froude's *History of England*, vols 7 and 8, and which Grove continued to read; and he retained a love for certain of his poems, most notably 'Lead Kindly Light'. But Grove grew increasingly distant from Newman's theological position, first as high church Anglican then as Catholic, and also became critical of his influence: 'to him, and to the stronger men who took the reins out of his hands, we owe the flood of rituals and material worship and magic that now fills our church, and I for one don't feel very grateful.... Our church is fast becoming... a mere magic mill for the production of Sacraments which are to act as charms.'[19]

Grove was much closer to Matthew Arnold, whom he knew well. He was the soulmate of Grove's later years (see Chapter 3). Arnold's larger concept of culture as expressed in his essays, and also his sympathy with music as embodying its qualities, found an immediate resonance with Grove. Some of Arnold's statements defining culture are pure Grove: 'Culture... shows its single minded love of perfection, its desire simply to see reason and the will of God prevail [and displays] the flexibility which sweetness and light give, and which is one of the rewards of culture pursued in good faith'; and likewise his definition of criticism: 'to try to know the best that is known and thought in the world, irrespective of practical politics, and everything of the kind'. Grove was also attracted by Arnold's churchmanship. Both esteemed a middle, liberal position in the Church of England and believed in the imagery and character of this church as embodying these values best. Arnold was reserved about the dissenting church, basically since he saw its political affinity with the new wealth and commerce and its capacity to pose an implicit challenge to the traditional English church order. '[Though] culture accepts the necessity of wealth-making... culture defines itself in opposition to false religious values.' Though he admired the Independents in some senses, he still criticized them in principle. 'Puritanism was perhaps necessary to develop the moral fibre of the English race, Nonconformity to break the yoke of ecclesiastical domination over men's minds and to prepare the way for freedom of thought in the distant future.' He agreed that the Oxford Movement had failed against middle-class liberalism, strongly influenced by Nonconformists, but argued that its ideal was better, that Puritanism was narrow. Grove was of similar mind, at least to judge by his reserved comments on his brother-in-law J.C. Harrison, a Congregationalist minister, and his pointed reserve towards the scholarship of Charles Haddon Spurgeon, the leading Nonconformist evangelical preacher of the day (and a fellow resident of the Crystal Palace district).[20]

Grove's London life had settled comfortably with the full-time position at Macmillan. Sydenham was his domestic and weekend social base; but the metropolis was his cultural scene, and membership of The Athenaeum had given him the flexibility to pursue it by providing a base when he needed it: the high period of cultural life in Sydenham had finished by the mid-1870s (see Chapter 2). Grove's many interests continued and blossomed as he rose in the social and professional world. One project reflective of this time, though never implemented, was for a Dictionary of Names, effectively a precursor of the *Dictionary of National Biography* (founded 1882), which Grove mentioned to John Murray in May 1860. One notable event which took place in 1878 was his visit to the USA with Dean Stanley, and Stanley's young doctor, Gerald Harper, a visit preceded by a visit to the Queen with Stanley. Grove, with Harper, was the lesser attraction and Graves notes how Grove put himself totally at the service of his esteemed senior throughout. They left Liverpool on 5 September and arrived at Boston on 16 September, an 11-day journey. They travelled extensively, from Harvard University, Cambridge, Massachusetts, where they met the President, to Newport, Rhode Island, to New Haven, where they met the president of Yale University; to New York, Baltimore, Washington, Richmond, Virginia, New York again, Albany, Niagara, Montreal; then back to New York via the Adirondacks, Lake George, the Berkshires, Concord, and Stockbridge. Stanley and Grove were particularly interested in American history and literature. Leading divines and academics played host to them throughout. At Boston they stayed with Phillips Brooks, rector of Trinity Church; at Philadelphia they were guests of G.W. Childs, and attended a black Methodist service, at Baltimore they met the president of Johns Hopkins University, Daniel Gilman, then in the process of raising money for a medical school (now one of the world's leading research and teaching hospitals). Finally in New York, the many events which ended the visit included sermons by Stanley at Trinity Church, Wall St, St Paul's Methodist Church, and Grace Church, Broadway and 10th St.[21]

Throughout this period Grove had continued to write his programme notes for the Crystal Palace and other concerts, and to attend its concerts regularly. The greatest musical counterpoint to his period at Macmillan was the creation of the *Dictionary of Music and Musicians*. But for all its focal importance in his creative life, it fell professionally under the umbrella of general editing for the firm. It represented the last of his dictionary activities, of the working out through his life of this particular approach and skill: at last, his own dictionary expressing his own deepest interest: the systematic gathering of a huge amount of information for eager consumers and responding to a clearly emerging need. He was uniquely placed to pull it off: a very wide knowledge, finely honed editorial skills, an awareness of and involvement with many of the issues of the time, together with a unique range of contacts. From the Macmillan period onwards he had very high musical status. One example of this is the extent to which he was invited to write prefaces for important new publications on musical subjects, usually in translation from German, to give them the stamp of authority for a still narrow world of consumers. In the case of Hiller's *Mendelssohn* he had the work serialized in *Macmillan's Magazine* (January–May, 1874). He wrote a preface to the English translation, and concluded it with a personal comment (written 25 June 1874):

> As I write news arrives of the death of Paul Mendelssohn, Felix's younger brother, and the last remaining member of the family circle to which he was so fondly attached. It is a double reminder – first that but for over-work and over-excitement Felix Mendelssohn might himself have still been with us, or but recently departed; and secondly that those who knew him personally, and to whom he was not only a musician but a living, loving friend, rich beyond measure in the gifts and powers of life, are fast passing away with their recollections and traditions out of the reach of the biographer.[22]

Director and Retirement 1882–1900

With his appointment to the RCM in December 1882 all the themes of Grove's life came together. He was able to take a major public position as an administrator of the newest and most forward-looking and hoped-for educational institution for music in the UK. And the ultimate public recognition, through his knighthood, came now in connection with his contributions to music on the day the college opened, 7 May 1883. He would receive a CB from the Queen on retirement for his contributions in the post. But it was more than his musical expertise that got him the job. The basic skills, the themes were still at work. As emerges in Chapter 9, Grove had become an intimate part of the public representation of the concept of a new college, though by no means universally welcomed and supported, and its spearhead at fund-raising. All the skills he used in the parallel situation for the establishment of the Palestine Exploration Fund were present here too. He was invited to become a member of the council of the executive committee of the proposed college in July 1881 and in March 1882 he took on fund-raising at the request of the Prince of Wales for six months. Again, his reputation for getting the job done went before him. It was arduous work touring to raise money by giving speeches all over the country: 'hard work for me and still harder work for my listeners', yet a latter example of the early value of 'getting your hands dirty.' On 20 October 1882 the announcement was made that Grove was Director-designate.

But if in retrospect Grove's appointment to the RCM can be seen as representing a natural culmination of his work as secretary, administrator and musical writer, it did not seem quite so obvious then to the music profession which took so much interest in the new project. There were those who thought it entirely inappropriate that the Director should not be a musician: the heads of the other two music conservatoires were leading composers and performers, both appointed to their posts in 1876, George Macfarren at the Royal Academy, and Arthur Sullivan at the National Training School, which the new college was to succeed. Expertise in musical scholarship was still not valued highly. Indeed, even at this late stage Grove was still regarded with reserve by many, for reasons that emerge from Graves's evaluation:

> in a musical performance, what chiefly impressed him was earnestness and simplicity. For the rest he was little concerned with the niceties of technique, and was infinitely more interested in the music than in the 'reading'. No doubt [his technical shortcomings] account for the disinclination of a certain number of highly-equipped professional musicians to regard Grove in the light of a serious authority on their art.[23]

Grove was 63 on appointment, an age at which many with his record of achievement might have been ready to retire. Though income was certainly one reason (Grove never had a high income or could afford a lavish lifestyle) the realization of his values was far deeper than raising money or running an efficient organization, even though the job was to be largely administrative and to have offered the biggest challenge of his life; he retained his position until retiring exhausted ten years later at the age of 74. He was very well placed to handle the initial responsibilities of appointing staff. One notes especially the commonality between the RCM staff and the staff of the Crystal Palace School of Arts, Science and Literature: of the seven members of the first Board of Professors, five had taught at the Crystal Palace. But he had to face problems with personalities and all his tact and patience was required. His letters show how much time he gave to college business. Above all he had to embrace the fact that he was a public figure in music education, and had to justify music nationally in what was often a philistine environment. Grove had raised much money for the college, but often felt national response to be niggardly. Music's needs were not always understood; and he found himself in dispute with the University of London concerning the national evaluation of teaching, which threatened the college's autonomy: in fact, he had had to face a similar challenge to the college's autonomy before his first academic year in the summer of 1883 when a co-ordinated protest was made by the universities at the college's right to award its own degrees by its royal charter. It was all very different from cultivating his musical passions in the quiet of his study at Sydenham, or the pleasure of concert attendance at the Crystal Palace.[24]

But behind it all, Grove did realize his educational ideals, in framing young lives in the environment of the experience of great music. His belief in the moral value of great music lay behind his approach to education and his relationship with the students; they were likely to have any advice laced with quotations from Beethoven or lines of poetry, and recommended reading and listening; above all, the sense of the privilege of experiencing great things. Through this period, the *Dictionary* also reached its final stage, though proceeding somewhat more slowly than in earlier years, to a four-volume completion in 1889. By now, Grove was far from interested in everything he had researched. He had much less interest in what would soon be termed 'Early Music', and was resistant to the pioneering work of the younger generation such as Arnold Dolmetsch, or Stanford's performance of Purcell's *Dido and Aeneas* in 1896 with students from the college. Whether he was against British music is less easy to ascertain: he gave every support to college composers, whether his colleagues or students, and received some dedications, for example of Coleridge-Taylor's *Hiawatha's Wedding Feast* set to the Longfellow text. But the German concert repertoire was the core of his interest and he eagerly attended new works, writing, for example, an important programme note for the first UK performance of Brahms' Fourth Symphony, conducted by Richter, in May 1886.

Finally, his cherished Beethoven research carried him into retirement and its culmination in *Beethoven and His Nine Symphonies* appeared shortly after in 1896. He began to slowly decline in health from 1898 and the winter of 1899–1900 saw him gradually slipping away. He was unaware of his surroundings for several months before he died on 28 May, in the first year of the new century which was to see the realization of so much that he had worked to achieve in the spread of musical knowledge and public familiarity with great works. He died appreciated: his efforts had been worthwhile. The remarks of his RCM colleague, the composer and conductor Charles Villiers (C.V.) Stanford made a fitting epitaph:

> Few Englishmen have been more universal in their sympathies, and more active in their developments than he. Engineer by profession..., explorer by circumstances..., musician by nature, he did more for Art while secretary of the Crystal Palace than any man of his time...His engineering developed into the mastery of men; his exploration into the discovery of the forgotten treasures of Schubert; his musicianship into the foundation and control of a great music school...There are few great advances in art for which we have not to thank him. He fought for everything worth fighting for, Beethoven and Schubert in especial. It was at his request that Parry wrote 'Blest Pair of Sirens...' He made many other suggestions to Parry; for he was always working for others, rather than for himself. In his later years he laid a sure foundation for English music in his directorship of the Royal College, and qualified for the post by an inaugural speech (unfortunately heard only by a few), which was worthy of Arnold at his best. A unique man, whom his friends will ever recall as a living force, and whom future generations will do well to emulate.[25]

Notes

1 A comprehensive survey of Victorian characteristics is included in Walter F. Houghton, The Victorian Frame of Mind, 1830–1870 (New Haven, 1957; 2nd edn,1985); the scope of British musical life in the period is the subject of *Music and British Culture 1785–1914. Essays in Honour of Cyril Ehrlich*, ed. Christina Bashford and Leanne Langley (Oxford, 2000).
2 George Granville Bradley 1821–1903; for Matthew Arnold, F.D. Maurice and A.P. Stanley, see Percy M. Young, *George Grove 1820–1900. A Biography* (London, 1980), p.26. F.G. Edwards, 'Sir George Grove C.B.', *Musical Times*, October 1897, 38, 654, pp.657–64; C.L.Graves, *The Life & Letters of Sir George Grove* (London, 1903), pp.213, 132.
3 Young, *George Grove*, p.23; See further, A. Pritchard, *The Life and Work of Charles Pritchard* (London, 1897), pp.47–8.
4 Graves, *Life & Letters*, pp.8–12; Young, *George Grove*, p.21; Pritchard, who had had a brilliant career at Cambridge, was destined to become Savilian Professor of Astronomy at Oxford from 1870–93. Young suggests that Grove 'lived out a sketch plan presented to him as a schoolboy'.
5 Young, *George Grove*, pp.13–19; works by Gordon [1802–68] include: *Historical and Practical Treatise upon Locomotion*...(London, 1832); *Treatise on Locomotion by Means of Steam Carriage* (London, 1832); *Observations on Railway Monopolies* (London, 1841); *Lighthouses of the British Colonies and Possessions Abroad* (London, 1848).
6 Young, *George Grove*, p.37; Graves, *Life & Letters*, pp.19–26; Robert Napier wrote *Machinery of the British and North American Royal Steamship 'Arabia'...constructed by Messrs. Robert Napier and Son* (London, 1855).
7 Graves, *Life & Letters*, p.26; Letter of Grove to Edith Oldham, 29 July 1893, quoted in Young, *George Grove*, p.44. Grove does not appear in the commemorative painting featuring the ten leading figures including Stephenson, Brunel and Wild. Nonetheless he was entrusted with writing the report of the successful completion of the bridge for the *Spectator* (see Chapter 3).
8 'Sir George Grove's Autobiography', *Musical Herald*, 628 (1 July 1900), p.195; Graves, *Life & Letters*, pp.26–7; Young, *George Grove*, pp.44–7.
9 'Sir George Grove's Autobiography', pp.195–6; Grove's contract with the Society of Arts allowed him to retain consultancies relating to railways for several years after he was appointed.
10 See the discussion in Young, *George Grove*, p.56.
11 The Society of Arts had held exhibitions of art manufacture in 1847–49. Concerning admission, see 'Commissioners Correspondence of the Great Exhibition, London (*c*.1849–1856)': letters to and from Grove: 20 February, 1851; 4 March 1851, 29 March 1851; 28 March, 1851; 14 April, 1851; 16 April 1851; 9 May 1851; concerning Messrs. Munday's contract: letters of 30 March 1850, 18 March 1850, 4 April 1850; 13 April 1850; 25 October 1851; 1 June 1852; 17 June 1850; and 1 June 1850. Other topics with which Grove was probably involved were the expenses concerning the removal of one of the large organs, an appointment to the Musical Instruments Committee and the casting of a commemorative medal. Grove was the last Secretary to live in the Society of Arts house: see D.G. Allen, *The Houses of the Royal Society of Arts. A History and Guide* (London, 1966), p.39.
12 'Sir George Grove's Autobiography', pp.195–6; The Crystal Palace is discussed and illustrated in Patrick Beaver, *The Crystal Palace* (Chichester, 1986), and Michael Musgrave, *The Musical Life of the Crystal Palace* (Cambridge, 1994), pp.11–23.

13 Letter of Thomas Carlyle to George Grove, 7 May 1852; quoted in Graves, *Life & Letters*, p.37. The Christian Socialists are comprehensively surveyed in Brenda Colloms, *Victorian Visionaries* (London, 1982) and Grove mentioned among them. Grove recalls a visit from Cardinal Manning on the subject of temperance, another major theme of the period (Graves, *Life & Letters*, p.218).

14 Graves, *Life & Letters*, pp.300, 171, 401.

15 *Ibid.*, p.49, n.1; Arthur Penrhyn Stanley [1815–81], *Sinai and Palestine in connection with their History* (London, 1856); Graves, *Life & Letters*, pp.48–9; '[Grove] rendered valuable service...not only by verifying the references, but still more by arranging the appendix on Hebrew geographical terms', *ibid*, p.103. Albert Way (1805–74), antiquary.

16 Graves, *Life & Letters*, p.103.

17 *Ibid.*, p.67.

18 There are more details of these incidents in Chapter 7 of this volume.

19 Newman's 'The Idea of a University' (Discourses V–VII) and *Apologia* are extracted in *Prose of the Victorian Period*, ed. William E. Buckler (Boston, 1958), pp.179–248; quoted passage at p.190; Letter of Dean Bradley, 30 October, 1890, Graves, *Life & Letters*, p.360; Grove never knew Newman closely, though he thought about inviting him to write an autobiography and left an interesting portrait of him prompted by one of his sermons (see Graves, *Life & Letters*, pp.218–19).

20 Matthew Arnold, 'The Function of Criticism at the Present Time', *Essays in Criticism, First Series*, ed., with introd. and notes by Sister Thomas Marion Hoctor (Chicago and London, 1964), p.17; 'Sweetness and Light', in *Culture and Anarchy*, ed. with introd. by J. Dover Wilson (London, 1935; 2nd edn, 1960), pp.56–62; Young, *George Grove*, p.36; Graves, *Life & Letters*, pp.55–6.

21 Graves, *Life & Letters*, pp.231–43; see also the summary in Young, *George Grove*, p.146.

22 Ferdinand Hiller, *Mendelssohn, Letters and Recollections*, trans. M.E. von Glehn (London, 1874): Editor's Preface, pp.xxxiv.

23 Graves, *Life & Letters*, pp.453–4.

24 Graves, *Life & Letters*, pp.369–70; the (unpublished) correspondence (June–August 1883) is preserved in the University of London Archives, Senate House: File RC4/18 ('Correspondence relating to the protest of the Universities at the right of the RCM to award degrees'). I thank Professor Brian Trowell for drawing this source to my attention.

25 C.V. Stanford, *Interludes, Records and Reflections* (London, 1922), p.137.

2
George Grove the Man

Celia Clarke and Michael Musgrave

Temperament and appearance

The familiar public image of George Grove accommodates his physical appearance to his well-defined public personality: a warm, friendly individual with a huge capacity for communicating his enthusiasms and responding to the interests of others. The artistic images invariably picture him sitting, with emphasis on his engaged attitude towards the outside world. The most familiar example of this is the 'Spy' cartoon of January 1891 when Grove was aged 70, which shows, side on, his inquisitive manner, as if generously considering and waiting to respond kindly to a speaker (see front cover of this volume). The posed portraits in oils (by Furse and Olivier), though in the former Grove is face forward and seated at a desk, capture the same engaged attitude, though with richer character and detail (Plate 2). However, Grove disliked both the formal oil paintings and the process of sitting. He preferred photographs for their greater immediacy. Most familiar is the half side view of 1890 (Plate 1) and several such posed photos appear from the period. However Grove's favourite was apparently that of 1890 where he appears at the back of the group portrait (Plate 3) taken for the laying of the foundation stone of the new building of the Royal College of Music (RCM), where, in contrast to the other posed individuals – most notably Parry – Grove seems at his most informal, indeed wearing a worried frown that confirms the moods of which we read during these years.[1]

Grove was not considered handsome. Graves recalls that 'he had no pretension to good looks, his features were too irregular for that, but the brow was open, the keen eyes and mobile mouth proclaimed him a humorist, and when his rugged countenance was lit up by the fire of affection or enthusiasm, it became quite beautiful to watch.' Stanford continues 'he was not physically beautiful but he had . . . charm and fascination, which was far superior to regular good looks'.[2] Nor did he cut a striking pose. 'In stature somewhat at under middle height, at once squarely but loosely built, and of spare habit, he redeemed the comparative insignificance of his figure by the vivacity of his mien and the engaging charm of his physiognomy'. Graves continues:

> It has been said that our characters are to be read in our features, and there was certainly much in Grove's outer man that harmonized with his eager, mercurial, versatile temperament. . . . Along with this varied play of facial expression he had, both in gait and gesture, a 'quicksilverishness' unusual in an Englishman. Even into old age he retained the habit, when in good spirits, of executing a sort of little chassé step when he came into the room. And thus, though he had at command an intense and fervid earnestness of manner, he was perhaps too vivacious to shine on great ceremonial occasions, too mercurial to be imposing, too sensitive to be dignified.

Stanford recalls that he was even described by one who saw him crossing the transept of the Crystal Palace as 'walking with two left legs and somebody else's arms'.[3]

Graves recalls that 'until the close of his life he was in the habit of taking a good deal of exercise, but he was active rather than athletic', and that 'he had quite modest tastes.' In the matter of dress he went back to his Puritan forbears; he was neither slovenly nor smart, avoided colours, aimed at an efficient simplicity of attire, and cordially disliked bejewelled women. It was the same with his diet; in the whole course of his life I have never come across a single written complaint of what he ate or drank. His taste in wine and tobacco was of the simplest. He 'hated champagne', drank Marsala, smoked cheap cigars, and, like Mr Gladstone, drank tea at all hours with impunity. He talked too much at meals to pay close attention to the refinements of gastronomy'.[4]

The friendly image of Grove was widely observed and admired. He always stimulated good responses in others, as in this tribute by a close friend E.H. Pember.

> The lovableness of the man, after all, was the dominant note in him. The love he was so ready to give drew attention no less than it provoked love. I have seldom known a man with sympathies at once so varied and so keen. Your sorrows and your joys he made his own. Whatever your art or calling might be, he always talked of it from the point of view of what it must be to you. If he told an anecdote he always gave you the notion, where it was possible, of laughing with the actors in it rather than at the situation. He essentially shared their fun.[5]

Similar appreciation came from the Rev. A.T. Davidson, when a young curate at Sydenham:

> There never was such a man as 'G' for not letting you feel unwelcome. You might go to him at any time, or any day, and he was always glad to

> see you. If he could not attend to you he would say so, but with such pleasantness, that you never felt you had had a walk for nothing. If on the other hand he had a minute or two to spare, he would throw himself into your news or your difficulty, whichever it might be, sympathize with you, cheer you up, promise to write to this person or that person for you (promises which he always aptly redeemed).[6]

This friendliness was more an expression of personal values than a matter of personality but Graves observes that 'he always preferred the attitude of the devotee to that of the critic', noting, from Mrs Wodehouse, his 'glorious enthusiasm' as the secret of his personality. He observed himself in 1865 that he 'always wanted to keep a boy's heart to the end of life.' For all his concern for editorial detail and accuracy he wanted to spread his own values of communication as much as possible. Thus his close collaborator on the *Dictionary of Music and Musicians*, Mrs Wodehouse recalls 'his hatred of pedantry and affectation is well known, and he did his utmost to cure all musicians by good humoured banter of this failing.'[7]

But Grove's temperament went beyond just warmth and enthusiasm. The mercurial aspect also denoted a highly strung personality and sometimes an over-abundance of energy of which his enthusiasm was the good side. Even this enthusiasm could occasionally get out of hand, as, for example, in requesting Frederic Leighton to suggest an example of an arabesque in world architecture and design to match or illustrate a passage in the 'Pastoral Symphony', to which Leighton responded 'What a wild creature you are' (though still doing his best with a clutch of examples). He also had quite a mischievous and 'larky' side as a young man that emerges, for example, in his high spirits in the company of his brother on a trip to Paris in 1848, and he always kept something of this quality later, as in his celebratory leapfrog with Arthur Sullivan at 2 a.m following their Schubert discoveries in 1867. He was highly emotional, with feelings often near the surface. Reading old letters, for example, would easily bring tears to his eyes.[8]

Behind the public smile there were indeed problems and unresolved tensions. Throughout his life he expressed doubts about his ability and focus: thought himself not tough-minded enough, and slow to get to the point. His self-analysis in the eve of his 55th birthday in 1875 is very revealing:

> Tomorrow I am 55 years old and what am I? As much a slave as I was at 35, as little near the attainment of any settled position of mind and spirit as I ever was. I am active and energetic and ready to do my best, but the day for that is gone. I ought now to be reaping the fruits and feeling like Stanley or Jowett, or other men of my own age that I am enjoying the harvest of my earlier years. You who know me well must feel how very far I am from that, and the thought presses on me very much. Of course you will say – no you won't say – but it might be said 'Shut up such

> grievances in your heart and don't confess them' – but to confess is with me a necessity; it does me good by the mere act and may get me useful advice. I ought not at my time of life to be a mere shuttlecock at the sport of all the people who employ me, or have the least claim on me. I ought somehow to have more weight and leisure – but I can't get it. And yet I feel in myself plenty of capacity.[9]

Grove's deeper unease could also manifest itself in much more than reflectiveness. He could be irascible, prone to deep depression, especially later when the responsibilities of the RCM weighed heavily and he felt his age. That there was actually only a fine balance between the two sides of his personality is shown in the comments of one of his closer circle.

> He had suffered much, as we all knew, and had his fits of depression and moments of discouragement, like any other; but his splendid cheerfulness overbore melancholy, and was in him, as I firmly believe, not merely the result of temperament, but the half conscious outcome of an inward acknowledgement that life, had after all, brought him more than it had cost him, and it behoved him to wear gladness as a robe of gratitude. His thankfulness was thus to him almost a continual feast.[10]

The sense of struggle was most apparent in the final years at the RCM when the bureaucratic aspects of the work got the better of him and he became easily exasperated and very bothered by meetings. He worried about how he would cope after retirement. Though he had no financial worries (the College had given him a fine pension close to his successor's salary), he knew he would miss the buzz of the College and this created a dilemma.[11]

In earlier years periods of pressure had revealed the same symptoms. The many close bereavements he suffered had profoundly depressive effects on him, which did not change over the years. One recurrent feature of Grove's life – his proneness to regular ailments and exhaustion seems a symptom of his psychological fragility, though he himself attributed much of it to overwork. He availed himself of regular holidays whenever he could, preferably abroad, and complained when he missed them. Wherever possible in later years, he went to his younger brother Edmund on the South Coast, after Edmund's retirement. He needed to get out and see new faces as a cure for worry, commenting 'If I lie in bed on a Sunday morning, I am [sure] to keep thinking. . . about all my worries, the letters I have not answered'; and he was most appreciative of letters that took him out of himself, as from old friends and especially from former students of the RCM.[12]

He frequently had bad coughs and colds. In later years he suffered severely from rheumatism and sciatica and sought 'the cure' at Ragatz, Switzerland, in one year, though with limited benefit. In later years he also sustained several injuries involving London cabs, perhaps a result of his awkward gait as much as increasing traffic. Grove's obituary in *The Times* suggests that he had been in poor health for some years, a reflection of his growing exhaustion after leaving the RCM, though he kept working with undimmed commitment, completing *Beethoven and His Nine Symphonies* in 1896. His final decline can be dated from a small stroke early in 1899, though he continued to send dictated letters until September. On 31 October 1899, Lady Grove wrote to Grove's intimate friend, the former student Edith Oldham, that Sir George had been unconscious for almost a month, and this did not change before his death on 28 May 1900.[13]

Family background

George Grove was born on 13 August 1820, the eighth child of the 11 born to Thomas Grove and Mary Grove (née Blades). His eldest sibling was 12 years his senior and his youngest seven years his junior; and his parents were respectively 46 and 36 at his birth. His father Thomas Grove (1774–1852) was a well-established 'fishmonger and venison dealer' with premises at 33 Charing Cross, where he had lived following his marriage in August 1807, and where his eldest six children were born. Thomas Grove (one of five brothers) had come to London from the family farm at Penn, Bucks, soon after his younger brother John. His father, George's grandfather Edmund Grove (1729–1823) was described by George as 'the last yeoman in Bucks', and had apparently become impoverished as a farmer. George Grove observes that as a lad his father had done manual work on the farm.[14]

Grove's mother, Mary Blades, came from the City of London of a family later in the printing trade. We learn from a letter to Eleanor Grove from her cousin William Blades (1824–90) that he 'loved to handle the works of the great typographers'. Her brother Joseph Blades became a principal of the printing firm of Blades and East of Abchurch Lane. Dean Bradley described Mary to Graves as 'somewhat austere but a woman of considerable brain'. She came from a more lettered background than he. Her nephew was the author of the classical biography of Caxton. 'Amid the cares of her large household, she found time – as subscriber to a Book Society – for a good deal of serious reading, and was not merely a lover of music but a proficient amateur'. Her combination of literary leanings and artistic gifts seem to have passed most strongly to George of all her children.[15]

The separation of home and business with the move to 74, Thurlow Terrace in Wandsworth Road, Clapham, in 1819 signalled both Thomas Grove's financial success and the needs of a growing family. Here Grove's immediate elder sister was born and the rest of the family. There were good reasons for the move. Clapham was rural but accessible to central London by coach or even on foot. Graves observes that 'all the way from Wandsworth Road to Clapham Junction the neighbourhood was a favourite residential resort for solid City people, the wealthiest living on Clapham

Common. But Clapham was thoroughly rural and not even semi-suburban in the 'twenties' and 'thirties'. Grove recalled in 1897 that

> in the days of our childhood, Battersea Fields were almost unoccupied. There was a farmhouse about midway between our house and the Thames...So clear was the air across Battersea Fields that we could see the coloured sails of the barges going up and down the river and could hear plainly the drums and fifes played by the Duke of York's boys in the Chelsea Hospital before they went to bed. It was an entirely open space.

This rural quality seems to have been much appreciated and to have contributed to the happiness of Grove's childhood. In due course the Blades family moved next door to the house named Thurlow Cottage.[16]

Yet, apart from occasional recollections of his father's youth on the farm and of his mother's musical influence in his youth, Grove mentioned his parents little. Though one does not sense a close relationship, in a large family the child's life would have been filled most immediately with his relationships with his siblings, especially those nearer his own age. Only one child of the family died in infancy, the elder Edmund, b.1817, sixth child and second son, who died in 1819. Grove mentions a girl, Kezia, born in this year of 1819, as having spent her life, after her parents' deaths, apart from the family in a *maison de santé* and dying in 1888; the fourth child and third daughter, Frances Moore Grove, died at 20 and is not mentioned. We know rather of Grove's three eldest sisters Mary Bithiah Grove, b.1808; Bithiah Blades Grove, b.1809 and Eliza Jane Grove, b.1815; of his elder brother Thomas Blades Grove, b.1812, and his younger brother Edmund Grove, b. 1823; and of his younger sisters Anna, b.1824, and Eleanor, b.1827.[17] Graves clarifies further: 'the four youngest children, George, Edmund, Anna and Eleanor, were specially united by their tastes and interests, as well as by their age.' Anna outlived them all, living until 1917, aged 92. But it was the youngest, Eleanor, of whom we know most and who was seemingly closer to Grove in interests. Eleanor became a suffragette and had connections with the University of London with regard to female education. Some letters survive connecting her with a range of important figures in London's educational life including Dame Millicent Fawcett, and she also spent time in Germany. Eleanor recalls that as children George and Edmund were always 'stirring up their sisters, impressing on them the value of sincerity and thoroughness, denouncing shams in dress and elsewhere, and infecting them with their enthusiasm for books and music'.[18]

Although Grove implies he had little to do with his elder sisters, this cannot have been entirely the case since Bithiah taught him to read until he was eight. But the sisters married by Grove's later teens and his life did not relate much to theirs thereafter. Nor was Grove ever very close to his eldest brother Thomas Blades Grove, eight years his senior. As the eldest son,

Thomas inherited the business on his father's death in 1852 and eventually became very prosperous. He remained a bachelor, living above the premises. In due course he purchased a house at Penn, Buckinghamshire, on land believed to have belonged to former generations of the family. Listed as 'Watercroft', the house subsequently passed into the hands of Walter Grove, George Grove's eldest son, since Grove, who inherited it, never lived there. Thomas was described as solid, and a pillar of the community at Penn. Grove could not share Thomas's interests with him, but in later years he grew much closer and liked to visit him at Watercroft. Grove took pride in notifying Thomas of his CB in 1894 and was very upset when Thomas died in November 1897.

In contrast, Grove was on very good terms with his younger brother by two years, Edmund. They were close as children and followed parallel careers in engineering for some years, travelled together and shared common interests. In fact, when Grove returned from the West Indies, it was Edmund's contacts that found him a job. Edmund outlived Grove and died in 1911. He was sympathetic to his more volatile brother's artistic and literary interests, though he stayed in engineering, becoming a partner in an engineering firm in Yorkshire and an Associate of the Royal Institute of Civil Engineers. He gave up his holidays to accompany Grove on some travels that included the study of church architecture in England. He was sympathetic to the RCM, had students to stay, and left the College a legacy. When Edmund retired from business, the bond drew closer, and Grove often visited him at his new home, first at Worthing, later at Preston Park near Brighton.[19]

By the time of Grove's birth, his father's income was comfortable and the children received the best education in the locality. The girls were probably educated at home; the boys were educated at schools in Clapham. To the account of Grove's education given in Chapter 1 can be added the first school he attended at the age of eight, run by one Mr Greaves, a Yorkshireman. This was subsequently described by one of Grove's contemporaries, Frederick Locker, later the poet Frederick Locker Lampson (1821–95), who listed it as having 'some 14 or more boys'. Though not given a flattering portrait, the school had good connections. Greaves had been Thomas Macaulay's first schoolmaster, and Grove's contemporaries also included the two sons of Sir Andrew Agnew as well as Rev. Charles Bradley's son, George, later headmaster of Marlborough College, Dean of Westminster, and Grove's lifelong friend. Bradley observes that Grove never shone at games or organized activities, such as cricket or football. While at Elwell's he learnt the Hebrew alphabet, perhaps from the Hebrew bible bought for him by his father.[20]

Marriage and children

Considering the range of Grove's professional activities and wide experience of travel as a young man, it is notable that he was to spend the latter fifty years of his life, from the age of 30 or so, only a few miles from his place of birth and upbringing. Although he could not have anticipated that, following his appointment to the Society of Arts in 1850, its then prime undertaking, the Great Exhibition of the Works of Industry of All Nations would soon lead to a permanent institution at Sydenham and that he would be appointed its first secretary, circumstances placed him back in familiar surroundings. For some time he still had close connections at Clapham through his own family and that of his school friend George Granville Bradley, whose father, Rev Charles Bradley, formerly the vicar of Glasbury-on-Wye was the incumbent of St James's Chapel, Clapham. Nor did he show any inclination to move to central London when he might have done so later in his career. Indeed, he was to marry into the Bradley family. He recalls 'Old Bradley had a very large family – 12, of whom my wife [the fifth daughter] was the youngest but one – his wife died; and after 12 or 14 years he married again, a delightful woman a third of his age, who still lives and is a dear friend of mine – and then had eight more children'. He got on well with them; as well as his close friendship with George, he writes affectionately to Andrew, the younger half-brother of George by Rev. Bradley's second marriage. He remained on terms of friendship with them after the family moved to Cheltenham. Grove was part of the family. It was even in terms of his friendship with George Bradley that George Grove later referred to his marriage: 'We took to each other at once, and I am happy to say we have never altered since. I married his sister.'[21]

Such a remark, made many years later, taken with the apparent lack of fulfilment Grove found in his marriage for most of its course, suggests that Grove undertook marriage as an extension of his background with some naiveté. He made assumptions about both his spouse and the institution in which he was disappointed. Harriet Grove plays no apparent role in Grove's creative or professional life. The social setting, of which their first relationship was a part, though it continued through their long life together at Sydenham, was to remain completely separate from his creative life, causing great unhappiness to him and, by inference, to Harriet, although we have no words of hers by which to judge. He had no apparent models for the larger professional and creative world into which he was entering with the appointment to the Society of Arts and later the Crystal Palace. His bride seems to have been a 'secure' choice. George and Harriet were married on 23 December 1851, just as he was becoming established at the Society of Arts house in the Adelphi, where they lived: a signal moment of professional success. Harriet would have fitted the bill of an acceptable wife for him. She was probably very well trained in housekeeping and prepared to raise a large family. Raised herself in a large church family, a devout student and lover of the Bible, she would have been ready to involve herself fully in the life of the parish, like many Victorian women of her class.

Yet there were obvious differences that surfaced through the years. Harriet does not seem to have been of an intellectual disposition, lacking the sceptical, analytical tendency he increasingly developed, and they apparently had no comparable interests or passions. She seems to have been unable to share fully what meant most to him, especially music; and she never came to the RCM or played any visible role as Director's wife. And she was obviously temperamentally very different: he was warm, volatile and mercurial, she was steady and cool; he must have been very difficult to live with, save in partnership with a like spirit. The relationship seems to have been adequate to begin with and they had children up to 1864. A key moment in the cooling of the marriage was the loss of their first daughter, Lucy. Grove commented on the death of their second daughter, Millicent, that 'my wife is stronger and more self-controlled than I am', surely a reference to her stoic reaction; he, typically, buried himself in work: 'I know that work is the great refuge.' She seems to have immersed herself in the work of the parish, but thereafter they did nothing much together apart from running the house and formal socializing. She played her social role to support Grove's responsibilities in entertaining important visitors to the Crystal Palace, and their place in the parish was publicly noted and accepted, as emerges in the various recollections of musicians and the clergy. She seems to have taken this very seriously and one senses a firm control of the affairs of the household and the behaviour of its members, as for example, when chastening Grove's musical assistant Fuller Maitland for the manner of his conversation at table, a reaction he apparently found too sharp. One can sympathize with her situation. Grove worked incessantly: she recalls him working right through the night hours in connection with the *Dictionary of the Bible* in the period 1857–63; and he always rose early to work: he noted on one occasion that she was going away with two of the children, and so he could 'work like fifty steam engines'. This was not a marriage of like minds.[22]

Yet he was a passionate man especially drawn towards people with like interests. He was naturally drawn to attractive and articulate women especially when they had artistic gifts. And he must have been a focus for them too as a central figure in the circle in which he moved. Thus, in Sydenham, he was greatly attracted to the talented daughters of his cultured neighbours, the families of Scott Russell and von Glehn, especially Louise Scott Russell, and Mimi von Glehn. His vivid recollection of his feelings for Mimi von Glehn show what love could mean for him; 'a perfectly pure though *most passionate* attachment' (and later) 'and with it came my first real insight into music, poetry, nature – everything.' He needed an outlet and he found it in emotional attachments and in work and the joy of music. After the decline of the Sydenham circle, and the death of his daughter Millicent, his contact with young women through his new life at the RCM was an inevitable source of substitute relationships, and he came to be emotionally dependent on trusted students, especially Edith Oldham, whose letters have been extensively discussed by P.M. Young. Even though sincere and largely paternalistic, Grove risked his public reputation by, for example, taking walks in Kensington Gardens with these trusted female friends. Harriet tolerated as much as she knew of the situation. As Young has shown, nothing is more telling of the calibre of Harriet than her handling of this relationship after Grove's death, which she seems to have accepted without comment. She wrote very formally to Edith when Grove was in his final stages of illness to keep her informed and destroyed valuable letters after his death. But the truth was never uttered publicly. Harriet's failure to attend his funeral was apparently due to illness: she had pneumonia. But equally, there is no sense of her memorializing him after his death and the crucial role she might have played in filling out the detail of his life as a prime source is conspicuously missing from the literature, especially Graves's biography.[23]

Given the reality of their relationship, one factor might have significantly enriched the lives of George and Harriet: the birth and development of their children. The Groves had five children: two girls and three boys, during the first 13 years of their marriage in the period 1853–64. But circumstances did not contrive to help, especially from Grove's point of view. Both girls predeceased their parents though they apparently played a more decisive emotional part in Grove's life than his sons, who survived their father. Both Grove and his wife were deeply attached to their first child, Lucy Penrose Grove, named after Francis Penrose. 'A singularly attractive and lovable girl,' her death from scarlet fever on 15 June 1863 was a complete 'bolt from the blue' and according to Grove represented a turning-point in his life: it was the first real challenge to his assumed beliefs and certainties, and made him more worldly wise. His postscript to a letter to Sullivan on the difficulty of coming to terms with Lucy's death shows that he did not share the burden with Harriet: 'I could not have imagined before I knew it from experience, how solitary one is under such a trouble as this. There is no companionship in these sorrows'. Grove's reaction to this death and the state of his marriage undoubtedly influenced his relation with his second daughter, Millicent Stanley. Born in 1862, she was the fourth child and carried the name of Dean Stanley, a tribute to Grove's friendship with the later Dean of Westminster. He was deeply attached to her also and she took over much of the role of a wife or companion: 'Milly' was his help and unofficial secretary, knowing where all his papers were, and she accompanied him on foreign trips, often involving research and music. Indeed his comments on her are very tender; almost more like those of a lover. She became ill and was recommended to recuperate in Italy, where she worsened and died in December 1886. She was buried in Alassio, both parents attending.[24]

The Groves' second child and first son, Walter Maurice, was born in 1857, and named after F.D. Maurice. He attended Marlborough College as a boarder from 1873, aged 16, a choice doubtless influenced by Grove's connection with George Granville Bradley, the former headmaster.[25] However, Walter developed a chest weakness and was, on medical advice, sent by the family to Australia in 1878, aged 21, where prolonged residence (as a sheep farmer) gave him a new lease on life: he eventually came back twenty years later, in 1898. But one can observe that Grove had no opportunity to form a relationship with Walter as a young man and to influence the professional life of his eldest son and heir. The second son, Julius Charles, also attended Marlborough as a boarder; and Grove saw more of him as an adult, apparently forming a close bond. Grove observed that he was never out of humour and he was known to the younger members of the family as Uncle Tundy. The third son and youngest child, Arthur, gave Grove little satisfaction: he found him feckless and extravagant.[26]

Professional Life

Grove's frequent attribution of his professional success to the role of friends, though a natural part of his affable personality, held much more than a grain of truth. The successful contacts had begun early, through his teacher Pritchard, his first employer Gordon, his brother's connections, the senior engineers in North Wales, and above all through the rapid transition from the Society of Arts to the Crystal Palace and everything that opened up for him subsequently. But friendly contacts were a fact of life in business, then as now, as Grove would have been the first to admit. He functioned in a small professional world where access to the right individuals opened up many possibilities. And given his easy social manner, what today would be called 'networking' would have come very easily and have been very beneficial. Abundant evidence exists of his behind-the-scenes activities on behalf of many he wished to advance and encourage, which is why so many people knew him and thought highly of him. Grove's election to the Athenaeum was endorsed by an exceptional number of people (Plate 14). Thus Grove's warm acknowledgement of the role of his friends in his career may be taken ultimately as an acknowledgement of his sense of good fortune in having opportunities where they might not have existed. But what is completely obscured by his generous references to friends are the two factors that transformed the conditions of modest success into a highly distinguished achievement, namely ability and ambition. He clearly impressed his employers from the first. Grove's career in the engineering world was not that of an undistinguished figure. He was given opportunities and responsibilities that suggest the recognition of high competence. And the Society of Arts and Crystal Palace positions fired his energies and ambitions as he found his deeper interests as well as his skills better suited to this new world. His reaction to the opportunities shows the extent of his drive.

Far from waiting until his developing interest in biblical scholarship and musical research led naturally to new commitments, Grove was clearly ready to move to other prestigious administrative positions. During the period

1860–75 we know he applied for or considered five positions: Directorship of the Patent Museum; Secretary of the East Bengal Railway Company; Keepership of the South Kensington Museum; Librarian to the House of Commons; and Secretary to Lloyd's of London.[27]

A brief and intense correspondence with John Murray, the publisher, in connection with the House of Commons position gives an indication of his directness in his own interests (Plate 13). He wrote on 17 April 1867:

> Dear Mr Murray, Don't you think I am a very fit and proper person to be Librarian of the House of Commons? If so can you help me? I only heard of the vacancy this morning and have written to APS [Arthur Penryn Stanley, Dean of Westminster], the Archbishop [of Canterbury], Layard, W[illiam] Smith, F.C Cooke and one or two others I think likely to help me. But I would fear that it was given away. Yours very truly G Grove.

He followed this up with this reminder on 25 April:

> Cooke told me that you were kindly going to write to the speaker in my favour. I hope this is true because I hear there is a vast number of candidates and if you wait to see him he may have pledged himself. I am very unwilling to break in on your holiday, but if you would kindly do this for me, I would be deeply grateful. I have a strong idea of your weight with him and should feel much happier if I knew you had written. I have had many kind replies from the Archbishop of York, Bishop of London and others to whom my friends or I have written. I sent in my formal application yesterday and referred in it to the Chairman of the [Crystal Palace] Company, Dean of Westminster, Dr Jowett, and you, which Cooke assured me might do. I think I stand a fairish chance as an outsider, but some 'dark horse' is likely to win – Still I say let us fight to the last. Pardon the haste in which I write.

The following day he scribbled another pencilled note on the train to keep Murray up to date that there were 40 candidates and that he needed more support.[28]

Grove's letter shows that his ambitions were backed by great self-belief and commitment. Even if he had occasional – and more than occasional – doubts about his capacities, partly as a result of endemic over-commitment, he believed in his judgement and – the one thing he could rely on in addition to his skills of personality – his sheer capacity for hard work. He had gained this by experience and discipline. Add to these qualities his boundless enthusiasm and he had the right to expect to succeed.

We know something of his skills from recollections of others. He was a fine and painstaking editor, as the earlier quoted comments from William Smith and Dean Stanley show. Grove was clearly very effective in handling detail and communicating sense. This was probably learnt and perfected in the writing of reports in his earlier life as engineer as his report on the Menai project shows; the same quality is expressed by Mrs Wodehouse in connection with the *Dictionary of Music and Musicians*. He was seen as quick and intelligent, with common sense and practicality – the ideal person to get something done. His skills of personality, though they helped facilitate professional interaction, could not have achieved this on their own. He always kept the wheels turning: persistent hard work is the strongest image we have of Grove.

His capacity for organization and the handling of responsibility is less clear. Grove often seems over-pressured, almost persecuted. Yet despite his extraordinary level of commitments, there is no evidence of delegation of work, or of the use of a personal secretary or assistants, until later years (some letters appear to have been dictated from the RCM and in the final years were definitely so, with some of his own annotations). He feared for the health of his stalwart Registrar at the RCM, George Watson, constantly feeling obliged to be on hand. What drove him? Grove knew that he was over-committed and that this condemned him to overwork. One obvious explanation is that the things he loved the most and felt the need to involve himself deeply in – biblical scholarship, musical research – could never provide him a living, at least outside the world of the academy, which he was not qualified to enter by education. And as for his greatest passion, music, he had no practical, employable skill at all. His talent was his enthusiasm, endlessly enquiring mind and dedication to ideals. Yet his need of income, sense of social position and self-esteem demanded that he hold a professional post of status, and he thus battled to harmonize these huge demands in his daily life.

Friendships and relaxation

The breadth of Grove's interests and activities makes it difficult to draw a sharp distinction between his professional acquaintances and personal friends. Grove's professional life brought him into contact with a wide variety of people and by his nature he made friends of many of them, and he had an emotional need for his friends, and got close to them, old and young. But certain figures stand out in the three clear aspects of his life: youth; his social life in Sydenham; and his professional life, especially in central London. One friendship stands out in Grove's youth, that with George Granville Bradley. They first met when Bradley was aged 10 and Grove 11 or 12, as fellow pupils of Elwell's school, and Bradley would outlive Grove to officiate at his funeral service at St Bartholomew's, Sydenham, after a life in which 'our own intercourse has never been interrupted for a moment.' As shown, it was to lead to crucial friendships and contacts in biblical research and the Church.[29]

Apart from the religious dimension, one reason for Grove's continuing devotion to life in Sydenham (his friends marvelled at his patience and energy at coping with the daily travel to and from central London in his later years), was undoubtedly its significant cultural aspects, important to him long after the focus of his professional work had moved to central London with his appointment to edit *Macmillan's Magazine.* Especially attractive to Grove in view of his artistic interests and the musical life surrounding the Crystal Palace were the families of Scott Russell and von Glehn. Scott Russell, Grove's predecessor as Secretary of the Society of Arts, and in connection with the Britannia Bridge project, was also one of the first directors of the Crystal Palace. A well-known Scottish engineer, and builder of ships, he took over Napier's London shipyard for construction of the *Great Eastern*; he had worked at a Greenock shipyard when Grove was in Glasgow, and he later contributed articles to *Macmillan's Magazine* under Grove's editorship. He married an Irish beauty and had five children with her, including three daughters who inherited their mother's looks and talent: Louise, Rachel and Alice. Grove admired them all but was especially taken with his 'very dear friend' Louise, though she died on 6 March 1878 from consumption. Their house, situated between Sydenham and the Crystal Palace, was called Westgate, and was a focus for cultural activity. It was at this house that C.V. Stanford first met Grove.[30]

Robert William von Glehn (1800–85) was a merchant from Revel (now Tallinn), capital of Estonia (then a province of Russia) who settled in England in 1835: Grove was especially close to his family. As a young man von Glehn was tall, distinguished, very musical, a dancer and much sought after by society. Deeply attached to Britain, he married a Scottish lady and established a home on Peak Hill, Sydenham – Peak Hill Lodge – that became a remarkable centre of artistic and intellectual energy, frequented by many distinguished people including the young Hubert Parry. They had 12 children, many of whom made a mark. Oswald, a painter; William, who married Sophie Löwe, a singer; Ernest, the husband of Marian Bradley, half sister to Harriet Grove; Olga, and Mary Emilie, known as Mimi; the youngest of the girls, Louise, married Mandell Creighton, later Bishop of London. Mimi was remarkably musically talented. Von Bülow thought her the best amateur player of Beethoven and Chopin he knew and she went to study in Hanover with him for two winters running for six weeks. 'Fragile, gifted and magnetic, the chief attraction', Grove was especially attracted to her. And she has a special importance in view of her knowledge of music allied to her mastery of German; she translated various German musical texts for which Grove wrote the prefaces. She died in 1886. Ernest had connections with Oxford University in 1868–9, apparently as an undergraduate, and was a founder member of the Bach Choir. Robert von Glehn's decline after the death of his wife was a turning point in the vitality of that era. Grove was very close to Ernest, and the latter recalls long walks deep in conversation after dinner to and fro between each other's homes till terminated by fatigue. In addition, in connection with Sydenham, two professional musical friendships stand out, important apart from their musical association: with August Manns and Arthur Sullivan.[31]

The Sydenham phase of Grove's career lasted for over 30 years from the 1850s and was very rich for Grove. But the death of the leading figures changed all that too. With his appointment to the RCM in 1883, his attention shifted more fully to central London. He had for long had strong links to the metropolis through his membership of the Athenaeum, which was a natural focus for those sharing Grove's artistic and literary interests. His proposal had been supported by two of his most prestigious friends Dean Stanley and William Smith in 1858. And 13 years later in 1871, as we have seen, when elected he was supported by an exceptional number of people by club standards, the names reflecting the breadth of his interests and influence. One of his supporters was destined to be very important in his artistic life. Frederic Lehmann was the youngest of five sons of a German artist who married a Scottish woman in 1852. Her mother had lived in Sydenham and was a celebrated hostess: in 1859 her guests included Clara Schumann, Joachim, Chorley, Viardot-Garcia, and well as Grove. In turn his London house in Westbourne Grove became a focus for artists and musicians. Other important homes for musical socializing were those of John Hullah, and of the painter and supporter of music, Felix Moscheles, son of the musician Ignaz Moscheles.

Grove's deep involvement with the publication of the *Dictionary of Music and Musicians* and the concept, founding and direction of the RCM made friends of many of his colleagues. He sponsored two young men on the *Dictionary* project, J.A. Fuller Maitland and William Barclay Squire, who became close friends. Hubert Parry, to whom he referred as 'my dearest Hubert' was to become his preferred successor at the RCM (where Parry taught composition and the history of music). At the College itself, he was in close contact with the leading piano teacher Franklin Taylor. Professional music included many prominent women; at the RCM, leading women musicians included the revered singer Jenny Lind-Goldschmidt (an admiring supporter of Grove) and, among other female pianists, the comparably distinguished Arabella Goddard. Grove's work on the *Dictionary* had brought him into close contact with Mrs Adela Wodehouse, of whom he was fond. He was also very grateful for the help of Lilly Henkel, a resident of nearby Honor Oak, who assisted in translation and proofreading.

Such a full life gave little time for rest, and, like his friendships, Grove's relaxations are difficult to separate from his work. Though he needed his annual breaks and recuperations they were generally associated with some other form of activity – the more relaxed aspects of his main preoccupations. The few activities that might appear as 'hobbies' were just the interests that he failed to develop or integrate into some formal study with publication in view. We read of an early interest in engraving shared with a friend at the British Museum and of a short but intense devotion to Chinese porcelain-collecting, on which he made extensive pocket-book notes.[32] But his only apparent means of physical relaxation was walking and sightseeing, though, as a competent horseman he rode the parish at Sydenham on horseback (his love of animals is also apparent in the several resident cats and dogs in the Grove home).[33]

The half-century of the Groves' intimate association with Sydenham was to continue through the 14 years or so of Harriet Grove's widowhood; she died in 1914. The family house was subsequently purchased in 1919 as a presybytery for the Roman Catholic Church of our Lady and St Philip Neri. The house was demolished in 1929 and the present presbytery built on the site, now adjacent to the church. A plaque on the garden wall in Sydenham High Road is now the only reminder of the site's legendary past (Plate 16).

Notes

1 The Furse portrait hangs in the RCM and the Olivier hangs in Grove's club, the Athenaeum. The bronze bust by Alfred Gilbert was commissioned by students of the RCM in 1895 and resides there. Grove only appears to have appreciated one portrait. This, by his Sydenham neighbour and friend Henry Phillips, in private possession, shows him as a studious young man reading and leaning on books. He appears to be only in his twenties or early thirties at most. But since the various dates attributed to this undated painting are all in the early 1860s when he was over forty, this was clearly intended by his friend as a romantic image, stressing his love of art and learning as the young secretary of the Crystal Palace. The painting is reproduced in P.M. Young, *George Grove 1820–1900. A Biography* (London, 1980), facing p.48.
2 C.L. Graves, *The Life & Letters of Sir George Grove* (London, 1903), pp.447–8; C.V. Stanford, *Interludes, Records and Reflections* (London, 1922), p.136.
3 Graves, *Life & Letters*, pp.447–8; Stanford, *Interludes*, p.37.
4 Graves, *Life & Letters*, pp.448–9.
5 *Ibid.*, p.451.
6 *Ibid.*, p.172.
7 Graves, *Life & Letters*, pp.457, 127; *ibid.*, p.460.
8 Lord Frederic Leighton 1830–96; Graves, *Life & Letters*, pp.396, 29, 147.
9 Graves, *Life & Letters*, p.214; the names Stanley and Jowett refer to Dean Arthur Penrhyn Stanley (1815–81) and Benjamin Jowett (1817–93).
10 Graves, *Life & Letters*, p.451.
11 *Ibid.*, p.437.
12 *Ibid.*, p.332.
13 *Ibid.*, pp.401, 333. Letter of 3 October 1899 quoted in Young, *George Grove*, p.267.
14 Graves, *Life & Letters*, p.3.
15 Letter from William Blades to Eleanor Grove, 14 October 1880. See Christopher Edwards, 'Antiquarian Books and Music', *Catalogue of Papers*... (London, 1998), section IV 'Letters to Eleanor Grove'; Graves, *Life & Letters*, p.4.

16 *Ibid.*, pp.4–6; Graves notes that the house was situated on the present site of the Wandsworth railway station, then the Wandsworth Road Station of the Chatham and Dover Railway, and that Grove revisited in later life and pointed this out to the station superintendent.
17 Young, *George Grove*, p.54; 13n.
18 Graves, *Life & Letters*, pp.6–18. 'Letters to Eleanor Grove', in Edwards, *Catalogue of Papers...*
19 Graves, *Life & Letters*, pp.408, 358–9; 337; 27–9.
20 Graves, *Life & Letters*, p.8.
21 'George Grove's Autobiography', *Musical Standard*, 628 (July 1900), p.195.
22 Graves, *Life & Letters*, pp.320, 156; see the remarks quoted in Young, *George Grove*, p.215.
23 Young, *George Grove*, pp.83–4; 269.
24 Lucy Penrose: 25 April 1853–15 June 1863; Walter Maurice Grove: 27 January 1857–13 April 1931; Julius Charles Grove: 8 April 1859–19 February 1937; Millicent Stanley Grove: 28 January 1862–16 December 1886; Arthur Stanley Grove: 22 July 1864–2 February 1942. Of Milly, 'Our journeys were like lovers' journeys' (Graves, *Life & Letters*, p.320).
25 Bradley was headmaster of Marlborough from 1852 until 1870, when he became Master of University College, Oxford.
26 Young, *George Grove*, p.165.
27 Graves, *Life & Letters*, pp.68, 70, 71, 108, 150; 164–5.
28 Quoted from letters of 17 April 1867 and 25 April 1867 (London: John Murray Archive).
29 'Sir George Grove's Autobiography', p.195.
30 See the summary in Young, *George Grove*, pp.82–4.
31 Agnes died 14 January 1881; Graves, *Life & Letters*, pp.42, 262, 168; Young, *George Grove*, p.83; 'As a young man Parry used to visit the von Glehns.... the rendezvous of the coterie of which 'G' was the central figure, and Miss Mimi von Glehn, fragile, gifted and magnetic, the chief attraction'. C.L. Graves, *Hubert Parry. His Life and Works* (London, 1926), vol.1, p.232.
32 'Sir George Grove's Autobiography', p.195; Graves, *Life & Letters*, pp.190, 202, 209.
33 Graves, *Life & Letters*, p 448. See John Coulter, *Sydenham and Forest Hill Past* (London, 1999), p.24.

3
Describing and Evaluating: Grove on Technology, Geography, Exploration and Literature

Michael Musgrave

For all the breadth of Grove's professional activities, we know him pre-eminently through his widely published musical writings. His extensive commitments to his professional fields outside music are reflected only partially in his correspondence and the range of his attainment is largely hidden. This is especially true of the earlier years of his professional training and first career in engineering. But some more extended writings do exist to give a better sense of his knowledge and experience in the two spheres that dominated his life: science, technology, exploration and travel, and the arts and literature. The rest of this chapter seeks to exemplify these preoccupations and skills and show some recurrent themes between them, further illuminating the many connections in Grove's thought and activities: first, his work on the Britannia Bridge, his *Primer of Geography*, and his reports of the archaeological explorations sponsored by the Palestine Exploration Fund and his role in it; then his interest in literature and approach to literary criticism.

Reporting technology: the floating of the Britannia Bridge

The construction of the Britannia Bridge across the Menai Straits at Bangor in North Wales was part of a complex of projects designed to extend the railway system to Holyhead, Anglesey, and connection to Ireland. The Chester General (Joint) Station, on which Grove had acted as Supervising Site Engineer on C.H. Wild's staff, was also an essential part of the rationalization of rail lines in the North West and was constructed and used by both the Chester & Holyhead Railway and the Chester & Birkenhead Railway. The Britannia Bridge was a further part of this scheme. Grove moved with the project, still attached to Wild's staff, as an assistant site engineer. It was the second major engineering project to span the Menai Straits, preceded in 1826 by Thomas Telford's pioneering suspension bridge for road traffic; the new bridge was situated a mile further down the Straits. The provision of a railway bridge posed a much bigger problem because the suspension method, so impressive in earlier engineering projects, would not provide the strength necessary to carry heavy railway trains. Stephenson's solution was the concept of a huge iron beam or tube, a technology involving many new issues in manufacture.

The project also involved much new technology in installation. There were 26 travelling cranes and six steam engines; 2,177 cargoes of stone; and five wharves and landing stages. A total of 700 men had been engaged in the stonework, 800 on the ironworks, and 700 in the floating operations, together with 36 on the delicate task of raising the great tubes of best wrought iron from Staffordshire. There was also a social challenge: the construction of 80 wooden cottages for 500 workers and their families, shops, school, Sunday school, and meeting houses. W.S. Morsom was resident director, Frank Foster resident engineer, and Wild and Edwin Clark assistant engineers, the latter responsible for the overall floating and lifting operations. By November 1848 all the towers were nearing completion. On 22 February 1849, the side towers were ready. The giant tubes, each more than a quarter of a mile long had been constructed some 2000 feet from the site of the bridge. (The floating of the second tube is illustrated in Plate 6).

On 19 June the first attempt to float the first tube into its raising position was made. Stephenson and some of his assistants, with Brunel, Joseph Locke, Captain Claxton and Sir Francis Head, were on the tube. But the first attempt to float it was unsuccessful; as was the second, made early the next morning. However, at 8 o'clock on the evening of 20 June the operation was satisfactorily completed.[1] The event was widely reported in the national press. Grove was the anonymous writer of the following report for the *Spectator* on 23 June 1849, which noted by way of introduction that 'the first of the four great iron tubes for the Britannia Bridge over the Menai Straits has been floated to its place. A correspondent supplies us with the following as a strictly accurate account of this interesting operation'. The correspondent's contribution read:

> The operation of floating the first tube of the Britannia Bridge from the place in which it was constructed to the foot of the towers by which it is at last to be supported, came off on the evening of Wednesday. The preceding evening was the one originally fixed on, but the capstan breaking after the hauling point a few feet, it was necessary to put off doing more till the following day. The tube was built at a distance from the bridge of about 2000 feet, and at a position along the shore at right angles to the line of the railway. It had therefore, after being borne down to very near the towers, to be slewed round across the stream, and finally adjusted to its place on the projecting shelf of stone at the foot of the piers. These evolutions were accomplished by ropes from capstans and crabs on the two shores and on the Britannia Rock: the men in charge of

> which were signalled to from the top of the tube. The final adjustment was a very delicate piece of work, as the width of the recess into which the huge mass had to be inserted is only an inch greater than that of the tube itself: however, it was managed with complete success. ...The whole operation occupied exactly one hour and three quarters; the order to haul out being given at 7.36, and the Anglesey end entering its recess at 9.22.
>
> On the tube with Mr Stephenson were his two assistants, and Messrs Brunel and Locke, who acted as his honorary assistants, Captain Claxton and Sir Francis Head. There was a general gathering of engineers, and a vast concourse of spectators, who lined the shores and platform on both sides of the Straits.
>
> The raising of the tube through the 100 feet between its present and its ultimate position will probably take place in the course of a few days. Its length is 172 feet, height at the centre tower 30, and its weight between 1700 and 1800 tons.[2]

Learning with Grove: the Primer of Geography

Grove retained a lifelong interest in the geography and geology of the natural world and had become a Fellow of the Royal Geographical Society by 1876; hence the relatively late appearance of his geography primer in 1877, when he had long passed any professional need for involvement in the subject. The skill and understanding with which it he lays out an account of the natural world for the general or school reader shows not only the thoroughness of his grounding in the subject, much rooted in Pritchard's teaching, but equally his skills as a teacher; this is the closest we come to Grove the teacher in action. His book was commissioned by J.R. Green as part of a series of 'History Primers' in various subjects doubtless inspired by the new educational requirements following the passing of the 1870 (Forster) Education Act.[3]

The book is structured in four major sections covering the following topics in 100 pages or so.

1. Maps and Map Making
2. The Earth: including the arrangement of the land and water; the structure of the old world and new world; comparison of the two; Europe, Australia, North America.
3. The Ocean: including its extent; the Atlantic, the Pacific, the Indian, the Arctic and Antarctic; winds, currents, Gulf Stream, bottom of the ocean, its heat, its saltiness.
4. Features of the Earth: including continents, islands, capes, mountains, volcanoes, valleys, plains, peninsulas, rivers, deltas, seas, water partings, watersheds, basins, coasts, gulf, strait, icebergs.

The book concludes with an Appendix including measures of length; knots in a degree of longitude in various latitudes; scales and symbols of ordnance maps.

One immediately notices the character of Part 1. The links to Grove's school interests and skills come clearly into view in the first of these sections: maps and map making – what a map is; how it differs from a picture; globes; poles; longitude and latitude; meridians; degrees and great circles; Mercator's chart; the Ordnance Survey and trigonometry; the mariner's compass, tropics and zones; axis rotation, time and travel. Equally, one notes how Grove continues to live out the principles of Pritchard's teaching in presenting the subject 'in a practical and interesting way, and as connected with common life, not the abstract world'; hence his focus on the necessity for the standardization of time based on his own wide experience of foreign travel and, at home, the consequences of railway travel (Greenwich Mean Time was only adopted as standard in 1884). The extract below, drawn from paras 47–57, covers 'the compass' and 'time'.

> 47 The compass was invented in the 12th or 13th century, no one knows by whom. Before its discovery ships crept about close to land, or if they ventured out, as St Paul's ship did, for an open course of 5 or 600 miles, were at once in the greatest uncertainty when the sun and stars were hid.
>
> 48 I said that the needle pointed *towards* the north, but it does not always point exactly *to* it. In fact there are only two lines on the earth's surface along which the needle does point to the true north, and neither of the two has any connection with parallels or meridians, but seems to cross them at haphazard. One of them sweeps up from the Antarctic circle, enters the east coast of South America, in S. lat. 24°, a little south of Rio de Janeiro, leaves it again at Cayenne, north of the mouth of the Amazons, crosses the Atlantic outside the West Indian Islands, enters North America near Cape Hatteras, and runs to a point north west of Hudson's Bay. The other line lies nearly opposite across the world, and is much more irregular in its course. It too comes up from the Antarctic Circle, and enters South Australia in E. long. 129°, S. lat. 32°, in the Australian Bight. It leaves it again in King's Sound, lat. 17° S., and long. 123° E., and, taking a sudden bend to the west passes outside of Java, Sumatra and the Malabar Coast, enters the continent of Asia in E. long. 60°, runs to the West of the Caspian, passes between Lakes Ladoga and Onega, and enters the arctic seas near the North Cape.
>
> 49 Along these lines there is no **variation of the compass**, but the needle points straight to the true north; and as you leave them on either side, it varies. To the east of them it points to the west of the true north, to the west of them it points east of the true north, more and more as you

forsake the lines of no variation. At the south of Greenland, the variation is 50 degrees West, and if you want to steer N.N.E. through Smith's Sound, as the Arctic Expedition did, you would have to set the ship's head South by West....The variation at London is 19°, 26′ West, at Cork, 24° West, and so on. The lines of variation all over the world are marked on the Admiralty charts, so no mistake can be made.

50 This variation is not always the same at the same place, but changes year by year or day by day. It was first noted by Columbus on September 13, 1492. In 1580, the variation at London was 11° 15′ East. In 1660 it had decreased to nothing and the needle at London then stood true, but it immediately began to vary on the other side, and increased till 1818, when it reached a limit of 24°, 30′ West; then it began to decrease, and now the variation there is 19°, 26′ West.

51 The lines of variation all come together at two places. One is north of Hudson's Bay, near Port Kennedy, in 75° N. lat., 100° West long. A second is in the Polar Sea, north of Nova Zembla. These points are called magnetic poles, and if you take the compass needle to one of them it will behave very strangely. It will not remain level but will dip and stand straight up and down, the north end down and the south straight in the air; also, if it is prevented from doing this and obliged to remain level, it will turn equally well to all points, just as a common piece of steel, not a magnet. The variation in the needle east or west is called its *declination*; the dip up and down is called its *inclination*.

52 **Time**. Another remark before we close this part of the Primer. We have seen that the circumference of the earth is divided into 360 parts or degrees. As it goes round on its axis once in 24 hours, its surface moves at the rate of 15 degrees an hour, since 15 times 24 = 360. I am not speaking now of the movement of the earth round the sun, but of its **motion on its axis** only, its **rotation** not its *revolution*. The sun is standing still at a distance, and the earth spins round once in 24 hours from west to east; and thus every place comes into view of the sun which is **sunrise**; arrives right opposite him, – which is **noonday**, and loses sight of him again, which is **sunset**. But move a short distance on either side of your own place, and each of these events will happen sooner or later than before. If you move to the East, sooner, if to the West, later. The difference made by moving one minute of longitude would be 4 seconds of time, and by one degree of longitude, 4 minutes of time.

53 And this explains why, when you go from the place where you live to one east of it, your watch seems to lose. It is not that your watch loses, but that you have arrived at a place when the sun comes into view of the earth, and comes to 12 o'clock, sooner than where you usually live. Suppose you go from London to Hamburg. Hamburg is east of London by 10 degrees of longitude. Now the earth turns once round, that is through

360 degrees of longitude, in 24 hours: and as from London to Hamburg is 10 degrees, when you are at Hamburg, you are one 36th part of 24 hours, or 40 minutes, nearer the sun than in London: that is to say, the earth arrives at sunrise and at 12 o'clock 40 minutes sooner in Hamburg than it does at London. But your watch keeps London time, and therefore when it is 12 o'clock at Hamburg your watch is 11.20 because at that moment it is 11.20 in London. In other words, London will have to travel 40 minutes further east before it comes opposite the sun for 12 o'clock. If, when it is 12 in Hamburg, if they were to telegraph the time from London it would be 11.20; and if when it is 12 in London, they were to telegraph you from Hamburg, it would be 12.40 there – Hamburg would have passed 12 o'clock, or the meridian line, by 40 minutes.

54 Go to a place west of London and the opposite happens. Take New York, which is 75° West longitude. Now 75 times 4 minutes is 300 minutes or 5 hours; that is to say, 5 hours after it has struck 12 o'clock at London, New York will have come whirling round to the same place at which London was 5 hours before, and will arrive opposite the sun, and have its 12 o'clock; and meantime, London will have gone on with its day, and its clocks will be striking 5 in the afternoon. And this accounts for the fact that telegraphs arrive in New York from London apparently before the hour at which they are sent off. Thus, say the Boat-race is won by Oxford at 1.35 p.m. The news is telegraphed to New York and arrives there, we'll say, by 2 London time. But at 2 London time it is only 9 New York time (5 hours earlier), so that New York actually hears of the event 4 hours and 25 minutes before the hour at which it happened!

55 After the railways were made it was found very inconvenient to have one time in London and another at Exeter or Birmingham, and so in all common matters, the towns of England sink their own correct time, and the clocks are set to that of London. Thus a train leaving London at 9 arrives at Bristol in 4 hours, and finds the clocks there exactly as they are in London; though if the clocks told the correct time they would show 12.50, Bristol being 2° 34' west of London, equivalent to rather more than 10 minutes of time. And communication will increase until the same thing that has been done in England will have to be done outside of it, and sooner or later all countries will have to keep London time.

56 As you go farther and farther round the world, the difference between the hour where you are and the hour at Greenwich will increase until it reaches 12 hours, and if you sail on till you get back to Greenwich again you will have gained or lost 24 hours, according as you sailed east or west – gained if you went east by the Suez canal, lost if you went west by America. In the first case, when you got back, if it were Tuesday on board the ship, it would be Monday on the newspapers in London; in the second

case it would be Tuesday on board and Wednesday on the newspapers. To correct this the log or journal of the ship is always altered when it arrives at the meridian of 180° (half way round the world from London), and a day is added or dropped in the reckoning as she has sailed East or West. But the old sailors were not always careful to do this, and some curious things happened in consequence. When Captain Basil Hall got to Manila (120° East long) he found that their Sunday was his Monday. At Tahiti the reverse has happened, and they keep Sunday on a Saturday. 'At Sitka in Russian America (W. long 136°) half the people are Russians who have arrived from Russia across Asia and half are Americans who have come from the United States. Hence when it is Sunday with the Russians it is Saturday with the Americans and the Russians are busy on Monday while the Americans are at their rest on Sunday, to the great interruption of business.' (See Clarke, *Geographical Reader*.)

58 Once more before we leave our globe for the earth itself, see how these scientific terms have worked their way into common speech. You have often heard the expression – 'angle of ninety degrees', 'angle of forty-five'. You remember that each meridian is divided into 360 degrees over its whole length. If, therefore from the Equator over the Pole, round by the Equator and South Pole to the starting point again was 360 degrees, it stands to reason that from the Equator to the Pole will be one quarter of that, or 90 degrees. From E to N is 90 degrees...– that which a stick makes with the floor when you stand it quite upright. And...an angle of 45 degrees,...is exactly half the angle of 90 degrees – halfway between level and being upright.[4]

Reporting exploration: the Palestine Exploration Fund

Grove's interest in the natural world and the technologies of map making, travel and description, came to a fruitful new synthesis with his abiding interest in biblical history and personalities. As a result of his contact with James Fergusson, Dean A.P. Stanley and William Smith, and his own visits to Palestine in 1858 and 1861 (during which he visited Nâblus and wrote a lengthy account of the Samaritans), Grove became deeply involved in the geographical and archaeological verification of the biblical narrative, in turn also part of the broader contemporary drive towards travel and exploration, more famously recorded in David Livingstone's explorations of Africa in 1841–56. The whole subject of biblical research had come to the fore as a result of the impact of science on traditional religious belief, a gradual process of which a focal point was the publication of Darwin's theories in 1859; within the Church itself a liberal theology was spreading as evidenced for example in such publications as Jowett's 'Interpretation of Scripture' in *Essays and Reviews*; and the study of the *Pentateuch* by J.W. Colenso, both of which were attacked for the beliefs of their authors, though both were supported by Grove. The publisher John Murray had created a whole community around Smith's biblical dictionary work with his regular Bible Dictionary dinners as a source of contact. Grove's organizing skills and energy gave however a special focus in the general interest through the foundation of the Palestine Exploration Fund to map and describe the Holy Land in detail for the first time.[5]

The focus of interest on Jerusalem had taken took a huge step forward through the preliminary survey of the city made in 1863–4 by Captain C.W. Wilson of the Royal Engineers. This had been undertaken ostensibly to organize a water supply, a project funded by Miss (later Baroness) Burdett-Coutts who provided £500 for the preliminary survey. Dean Stanley, intimately interested in the field through the research embodied in his recent book *Sinai and Palestine*, applied to Sir Henry James, Head of the Ordnance Survey (Wilson's superior) for the services of a Royal Engineer party to be paid from the sum provided by Miss Burdett-Coutts. Grove had become particularly interested since reading the book *Jerusalem Explored* by Pierotti, about which he wrote to *The Times*. Grove met with Fergusson and David Roberts at the Crystal Palace, and apparently before the end of 1864 had hatched the plan of a larger project (the Palestine Exploration Fund); the later recollections of Walter Morrison confirm Grove as the motor behind this project.[6]

James wrote to *The Times* about the survey on 31 December 1864, specifying the discoveries made by the expedition, and hoping for funds to complete the investigations and report on the relative levels of the Mediterranean Sea, Jerusalem and the Dead Sea. Grove responded immediately, commending, in his letter published on 3 January 1865, Captain Wilson and these aims, but with the following further demands:

> There are other matters, also, that are crying out for accurate investigation and which I earnestly hope means may be found to enable Captain Wilson to examine. I will name only four, though it would be easy to swell the list. 1. The excavation of the remains of the so-called Frank Mountain – the Herodium, or fortress built by Herod and described by Josephus. 2. The exploration of the tombs of Tibneh, a little west of the main north road at Jifneh, a few miles above Jerusalem. These are nearly, if not quite, as important as the well-known 'Tombs of the Kings' at Jerusalem, and one of them is probably the tomb of Joshua in his inheritance at Timnath; 3. A correct plan of the remains of the great temple and of the Samaritan Holy Places on Mount Gerizim – the Mount Moriah of Abraham; 4. The exact latitude of the spots at which the Wady Zerka and other torrents on the East side of the Jordan enter that river. The want of this knowledge is a sad bar to any accurate map making in that locality.

He adds in conclusion that there must be many who would support this project 'if some proper channel were found for their liberality' and proposing 'the unused balance of the funds for the The Assyrian Excavation Fund founded in 1853 by Mr Layard, M.P and the late Mr S. Phillips' as a basis, in the hands of the treasurer, Mr John Murray, commenting 'but why should it not revive to the kindred work of Palestine exploration?'

Grove had thus widened the scope of the possibilities for exploration at a stroke. To further his aims, he approached a number of friends and contacts and encouraged them to support a preliminary meeting held on 12 May 1865. He already knew Austin Layard, the explorer of Nineveh, who, in 1865, was Foreign Under-Secretary. Grove broadened the base of support by encouraging scientific interests, resisting the clerical emphasis that Charles Kingsley, in a letter to Grove, had suggested would limit proper scientific discussion, though ensuring a wide representation across the religious community. The Fund was then launched at a meeting on 22 June 1865, at Willis's Rooms at St James's, with the Archbishop of York in the chair and Grove as Hon. Secretary – the Archbishop commenting that it was their aim 'to apply the rules of science, which are so well understood in other areas, to the study of the Holy Land'.[7] On 11 August Grove informed Layard that a resolution had been passed with instructions to Wilson to concentrate on certain sites near Damascus, at the north eastern corner of the Lake of Galilee, and in Jerusalem. There was, of course, a political and diplomatic dimension to be considered: Wilson wanted favour to be shown to the Pasha for permissions to excavate the holy places; and already work on excavating a well at 70 feet had had to be stopped for lack of funds.

Grove now set about gaining public support through words and speeches. He spoke in Birmingham in September 1865 to the Geographical Section of British Association on the need for 'systematic, leisurely and thorough-going investigation of the Holy Land', and raised £100 as a result. By February 1868, in speaking to the Institute of British Architects, he was inclining his words towards the interests of his listeners as concerning a subject 'which could not fail to be interesting to his audience, as their accomplishment would necessarily conduce to the promotion of architecture and the kindred arts'.[8]

The first party had set off in December 1865. Its progress was regularly communicated to the public through Grove's summaries of Wilson's reports (Wilson was 'working assisted by Lieutenant Anderson R.E., an officer, like himself, of much experience in surveying and observing, and a corporal of engineers who is a first rate photographer', as Grove records). In a letter to *The Times* of 17 January 1866, Grove emphasized the range of the technical equipment provided (one of its providers was Charles Pritchard):

> They are well provided with chronometers, barometers and other meteorological and surveying instruments [and] are also furnished with every requisite for maintaining and preserving of collections in botany, natural history, geography etc. Few private expeditions have probably gone out of the country better provided. The object of the expedition is in the main tentative. To ascertain what special lines of exploration may be followed out in more detail.

Grove then outlined the places and their relation to the biblical narrative; for example:

> at Banias, the sources of the Jordan will be investigated, and an attempt made to find Lake Phiala of Josephus, the present identification of which ...is more than doubtful. Descending the Jordan, Kedes – the Kedesh of the story of Sisera – will be explored, and an attempt made to discover the site of Hazor. The first serious halt will be the upper end of the Lake of Galilee, where an endeavour will be made by careful examination of the ruins at Tell Ham, and by exploration and excavation at Khan Minyeh and at Ain-el Madawara (the round fountain) to elucidate the situation of Capernaum, Bethsaida, and the other towns of the Gennesarat. It seems more than possible that among the extensive remains of architectural fragments which strew the ground at Tell Ham, some inscriptions may be found to throw a new light on this vexed and hitherto hopeless question, of such deep interest to all readers of the gospel narrative. While here explorations will be made on the eastern side of the lake, with a view to reconciling the curious discrepancies pointed out by the Dean of Westminster [A.P.Stanley] (*Sinai and Palestine* ch. 10), and thus throwing light on the spot where the healing of the demoniacs and the destruction of the swine took place.
>
> The level of the Lake above the Mediterranean will also be taken....Nâblus ...will be the second halting place...Proceeding southwards from Nâblus, several places of promise will be explored. Seilùun (Shiloh), so long a sanctuary and a seat of the Tabernacle; Tibneh, probably Timnath, possibly the burial place of Joshua, containing extensive and elaborate tombs, hitherto only cursorily examined...but promising to be both interesting and important; Beitin (Bethel), abounding in ruins. At Jerusalem Wady Bittir (possible the ancient Berher), and the Frank Mountain, the Herodium, or fortress of Herod, will be explored. In Jerusalem itself, what can be done will depend much on circumstances, and must be left to the judgement of Captain Wilson....

Between December 1865 and May 1866 no less than 49 different places, the positions of which were previously unknown had been fixed and detailed sketches for maps published under Grove's supervision by John

Murray. In August 1866 at the Nottingham British Association meeting, Grove announced the intention to persevere until every square mile of Palestine had been properly and accurately surveyed and mapped:

> Till every mound of ruins has been examined and sifted; the name of every village ascertained, recorded and compared with the lists in the Bible; till all the ancient roads has been traced, the geology made out; the natural history and botany fully known.[9]

On 21 May 1866, *The Times* reported on Grove's lecture to the Institute of British Architects, noting that he could

> say without hesitation that nothing definite or certain was known about the places of which [he] was speaking until a year or two ago. Up to that time the geology had been conjectural; and the maps of the Holy Land, though they looked well enough, were anything but accurate in detail. The dearth of articles connected with the archaeology of Palestine [was] remarkable in the highest degree.[10]

The second party had set out under Lt Warren in January 1867, focusing on Jerusalem. Such exploration could not proceed without gaining a political dimension, involving the observation of local customs and the obtaining of permissions to enter the holy places. The Archbishop of York became involved in this, and Grove in due course made public the issues in a letter to *The Times* of 5 August 1867.

> When the Palestine Exploration Fund sent out their second party to the Holy Land in January 1865 under charge of Lt Charles Warren they gave him general instruction to make Jerusalem his headquarters and to investigate in and about the city as much as possible, especially in the sacred enclosure of the Harem-es-Sherif; and Lord Stanley was then good enough to apply to the government of the Porte for a Vizierial letter authorizing such explorations to be made within that sacred spot. The letter was duly sent to Lieutenant R.E. Warren in accordance with Lord Stanley's request, but unfortunately on its arrival it was found to contain a clause expressly excluding the Haram-es-Sherif and all other sanctuaries from our examination. Lieutenant Warren therefore wisely determined not to make use of so imperfect a weapon, but to proceed with his investigations as best he could without such aid. The result is that outside the walls of the sacred enclosure he has made as discovery which is almost, if not quite, as important as any that have ever been made about or in Jerusalem, and which cannot fail to be fruitful parent of many more. He has found that the south wall of the Haram, which rears its venerable face to a height of 80 feet above the soil, descends to

no less than a depth of 50 feet below it – the solid rock of Mount Moriah on which it is founded being covered with an immense thickness of débris. Thus this wall must have originally stood at a height of 130 feet above its foundations, fully justifying the expressions of Josephus, who says concerning it that 'if anyone looked down from the top of the battlements into the valley he would be giddy, while his sight could not reach to such an immense depth' (Ant xv., ii., sec. 5).

The foundations and the unworn masonry of the buried portion may be expected to disclose many a secret affecting these venerable walls, secrets which Lieutenant Warren is now diligently occupied in revealing. But that is not all. He found two other things. He found, first, that the eastern wall is prolonged beyond the southern face, and continues in the general direction of Siloam, with all the solidity and antiquity which characterize its known portions. How far it continues and what are its exact direction and extent, I expect to hear shortly from Lieutenant Warren. He found, secondly, that below the débris a second south wall exists 20 feet distant from the known one, and of slighter workmanship. How far this walls goes, what its purpose may have been, its relation to the 'triple gateway' and the staircase which M.de Saulcy believed he had discovered to descend from the triple gateway, how this discovery may affect the piers of the arches below the southeast corner of the enclosure, are questions I await further information to be able to answer.

Meanwhile, such discoveries outside naturally whetted the appetite of the committee for what existed inside the enclosure, and at their recent meeting on the 19th July, in the Jerusalem chamber at Westminster, it was resolved to apply to the Fuad Pasha for an interview, either with himself or with the Sultan, at which the intentions of the committee might be laid fully open, and any power or influence possible obtained. I now leave the Archbishop's letter to tell its own tale:–

'I stated,' says his Grace 'that our committee desired every facility should be given then for the explorations; that we disclaimed all wish to proselytise through them; that we were acting in the interests of religious literature and history only, and that we earnestly desired to excite no hostility. Fuad Pasha observed that the Turkish government desired to be perfectly tolerant, and that the only limitation of their power to be so lay in the danger of fanatical outbreaks, which arose, not from the Turks, but from the Christian population, and the natural jealousies of the three great divisions of Christians. So far as was consistent with order, the Government would give every help to the exploration. A little distribution of money here and there to the custodians of these places would do much to smooth away difficulties. He observed that the Turks no longer knew the Protestants only through the representation of other sects, but understood them better than formerly, and were aware that they did not lend

> themselves to any political object: He said…I will desire that every possible facility be given to the explorers, believing that they are, as you say, discrete and desirous to avoid disturbance. I shall be glad at any future time to hear from you as to your wishes, and shall do all I can to promote them'.

Grove concluded:

> Nothing could be better than this, and I feel confident that before long the secrets of these most venerable and interesting places (surely the most interesting in the world) will have yielded themselves up to the reverent and intelligent examination and the exact record, of Lieutenant Warren and his Sappers.

After an appeal for money he concludes:

> The Palestine Exploration Fund is the first organized attempt to do what four-fifths of the educated Englishmen of the last 50 years have longed, have tried to do for themselves. Who is there that has ever had the opportunity of going to Palestine who has not eagerly embraced it, and who is there that has not found the speed, the language, the heat, the ten thousand drawbacks of the place too much for him, and returned with a new idea, a new feeling, certainly, but still with hardly more? At last this society was started with the object of doing at leisure, and in a systematic and thorough manner, what everyone tries and fails to do hastily, fragmentarily for himself.

He continued in like vein in a letter to *The Times* of 14 November 1867, again seeking public financial support.

> I am well aware that discoveries of the kind I have named are barren and uninviting to the majority of readers, even to many who are keenly interested in the Holy Land and Holy Writ. They find little in them to throw direct light on the lives which they so cherish, and every detail of which they so dearly prize. True; but it must be recollected that exploration in Jerusalem is at present in a condition of a puzzle or joining map in which only half-a-dozen pieces are found out of 60 or 70. Find the others and the whole can be put together and it will be intelligible enough. Extend to the other parts of the city the researches here begun, and the sites of the Temple, Calvary, the Holy Sepulchre, the Pool of Bethesda, will be problems no longer. I may therefore, with good reason, beseech all who are interested in Biblical Studies to give their aid to the Palestine Fund for this work. …The Fund has been in existence two years and under all the difficulties of a first enterprise we have succeeded in making an Ordnance Survey of 2,300 square miles, in obtaining 340 photographs, and in

> making the discoveries which form the immediate subject of this letter. In this work, £3,242 have been expended, a sum which no one conversant with the subject will think extravagant. I entreat the public of England not to let it drop. Mr Warren estimates his expenses at £200 a month for six or eight months £1,500. What is this to raise in England from the very large number of persons who take an interest in researches bearing so directly on the illustration of the Bible?

Grove's interest and active involvement as Hon. Secretary continued for many years, though by 1868 Walter Besant became Executive Secretary, and Grove was eventually succeeded as Hon Secretary by F.W. Holland. Grove was always available for important issues. For several years from 1871 he supported the application of Clermont Ganneau to obtain leave of absence from the French Government to participate in the extensive survey of Western Palestine, which had begun under Captain Stewart, was continued by C.R. Conder, with Lt Hubert Horatio Kitchener as his assistant, and was completed by Kitchener (in due course Field Marshall Kitchener) in 1877. The party learnt much from these experiences though it was withdrawn for two years after local attacks in 1875, a reminder of the constant threat to this work. A total of 26 sheets were published in 1879 in four colours, a feat of map-making that remained the standard source until 1956 when a new series was produced. All this work was expanded into a comprehensive book written by Conder and Kitchener as *The Survey of Western Palestine, 1882–1888, including a Survey of Eastern Palestine,* which remains the primary source for the study of Palestine, and has recently been issued in a facsimile edition by the Fund, which continues its work to this day.[11]

Grove was doubtless greatly heartened to receive the following letter from his sister Ellen in 1877, which captures the popular response he sought, as well as throwing some fresh light on the family background and his closeness to her. It was written in response to a request for Grove to give a lecture on Palestine.

> Don't you think people would like much to hear the new discoveries with regards to the geography of Palestine? One's ideas about it have been so completely <u>untergraben</u> [undermined] of late years that one does not know where the old towns and places about which we spoke to our Sunday school children with such comfortable certainty in old days have wandered to. I only put this out as an idea, but so <u>many</u>.... teach in Sunday Schools that such an explanation of matters would be both necessary and interesting...; But perhaps there is not enough matter for a course?
>
> Your loving sister, Ellen.[12]

Literature and literary criticism

Grove's wide circle of friends and acquaintances brought him into contact with many aspects of artistic as well as scientific life. He regularly attended the major art exhibitions and was clearly very familiar with foreign galleries and their treasures from his many travels. As well as the music-loving Lord Frederic Leighton, pre-eminent in London's artistic life during Grove's period as the long-serving president of the Royal Academy, he was close to Felix Moscheles, the painter son of the pianist and composer Ignaz Moscheles, who was likewise devoted to music, and friend also of the Lehmann family, whose house in Westbourne Grove, as we have seen, was a 'focus of artistic, literary and musical activity'.[13]

Grove's greatest preoccupation of the imagination outside music was with literature. He read voluminously and loved to respond, in letters to friends or to the press, to emerging critical issues in many fields, whether in response to writings on history, contemporary events, or religious and social matters. One would stress that his compulsive writing of letters is really the mirror of his reading as a crucial means of contact in his communication with others. He read partly to satisfy an insatiable appetite for knowledge and understanding, but also with a writer's and a scholar's eye and analytical sense of substance and aptness of expression. Graves observes that

> many of his books bear the unmistakeable impress of his eager mind, for not only are the margins crowded with notes containing cross references, comparisons of different editions, corrections or exclamations, but he also constantly made his own index, fixing in extra blank pages at the end of the volume for the purpose.

In an age before mass communication, the written word served many purposes for communication, and basic themes and issues permeated novels, poetry, essays, and criticism. Records of his reading at various times show a remarkable range. At random, Graves notes of the year 1863, for example, that his reading included Arnold's Poems; Landor's *Imaginary Conversations*, Kinglake's *Eothen*, Austen's *Faust*; Lewes's *Goethe*; Lecky's *History of Rationalism*; Herder's *Spirit of Hebrew Poetry*; Mrs Margaret Oliphant's *The Chronicles of Carlingford* and Dickens's *Our Mutual Friend*, as well as Carl Engel's *Music of the Ancients*; the records invariably include Shakespeare and the Psalms of David (to whom he often refers as David).[14]

Major works of commentary on the present and recent world and its great figures, especially when involving religious and social issues were a central preoccupation, for example, his enthusiastic reception of Thomas Carlyle's *The French Revolution* and *Frederick the Great*; James Anthony Froude's *History of England*; Benjamin Jowett's *Sermons*. He read novels very widely, though his temperamental limitations denied him the full scope of the modern novel.

> I have just been reading The Mill on the Floss. I never read it but once before, and the remembrance of the deep tragedy of it has always kept me away from it since. It's wonderfully true to nature and in parts wonderfully fetching; and certainly the tragedy is as great as I recollected it. Yet Tom [Tulliver], true to life as he is, is to me very repulsive – and yet what a fine character for conflict with the world!

Grove always looked for strong characterization and description. His favourite English novelist was Thackeray. Here he could also revel in the social observations: and he even envisaged issuing a revised edition of *Vanity Fair*, 'correcting various errors and inaccuracies, due chiefly to careless proof reading in the original edition, which had long…been thorns in his flesh'. He was attracted to Trollope well before Trollope's greater popularity, commending *The Duke's Children*, which he thought 'very good…not elevating, not exciting, but a thorough good piece of painting of character and manners'.[15]

He also read foreign novels. Grove had studied German early on in his musical studies, and had sufficient French to read Zola's *Le docteur Pascal* almost immediately after its publication; he was impressed by the veracity of its descriptive force, though commenting in due course 'but we can't live on psychology, especially when it all tends to filth – so I think "je jetterai au feu"'. Of Russian novels, he was greatly attracted to the novels of Turgenev (in translation) – 'so little padding, so much like real life' and 'one of the greatest artists of our time'; at one time he would 'never go on a journey without taking *Pères et Enfants* or the *Nichée de Gentilshommes* in his pocket'.[16]

The core of his reading was used for intimate artistic and spiritual experience, companionship and comfort. Here poetry held the key, because it combined two aspects essential to Grove: a musical, sonorous quality, and a preoccupation with the numinous, with the deeper mysteries of life. He advised his students one 'should always have a stock of poetry to hand'. There are many examples of his referring to particular lines when something pressing was on his mind; even when depressed in later years, memories of poetic lines would accompany a rise in spirits, as, for example in response to the coming of spring:

> How lovely the Spring is! The mere look of the golden young lime-leaves against the pale blue sky in the morning is enough to make one thankful for all the beauty and joy that one sees around one. And then the sounds! And the delicious faint smells: as Tennyson says: 'Sympathies how frail/ In sound and smell'.[17]

That which moved and satisfied him most profoundly was invariably celebrated by analogy with great music: he loved that which was most like music – instrumental music – that which was beyond rational explanation and moved one primarily emotionally: the capacity of poetry to capture a unique and sensitive mood was analogous to music's ineffable quality. He was fascinated by the common elements: rhythm, balance, the quality and quantity of stress, and was greatly interested in scansion: he obviously memorized the sonic, aural quality of poetry. Graves notes that 'of his favourite [modern] poets.... he knew a great portion by heart' – and though one can observe that he did not always recall them perfectly, his retention was (like the range of what he read) very notable.[18]

It was nineteenth-century English poetry, however, essentially that of his contemporaries, and that of the immediately preceding and following generations, that attracted him by combining musical qualities with a mirror of his own emotions and concerns, especially loss of faith in religion, and issues of the fate of loved ones. Grove claims that his first insights to poetry came in 1865 when he penned his own lines of verse associated with personal loss and tragedy at what he called 'the problem time of his life', at the first challenge to his religious belief with the death of Lucy.[19]

Graves observes that Grove's favourite (modern) poets were Tennyson, Matthew Arnold, Clough and Wordsworth. Tennyson was by far his favourite, for whom he had no reservations and most admiration and to whom he was closest in the musical and spiritual qualities of his work. Grove knew Tennyson personally from his thirties. Analogies occur more often in Grove's writings between Tennyson and great music and great feelings than with anyone else. He believed him to be the greatest poet since Shakespeare. Grove's response to Tennyson through an extensive poetic criticism concludes this chapter.[20]

Second only to Tennyson in Grove's estimation was Wordsworth. Like many critics, Grove found Wordsworth's output mixed:

> I have an intense admiration for a few things of Wordsworth's, but I cannot be called a Wordsworthian. The set ponderousness and even commonplace style of the majority of his poems repels me; and the entire absence of the passion of love robs them of one of the main elements of poetry.

It was the early works and the expression of the beauty and elements of nature that inspired him.

> I like best the 'Daffodils' and the poems on Lucy, and of all others the Highland Reaper [The Solitary Reaper] who was filling the valley with sound and on whom there is that exquisite simile about the cuckoo-bird
>
> 'Breaking the silence of the Seas
> Among the furthest Hebrides – '

With the next stanza:–

> 'Old, unhappy far-off things
> And battles long ago.'

He found particular solace at the time of his own Lucy's death in the poem 'She dwelt among the untrodden ways'.[21]

Of poets closer to his own generation, Robert Browning had a special place. Though Grove firmly asserted Tennyson to be superior to Browning, he still thought very highly of his work and commented:

> I don't know very much of him, but what I do know I know well. It is confined to Men and Women, Christmas Day [Eve] and Easter Eve [Day] and a few of the earlier poems outside these books... In Men and Women my favourites are 'Love amongst the ruins', two in the Campagna [both actually in 'Lyrics'], Karshish (your friend)...*In a balcony* [in Tragedies]. But the gem of all is the last poem, One word more. It wants browsing; like a piece of Beethoven.

Grove was much better acquainted with Browning than with the older Tennyson, and counted him as a friend of his London circle, Browning enthusiastically supporting him for his election to the Athenaeum in 1871. This was doubtless partly due to Browning's musical interests. Browning was a keen amateur player and improviser on the piano, and, like Leighton, Lehmann and Moscheles (and also George Eliot's companion G.H. Lewes) was present with Grove for the British premiere of Brahms's first symphony at Cambridge on 8 March 1877.[22]

Grove became more attached to the poetry of Matthew Arnold and Arthur Hugh Clough with age and growing loss of certainty of belief. Like Browning, Arnold was a member of Grove's circle and, as shown earlier, Grove was greatly influenced by his thinking. But Grove found Arnold's poetry lacking in the musical quality which facilitates memorizing. The attraction in it mainly lay elsewhere for him: it appealed to his need for a like mind. A letter to Edith Oldham shows the intensity of his response, and also what he looked for in poetry.

> I have been reading a good deal of Matthew Arnold's poetry of late. How very difficult his poetry is to learn! It gives me greater trouble than any other. I have been committing to memory (Macaulay's term) one of his mystic poems, and will write it out here first to see if you know it, and secondly because you will like it. It is a sort of comparison of life to a multitude of islands scattered over a vast ocean.
>
> 'Yes! In the sea of life enisled,
> with echoing straits between us thrown,
> dotting the shoreless watery wild,
> we mortal millions live alone...

There were musical problems in the later part of the poem for him: 'the last stanza is clumsy (except the last lines of all, which are superb) and the 'nights' and 'nightingales' come perilously close in verse 2, but it's a beautiful poem. Isn't it?'[23]

Grove had first 'learnt to love' the poetry of Clough in the 1860s 'at the turning point of my life' (the death of Lucy), and re-read it 'in the dead hours of night with the greatest delight'. Like Arnold's, the poems were a little too close to life to be revered. 'I have always had the greatest admiration for (no sympathy with) them: the feeling is too much part of myself to be admiration.' Again, musical qualities had been sacrificed to the substance. He writes to Mrs Wodehouse:

> the poem you mean [which he does not identify] is by Clough and is one of the sweetest pieces in the world. The third stanza is a little faulty, but when Beethoven played we should not have minded a phrase played clumsily here and there; but indeed Clough's part in the vol. is full of the highest poetry. The two ships [he means 'O ship, ship, ship'] is particularly dear to me; I heard Arthur Stanley quote two stanzas at a Rugby dinner, when I was at the turning point of my life and I have myself used them in a sermon at College.[24]

Of Tennyson's poetry, Grove's greatest admiration was reserved for 'In Memoriam'. He commented:

> A man who can write such a gospel as there is in 'In Memoriam' – you know how I value that book – must know all about it, but where I ask did he get the art to build so vast and bright an edifice out of such slender materials and so gloomy a foundation?'…that wonderful poem, and the few scattered pieces connected with it, contain the most complete answer to the sweet seduction of 'Tears, idle Tears'.

The latter poem, with 'Ask me no more' was the subject of two criticisms he published in 1866: 'On a song in The Princess' in the *Shilling Magazine* in February 1866 ('Ask me no more') and 'On Tears, Idle Tears' in *Macmillan's Magazine* for November 1866. We gain a special insight into his intense relationship to poetry through these criticisms, of which the latter is reproduced below. Here several major themes come together: loss, stimulated by the death of Lucy; religious doubt, and possible spiritual responses to it; loneliness and friendships; sex and passion – with clear reference to his personal life. The presentation of Tennyson's 'Tears, Idle Tears' (quoted in full on pages 59–65 below) is starkly revealing of Grove's emotions and experiences for a published piece, and reveals another facet of his nature.[25]

'Tears, Idle Tears': A Commentary

Tears, idle tears, I know not what they mean,
Tears from the depths of some divine despair
Rise in the heart, and gather in the eyes,
In looking on the happy Autumn fields
And thinking of the days that are no more.

Fresh as the first beam glittering on a sail,
That brings our friends up from the underworld,
Sad as the last which reddens over one
That sinks with all we love below the verge;
So sad, so fresh, the days that are no more.

Ah, sad and strange as in dark summer dawns
The earliest pipe of half-awaken'd birds
To dying ears, when unto dying eyes
The casement slowly grows a glimmering square;
So sad, so strange, the days that are no more.

Dear as remember'd kisses after death,
And sweet as those by hopeless fancy feign'd
On lips that are for others; deep as love,
Deep as first love, and wild with all regret;
O Death in Life, the days that are no more.

'Idle Tears' they may be – for what tears in this world are not idle? – but still the saddest that ever flowed from human eye. Tears of joy, tears of pity, are to be found elsewhere; but such tears of desolate, hopeless, unrelieved misery are recorded in no literature, are preserved in no lachrymatory, ancient or modern. Each stanza contains an image or images, and each hopelessly, irretrievably mournful, drawn from the very abyss of sorrow. Even the 'happy autumn fields' and the bright beam of morning, glorifying our friends' return, borrow the despairing hues of the rest.

The theme is the irrecoverable past – 'the days that are no more ' – exhibited to us in the several aspects of their freshness, their sadness, their strangeness, their dearness, their sweetness, their depth and their wild regret.

The key-note is clearly and beautifully struck in the first stanza. Nothing moves the spirit of man so profoundly as some of the appearances of nature; more profoundly, because it is often impossible to explain why it should be so. The vague but intense yearning, the feeling of vastness and longing, which possesses one at the sight of certain aspects of the sunset, has been felt by almost everyone. It is a mere commonplace, but a commonplace that is unexplainable, and which is a stronger evidence, to those who feel it, of the immortality of the soul than all the demonstrations of natural theology. So it is, too, with the awe excited in the mind by the starry heavens in all their clearness and immensity; by the rare and most touching spectacle of the waning moon; or by the ascent of the dawn, in the hush and chill of daybreak. The same kind of feeling, only more personal, and less vast, and coloured rather by wild passionate human regret, is apt to seize the mind in autumn, in viewing some scene of sweet, rich, peaceful beauty, like the 'happy autumn fields' of this poem. The feeling may be due in part to the universal spectacle of things passing away – corn ripe and cut, leaves gradually 'reddening to the fall', all things drawing slowly but surely to their appointed end. The very look of the clouds in the autumn afternoons, so round and calm and still, so ethereal in their tints, so unutterably soft and mellow in their lights and shadows, contributes to the general impression of rest and peace. But the real ground of the melancholy which autumn inspires is something deeper, some instinct of which we know only the effect, and cannot even conjecture the working, and which, from that very vagueness, stirs the spirit more deeply than any more definite cause would do.

However this may be, certain it is that, at such moments, the transitoriness of life and all around will suddenly impress itself on the mind. The key-note of 'some divine despair' in the heart is touched. Persons and incidents, fraught with unutterable recollections, and worth all the world to one – a dead child, a lost love, a sudden look, a parting, a difference, a reconciliation – present themselves with particular power. It is, perhaps, long since we had to do with them, but they come back as 'fresh' as if it were yesterday; they fill the mind as if present, in all their sweetness and familiar tender dearness, and the pang of absence, and the maddening sense of the utter irrecoverability of the past rushes in after them with the 'wild regret', and the tears, the 'idle tears' – not idle in themselves, but idle only because 'we know not what they mean', – 'rise from the depths' of our 'divine despair' – 'divine' because so utterly beyond all human reason or knowledge, – and gather, smarting, in the eyes of the gazer.

The images in which this grief of the mind is presented are not only very original, but they succeed one another in a progression as subtle and delicate as it is admirable. The key, so to speak, in which the poem starts, is adhered to, with a slight departure only, through the second and third stanzas. The natural and external image of the 'happy autumn fields' is continued in the wide expansion of the ocean, the ships, and the sunbeams striking across the world, all external to the observer. It is again continued in the next stanza, in the rising of the 'dim dawn', 'loud with the voices of the birds' outside the casement, though here intensified and made more solemn by the introduction of the slowly dying man, on whose dull eyes and feeble ears these sights and sounds strike for the last time. The outward-bound ship, bearing off 'all we love', is mournful enough, as in the chill damp air which foreruns the night we watch the last red tint on the sails, and wait for the sun to drop below the sea-line, and all to assume, as if by magic, one dull, leaden, indistinguishable hue. This is mournful, but the picture which follows it – the dying man on his death bed, watching the faint beginnings of his last day on earth – is surely one of the most desolate in all literature or art.*

Even this, however, can be surpassed, So far we have been spectators only – looking at that which is outside of us. In the fourth and last stanza we encounter a sudden modulation; and by a transition, than which Beethoven himself never imagined anything at once more sudden and less violent, we are landed in a region quite remote from the former one – the region of our own selves, and amongst images that transcend those that precede them, as much as that which is personal and passionate must surpass that which is merely external and passive. Sad as is the departure of all we love across the waste of ocean, desolate as are the loneliness of the long daybreak and the dim sounds of life to the dying man, the sting of kisses remembered when the loved one who kissed us is gone for ever is still sharper:– '– a sorrow's crown of sorrow is remembering happier things'.

But even this again may be exceeded. There may be a union of sweetness and mad anguish in repeating in fancy the caresses of lips, once all your own, and now lost forever – lost, not by death, or any such divine decree, but by human faults, by faithlessness or misunderstanding, or social difference, or some other cause which infuses a rankling sense of injustice into the pain of the loss. As it is the thought of death that forms the link between the two stanzas – the dying man leading on to the dead love – so it is the introduction of the element of love which gives the last stanza its special keenness, which makes it so truly the climax of the poem. For love is the crown of all human things, and gives the last bitterness to sorrow, the highest culmination to joy; and, in comparison to it, absence, and friendship, and kindred, and death, and all other ills,

* Wallis's picture of Chatterton is full of desolation; but it is far below this poem, because *there* the struggle is over – *here* it is still going on. Schumann's overture to Manfred is equally gloomy, and equally touching. It is, however, a more extended work in every way. The nearest parallel in music must, perhaps, be looked for in Schubert's works – at the base of which, almost without exception, there lies a profound melancholy. The songs of 'Das Wirthshaus' or the 'Todesmusik' (op. 108), are those which occur to me as the most suitable. But, indeed, such parallels are never quite satisfactory, if only from the fact that, owing to the necessary form, there are fewer ideas in music than in poetry, though perhaps as many emotions.

and all other delights of earth, are as nothings, as mere passing vanities. Nor is it love alone that is introduced, but its very acmé – the kiss, the 'meeting of the lips', when 'spirits rush together,' and soul closes with soul on fire.*

Thus pointed as thus presented, the memory of the 'days that are no more' become indeed a very 'Death in Life'.

So, hopeless and forlorn, ends this most lovely, but most sorrowful of poems. And if this 'moan about the retrospect' were all that could be said about the 'days that are no more', what would there be for us but to lie down and die, and so purchase a swift immunity from such unavailing regrets? And it is undeniable that such a view of the past has at times, more or less often, been taken by every man and woman of sensibility. More or less often, but, thank Heaven, not always. There is another aspect, brighter, and better, and healthier than any of these yet presented to us. 'Sweet' as they are – and there is no denying their sweetness, even the stern Princess herself is compelled to allow that – sweet as they are, they are yet truly 'vague' and 'fatal to men' – 'fancies hatched in silken-folded idleness'. Memory may be – perhaps always must be – 'memory with *sad* eyes', but we must not forget that what she supplies us with would, but for her, be lost for ever; her gifts are not only so much saved from the wreck of life, but, once possessed, they are ours for life. That which has once happened to us becomes a part of our being, and, though for the time forgotten or overlooked, is still there, in the storehouse of the mind, always ready to start into action when the proper chord is touched – and to present itself in its original force and freshness, mellowed perhaps, but hardly weakened, by the enchanting effect of distance. Such memories are a part of our very selves, and can only be taken from us by the failure of our powers, the positive loss of the faculty of recollection. Cherish and encourage them! Nothing can make up for their loss, nothing can surpass their power and sweetness. They are the one certain possession granted to us; nor only certain, but personal and exclusive in the highest possible degree. No one can take them away, and no one can share them:– 'Mine they are, ever mine, mine alone'.

As long as they remain there is still an Eden for men. 'Memory' says Jean Paul, 'is the only Paradise out of which nothing can ever drive us'.

---

* Methinks if I should kiss thee, no control
Within the thrilling brain could keep afloat
The subtle spirit - even while I spoke
The bare word KISS hath made my inner soul
To tremble like a lutestring, ere the note
Hath melted in the silence that it broke.
Poems 1833

And surely to remember and ponder over the joys of life, even when those joys are no longer ours, is full of unspeakable comfort. True, the caresses of the loved one, which were 'sweeter, sweeter than anything on earth', are gone for ever; but we possess their memory, the memory of the supreme happiness which they brought to us, and to her who loved us, on their heavenly wings. We may meet again, and we may not, in the land of peace and brightness, which we were taught from our childhood to believe in. We may not. Alas! that the doubt should obtrude itself on those to whom the contrary belief would be the greatest blessing! But the very shadow of the doubt should make us prize only the more ardently the certain memory which we hold, and with which we may solace ourselves during the few short years which yet remain to us on earth. Whatever our future may be, *this* we *have*, *this* nothing can take away. We can go over every circumstance of the past, recall every look, every word, every touch, of each interview, each meeting, and each parting, and in so doing feel what alleviations there are to the immense inevitable ills of life, how carefully each privation is accompanied by a gift, how true it is that we have here a joy that nothing can take away:–

Come foul, fair, or rain, or shine,
The joys I have possessed in spite of fate
are mine;
Not heaven itself upon the past has power,
But what has been has been, and I have
lived my hour.

A view so opposite to that of the song before us could hardly have been embodied without violating the dramatic intention and course of the poem. But it is a great lesson, and one which might well be enforced. Indeed, Mr Tennyson has elsewhere done it in the noblest, most complete manner. If we want to see how, by a great loss, a man can be plunged headlong into the very depths of grief and despair; how, out of the listlessness which follows so stunning a blow – when the paralysed 'tongue' refuses to 'utter' the vague 'thoughts that arise' in the mind; when all earthly things, from the stately ships and the everlasting 'hills', to the 'fisherman's boys', seem as nothing in comparison to one 'touch of the vanished hand' – how out of even these depths, he can lift his head gradually above the wave, and from reviling and repelling his sorrow (under the aggravation which is the next stage of the mental conflict) as a 'cruel fellowship', a 'priestess in the vaults of death' can come to entreat her to 'dwell with him', 'no casual mistress, but a wife', – can at length look calmly back on what has been, and 'two and thirty years' after the 'fatal loss' can see the mist rolled away, and all stand before him in perfect symmetry and perfect loveliness – if we want to see this, then look at 'In Memoriam'. That wonderful poem, and the few scattered pieces connected with it, contain the most complete answer to the sweet seductions of 'Tears, Idle Tears'.

But 'In Memoriam' deals with a larger and more complicated past than that which is reflected in the little poem we are considering. Is it too much to hope that Mr Tennyson may some day take up the task, and compose a pendent to 'Tears, Idle Tears', setting forth, in his own exquisite language, and with images as suggestive and touching as those now before us, the happy aspects of the past – the comfort and satisfaction conferred by those purely personal recollections, which are of more real value to each individual man and women than anything outside of us can be; and thus give us, in the forms and feelings of our own time, a companion to that striking Ode just quoted, in which the nervous and energetic genius of Dryden embodied the sentiments of his coarser and more material age?

One remonstrance I desire, though with greater deference, to make, before concluding this part of my subject. It refers to the expression 'deep as first love'. Of course there are exceptions to the general rule, and it may be a man's fortune not to love till his faculties are mature; but, generally speaking, 'first love' occurs in youth, or immature age, and in that case 'holding' as it does all the 'promise of the golden hours', and brilliant and fresh as it may be – and surely nothing can compare for freshness with the bloom and dew with which one's first passion invests all the world – brilliant and fresh as it may be, it cannot be so 'deep' as the love of a man of ripe age and maturer powers, who has kept his 'boy's heart' so long as still to love ardently, but joins to his ardour the knowledge, the firmness, the persistence, the power, with which years have endowed him. These – and they are not of infrequent occurrence – these are the grand 'deep' passions of life, so powerful as to modify, and sometimes completely to change, even a character long fixed and settled.

The form of the Song is not one of the least remarkable things about it. It is of four stanzas, each of the usual number of five lines. Like the general body of the poem, the stanza consist of ordinary ten-syllabled unrhymed lines; and the Song is distinguished from that which precedes it and follows it merely by the fact that the sense comes to an end at the end of each stanza, and that each closes with the refrain, 'the days which are no more'. It is a form which has not, I think, been employed by other poets, though by Mr Tennyson himself it is used on two other occasions – first in the song of triumph sung by the Princess, in the opening of the sixth canto of this very poem, and again in the 'measured words' of the 'Golden Year', a piece inserted in recent editions of the 'Poems'. In each of these a similar artifice is employed to mark the recurrence of the stanza, each has a refrain 1 – in the former at the beginning of the verse, in the latter at the end; but they are both far inferior (the war-song naturally so) in flow and finish to the masterly work before us. In this case, owing to some hidden secret of workmanship, which I am unable to discover, save by its effects, some subtle fragrance breathed over the song, so perfect is the cadence of the lines, and so sweet the music of the syllables, as to give all the effect of the rhymes which the stanza-form naturally suggests, and which the ear, in this case, fails to miss.*

The diction and workmanship are as choice, as delicately appropriate, and as minutely finished as those of Mr Tennyson's usually are. Such lines as

> 'Tears from the depth of some divine despair'
> or
> 'Sweet as those by hopeless fancy feigned'
> or
> 'Deep as first love, and wild with all regret,
> or again
> 'That sinks with all we love below the verge,'

where the slow, heavy monosyllables are almost like earth dropping on to a coffin – lines like these, in which the force of the thought is preserved through all the labour necessary for such high finish, would make the fortune of any other poet. Every one knows that they are to be found in hundreds in the work of Mr Tennyson, one of whose most remarkable characteristics is the power he possesses of uniting the most exquisite beauty of detail with force and completeness of general effect, a power which forms one of the strongest guarantees for the endurance of his poetry.

I have only to add that this Song has never been altered; but remains exactly as it was in the original edition of 'The Princess'.[26]

* A refrain is also used in the song in the last canto:– 'Now sleeps the crimson petal, now the white', – though its consists only in the single word 'me'. There are beautiful examples of this charming artifice also in the first song – 'As through the land', the Cradle Song, and the 'Bugle Song', on which I hope to be able to speak at length on a future opportunity, as well as in 'Ask me no more', which I have already attempted to examine.

Notes

1 See Edwin Clark, *The Britannia and Conway Tubular Bridges* (London, 1850); Asa Briggs, *From Iron Bridge to Crystal Palace* (London, 1979), pp.92ff.; also the account in Percy M. Young, *George Grove 1820–1900. A Biography* (London, 1980), pp.48–9; Graves discusses Grove's life at Chester and at Bangor, in *The Life & Letters of Sir George Grove C.B.* (London, 1903), p.27, as does Young, *George Grove*, pp.43–9.

2 The *Spectator*, week ending Saturday 23 June 1849, no. 1095, p.579: 'The Provinces'. Grove also wrote a 'popular account', which was sold on the spot. See Graves, *Life & Letters* p.30.

3 Green and his wife were fellow-residents of Sydenham and close friends of Grove, with whom Grove travelled to Germany in 1878: see further, Graves, *Life & Letters* p.245; and Young, *George Grove*, p.152.

4 *Geography, with maps and diagrams, by George Grove FRGS*. History Primers, ed. J.R. Green (London, 1876), pp.34–40.

5 George Grove, 'Nabloos and the Samaritans', in F. Galton, *Vacation Tourists and Notes of Travel in 1861* (Cambridge, 1862), pp.241–58; Benjamin Jowett, 'Interpretation of Scripture', *Essays and Reviews*, 12th edn, (London, 1865); J.W. Colenso, *The Pentateuch and Book of Joshua Critically Examined*, 7 vols, (London, 1862–79); the Bible Dinners are mentioned in Graves, *Life & Letters*, p.67.

6 Miss Angela Burdett (later Baroness) Coutts (philanthropist and banking heiress, 1814–1906); the background is discussed most thoroughly in V.D. Lipman, 'The Origins of the Palestine Exploration Fund', *Palestine Exploration Quarterly*, vol.120 (January–June 1988), pp.45–54; Graves gives an outline of Grove's involvement, *Life & Letters*, pp.118–122; the Pierotti controversy is discussed on p.118.

7 Kingsley is quoted in Young, *George Grove*, p.90; Lipman outlines the breadth of the religious representation in 'The Origins of the Palestine Exploration Fund', pp.47–8.

8 Young, *George Grove*, p.91; report of the RIBI meeting in *The Times*, 21 February 1866.

9 Quoted in Young, *George Grove*, p.277.

10 Wilson wrote his own account. Sir Charles Wilson, *The Recovery of Jerusalem*, ed. W. Morrison, with an introduction by A.P. Stanley (New York, 1871).

11 Grove thought Ganneau 'a much better Arabic scholar than Warren': letter of Grove to Besant, 3 October 1873: Archive of the Palestine Exploration Fund WS/56; *The Survey of Western Palestine 1882–1888, including a Survey of Eastern Palestine*, facsimile edition (London; Archive Editions in association with the Palestine Exploration Fund); Grove wrote several letters to *The Times* in 1870 concerning the discovery of the 'Moabite Stone'. See also the references given by Graves, *Life & Letters*, p.187.

12 Letter of Ellen Grove to George Grove of 20 February 1877: BL Add MS 55255, fol. 6.

13 Grove's first published work was his translation of F. Guizot's *Essai sur les beaux Arts* (Paris, 1852) published as *The Fine Arts, their Nature and Relations* (London, 1853); Graves, *Life & Letters*, p.97.

14 Graves, *Life & Letters*, p.117.

15 See Graves, *Life & Letters*, pp.329, 438; he also deplored Robert Elsmere because of Mrs Humphry Ward's having 'trodden the paths of display and pretension' (Young, *George Grove*, p.288).

16 Young, *George Grove*, p.287; Young also discusses Grove's 'love-hate' relation with French poetry and his interest in Turgenev and Pushkin; Graves quotes Grove on Tolstoy and Turgenev, in *Life & Letters*, pp.424, 461.

17 Graves, *Life & Letters*, p.461. The poetic references indexed in *Beethoven and His Nine Symphonies* are a sure guide to what moved him most in poetry. Tennyson and Wordsworth references appear frequently.
18 *Ibid.*
19 Graves notes that Grove began to read French poetry in 1865 (*Life & Letters*, p.128); Grove was also well acquainted with the work of the American poets Harte, Longfellow and Poe; Young quotes Grove's own lines and notes their 'Tennyson echoes', in *George Grove*, p.86.
20 Graves, *Life & Letters*, p.46. Grove first approached Tennyson as Poet Laureate in 1852 for an Ode for the opening of the Crystal Palace in 1854; he later became well acquainted with the poet, visited him and travelled with him to Switzerland (Graves, *Life & Letters*, p.44ff); See further on their connection through *Macmillan's Magazine* in Chapter 7.
21 Graves, *Life & Letters*, p.355; Young, *George Grove*, p.156; see *The Poetical Works of William Wordsworth*, ed E. de Selincourt and H. Darbishire, 5 vols (Oxford, 1946–69), vol.2, pp.30, 214.
22 Letter of Grove to Edith Oldham, 15 September 1887; Young, *George Grove*, p.284; Graves, *Life & Letters*, p.191; *The Poetical Works of Robert Browning*, 8 vols (Oxford, 1983–2001): vol.5 (Men and Women), ed. I. Jack and R. Inglesfield, and vol.4, ed. I. Jack and R. Fowler, pp.331–419.
23 'To Marguerite, on returning a Volume of the Letters of Ortis' (first published title): *The Poems of Matthew Arnold*, ed. Kenneth Alcott (New York, 1965), pp.123–4; Graves, *Life & Letters*, p.374–5.
24 *The Poems of Arthur Hugh Clough*, ed. F.L. Muhlhauser, trans. Jane Turner (Oxford, 1974), p.351; Graves, *Life & Letters*, pp.304–5; 424.
25 Graves, *Life & Letters*, pp.134–40; see *Poems of Tennyson*, ed. Christopher Ricks, 3 vols (London, 1969; 2nd edn, 1987), vol.2, p.232.
26 *Macmillan's Magazine* (November 1866), pp 67–72.

Part 2

The Scholar and Writer

4

'The Other Dictionary': Grove's Work in Editing Dr Smith's *Dictionary of the Bible*

Percy M. Young

A Background of Exploration and Writing

On an April day in 1895 Grove gave this lively response to a letter from his friend Edith Oldham:

> Fancy your reading about the Hittites! It is delightful. I am remembered here for having said in a lecture which I gave 30 years ago that the Hittites were one of the most interesting peoples of the Antient World. – that was because of the physiogenies of most of the old races – but that 'if I could see the face of a Hittite I would die happy'. Then nothing or next to nothing was known of them...[1]

A month later he returned to the defining source of his information:

> Happened just now to look at one of my articles in Smith's Dictionary of the Bible, when I was near to them. I was astonished at the style of the notes and the extraordinary go & pace of it all.
>
> Our first introduction to the Hittites is in the time of Abraham, when he bought from the Benecheth 'Children of Heth' – such was then their title – the field and the cave of Machpelah, belonging to Ephron the Hittite. They were then settled at the town which was afterward, under its new name of Hebron, to become one of the most famous cities in Palestine, then bearing the name of Kirjatharba, and perhaps also of Mamre. The propensities of the tribe appear at that time to have been commercial rather than military. (Genesis xxiii 19; xxv 9)[2]

Before William Smith and before George Grove there were more than two hundred years of exploration of the territories of the formerly Roman 'Palaestrina', broadly described as 'The Holy Land', sometimes for commercial and sometimes for political reasons, and otherwise out of curiosity. The line of discovery took in merchants, soldiers and sailors, dedicated clergy, American and German scholars, travellers and some few well-known ladies of leisure, among whom were Lady Mary Wortley Montague and Lady Hester Stanhope. A notice of the most conspicuous sources of information indicates why and how Smith saw opportunity in his project and suggests how it was that, without Grove, his intention would not have arrived at fruition.

The first guidebook to the Holy Land, published in England in 1615, contained the travels of George Sandys (1578–1644), youngest son of Edwin, Archbishop of York, and brother of Sir Edwin Sandys (1561–1619), founder of the colony of Virginia. George Sandys matriculated at St. Mary Hall, Oxford, and, after the death of his mother in 1610, undertook an extensive tourist programme, spending time in France and Northern Italy before reaching Turkey. From here his immediate travels, including Greece, Egypt, and Armenia, brought him into the Holy Land – the *terra sancta*. At that time this was divided into three regions: Judea in the south, Samaria in the middle, and Galilee, which spread from the Mediterranean to the Jordan. In 1615 he published *Sandys' Travels*, dedicated to his friend, the then – 'Prince Charles'. In this Sandys carefully observed the hazardous present, while paying due reverence to a distant past. Across the lands through which he had passed in preparation for a climactic ending he began by deploring the terrible conditions that widely prevailed, even…

> ..where God himself did place his own Common-wealth, gave laws and oracles, inspired his Prophets, sent Angels to converse with men; above all, where the Son of God descended to become man, where he honoured man with his beauteous steps, wrought the work of our redemption, triumphed over death and ascended into glory, which Countries once so glorious and famous [with]…large territories dispeopled, or thinly inhabited; good cities made desolate; sumptuous buildings become ruins, glorious temples either subverted, or prostituted to impiety…so far as convenience might permit, [all that we saw] presented a brief view of the former estates…those people and countries.[3]

This energetic description George Grove might well have taken as 'the extraordinary go and pace of it all'. A careful disposal of time and place, however, allowed Sandys an area of flexibility, the narrative always coming alive in picturesque imagery: so that with an *O sola magnarum urbium, Magna Bethlehem* as introduction, with borrowing from St Luke and later sources, he set the following, not entirely familiar, narrative before his reader:

> For when Augustus Caesar had appointed that all the world should be taxed, every one repaired unto the Citie of his family; and Joseph with Mary came up to Bethlehem, where in a Grot at the East-side of a Citie,

> imployed for a Stable (the Inn being pestr'd with strangers) she fell in trauell, and produced unto the World a Saviour. In this cave from the time of Adrian, unto the reigne of Constantine they celebrated their impious lamentation of Adonis (much honoured by the Syrians) who aboue had his Statue shadowed with a grove of Myrtles. Which the vertuous Helena subverted and erected thereupon this goodly temple (yet entire...& possessed by the Franciscans of Jerusalem, of whom some few are here continually resident) and called it Saint Mary's of Bethlehem.[4]

Three pages later the legendary 'three wise men' arrive in Bethlehem. Within this Temple, in the Chapel of the Nativity, there is:

> on one side of grotto – a bench in the Rock, not unlike to an Altar where the Magi of the East, that were conducted here by the starre, disposed, as they say, of their Presents: for Myrrha, teares; for Frankinsense, impart submissive prayers; for Gold, a pure heart.[5]

The better to understand the scene, Sandys includes a drawing, labelled:

> A The Altar of the Nativity,
> B The Manger,
> C The Altar of the Magi,
> D The stairs that ascend into the Temple above,
> E The picture of the imagery figure of St Jerome.[6]

George Sandys was also a poet, publishing in 1638 a version of the Psalms of David, as *A Paraphrase upon the Divine Poems*.[7] In turn Milton owed these lines of *The Passion* to Sandys:

> Mine eye hath found that sad Sepulchral rock
> That was the Casket of Heav'ns richest store,
> And here though grief my feeble hands up-lock,
> Yet on the soft'n'd Quarry would I score
> My plaining vers as lively as before.[8]

Between this scene, and its restatement and analysis by Grove, is a bridge across which travellers from many countries passed – some curious, some inspired by faith, some by trade, and some with malice. Throughout this time these lands were subject to the rule of the Turkish Empire. In 1581 a Charter was granted to the Levant company in London to trade with Constantinople (Istanbul) and its territories. This trade was active from about 1592 until 1825. In 1697 Henry Maundrell (1665–1701), an Oxford graduate and a curate at Bromley in Kent, was elected by the Company of the Levant Merchants to the Chaplaincy of their Factory in the Muslim city of Aleppo – then a great trade centre between Europe and Asia. Maundrell's account of how, with 14 of his company, he was able to celebrate Easter in 1697, in Jerusalem, was described in rich and humourful detail in his book *From Aleppo to Jerusalem*, published in Oxford in 1703 with the imprimatur of the Vice-Chancellor.[9] Beginning with a drawing entitled Prospect of Aleppo, the book may be described as well illustrated. Mandrell precisely writes: 'We set out from Aleppo Friday Feb. 26, 1696, at three in the Afternoon, intending to make only a short step that Evening, in order to prove how well we were provided with necessaries for our journey'. Before long, however, early problems induce a note of caution:

> It must here be noted, that in travelling this Country, a Man does not meet with a Market-Town, and Inns, every night, as in England; the best reception you can find here is either under your own Tent, if the season permit, or else in certain publick Lodgments founded in Charity for the Use of Travelers. But [one] must expect nothing here generally but bare walls: as for other Accomodations, of Meat, Drink, Bed, Fire, Provender; with these it must be everyone's care to furnish himself.[10]

After travelling for a year Maundrell and his companions arrived in Jerusalem in time for the celebration of Easter. His account of the events of this holy season in and about the supposed Church of the Holy Sepulchre is, in effect, an essay in disbelief. The Easter services acted out by Greek and Armenian religious, whose piety was secured by the periodic burning of holy fires, the flight of sacred birds (purposely let fly by the Greeks to deceive the people that it was a visible descent of the Holy Ghost), and by the violent discipline imposed on disputing worshippers by Turkish strong men with huge clubs. Outside of the church one holy place jostled with another for public entertainment. Near to St Peter's prison was a gate that opened of its own accord; nearby a font once used by the Apostles for public baptizing. On Easter Monday the English visitors joined others on tour to Jordan as guests of the Muslim Governor of the city, paying him $12 per person. This narrative exemplifies the pleasures and problems of tourism in the seventeenth century. Even in 1767 Maundrell's book was still available, now in its 17th edition: a hundred years later, in an uncertain translation published by Bohn, it was praised by Grove.[11]

At that time, against what might have been regarded by some as mere dilettantism, pioneer geographers were demonstrating the hazards of exploration in unknown territories and languages. The extraordinary account of a scientific mission through Egypt, Arabia and Syria, begun in 1761, financed by the King of Denmark, led by Carsten Niebuhr (1733–1815), a German, was published in 1772 as *Beschreibung von Arabien*. An English translation by the Scotsman, Robert Heron, with the title *Niebuhr's Travels Through Arabia and other Countries in the East*, was published in Edinburgh, in two volumes, in 1792.[12] Four seafaring geographers began that expedition in 1761. Two of them, exhausted by the climate, the unwholesomeness of the food, and exhaustion, died in Arabia. The end of the expedition came when, sailing to India, a third man died 'after long languishing'. Niebuhr alone survived, never to be forgotten for the extent of his researches. The next important project was undertaken by the Anglo-Swiss explorer, John Lewis Burckhardt (1784–1817). For this he prepared himself by learning to speak Arabic – as fluently, it was said, as a native. He discovered the sites of forgotten cities in the Yemen and he surveyed the outline of the Arabian coasts. Much of the content of his *Travels in Arabia* (1829), came from personal contacts with native people. His *Travels in Syria and the Holy Land* (1822) was also issued in German translation.[13]

The nineteenth century brought a broader interest in the the Holy Land, sometimes with political, sometimes with geographic, and sometimes still with tourist interest. Scholars of different countries and denominations, as well as sailors – including officers of the Indian Navy (British) – were now beginning to assess more accurately the shape of Arabian coastlines. Among the intrepid travellers were the military, among whom there were those whose duties obliged them to travel in the Holy Land and those stationed elsewhere, who, with generous periods of leave, could make scholarly use of periods of professional inactivity. Henry Light, Captain of the Royal Artillery, in garrison in Malta, in the year 1814 obtained sufficient leave to travel widely in the Holy Land. Zealous in keeping account of the countries visited, he was able eventually to have his papers edited and published as *Travels in Egypt, Nubia, Holy Land, Mount Libanon & Cyprus in the Year 1814*. From his account of places visited it is possible to determine how far legends and wilful misrepresentations continued to disturb the truth. For example, that in the Church of the Holy Sepulchre in Jerusalem, everything concerning the Crucifixion was under one roof, where the Crucifixion took place, where the crosses of our Saviour and the malefactors were found, 'where St Helena found the Cross'…'the tomb of Nicodemus the Jew', with contents shared out between the different sects, each with the right to purchase from the Turkish chiefs 'who are of course anxious that such contests should occur'.[14]

In 1837 Major James Skinner's *Adventures During a Journey Overland to India* – with a hint of *Boys' Own Paper* – appeared. Like Henry Light, however, Skinner was amazed at what local influences were doing to history. But under the heading of 'Eastern Mendicants' he offers a gentle interpretation of what he found:

> The holy spots are so well known, that I shall not follow my guide in the narration of traditions that appear to me to be interminable. The implicit faith of those who undergo so much to visit them, in the authenticity of all they bow before, is too interesting a spectacle to talk lightly of.

> I preserved a sober and credulous demeanour throughout the day; for I would not shock the feeling of real devotion about me by an appearance of doubt regarding any of them.[15]

The two volumes of *Letters on Egypt, Edom, and the Holy Land* by Lord Lindsay of Balcarres contained much political interest, for he had asked John W. Farren, then Consul-General in Syria, to prepare for him an official statement on conditions in Syria. This was duly printed in the second volume. (Letters otherwise were personal: to Lt. Colonel Lindsay, at Cadiz and Gibraltar, to his mother, and to his sister Anne.) Somewhat like Sandys, Lindsay writes with a degree of elegance coupled with compassion. He writes to his mother from Damascus in July 1837:

> Throughout the Holy Land we tried every spot pointed out as the scene of Scriptural events by the words of the Bible, the only safe guide-book in this land of ignorance and superstition, where a locality has been assigned to every incident recorded in it – to the spot where the cock crew at Peter's denial of our Saviour, nay, to the house of Dives in the parable. Yet, while I question the truth, I would not impugn the poetry of some of these traditions, or deny that they add a peculiar and most thrilling interest to the scenes to which they are attached – loco sancta indeed, when we think of them as shrines hallowed by the pilgrimages and the prayers of ages.[16]

On 23 September 1841, Dr Thomas Arnold (1795–1842), Headmaster of Rugby School, writing to Sir Thomas Sabine Pasley, Bart. (1804–84), brought the matter of the Holy Land towards the centre of ecclesiastical politics with wider connotations.

> The first Protestant Bishop of Jerusalem is to be consecrated at Lambeth next Wednesday. He is to be the legal protector of all protestants of every denomination towards the Turkish government, and he is to ordain Prussian clergymen on their signing the Augsburg Confession and adopting the Prussian Liturgy, and Englishmen on their subscribing to our Articles and Liturgy.[17]

This accommodation of different religious denominations naturally encouraged a cross-current in the study of the Bible in a challenging period of independent research. The inspirational legends of the Holy Land now called on new methods to test the evidences of history. One observer of changes in the nature of German theology in respect of the continuing discoveries being made was Rev. Charles Forster, formerly domestic chaplain to Bishop Jebb of Limerick. With the approval of the Bishop, Forster had spent some ten years in the Holy Land before his completion of a major work in two parts, *The*

Historic Geography of Arabia, or the Partriarchal Evidence of Revealed Religion, published in 1844.[18]

Heinrich Gesenius (1788–1842), orientalist and Old Testament scholar, was educated in the University of Göttingen and subsequently became Professor of Theology in Halle, and later in Breslau. A very rare tribute was paid to him by the chronicler who recorded that at times as many as 500 students came to hear Gesenius lecture. He was an expert in Hebrew speech, in interpretation of dialects and inscriptions, he reported on his discovery of a Himyaritic alphabet and inscriptions to the Journal of the Royal Geographic Society in London.[19] Emil Roediger (1801–74), son of an organist in Sangerhausen, was educated in school and university in Halle where, in turn, he became Professor of Oriental Languages and Theology. Expert in Arab, Persian and Syrian handwriting and in translations from those languages, in 1860 he was elected a Member of Academy of Scholars in Berlin. During a period of controversy concerning the interpretation of architectural remains in Jerusalem, he so approved the content of articles written by the English scholar, George Williams, to have them translated and published in Halle. Dr Lobegott (Friedrich Constantin von) Tischendorff (1815–74), also a native of Saxony, unusually took no academic posts, but was a vigorous preacher, and a perpetual author of works of diverse character. One episode illustrates the sometimes fugitive nature of important manuscripts as he recounts how, in 1848, he rescued 48 sheets of manuscript from a waste deposit in a cellar in the Franciscan Monastery on Mount Sinai, which, with added material in 1862, was designated *Codex Sinaiticus*. A strong supporter of the United Bishopric of Jerusalem, Tischendorff was praised by George Williams for his judicious approach to matters not directly concerning religion.[20]

No subject occupied more attention than the authenticity of the ancient, and much disturbed, Church of the Holy Sepulchre in Jerusalem on which the authority (for the time being) was Dr Ernst Gustav Schultz, the Prussian Consul in Jerusalem, who had for the three years of his office 'applied himself to the study of its archaeology, with an industry and intelligence truly national'.[21] A collection of views on this topic from many sources, informed and ill-informed, was stopped in its tracks when, in 1847, a new theory concerning the structure of the Holy Sepulchre emerged from a Mr Fergusson, who, in an 'Essay on the Ancient Topography of Jerusalem', claimed to have proved that the building universally regarded as a Saracenic structure, and popularly called the Mosk of Omar, was the actual Church of the Holy Sepulchre erected by Constantine over the tomb of our Saviour and not the present church of the Holy Sepulchre!'[22] As a young man James Fergusson (1808–1886) worked in the family firm of Merchants-Calcutta. Through travelling in India as a business man he discovered a great fascination in Indian architecture. When this so occupied his time, he sold his business interests and thereafter turned his energies to becoming an acknowledged authority in unfamilar areas.[23]

William Smith and George Grove

In 1850 George Grove moved from engineering to the Secretaryship of the new Society of Arts. The Arts – now being allowed a broader definition, embracing pure as well as applied arts – revelled in the multi-cultural Great Exhibition of 1851 and the building of the Crystal Palace (the Millenium Dome of that age!) at Sydenham. To this London suburb, at the end of that year, Grove brought his wife Harriet, fifth daughter of George Bradley – who, like Grove himself, was a former pupil of Clapham Grammar School. Earlier in the same year Grove had visited his brother Edmund, also an engineer. Through Edmund he met James Fergusson, whom he remembered later as 'one of the *fullest* men I ever knew'.[24]

In the meantime there was ever increasing interest in the Holy Land, helped in 1841 by a notable contribution from the diligent American scholar Edward Robinson, Professor of Biblical Literature at Union Theological Seminary in New York, whose examination of sites in the Holy Land, and his clarity of exposition, set a high standard in scholarly judgement. Robinson's 'high geographical powers' were praised by Arthur Penrhyn Stanley, now a Canon of Canterbury – who also set out for the Holy Land with the purpose of bringing together the history and geography of the region. Three friends, Theodore Walrond, Thomas Francis Fremantle and William Benjamin Findlay, accompanied him. With the material for a book ready to be edited, he was advised by their mutual friend, George Bradley, to turn to George Grove. Stanley's book was published in 1856, carrying this acknowledgement: 'For the arrangement of the Appendix, as well as for the general verification of references and correction of the press, I am indebted to the careful revision of my friend, Mr. Grove, of Sydenham.'[25]

At this time, education, beginning to be revitalized, brought a feeling that, while knowledge of the Bible would promote virtue, its contents would be better understood with the aid of an accompanying dictionary. For this an Editor was already in place, so to speak, in the person of Dr William Smith, Classical Examiner in the University of London, who, by 1848, had provided the public not only with a *Dictionary of Greek and Roman Antiquities* but also with a heavily revised version of same (for as many as 300 articles had necessarily been rewritten).[26] It was, Smith claimed, 'inevitable that many defects would be found in the first Edition' of such a work, and 'those which had not been rewritten have been carefully revised'.[27] Even so, a major contributor, George Long, confessed that he considered 'some apology necessary in respect of what he had contributed..., ' for, despite writing the article on Roman Law, he 'had never had the advantage of attending a course of lectures on Roman Law...'[28]

Smith's idea of a dictionary was a sequence of articles, written by appropriate authorities, set out in alphabetical order and illustrated by occasional drawings. From his first *Dictionary*, now purged of error of the more abstruse contributions, Smith went into school books. The consequent *Smaller Dictionary of Greek and Roman Antiquities*, with shortened articles, achieved four editions by 1860. The editor added this commendation: 'The Abridgment was undertaken at the suggestion of the head-master of one of our great public schools, and no pains have been spared to adapt it to the class of persons for whom it is more especially intended'.[29] William Smith passed painlessly from MA, through LL.D, and on to a knighthood.

With his credentials for research into the subjects so well noticed in his diligent editing of Stanley's *Sinai and Palestine*, there was no other candidate for Smith's second-in-command of the proposed dictionary of the Bible than Grove. Knowing Smith's previous methods in dictionary practice, we can see how essential Grove's participation was to be. For his new enterprise,[30] Smith's editorial policy was defined in a Preface:

> It is a Dictionary of the Bible and not of Theology. It is intended to elucidate the antiquities, biography, geography, and natural history of the Old Testament, New Testament, and Apocrypha; but not to explain theology, or discuss points of controversial divinity.[31]

The first stages of the enterprise, including the selection of other contributors, went smoothly. In the first scheme of allocation of subjects Grove was to be responsible for Names, of which Smith advertised that names of all persons and places – in the Old and New Testaments and the Apocrypha – would be included. For some such entries he had material left over from his researches on Stanley's behalf, and also from Fergusson, whose descriptions of tombs and accounts of the Holy Sepulchre were already available. There was, however, tension at home. Harriet, Grove's wife, in an early burst of twentieth-century determinism, went so far but no further when initiated into the duty of listing names on her husband's behalf.[32] However, in the summer of 1858, following the example of the American scholar Dr Robinson, Dr Dobler, Ms Guerin, and others, the Groves shut up house and departed for the Holy Land, to search the subject at first hand.

The first volume of the *Dictionary of the Bible* was published in 1861. In his Preface to this, dated 15 March 1860, Dr Smith wrote:

> The Editor cannot conclude this brief explanation without expressing his obligation to the Writers of the various articles. These names are sufficient insurance for the value of their contributions; but the warm interest they have taken in the book, and the unwearied pains they have bestowed upon their several departments demand from the Editor his grateful thanks. There is, however, one Writer to whom he owes a more special acknowledgment. Mr. George Grove of Sydenham besides contributing the articles to which his initial is attached, has rendered the Editor important assistance in writing the majority of the articles on the

> more obscure names in the First Volume, in the correction of the proofs, and in the revision of the whole book. The editor has also to express his obligations to Mr. E. Stanley Poole for the revision of the Arabic words.
>
> It is intended to publish shortly an Atlas of Biblical Geography, which, it is hoped, will form a valuable supplement to the Dictionary.[33]

The remainder of the *Dictionary*, in two volumes, appeared in 1863.

Grove's mark on the *Dictionary* was magisterial, but his text was never far away from noticing values beyond the reach of scientific absolutism – also with frequent suggestions that a necessary ingredient was a sense of imagination. In this, in respect of Bible studies, he was not alone. *Eothen* (the Greek equivalent to the beautiful German *Morgenland*, meaning 'dawn' or 'looking towards the East'), a travel book attributed to Alexander Kinglake (1809–91) and written between 1834 and 1844, was a unique work, its sensitivity reflected in a passage which reads almost as a continuation of George Sandys:

> The village of Bethlehem lies prettily couched in the slope of a hill. The sanctuary is a subterranean grotto, and is committed to the joint-guardianship of the Romans, Greeks, and Armenians: these vie with each other in adorning it. Beneath an altar gorgeously decorated and lit with everlasting fires, there stands the low slab of stone which marks the holy site of the Nativity; and near to this is a hollow scooped out of the living rock. Here the infant Jesus was laid. Near the spot of the Nativity is the rock against which the Blessed Virgin was leaning when she presented her babe to the adoring shepherds.[34]

Ten years later Grove brought the scene strikingly up to modern times in his text for Smith's *Dictionary*, drawing on the second-century writing of Justin Martyr based on Isaiah xxxiii, vv.13–19:

> But the step from the belief that the Nativity may have taken place in a cavern, to the belief that the present subterranean vault or crypt is that cavern, is a very wide one. Even in the 150 years that had passed when Justin wrote, so much had happened at Bethlehem that it is difficult to believe that the true spot could have been accurately preserved. In that interval – an interval as long as that between the landing of William III and the Battle of Waterloo – not only had the neighbourhood of Jerusalem been over-run and devastated by the Romans at the destruction of the city, but the emperor Hadrian amongst other desecrtions, had actually planted a grove of Adonis at the spot. In the plain below and east of the Convent, about a mile from the walls, is the traditional scene of the angels' appearance to the shepherds, a very poor village called *Beit-Sahur*, to the E. of which are the unimportant remains of a Greek church.[35]

The illustrative power of Grove's prose and the skill of his teaching is demonstrated in his presentation of some familiar biblical topics: Elijah; the Mount of Olives; the Kedron brook; Reuben and the Reubenites, Mount Carmel. He explains the character of Elijah and his people in 16 columns of small print with 50 footnotes.[36]

> Elijah the Tishbite of the inhabitants of Gilead has well been entitled 'the grandest and the most romantic character that Israel ever produced'. His rare, sudden, and brief appearances – his undaunted courage and fiery zeal – the brilliancy of his triumphs, the pathos of his despondency – the glory of his departure, and the calm beauty of his reappearance on the Mount of Transfiguration – throw such a halo of brightness around him as is equalled by none of his compeers in the sacred story.[37]

Nothing is known of the prophet's family, even of his parentage, but he came from Gilead. Grove relishes staying awhile in his commentary, so bringing his readers into familiar scenes:

> Gilead was the country on the further side of the Jordan – a country of chase and pasture, of tent-villages and mountain-castles, inhabited by a people not settled and civilized like those who formed the communities of Ephraim and Judah, but of wandering, irregular habits, exposed to the attacks of the nomad tribes of the desert, and gradually conforming more and more to the habits of those tribes; making war with the Hagarites, and taking the countless thousands of their cattle and then dwelling in their stead. ...To an Israelite of the tribes west of Jordan the title 'Gileadite' must have conveyed a similar impression, though in a far stronger degree, to that which the title 'Celt' does to us. What the Highlands were a century ago to the towns in the Lowlands of Scotland, that, and more than that, must Gilead have been to Samaria or Jerusalem.
>
> *footnote:* Although it may seem out of place in a work of this nature, yet the writer cannot resist referring to the Oratorio Elijah written by Mendelssohn, one of the most forcible commentaries existing on the history of the Prophet. The scene in which the occurrences at Beersheba are embodied is perhaps the most dramatic and affecting in the whole work.

Elijah leaves Beersheba and takes leave of his servant before taking his journey across the desert: Mendelssohn's reading of the climax of that scene – 'Es ist genug! So nimm aus, Herr, meine Seele, ich bin nicht besser denn meiner Väter, es ist genug!' [It is enough. So, Lord, now take my life, for I am no better than my fathers] was for Grove contemporary music.

The Mount of Olives receives 12 columns with commensurate notes:

> 'The lasting glory of the Mount of Olives', it has been well said, 'belongs not to the Old dispensation, but to the New[']. Its very barrenness of interest in earlier times sets forth the abundance of those associations which it derives from the closing scenes of the sacred history. Nothing, perhaps, brings before us more strikingly the contrast of Jewish and Christian feeling, the abrupt and inharmonious termination of the Jewish dispensation – if we exclude the culminating point of the Gospel history – than to contrast the blank which Olivet presents to the Jewish pilgrims of the Middle Ages, only dignified by the sacrifice of 'the red heffer;' and the vision too great for words, which it offers to the Christian traveller of all times, as the most detailed and the most authentic abiding-place of Jesus Christ.[38]

In his related image of the brook of Kedron (six columns with notes) Grove's old self, the engineer, usefully emerges:

> [At a bridge across the deep valley lying between Jerusalem and the Mount of Olives] two subterranean drains [enter] from above; one of which comes from the sunken court of the Virgin's Tomb, and the other from the fields further to the north-west. The breadth of the valley at this point will appear from the measurements which I took from St. Stephen's Gate to Gethsemane along the path, viz. [in English feet]
>
> 1 From St. Stephen's Gate to the brow of the descent, level 135;
> 2 Bottom of the slope, the angle of the descent being $16\frac{1}{2}^{\circ}$, 415;
> 3 Bridge, level 140;
> 4 N.W. Corner of Gethsemene, slight rise 145;
> 5 N.E. Corner of Gethsemane, slight rise 150.
>
> The last three numbers give the breadth of the proper bottom of the valley at this spot, viz. 435 feet, or 145 yards';[39]

The topic of 'how wide a gap' already existed between the ideas of the Reubenites (who relinquished the worship of Jehovah) and those of the Western tribes is also made contemporary.

> The pile of stones which they erected on the western bank of the Jordan to mark their boundary – to testify to after ages that those separated by the rushing rivers from their brethren and the country in which Jehovah had fixed the place where He would be worshipped, they had still a right to return to it for His worship – was erected in accordance with the unalterable habits of Bedouin tribes both before and since. It was an act identical with that in which Laban and Jacob engaged at

> parting, with that which is constantly performed by the Bedouins of the present day.[40]

Of Mount Carmel, intimately connected with Israel's two great prophets Elijah and Elisha, Grove observes in his five-column entry:

> A mountain which forms one of the most striking and characteristic features of the country of Palestine. As if to accentuate more distinctly the bay which forms the one indentation in the coast, this noble ridge, the only headland of lower and central Palestine, forms its northern boundary, running out with a bold bluff promontory all but into the very waves of the Mediterranean. From this point it stretches in a nearly straight line, bearing S.S.E. for a little more than twelve miles, when it terminates suddenly by a bluff somewhat corresponding to its western end, breaking down abruptly into the hills of *Jenín* and Samaria which form at that part the central mass of the country.[41]

From that serene reference one is reminded of the purpose of the whole *Dictionary of the Bible*: to deliver the high significance of the *terra sancta*. Grove's monumental article on Palestine stretches over 35 pages of double-columns.

The closing text of 'The Other Dictionary' ends suspiciously with a barely concealed show of humour. The last main entries of the third volume by Grove, concern the problematic etymology and locations of the 'Land of Zuph' and the people named the Zuzim and Zamzummim. Grove happily notes that Gesenius characterizes the name 'Zuph' to mean honey. Of the rest he comments:

> the Zumim, who inhabited the country of the Ammonites, and were identical with the Zamzumimm, who are known to have been exterminated, and succeeded in their land, by the Ammonites. This suggestion has already been mentioned under Zamzumimm, but at the best it can only be regarded as a conjecture, in respect to which the writer desires to say with Reland – and it would be difficult to find a fitter sentence with which to conclude a Dictionary of the Bible – 'conjecturae, quibus non delectamur'.[42]

One may not say that without the experience of the *Dictionary of the Bible* there would have been no *Dictionary of Music and Musicians* (it is perhaps surprising that Dr Smith did not pursue the possibility). In Grove's prescription for the *Dictionary of Music and Musicians*, however, there are distinct echoes of the former work.

Notes

1 Letter of Grove to Edith Oldham, 2 April 1895: RCM MS 6864/415.
2 Letter of Grove to Edith Oldham, 6 May 1895: RCM MS 6864/417.
3 George Sandys, *A Relation of a Journey begun in An. Dom. 1610 in four books containing a description of the Turkish Empire, of Egypt, of the Holy Land, of the remote parts of Italy and islands adjoining* (London, 1615), p.138.
4 *Ibid.*, p.177.
5 *Ibid.*, p.180–1.
6 *Ibid.*
7 George Sandys, *Psalms of David, as A Paraphrase upon the Divine Poems, set to new Tunes for Private Devotion, And a Thorow Base, for voice, or Instrument, By Henry Laws, Gentleman of the Chapel Royal (1596–1662)* (London, 1638).
8 Ode 'The Passion', st. 7, ll.1–5. *The Complete English Poetry of John Milton (Excluding His Translations of Psalms 80–88)* [the Stuart Editions], arranged in chronological order with an introduction, notes variants and literal translations of the foreign language poems by John T. Shawcross (New York, 1963), p.54.
9 Henry Maundrell, *The Journey from Aleppo to Jerusalem* AD *1697* (Oxford, 1703).
10 *Ibid.*, pp.1, 2.
11 It was published as 'The Journey of H. Maundrell from Aleppo to Jerusalem AD 1697' in *Early Travels in Palestine*, ed. with notes by Thomas Wright (London, 1848), pp.383–512, and included in H.G. Bohn, *Antiquarian Library* (44 vols, London. 1847–1913).
12 Carsten Niebuhr, *Beschreibung von Arabien aus eigenen beobachtungen*... (Copenhagen, 1772), trans., Robert Heron, as *Niebuhr's Travels Through Arabia and other Countries in the East*, 2 vols (Edinburgh, 1792).
13 John Lewis Burckhardt, *Travels in Arabia* (London, 1829); *Travels in Syria and the Holy Land* (London, 1822), trans. as *Reisen in Arabien* (Weimar, 1830).
14 Henry Light, *Travels in Egypt, Nubia, Holy Land, Mount Libanon & Cyprus in the Year 1814* (London, 1818), p.161.
15 James Skinner, *Adventures during a Journey Overland to India by way of Egypt, Syria, and the Holy Land, 2 vols* (London, 1837), vol.1, p.206.
16 Lord Lindsay of Balcarres, *Letters on Egypt, Edom, and the Holy Land*, 2 vols (London, 1839), Letter 10 from Damascus, vol.2, p.60. The seventh of his letters was written to his sister, from the Convent of St. Catharine, on Mount Sinai: '...finding a Polish pilgrim here, about to return to Cairo, I seize the opportunity of letting you and my dear mother know, a month sooner than I otherwise could, how well we have got on hitherto and under what peculiarly favourable circumstances we are likely to continue our journey by Petra to Jerusalem' (vol.1, p.249).
17 Letter of Thomas Arnold to Sir T.S. Pasley, 23 September 1841. *The Life and Correspondence of Thomas Arnold D.D. by Arthur Penrhyn Stanley*, 2 vols, 12th edn (London 1881), vol.2, p.238.
18 As cited in n.13 above.
19 Heinrich Gesenius, *Journal of the Royal Geographic Society in London* (*RGS Journa*l), 11, 1841. Gesenius also translated the *Codex Sinaiticus*, the ancient biblical manuscript now in the British Museum (London, 1934).
20 Here I must mention Grove's close knowledge of Tischendorff's editions of the New Testament and his reviewing them in *Macmillan's Magazine*.
21 George Williams, *The Holy City* (London, 1845; 2nd edn 1848), p.xii. For Ernst Gustav Schultz (1811–51), diplomat and orientalist, see *Jerusalem. Eine Vorlesung*

von Dr Ernst Gustav Schultz (Berlin, 1845). Schultz made full acknowledgement to Williams's work in the appendix to his second edition (Berlin, 1849), as did Williams to Schultz in the text of his second edition (cited above).

22 See also Chapter 1, pp.10,12.

23 Among his published works were *The Illustrated Handbook of Architecture* (London, 1855); *History of the Modern Styles of Architecture* (London, 1862); and *A History of Indian and Eastern Architecture* (London, 1876), all published by John Murray.

24 Percy M. Young, *George Grove, 1820–1900. A Biography* (London 1980), p.69.

25 Arthur Penrhyn Stanley, *Sinai to Palestine, in Connection with their History* (London, 1856), 'Advertisement', p.ix.

26 William Smith, *Dictionary of Greek and Roman Antiquities* (London, 1842, 2nd edn 1848), Preface, pp.vii, xi–xii.

27 *Ibid.*, Preface, p.vii.

28 *Ibid.*, Preface, pp xi–xii.

29 William Smith, *A Smaller Dictionary of Greek and Roman Antiquities* (London, 2 vols, 1853), Preface.

30 William Smith, *A Dictionary of the Bible, Concerning its Antiquity, Biography, Geography and Natural History*, 3 vols (London, 1860–63). See list of Grove's published works in Appendix 1.

31 Smith, *A Dictionary of the Bible*, Preface to vol.1.

32 Having, in fact, listed an uncountable pile of names for my present purpose, my sympathy lies with Harriet. George, I suppose, had assumed her task to be not duty but pleasure. In a macabre way, I see his point of view.

33 Smith, *A Dictionary of the Bible*, Preface to vol.1.

34 'Terra Sancta', in Alexander W. Kinglake, *Eothen* (London, 3rd edn, 1845), p.157.

35 Smith, *A Dictionary of the Bible*, vol.1, pp.203–4.

36 Smith, *A Dictionary of the Bible*, vol.1, pp.524–7.

37 The quotation is from *Sinai and Palestine*, p.328. Grove's footnote read: 'Omnium suae aetatis prophetarum facile princeps.' Grove gives the Greek equivalent as Eliyahu.

38 Smith, *A Dictionary of the Bible*, vol.2, p.629, 'Olives, Mount of'. The 'red heffer' is explained in a footnote on 'Sin-offering' in the third volume, p.1324, note b.

39 *Ibid.*, vol.2, p.15, 'Kedron, the Brook'.

40 *Ibid.*, vol. 3, p.1033, 'Reuben'.

41 *Ibid.*, vol.1, p.278, 'Carmel'. Grove notes that the name is nearly always given with the definite article, i.e. 'the park' or 'the well-wooded place'; and that, in Kings, Carmel is generally given as 'Mount C' (in Greek, 'Mount Carmelos') and in the Prophets, 'Carmel'.

42 *Ibid.*, vol.3, pp.1861–62.

5
The Making of a Scholar: Grove's Beethoven, Mendelssohn and Schubert

Michael Musgrave

'An Amateur of Music': the context of Grove's scholarship

> This book is addressed to the amateurs of this country, who have so immensely increased during the last fifty years with the increase of good and cheap performances...It would be presumptuous in me to attempt to interest professional musicians, who naturally know already all that I have been able to put together, and much more; and in a more complete and accurate manner.[1]

Thus Grove introduced his *Beethoven and His Nine Symphonies* of 1896 (Plate 15), expressing a sentiment he very often repeated. It prompts two immediate responses. First, his obvious sensitivity to the fact that he was not a professional musician and lacked professional training or skills in music; second that his writings lacked technical detail, possessing rather descriptive and responsive quality, a feature for which he had earlier received criticism, as we read from Shaw. Indeed, of his education in music, Grove freely admits that he never learnt the piano: 'neither I nor my brother could ever play more than a 'psalm tune quick' like Punch's Italian [organ-grinder]. We were to be engineers and get too soon into the world': this in contrast to his younger sister, Eliza, who followed her mother, in accordance with social custom, as a capable pianist. Graves adds that 'he was no "executant", though as a boy and a young man he had played the piano a little and sung in choral classes'.[2]

Yet Grove also reveals self-confidence: he could afford to be open because by the time he wrote *Beethoven and His Nine Symphonies*, his position as an authoritative communicator for the concert-going audience he sought – and had helped to build at the Crystal Palace – was unique in England and highly regarded abroad. Indeed, such a leading musician as the conductor Hans Richter declared to Graves his conviction that 'the services rendered by Grove in his picturesque and genial analysis of the symphonies of Beethoven, Schubert, Brahms &c. were of incalculable value in educating the public'.[3]

The evidence of Grove's musicianship is rather of a remarkable capacity to absorb the shape and essential character of music as a listener.

> [H]e could find his way well enough about the full score of a work that the had heard three or four times. By that time, the written page became luminous, so to say, in his mind. The mere mental perusal of the score of a brand new work conveyed as little to him as it does to most amateurs...Later on he generally had the talent of the best professionals and amateurs at his disposal – if he wanted to hear anything in particular.

He was open in his confession that he internalized poetry more intimately:

> You who execute music have an immense advantage over us who only listen to it. You don't realize how much you gain by having to go over and over a song till you can really sing it – till it becomes to you what many of the poems in In Memoriam are to me. I often think of that, and lament that with all my love, my knowledge of music is so much less intimate than it might be...

Indeed, his analytical approach was with an essentially broad brush.[4]

Circumstances were to make Grove's musical education self-education, and he began it through the traditional route of the copying out of music, involving the understanding of figured bass and vocal score reading. His studies continued irrespective of his current location: he studied whenever he could: his first commonplace book is addressed from Glasgow (see his comments given in Chapter 1, page 6). He frequented the British Museum from the opening of the new Reading Room in 1838 and continued his studies right through his period of travel, including his work in the West Indies. His first focus was on choral music, of which he made lengthy extracts, his transcriptions including frequent comments on the character of particular chords and effects. His appetite for garnering documentary material and gaining a comprehensive background to the composers is clear in his listing of sources and making of his own indexes, as well as the sources of his further reading and critical judgements. Subsequently his interest focused particularly on the organ music of J.S. Bach in the new Griepenkerl edition (he knew the music well from childhood, as he recalled to F.G. Edwards), to which he provided his own handwritten list of contents. Grove was deeply devoted to Bach into the 1860s, but the enthusiasm then took second place to Beethoven, Mendelssohn and Schubert. The depth of Grove's emerging interest required a knowledge that went far beyond what the conventional theory of harmony and counterpoint could provide; and once at the Crystal Palace, Grove had unrivalled opportunities to experience intimately the emerging concert repertory through live daily performance and rehearsal – and he had already gained a thorough knowledge of performed repertory in England when he wrote to August Manns in 1855 concerning his appointment as Director of Music.[5]

But there is a broader perspective to be added to Grove's comments. The focus on music documentation – which was to be a crucial element of Grove's contribution alongside his discussion of the music itself – was new and came about in response to the growing reputation of certain composers through the emerging repertory of public concerts. Some of Grove's greatest contemporaries – his generation is identical with that of the founding figures of musicology – were also 'amateur' in the sense that their professional training and activity were in another field. However, the term must not be taken in the modern pejorative sense, devalued through the subsequent 'professionalization' of such study. The precision and discipline of method and thought they brought to their documentary work was professional, and the achievements of this generation relative to the size of the task outstanding. Here Grove worked with a much sharper point.[6]

The breadth of Grove's professional commitments was, however, unique, even by comparison with these contemporaries, and his background and circumstances inevitably determined a different scholarly product. Grove was never able to produce the books embodying all he knew in focused scholarship: his intended books on Beethoven, Mendelssohn and Schubert, based on his dictionary articles, never materialized. Thus, there is no documentary equivalent in Grove's output in his primary area of specialization – Beethoven – to the work of Nottebohm and Thayer, whose names have survived through the revision of their work, and Grove's scholarly importance is significantly lessened for the modern reader as a result: he is now known to scholarship only as the founder of his *Dictionary*. His book on the Beethoven symphonies was only produced at the end of his life as a final stage of his constantly updated programme notes on the works, and takes a detailed and personal account of the music as its focus. His three major articles were part of a much larger dictionary and were, for all their detail, not designed for full analysis of music and biography.[7]

The channel for the emergence of Grove's documentary work was his programme notes for the Crystal Palace concerts, a vital accompaniment to the emerging new repertory of public classical music (see Chapter 6). Grove typically added much more than was to be found in the notes of more academic writers. As well as discussing the music itself, he communicated new material on both the documentary sources of the music and the composers' lives. The notes sometimes bear almost the character of a progress report on the state of discovery, an educational dimension further apparent through his quoting of his sources and recommendations for further reading. This, as it were, communal spirit, arose from the atmosphere of the Crystal Palace.

Grove's capacity to express all this in a vital ongoing narrative of the music comprehensively illustrated with precise music examples gave his notes a value to professionals as well as a unique quality for the general reader. However, his stated aim was simply 'to make the music itself more intelligently heard and better understood', and his primary method the tracing of the outlines of form and structure by theme and motive: his text was richly illustrated with music examples as guide, and focuses on features of special interest. One notes his emphasis on orchestral features, tacitly acknowledging that his listeners would rarely hear these works in live performance, but would know them better through arrangements for piano duet. What his presentation lacked in technical detail and terminology, he made up by his capacity to give a larger view of musical issues, and he is still worth quoting today, as in addressing the thematic significance of the first movement of Beethoven's Third Symphony:

> The Eroica first shows us the method that was to so revolutionize that department of music – the continuous and organic mode of connecting the second subject with the first, the introduction of episodes in the working out, the extraordinary importance of the Coda.

But his interest in thematic aspects went well beyond the unity of single movements or works. He was a virtuoso observer of significant thematic similarities between works, symptomatic of his view of musical tradition as an 'apostolic succession of great composers' and these links as evidence of it. This special interest is manifest in his only extended work of a theoretical nature, the lengthy series of articles on the varied historical manifestations of a single figure especially familiar as the opening motive of the finale of Mozart's Jupiter Symphony.[8]

Grove could never have begun to conceive of the *Dictionary* without the wide knowledge he had gained from his extensive studies from his youth to the 1870s, and must have anticipated how much he would have to cover between the contributions of his invited specialists, even before the project began to expand beyond the two volumes originally planned. As editor, he ended up as the backstop contributor and his own tally amounted to around 1,600 entries on an extraordinary range of topics from obscure composers to technical devices in music. But this work relied largely on secondary sources. For the essays on his revered three major composers of the modern concert hall – Beethoven, Mendelssohn and Schubert – he went much further, undertaking original research, gaining an intimate critical knowledge of the rapidly emerging literature, offering opinions of great authority and effectively becoming a tastemaker in his promotion of them. These were the vehicles on which he wanted his scholarly reputation primarily to stand. And these composers had an added dimension by comparison with much of his other work: they were already part of a living tradition, both in that their music formed the basis of the emerging canonical repertory, and in the number of individuals still living who had been acquainted with them. Original research required travel and access to contacts and sources. Grove made three main research trips: to Vienna in 1867 and 1880 for Schubert; and in 1889 for Beethoven; and included visits to contacts and to musical events on regular trips to Germany; he also had his colleagues undertake research work for him – C.A. Barry and C.V Stanford notably.[9]

Each of his three main composers presented Grove with a different task. This Chapter outlines the main contour and context of the innumerable details of his research work: how things stood in the field of documentary research on these composers, and Grove's contributions through his three articles, published in the volumes of 1879, 1880 and 1883 respectively, and in *Beethoven's Nine Symphonies* of 1884, its greatly expanded sequel *Beethoven and His Nine Symphonies* of 1896 and other publications.

Beethoven

By the time Grove prepared the Beethoven article, he was able to draw on a wide range of primary biographical sources, beginning with the reminiscences of Seyfried, Wegeler, Ries, Schindler and Breuning, as well as the extensive collections of letters which began to appear with Nohl's first collection in 1865, all of which he lists; and also more fragmentary sources and subsequent early literature of importance, including newspaper reports.[10]

In the field of critical documentation, the first Breitkopf und Härtel thematic catalogue had appeared in 1851. In 1868, Nottebohm produced a second and greatly expanded edition in order of opus number; this had been preceded by the transcription of a sketchbook with commentary in 1865, and followed by a series of articles, and a further transcription of sketches in 1872–3. Thayer began the first major critical biography of Beethoven in 1866 (drawing on Jahn's unfinished work), preceded in 1865 by his own chronological index which included works in composition order and also unpublished works, as precursor to his biography. Grove also lists modern biographical writing beginning with Fétis and von Lenz.[11]

The works of Nottebohm and Thayer were the foundation of Grove's documentary knowledge and were regarded by him as almost definitive. They significantly constrained what he could add to the field, and the first edition of *The Dictionary of Music and Musicians* (hereafter *Grove 1*) is deeply indebted to them. Grove's Beethoven work was to come to full fruition only years afterwards, in *Beethoven and his Nine Symphonies*, and the work-listing in the appendix to *Grove 1* (1889), and other writings. Grove's reference to source material had to be based on limited access to documents and contacts. In London he could consult a few Beethoven autographs only. The British Museum had possessed sketches of the Hammerklavier Sonata since 1843, the so-called Kafka sketchbook since 1876, and sketches for the

Pastoral Symphony since 1880–1; the Philharmonic Society had the copy score of Ninth Symphony made by Beethoven 'for the society'; Grove notes autograph material in the hands of several private individuals in England: a score of the B flat Piano Concerto; a letter to Broadwood; the Heiligenstadt Testament; and a sketchbook owned by Joachim. First-hand contacts also occasionally came his way in England: he was visited at the Crystal Palace by Karoline Unger-Sabatier, who as Karoline Unger had sung the contralto part in the premiere of Symphony No.9, and recalled Beethoven's inability to hear the applause he received.[12]

Vienna offered much more. On Grove's first visit in 1867, he had access to manuscripts in the Gesellschaft der Musikfreunde collection, through the society's archivist, C.F. Pohl, including the autograph score of Symphonies No.3 and No.6. Through the publisher Spina, he had access to uncatalogued letters, one of which was given to him by Spina. He recalls that Spina said:

> I am now going to show you something of real interest. Come down with me. And he produces about 12 letters from Beethoven from Diabelli, never printed or seen before by profane eyes and reads them to us – as they are worse than Hebrew to make out... At last Spina selected one with a clearer signature than the rest and begged me to keep it as a souvenir.

Of first-hand personal contacts he met Spina's manager Franz Doppler, whom both Grove and Sullivan recall as describing his mode of dress; how he used to communicate using a slate with Czerny, Seyfried, Stadler, and his unawareness of his surroundings. Of locations, Grove had in 1867 visited the graves of Beethoven and Schubert, recently reinterred in 1863. But in 1889, in final preparation for the Beethoven book, he visited many more places. Now in the company of Pohl's successor, Eusebius Mandycewski, he visited Gneixendorf, where the composer spent his last autumn; the valley called Brühl near Mödling where Beethoven wrote the Pastoral Symphony and the Mass in D –

> just as it was in 1815...one of the most beautiful spots even now and the old taverns and houses are just as they were, including the Two Ravens where the band used to play which he caricatured in the scherzo of the Past[oral] Symphony

– and Döbling, to visit the rooms where Beethoven wrote the Credo of the Mass in 1820, which Grove measured.[13]

This material was worked into the article and later, more fully, the book alongside complementary matter from published sources, compared with each other for accuracy. Although Grove's contacts and travels enabled him to add supporting information to the available documentation of the composer and his work, his major contribution had to be critical, based on his special expertise: his knowledge of the music and the scores; and of the major sources and writings upon them. This was to be a long process. Despite the scope of the Beethoven article in *Grove 1*, it had only a simple summary of works by genre (merely subdivided into Instrumental or Vocal) with no dates or details – perhaps reflecting both Grove's deference to the work of Nottebohm and Thayer (since the article itself contains many such details) and the pressure of completing such a major piece so early in the *Dictionary*. But with greater time over later years, he significantly extended Nottebohm's documentation of sources, though without providing incipits (Nottebohm had died in 1882). The listing provided in the Appendix to volume 4 of 1889 (and taken into the second edition - *Grove 2)* is described as 'based on Nottebohm's catalogue of 1868, the letters, the works themelves and other sources' and was the most comprehensive at the time, adding, where known, datings of composition, dates of first editions and publishers, locations of the manuscripts of unpublished works, names of dedicatees, drawn from direct enquiries of publishers and private individuals, and from the autographs themselves. Additionally, Grove extended the series of opus numbers from the existing op.138 to op. 256. Both the *Grove 1* article and *Beethoven and His Nine Symphonies* provided information on early performance history in Germany, England, USA and France on the basis of the first-hand reminiscences of his contacts and published records including the concert histories written by Hanslick, Pohl, Hogarth and others.[14]

Grove's article and his book show the extent of his critical examination of published writings, especially of the work of Nottebohn and Thayer. He carefully compared Nottebohm's various publications for discrepancies, and notes, for example, an implicit discrepancy as between his remarks in *Beethoven Studien* and *Zweite Beethoveniana* concerning the identity of sketches he had at first identified as for Symphony No.1. And in examining Thayer's work, he compares the programme given for the first performance of Symphony No.2 with the report in *Allgemeine Musikalische Zeitung*, noting differences. Of dating, for example, he queries both Thayer and Nottebohm's acceptance of the word 'Mai' for the month unclearly given on the autograph of Symphony No.7, considering that June and July were equally possible readings. He added to Thayer's quoted source for Beethoven's notice of 30 October 1802 in the *Wiener Zeitung* another source from the *Wiener Intelligenzblatt*; and Grove also applied his criticism to the first-hand sources where it seemed appropriate. For example, he compares the treatment of the same details as between Ignaz and Charlotte Moscheles's record. He challenged Schindler's authority by querying the name of General Ham in the literature by asserting 'I have ascertained, by courtesy of the authorities at the War Office, the Record Office and the Foreign Office, that no such name is to be found in the British Army Lists or other official documents of that day.' More generally he observes that 'one of the few defects of Mr Nottebohm's thematic catalogue…is that there is no indication of what the various publications are. It is often impossible to tell whether they are score or parts', a criticism repeated later.[15]

However, Grove's greatest critical focus was on the scores themselves, both on the accuracy of the autographs and on how problems persisted in the first published editions. As well as the autographs in the Gesellschaft der Musikfreunde, he saw the autograph scores of the symphonies (always his primary focus) Nos 4, 5, 7, 8, 9 in Berlin in 1891 (Nos 4, 5 and 7, were in the possession of Ernst Mendelssohn; Nos 8, 9 at the Imperial Library). Grove believed that the original editions of the Beethoven symphonies 'were issued with Beethoven's approval and 'errors excepted' are to be taken as correct'. And he pointed out these errors in various of his publications: for example, in Symphony No.5, he points out two redundant bars about which Beethoven wrote to his publishers before publication, asking for them to be removed, a request not acted upon until 1846; also the suppression of the dedication of this work on publication; and in Symphony No.9, the omission of the Da Capo marking after the Trio, which was omitted in the first proofs and corrected by Beethoven.[16]

Mendelssohn

In sharp contrast to the biographical sources of the Beethoven article, most of the Mendelssohn source materials had only begun to appear in the twenty years or so before Grove's Mendelssohn article of 1880, and he notes there the Mendelssohn literature as 'not yet very extensive'. It lists (though not in chronological order) the recollections and anthologies of Lampadius, Benedict, Devrient, Carl Mendelssohn Bartholdy, Hiller, Polko, Sebastian Hensel, Hogarth, Moscheles, Schubring, Horsley, Dorn, Chorley, Marx, Rellstab, Lobe. Mendelssohn's letters also began to appear in the 1860s, with two major collections, as well as many items within the above sources and anthologies, and were extensively translated into English.[17]

In the critical documentary literature, the first thematic catalogue had appeared before Mendelssohn's death in 1847: the first Breitkopf und Härtel catalogue was in 1841, the second in 1846, new edition 1853. More works were added in Julius Rietz's listing as the appendix to the English translation of the *Briefe aus den Jahren 1853–47*, trans. 1864. The second and more comprehensive Breitkopf und Härtel catalogue appeared in 1873.[18]

Thus, by the time these materials had begun to appear, Grove had already had good opportunities to do his own research and to become intimately associated with the emerging documentary field. Not of least value to him was the fact of Mendelssohn's close associations with England. This gave him both personal contacts and access to musical material. The fifty or so names he acknowledges in the article begin with the Mendelssohn family itself. He knew Mendelssohn's brother Paul, the sons Paul and Carl as well as the daughters, Marie Benecke and Lili Wach, to both of whom he was close, the nephew

Ernst Mendelssohn (son of Paul) and nephew Sebastian Hensel (son of Mendelssohn's sister Fanny Hensel), and members of his circle: Charlotte Moscheles, Livia Frege, the family of Conrad Schleinitz, who had been director of the Leipzig Conservatoire, Charles and Sophy Horsley, Dr Klengel (tutor to Mendelssohn's sons), Joseph Joachim and Clara Schumann, Ferdinand Hiller, Otto Goldschmidt and Jenny Lind, the Sterndale Bennett family, George Macfarren. These however were only some of the names cited as sources of original material in the body of the article; there are many references to others who provided him with original material.

Of musical materials, the British Museum held the string quartet in E flat, first performed in 1879 and published in 1880 and two fugues, one for organ, one for piano; Mendelssohn had dedicated the symphony 1 in C minor to the Philharmonic Society, and the Society owned the autograph. The Sacred Harmonic Society had given first London performances of *Elijah* and *St Paul* and had documentation which was made available by the Secretary W.H. Husk; the head of Novello, Henry Littleton, possessed the autograph score of *Elijah* (later in the Bodleian Library). Grove appears to have had access to the compositions in the Green Books through the family before the musical part went to Berlin: he notes, for example, the permission of Marie Benecke to reproduce a passage from the incomplete C major Symphony (also subsequently in Bodleian). The article shows Grove's intimate knowledge of the entire field of MSS owners and locations, not only in England but abroad, though he notes difficulties of access.[19]

Thus, Grove was in a position to produce a much more comprehensive list than previously existed. Although the *Grove 1* article merely states it was based on the 1873 Breitkopf and Härtel catalogue 'with the addition of the dates of composition, where discoverable, and the names of the dedicatees' (drawn from autographs, letters and other sources), its third and final section includes far more material, listing posthumous works, works since published and performed, with first performance dates, and also the unpublished works in the Green Books – this listing also far exceeded that of the next Breitkopf and Härtel catalogue 1882, which was restricted to published works, with and without opus numbers. Since the catalogue was never again revised, but simply reissued (to the present day), Grove's list remained preeminent. But, as with his work on Beethoven, the following twenty years or so provided much more material. Although the format in the *Grove 2* article followed that of *Grove 1*, and likewise claimed the preceding *Breitkopf und Härtel* catalogue as its basis (here 1882, and likewise with dates of composition and dedicatees, though, as the editor adds, 'also the original German and English publishers insofar as they can be traced') – this final listing was far more extensive in its entry detail, including additional items within the categories of works without opus number, and works 'not included in the thematic catalogue'.[20]

Grove's contacts enabled many biographical details to be included in the article itself, not least from English sources. Charles Horsley provided a description of Mendelssohn, added to by others. A rich field concerned Mendelssohn as a performer: Grove obtained first-hand descriptions from Mendelssohn's friends and former pupils about his piano and organ playing and his conducting, and records of his teaching style in Leipzig. Grove's primary sources for the piano playing were Otto Goldschmidt, Clara Schumann and J.W. Davison. English organists, who also noted which Bach works he played, included E.J. Hopkins and James Turle: Grove compared published recollections, for example those of H.J. Gauntlett (*Musical World*, 15 September 1837) with Hopkins's recollections. The critic Henry Chorley had left a vivid recollection of Mendelssohn in August 1847, playing to him on the village church organ at Ringgenberg near Interlaken, pieces by Bach as well as his own improvizations. Grove visited this church many years later with Walter Parratt, where they shut themselves in, just as Mendelssohn 'used to shut himself in and play to his heart's content after he lost his sister...and had quite a solemn little service, Parratt playing three pieces by Bach and three by Mendelssohn'. Of Mendelssohn's conducting, George Macfarren made available to Grove his own unpublished recollection of the first performance of the Scottish symphony. Grove had sent him one of his own essays, and Macfarren replied 'I have personal knowledge of some incidents in the symphony's history which in order to define some lines which are wavy in your account I will repeat'. He then set down a precise recollection of the first performance under Mendelssohn on 13 June 1842, which Grove used (including references to the lack of pauses between movements).[21]

Prior to the completion of the article, Grove had already published some of his research findings. He described and illustrated the 11 String Symphonies for the first time in 1871; and had written in response to reaction to his programme notes on the so-called Trumpet Overture in a letter to *The Times* clarifying his understanding of its provenance. As a result of his contacts, Grove himself came to possess several original items, including portraits, which he later gave to friends, chiefly to F.G. Edwards.[22]

Grove also contributed to the publication of the music itself. As well as commissioning (from Dannreuther) a short score piano transcription of the first movement of the unpublished C major symphony obtained through Marie Benecke, published for the first time in the *Grove 1* article, he added a concluding movement to Mendelssohn's published setting of Psalm 95 for SATB and organ accompaniment. The new publication was prefaced with this information:

> The chorus which here concludes the Psalm ['For his is the Sea'] and which is now published for the first time, was discovered among Mendelssohn's autograph MSS before they left this country for the

> Imperial Library at Berlin, where they are now deposited. It is dated by its author '11 April, 1839' i.e. some weeks after the first performance of the work at Leipzig on the 21st of the preceding February. It appears likely that the newly discovered Chorus had been written to give a more complete finish to the Psalm than is given by the present Andante in G minor; and with this view the permission of Mendelssohn's family was obtained for its publication.

Grove took the opportunity offered by the Crystal Palace concerts for the first performance of the Psalm on 26 February 1876 under Manns.[23]

Grove's intimate knowledge of the field placed him in an excellent position to sit in the critic's chair on emerging literature. As with Beethoven research, he carefully compared his sources for accuracy of information. The natural focus for new information was the appearance of the large collections of letters. Grove made his first important public statement on Mendelssohn research in 1865 when he castigated the editors of the first volume of letters for the inadequacy of their choices and editing. He wrote to E.M. Oakeley on 30 December 1865:

> The charge against the editors of Mendelssohn Letters is wider than you seem aware of. They have suppressed *all mention* of many of the most prominent of his contemporaries and the dearest of his friends. It is hardly credible that the names of Jenny Lind, Joachim, Sterndale Bennett, J.W. Davison, Robert Schumann and Clara Wieck, with whom he was in the closest intimacy and constant correspondence, should either not be found at all in either of the volumes or else only be mentioned in some such terms as 'The Schumanns are here', 'Bennett has just arrived', and so on. What the motive for this exclusion is, I do not know. I can only observe one fact: that Mendelssohn had a very high opinion of these persons and therefore that if he had mentioned them it would always be in terms of praise. Now very few of the letters printed contain praise of his contemporaries. This seems to have been one guiding principle in selecting the letters and it is a very reprehensible one, because it not only suppresses Mendelssohn's good opinion of the various persons, but also leads one to believe that he was jealous of his rivals – which are the reverse of the truth. Quantities of letters exist full of praise of Jenny Lind, Joachim, Schumann &c.

Grove was also a sharp critic of Lady Wallace's translations, as he was of her Beethoven letters. Of the reminiscences of Elise Polko, also translated by her, he referred to them as 'poor, gushing stuff' (though he still drew on them for his essay). Grove's great authority in the field led to his being asked to write prefaces to several books on the composer (see list of published works in Appendix 1). He also translated a poem by the composer.[24]

Schubert

The situation with Schubert documentation was totally different from that of either Mendelssohn or Beethoven. Grove's observation that the literature was 'by comparison with other composers, not extensive' was a typical understatement. It was virtually unknown when Grove began his work in the mid-1860s because much of Schubert's large-scale music was unpublished or rarely if at all performed. The modern perception of Schubert as a great composer of the classical instrumental tradition did not yet exist; most audiences knew him only by a few songs. The brief early reminiscences were little known outside Vienna, and Grove did not know them all: he acknowledges, for example, that the *Recollections of von Spaun* published by Köchel were known to him only through C.F. Pohl in Vienna; and though he lists or mentions those of Ferdinand Schubert, Johann Mayrhofer and Eduard Bauernfeld; Anton Schindler; Sophie Müller, Helmina von Czézy; Ferdinand Hiller, Anselm Hüttenbrenner and Rellstab, he does not cite those of Sonnleithner or Zedlitz.[25]

Extended literature on Schubert only began to appear from the mid-1860s with biographies and some later published reminiscences in various sources: beginning with the first extended biography of the composer by Kreissle von Hellborn of 1865 (full English translation with new appendix, 1869), followed by biographies by Barbedette, Reissmann; the article in Wurzbach's *Biographisches Lexicon*, 1876, Niggli, Gumprecht, and La Mara. Additionally Grove cites the performance histories cited in the Beethoven article. There were far fewer letters to appear than in the case of Beethoven and Mendelssohn. By the time of Grove's article, few had been published; *Grove 1* (vol.3) notes them individually, a list unchanged in the second edition.[26]

Reception in England was particularly slow. Indeed, so little was known of Schubert in England before Grove's initiatives that he explained the situation in detail in his first Schubert publication, the appendix he provided to the English version of Kreissle: that it was only in 1846 that he heard his first Schubert songs (of which only the most familiar were known); and not until Manns's Crystal Palace performance of Symphony No.9 in C major in 1856 (given in two stages on successive weeks) that he heard any orchestral music; and then the same work again only in 1865; that Manns had the 'overture' to *Rosamunde* in his repertory (it had been played in 1856 and 1866: see below). Of orchestral music, only Symphony No.9 had been published in score (in 1840) by the time of Kreissle's book.[27]

Of critical documentary material, the Diabelli thematic catalogue 1852 was completely inadequate; it was to be greatly augmented by Nottebohm's revision of 1874, listing works with and without opus number (based on the listing in Reissmann), unpublished works, with lists of publishers, portraits and books to standards which Grove greatly admired.[28]

Yet before almost any of this material had appeared, Grove had already made a major contribution to Schubert research through his response to Kreissle's book in its German original of 1865, which gave him the chance to make his scholarly mark whilst also satisfying his curiosity and new passion for Schubert's works. The book had included within each compositional category a list of unpublished works. By the time Grove had followed up on this information by visiting Vienna and had produced a thematic catalogue of the symphonies and some other works, describing the manuscript sources with musical examples, and with references to other works in his appendix to the English translation published in 1869, he had himself become a figure in the emerging tradition, and he then also drew fully on the available literature for his article published in 1883.[29]

Grove's journey to Vienna had been essential to establish the facts, since little information was available elsewhere, and its consequence became part of the musical heritage of the Crystal Palace. Grove had first written to the publisher Spina concerning the Entr'actes of the drama *Rosamunde*, which were described in Kreissle. Spina told him that several numbers were in his possession and that and two were in the press (the Entr'actes in B minor and B flat, between the first and second, and third and fourth acts respectively), and the printed score and parts were sent by the end of October 1866 (Plate 12). Soon after, MS copies of No.2, 'Ballo', and No.9 'Ballet Air' were also sent. Spina also sent MS copies of the overtures to *Alfonso und Estrella* and *Fierrabras* (also in press), and soon appeared the overture 'In the Italian Style' in C, also in press. All these works were quickly performed at the Crystal Palace by Manns, as was, in the spring of 1867, the newly published Symphony No.8 in B minor. But enquiries regarding orchestral accompaniment to the three pieces with piano accompaniment were not successful. In Vienna Grove, with his companion Arthur Sullivan, also met Eduard Schneider, the son of Schubert's sister Theresa, possessed of a cupboard of MSS including Symphony No.4 in C minor, and No.6 in C. They also made notes on the scherzo opening of the Symphony in B minor, bars 1–9, and on the 'Great' C major symphony; a second call to Schneider found the *Rosamunde* part books from which copies were taken, and an index made of the complete *Rosamunde* music.[30]

Grove's enthusiastic enquiries regarding the symphony left in sketch form by Schubert, 'No.7 in E major' had finally reached Paul Mendelssohn, the composer's brother, who had inherited it from Felix Mendelssohn, to whom it had been entrusted by Schubert's brother Ferdinand Schubert in the hope that he could orchestrate it. Grove describes the score, that the first 109 bars are fully scored, and the rest in sketch, but that the entire score is set out with instruments and bar lines, and tempo indications (Plate 11). He gained access in sufficient time to include the work in his Appendix to the translation of Kreissle's book in 1869. But symphonies Nos 1–6 were not published, nor to be so until they appeared in the *Breitkopf und Härtel* collected edition in 1884 and 1885, edited by Brahms. However, Grove's excellent relations with the manuscript owners and with C.F. Pohl enabled him to obtain copies and thus to give performances. Grove's circumstances at the Crystal Palace made him able to continue to promote concert performance of the many unknown orchestral works. Manns performed them as follows: Symphonies Nos 4, 6, 1868; No.5, 1873; No.2, 1877; Nos 1, 3, 1881. Of these Nos 1–3 were claimed as world premieres; and in 1880 a complete cycle was given, the first anywhere.[31]

Grove's Vienna visits had yielded first-hand recollections of the composer (as with Beethoven). At Spina's in 1867, Franz Doppler had claimed close connection with Schubert (he was born in the same town) and said that he was present at Schubert's christening. Grove sought further information through the family by approaching Schubert's great-niece, Carola Geisler-Schubert. She recalls how Grove wrote 'begging her to ask her grandmother for any particulars she remembered about her brother -in-law the composer'. After his visit to Vienna in 1880, he wrote to thank her for 'the exact room in which Schubert was born, which is not stated in any of the biographies' and asking to publish a letter she had found in his biography [article] 'for the first time'. She then sent him a photograph, and he wrote back about what he had been able to draw from it, both for dating and biography.[32]

Thus Grove came to the Schubert article not only with access to virtually all the available literature, but already very familiar with the manuscript sources and as a real influence in the promotion of the music. This rich background helped to give the Schubert article its great authority and value. Grove now offered by far the most detailed available listing of works, much greater than that of Nottebohm. Although he notes the latter as 'admirable ...comprehensive and accurate...and a model of what a catalogue should be', he added to it. Nottebohm gave only the incipit, brief history, editions, with dates and prices of scores, and transcriptions, likewise, and these only of printed music. Grove's listing took six sources as a starting point, both published and in manuscript sources. To Nottebohm's listing, Grove indicated as added the Chronological Collection of Songs from 1811–1828 in the Witteczek collection of the Gesellschaft der Musikfreunde, Vienna; his own notes taken from the archives of this collection; the list given by Reissmann (see above); occasional information in letters; all other sources available to the compiler which comprised an 11-column list of works listing 1,131 compositions. These were laid out by genre not chronology, with an independent alphabetical listing of songs and part songs, as well as dates of composition, publication, opus number or name of publisher. It therefore had an analytical, educational character, in showing the full shape of the output by adding unpublished works and new publications. Grove's accompanying article synthesized all the available information with his own first-hand knowledge which exceeded all previous biographical work on background and performance history, and manuscript ownership.

Together with the Crystal Palace performances it undoubtedly had significant influence on the promotion of Schubert's music and probably on the production of a collected edition by Breitkopf und Härtel, a remarkable initiative in recognizing the composer's importance so soon after the first performances, since some major works were here published for the first time, including most of the symphonies, under the editorship of German scholars including Brahms and Mandyczewski.[33]

Thus the nature of Grove's critical work in this field was rather different than that with Beethoven and Mendelssohn. It was not just a matter of critically comparing writings, even publishing some works, but of studying from the sources themselves, and obtaining professional copies for first performances. It was perhaps inevitable, given the amount of unpublished and incomplete works in Schubert's output, that the prevailing climate of discovery led to speculation as to further missing works, most famously with regard Grove's belief in the possible existence of a late symphony written before then present Symphony No.9. During Grove's final preparations for the article, he had pondered Bauernfeld's diary entry of an '1825 grand symphony' 'for the Society' (Gesellschaft der Musikfreunde) written at Gmunden and Gastein, and in 1826 offered to the Society, and mentioned in letters, of which there was no record. He wrote a letter to *The Times* published on 28 September 1881 proposing it as an unknown work. Although Grove's by now old friend the archivist of the Gesellschaft der Musikfreunde C.F. Pohl protested and published his letter to Grove in the *Neue Freie Presse* of 7 October 1881, saying that such a symphony would have been entered in the Society's records, Grove pressed on, arguing that the onus of proving the non-existence of a new work rested 'with the Viennese people…and that must be my next point. I wish them joy', following this with another letter to the Athenaeum on 19 November 1881. We can sense Grove's opportunism as he writes to William Barclay Squire: 'was not that Gastein a lucky find for me?' as also in his subsequent re-numbering of the 'Great' C major, completed in 1828, as No.10 for its many subsequent performances at the Crystal Palace. Grove's argument was controversial, since the mere lack of contradictory evidence could not be taken as proving a hypothesis, and, amongst others, C.V. Stanford, like Pohl, disagreed with Grove from the start. Equally, Pohl's presentation of the evidence did not remove all doubt and thus the matter lay open in Grove's lifetime and beyond.[34]

Legacy

Subsequent evaluation of Grove's documentary work has inevitably been influenced by scholarly emphasis since his time. Of his three composers, the greatest attention by far has been given to Schubert and Beethoven through the comprehensive thematic indices of Deutsch and Kinsky-Halm respectively, and various documentary works, all appearing from the post-war period. Most attention was naturally directed to Grove's Schubert work in view of its greater role in the creation of the documentary base, his listing and biography remaining the major source until the appearance of the work of Deutsch and Maurice Brown. Both acknowledged Grove's importance, Deutsch speaking of his 'excellent article' and Brown offering his revisions with reluctance. Indeed, part of Deutsch's original project had been the publication of a revision and translation of Grove's article. Their research made it possible to reconsider Grove's datings, locations and other factual details based on his interpretation of the known circumstances, and even including his claims for missing manuscripts; and similar revisions have appeared in the literature as appropriate since. Despite Deutsch's systematic revisions, however, not all his criticisms have been sustained. His statement that there is 'no confirmation for Grove's dating of the Trio in B flat Op.99 as October 1827' has subsequently been challenged on the grounds of paper type and Grove's view supported. Most interestingly of all, Deutsch himself does not ultimately challenge Grove's claims for the existence of the 'Gmunden Gastein' symphony, leaving open the possibility of a lost work and simply reproducing Grove's documents in favour with those from others against. Although the issue has tended to resolve itself for many critics simply because no such major manuscript has ever come to light, it is notable that the editors of the Schubert work list for the *The New Grove* of 1980 and *New Grove II* of 2001 have continued to retain it.[35]

Because of the greater ongoing work on Beethoven, the many details of Grove's contributions, including his comments on the work of Nottebohm and Thayer were absorbed into the literature over the years and little survived for comment in the post-war period. However, Grove remains recorded as source in Kinsky-Halm in several cases: as providing the evidence for the melting down of the plates of the first edition of Symphony No.9, evidence derived from the publisher; and for details of the first performance in London by the Philharmonic Society from the copy sent by Beethoven 'for the Society'; in identifying the former owner of WoO 137 *Lied aus der Ferne* (now in the British Library); and on the first London edition of Op.22. Revisions to his work in this source have included the replacement with WoO numbers of his added opus numbers to unpublished and posthumous works; other literature has made further revisions.[36]

In total contrast, documentary work on Mendelssohn has lain fallow from Grove's time until recently. Following the third edition of the Breitkopf und Härtel thematic catalogue of 1882 no listings within studies of the composer supplanted the thoroughness of Grove's final listing in *Grove 2*. No complete list accompanied the complete edition of his works published by Breitkopf und Härtel under Rietz's editorship; nor has any appeared with the new Leipzig edition of composer's works. Only since the completely expanded listing in *The New Grove* in 1980 and *New Grove II* in 2001 took cognisance of the huge amount of music since discovered or published has a fuller indication of his output become available though without the thoroughness of a full thematic catalogue. Thus there has been no focus for systematic correction to Grove's information in subsequent scholarship: rather, informal corrections have been made. However, an early example, Eric Werner's querying of Grove's assertion for the existence of a symphony in B flat major is mistaken, as such a symphony exists in the Deutsche Staatsbibliothek, Berlin: more recently, corrections have been made to his details concerning the first performance of *Elijah*; and concerning his death, through the record of his wife.[37]

If the establishment of such basic documentary facts was largely a finite activity, determined by available evidence, the larger image of a composer's nature and significance was determined by much broader cultural factors, then as now. The images established by the first generation of scholars have lingered long, reflecting powerful contemporary assumptions. Grove's world of great modern orchestral music was bounded by a small number of great figures, and their achievement inevitably tended to be evaluated by comparison with each other rather than for themselves, with Beethoven as the constant point of reference, though the comparison could easily lead him into verbal difficulties, as with his responses to Schubert's 'Unfinished Symphony': 'It is not that it is *greater*. It is dearer, nearer'. And comparisons also invited inadequate stereotypes, in which the effect of the music played a crucial role in determining Grove's assumptions about the man. The inadequacies of the consequent evaluations can be found in passing, but telling, contradictions in his text.[38]

The most exaggerated of Grove's pictures was that drawn of Schubert, both for powerful reasons occasioned by the remarkable circumstances of its late discovery and Grove's role in it; and for what was seen as the elusive aspect of the subject: that little was known – and believed able to be known – of his inner nature and brief life, and for his huge output and many unfinished major works. Entranced by Schubert's music, Grove saw him as an entirely natural composer, spontaneous and very speedy in his working out and writing down, and he repeated the assertion that Schubert never altered or corrected his manuscripts (based on the neat condition of the manuscripts he had seen).

> Remember the splendid effects, the beautiful instrumentation, &c, and then recollect that every piece was written without note or sketch as hard as his pen would go, and you form some idea of the skill and technical ability of the man with all his want of learning.

Thus his striking originality: that in 'pouring out what he has to say [he] gets into all kinds of irregular keys and excrescencies'. Thus, limitations of 'learned technique' were especially imputed to him: that, for example he was 'deficient' in counterpoint, a view prompted by his application to

Sechter for counterpoint lessons, and because there are fewer fugues and canons in his output than those other 'classical' figures. Grove saw Schubert as a vulnerable and noble outsider and applied the appropriate stereotype: 'Failure is the lot of artists. The world kept him in his harass and poverty, till he died of it'.[39]

Yet Grove did not merely describe a simple man. He quotes Schubert as making the challenging statement that his music had the consequence of 'my genius and my misery', and that which he had written in his greatest distress was that the world seemed to like best. Yet Grove never pursued the aspect of hidden struggle in Schubert. Despite the power and unease in so many of the works (which, indeed, he touches upon, though not with sufficient emphasis in the article), he still retained a controlling view of the music as paralleling the life of 'our simple, genuine composer.' And even when he acknowledges the power of such a movement as the finale of the Symphony No.9 in C as an exception (to which many other examples can be added in the late works, for example the finales of the late string quartets in D minor and G major) the implication that there exists a more complex picture to be completed never emerges.[40]

If Grove's portrayal of Schubert was not without criticism at the time (the critic H.H. Statham drew from it that Schubert was of low social class, undeveloped as a composer, and not worthy of serious attention beyond his songs), Grove's advocacy presented a picture that remained standard for many years, especially in England. Its value was in presenting Schubert as a major composer, complementing Beethoven and of comparable quality, at a time when even accomplished amateurs in the UK, at least outside the orbit of the Crystal Palace, knew only the most hackneyed of his songs. But his picture of an innocent master who lacked all Beethoven's intellectual skill and the discipline to control his gifts lingered on till modern times.[41]

In contrast to the slow general reception of Schubert's music and the creation of a more realistic view of him, the rapid change in Mendelssohn's reputation even in Grove's lifetime rendered his image of the composer more rapidly out of date to the more informed musician: from the composer revered in Grove's youth as the major modern master after Beethoven, to one increasingly regarded as facile, even sentimental, a view current till only recent years. By the time Grove's article had appeared in 1880, the *Musical Times* had already presented one entitled 'Is Mendelssohn in Danger?', reflecting criticism of the composer. The language of modern music had now advanced greatly: the elegance and clear social context of Mendelssohn's music was now a problem in maintaining his position as a representative modern figure. Furthermore, in the era of the rediscovery of the riches of the classical heritage, Grove's apportioning of all of 58 pages to Mendelssohn, as against Mozart's mere 32 pages and Bach's sparse five, caused criticism (though this well reflected the actual proportions of concert programming at the Philharmonic and Crystal Palace at the time). However, as well as being warmly regarded by those who subscribed to the same admiration, it has remained highly regarded by scholars to the present day, though implicitly for its important documentary value.[42]

For all the latter criticism of Mendelssohn's music, it was much more difficult to challenge the picture that Grove drew of his character and personality. Mendelssohn was infinitely better known, and to a vastly larger number of people still active in Grove's time, than were Schubert or Beethoven. Not only was he the greatest modern composer of the age in popular esteem – for all of 40 years 1840–80 in England – but he was a manifestly fine person, who worked with total dedication as performer and composer, not least in England. Indeed, Grove sympathetically observed in 1874 that 'but for over-work and over-excitement [he] might have been still with us, or but recently departed', and elsewhere comments that with all his commitments 'we may almost be pardoned for wondering how he can have found time to write any music at all'. Taken with his religious convictions and religious music, Mendelssohn was a model figure in Grove's world. Again, the music mirrored the man. Grove highly esteemed the 'habitual cheerfulness and absence of misery or sorrow' in Mendelssohn's music:

> Surely there is enough of conflict and violence in life and art. When we want to be unhappy we can turn to others. It is well in these agitated modern days to be able to point out one perfectly balanced nature, in whose life, whose letters, and whose music alike all is at once manly and refined, clever and pure, brilliant and solid.[43]

But for Grove these qualities were implicitly part of an unchallenged life. Drawing on a biblical metaphor, he states that Mendelssohn was not, by implicit comparison with Beethoven and Schubert, 'tried in the fire'. But if not so tried, Mendelssohn worked very hard to realize his extraordinary gifts, and Grove acknowledges this elsewhere in observing, approvingly, the 'innumerable corrections and alterations and afterthoughts…he always gave his works' (a Beethovenian quality for Grove). This was something of an understatement: there were major revisions to, for example, one of the most 'natural' of them, the *Hebrides* overture, as Grove points out in his posthumously published analysis. In his reference to Mendelssohn's skill in counterpoint as 'an indiscretion of youth he outgrew', he seems to contradict his censure of this lack in the work of Schubert – or, rather, reinforces the view of Schubert's failure to measure up to Beethoven, according to Grove's notion of the requirements of musical greatness. And all of a piece with this subjective view is the fact that he makes something of an exception to this lack of struggle in viewing the religious music. He particularly admired the history of the Mendelssohn family in their development to prominence in moving out of the depressed position of many Jews in the eighteenth century. Of the eight-part motet 'When Israel out of Egypt came', he observes that

> the Jewish blood of Mendelssohn must surely for once have beat [sic] fiercely over this picture of the great triumph of his forefathers, and it is only plain truth to say that in directness and force his music is a perfect match for the splendid words of the unknown psalmist

– and he regarded *Elijah* as the greatest oratorio of the nineteenth century.[44]

Of his three composers, Grove's view of Beethoven has changed the least over time. Beethoven still stands as the commanding figure of the classical concert repertory, seen as a hero in his personal life, in overcoming deafness, and a transcendental master of musical materials, the two aspects invariably seen as connected in an effort of the will; further he now commands an ethical dimension through the verbal message of the finale of the Ninth Symphony, that carries an even more 'religious' quality in a secular age than do the sacred works formerly representative of this role, such as those of Handel or Bach. This image of struggle and overcoming was reinforced for Grove by his knowledge of the effort that Beethoven put into his works, the labour through which he clarified his ideas, as exemplified by the huge number of sketches. Beethoven possessed all the masculine characteristics by which others were judged and his artistic qualities became normative. But though Grove was prepared to accept that Beethoven was possessed of a somewhat more robust temperament and personality than might pass for his ideal of gentlemanly behaviour, his placing of Beethoven on a moral pedestal had inevitable consequences in the face of the facts of Beethoven's personal life. Grove was not prepared to make the leap into exploring his private life too closely. The hero had to remain a hero. Thus the inconsistencies in Grove's discussion of his illnesses: Grove added a footnote to his discussion to acknowledge that Thayer had informed him of the presence of two prescriptions from which Grove's friend Dr Lauder Brunton diagnosed syphilitic infection, stating in his main text 'the whole of these appearances (in the post-mortem examination) are most probably the result of syphilitic infection at an early period of his life. ...' Yet only a few pages earlier Grove declared that 'one thing is certain. ... that he (Beethoven) had no taste for immorality'. This, at least to a Victorian churchgoing Christian like Grove, should have indicated a contradiction, as has been observed. On the one hand, he argues on the basis of relationships he cites, that Beethoven behaved honourably towards the women to whom he was attracted, a facet of the presentation of a noble and heroic figure; on the other, in the pursuit of factual thoroughness in providing information that Thayer was not prepared to provide in his biography, he, ironically, compromises his argument in the name of scholarship.[45]

Conclusion

Original research is quickly absorbed into the mainstream: no one knew this better than Grove, who would doubtless have welcomed the review of his work with sympathetic enthusiasm. He knew that the scholar's capacity to verify all his evidence necessarily varies, not least with the most valuable, observing of the early biographical sources for Beethoven that 'many must be taken with reserve, as written long after the event, and with strong bias', and of Schubert that 'recollections written so long after the event must always be taken *cum grano*.' He even admitted in print that there were problems he could not resolve in the absence of further evidence. Indeed, many familiar images of these composers are only now being systematically re-examined: for example, the image of the defiant dying Beethoven quoted by Grove from Schindler, but only now seriously challenged by comparison with different reports of his death.[46]

Yet Grove still stands out for the rigour with which he treated the facts he did have in the light of his assumptions of their value, observing as the true principle of biography to 'find out all the facts of the lives in which the works were produced, and which must have the closest connection with them, and to leave criticism alone', a principle that applied more broadly. He added to the trend. And in the two areas where he could make a factual contribution without equivocation, he did so: in the comprehensiveness of his listing; and in the sovereignty of the score for the accuracy of performance. His final listings add an amount of detail lacking in contemporary sources and were prescriptive for later listings in the provision of such detail as the dedicatees of each work where known, and the publisher's name and place and date of publication. Moreover, in an era well before today's concern with the relation between the score and the unknown aspects of historical performance style, as well as the nature of the instruments for which the music was written, the central issue was establishing the text free of performer interpretation: this was the forward-looking position. Though he welcomed a new era of collected and edited texts, symbolized in the Breitkopf und Härtel collected edition of Beethoven, he subjected it to his own close criticism and added much to the record.[47]

It is no coincidence that Grove's last piece of scholarly writing should have concerned these issues in Beethoven's Ninth Symphony, a final plea for the values he cherished. Here he took as focus the errors he perceived as emerging in the 1867 Schott octavo edition in a paper to the Musical Association in 1896, noting where they were taken into the later Breitkopf und Härtel collected edition. These errors involved such features as expression marks, slurrings, repeat marks, and the inaccurate reproduction of notation, on the basis of his close reading of Beethoven's correspondence with the publisher. Grove noted, for example, how in the scherzo the metronome mark of dotted minim = 116 has become in 1867 a dotted breve through the misreading of the very indistinct stem in the first edition, this resulting in doubling the speed and consequently impossible writing for the horns; in the finale he notes the amended position of the change of key signature to five sharps, stressing again Beethoven's extreme care in the placing of markings; he notes Beethoven's habitual distinction between *Striche* (dashes) and *Punkte* (dots) for the strings as having been standardized to *Punkte* only, in the 1867 edition; elsewhere he was also concerned about the lack of a pause after the slow movement; of the verbal text of the finale, he notes how Beethoven substituted in Schiller's text of the 'Ode to Joy' the word *frech* for *streng*, but that this has been reinstated in the octavo and subsequent editions (his concern for the spread of errors was one reason for his wanting a bibliography of published editions). In looking forward to better editions, he supported the emphasis on the importance of the reproduction of scores as Beethoven had left them (with obvious errors, of the kind already noted, corrected). This was best done through the newly emerging technique of high quality facsimiles. He was especially enthusiastic about the facsimile of Beethoven's op.26 Sonata by Dr Erich Prieger (Bonn, 1895).[48]

The ultimate purpose of all these safeguards was for proper performance practice and tradition. Grove was constantly thinking about the details of performance, either stimulated by the scores themselves, or by any performances that raised the issues. Doubtless, he was greatly stimulated by the very similar views of August Manns and his opposition to amendments to the score, for example those of Wagner. Grove especially acknowledged Sullivan in his playing of the Ninth symphony with regard to his treatment of pauses between movements. In 1883 Grove made the observation that

> every movement of the choral symphony ends with a [fermata] except the slow movement, which has the necessary rests after the last note, but then goes on to the presto. The inference is obvious, that Beethoven intended the lovely dream of the Adagio be broken up by that horrible clangour *as suddenly as possible.*
>
> By the time of the Leeds Festival in 1889, he felt vindicated in observing that Sullivan omitted the customary pause at the end of the slow movement, commenting with rewarded satisfaction. 'On the present occasion ...for the first time, to the best of my knowledge, Beethoven's intention was strictly carried out; no pause was made, and the effect was new, extremely dramatic, and to my mind, convincing'.[49]

Notes

1 George Grove, *Beethoven and His Nine Symphonies* (London, 1896), Preface.

2 George Bernard Shaw, 'Beethoven's Symphonies', article reviewing the above in the Saturday Review, 14 November 1896. Shaw observes that Grove had been 'one of the best ridiculed men in London' for his vivid and non-technical response in his earlier years of programme note writing, a quality that Shaw greatly esteemed just as he denigrated the academic approach. Grove adds: 'I began music by my mother playing Messiah to us out of an old score (voices and figured bass). Then came Bach's 48

and the Sacred Harmonic Society Concerts': Letter to F.G. Edwards, 14 October 1897, BL Eg. MS 3091, f. 203, quoted in P.M. Young, *George Grove. A Biography* (London, 1980), p.26; compare Edwards's presentation in 'Sir George Grove', *Musical Times*, Vol.38, No.656 (October, 1897), p.658; Rev. A.T. Davidson mentions him later 'talking a share in any music that was made' in Sydenham: C.L. Graves, *The Life & Letters of Sir George Grove C.B.* (London, 1903), p.172; Graves makes it clear how much Grove was surrounded by music at home, and the prompt to study it, especially shared with his sister Eleanor: *Life and Letters*, p.8.

3 Graves, *Life & Letters*, p.454. Not only the public: scholarship has also benefited from, for example, his illustrated account of the original slow movement of Brahms's First Symphony for the Crystal Palace programme of 31 March 1877, a movement completely revised by the composer in its published form.

4 Graves, *Life & Letters*, p.453–4. It is in listening mode that Grove is pictured in the 'Spy' cartoon (see cover of this book); Macfarren noted Grove's special capacity at 'bar counting' in a score; Young, *George Grove*, p.130, note.

5 For illustration and discussion of some of these extracts, see Young, *George Grove*, pp.38–41. One commonplace book (of 47 numbered sides and two unnumbered) was jointly signed 'Ellen and George Grove, January 1843' (RCM MS 1142). The extent of his knowledge of the performance of works in London is revealed in his comment to Manns quoted in H. Saxe Wyndham, *August Manns and the Saturday Concerts* (London, 1907), pp.31–2.

6 Otto Jahn (1813–69) was a classical scholar and archaeologist; Carl Ferdinand Pohl (1819–87) was trained as an engraver; Alexander Wheelock Thayer (1817–97) studied law, and was a librarian and editor, and later US Consul in Trieste, whose work was significantly constrained by insufficient funds; Friedrich Chrysander (1826–1901) began as a private tutor and school teacher and finally funded some of his work from the proceeds of his market garden; the slightly younger Hermann Deiters (1833–1907), who translated Thayer's Beethoven biography into German (see later in this Chapter) taught Philology in various German universities throughout his career. Closer to home, William Pole (1814–1900), a major contributor to the first *Dictionary of Music and Musicians* was, like Grove, an engineer by training, and his colleague on the Britannia Bridge project.

7 Gustav Nottebohm, *Thematisches Verzeichniss der im Druck erschienenen Werke von Ludwig van Beethoven* (Leipzig, 2nd edn, 1868, rept 1968); Alexander Wheelock Thayer, *Ludwig van Beethovens Leben*, ed. and trans. H. Deiters, 4 vols (Berlin 1866–79), 2nd edn, 1901; 3rd edn, 1917; vols II and III, trans. H. Krehbiel (New York, 1921) and E. Forbes (Princeton, 1964, 2 vols, 2nd edn, 1969); *Beethoven and His Nine Symphonies* was reprinted twice in the remaining four years of Grove's life (2nd edn, 1898; rept 1962). The book is an extended version of *Beethoven's Nine Symphonies* (Boston, 1884), with a preface by Georg, later Sir George Henschel, then conductor of the Boston Symphony Orchestra.

8 *Beethoven and His Nine Symphonies*, p.70; Lewis Lockwood quotes Grove's words on the *Eroica* [*ibid.*, p.50] in 'Eroica Perspectives. Strategy and Design in the First Movement', in *Beethoven Studies*, ed. A. Tyson (Cambridge, 1982), p.90; George Grove, 'The History of a Musical Phrase Attempted', *Musical World*, 64, 39 (2 October 1886), p.627, serially to 65, 20 (14 May 1887), p.371.

9 *Dictionary of Music and Musicians*, 4 vols, ed. George Grove (London, 1889: hereafter *Grove 1*): contributors' entries are listed at the end of the index of vol.4, pp.181–2 (and likewise in the independently issued index volume: *Index to the Four Volumes*, ed. Mrs Edmond R. Wodehouse, London and New York, 1890). Grove's three large

articles stayed in the *Dictionary* (though not with all their lists) through the first four editions. When Eric Blom, as editor of *Grove 5* of 1951, replaced them, he reissued them in recognition of their value, with corrections noted in brackets, in an independent book. See *Beethoven, Schubert, Mendelssohn by Sir George Grove, with an introduction by Eric Blom* (London, 1951). For discussion of the issue of the emerging canon of orchestral music, see William Weber, *The Rise of Musical Classics in 18th Century England. A Study in Canon, Ritual and Ideology* (Oxford, 1992).

10 Grove lists beginning as follows: I. von Seyfried, ed., *Ludwig van Beethovens Studien im Generalbass, Contrapunkt und in der Compositionslehre*, Anhang (Vienna, 1832, 2nd edn, 1853, trans. 1853); F.G. Wegeler and F. Ries, *Biographische Notizen über Ludwig van Beethoven* (Coblenz 1838, with *Nachtrag* by Wegeler, Coblenz, 1845); A. Schindler; *Biographie von Ludwig van Beethoven* (Munster, 1840, enlarged, 1845: trans. I. Moscheles as *The Life of Beethoven* 1866); G. von Breuning, *Aus der Schwarzpanierhaus. Erinnerungen an L van Beethoven aus meiner Jugendzeit* (Leipzig and Vienna, 1874); Hiller, *Aus dem Tonleben unserer Zeit* (Leipzig, 1868–71); L.Spohr, *Selbstbiographie*, I–II (Kassel and Göttingen) 1860–61, trans. 1865. Of letters, Ludwig Nohl, *Briefe Beethovens* (Stuttgart 1865), trans. with additional letters by Lady Wallace, 2 vols (London 1867); Ludwig Nohl, *Neue Briefe Beethovens*, including contents of L. von Köchel, *Originale Briefe...an den Herzog Rudolf*, Vienna, 1865; Schöne, *Briefe...an Grafin Erlody und Max Brauchle*, Stuttgart 1867 (Stuttgart, 1867). For further items, see *Grove 1*, Vol.1, pp.207–8.

11 *Thematisches Verzeichniss der im Druck erschienenen Werke von Ludwig van Beethoven* (Leipzig, 1851); Gustav Nottebohm, *Thematisches Verzeichniss der im Druck erschienenen Werke von Ludwig van Beethoven* (Leipzig, 2nd edn, 1868); *Ein Skizzenbuch von Beethoven* (Leipzig, 1865; 2nd edn, 1924, rept, 1970; *Beethoveniana* (Leipzig, 1872); *Beethoven Studien* (Leipzig, 1873); Alexander Wheelock Thayer, *Chronologisches Verzeichniss der Werke Ludwig van Beethovens* (Berlin,1865); *Ludwig van Beethovens Leben*, ed. and trans. H. Deiters, 4 vols, (Berlin 1866–79), 2nd edn, 1901; 3rd edn, 1917), vols II and III; English translation H. Krehbiel (New York, 1921) and E. Forbes (Princeton, 1964, 2nd edn, 1969); F.J. Fétis, entry 'Beethoven' in *Biographie universelle des musiciens* (Brussels, 1835–44, 2nd edn, 1860–65), vol.1, pp.314–18; W. von Lenz, *Beethoven et ses trois styles* (St Petersburg, 1852; 2nd edn, Paris, 1855); Grove's listing in *Grove 1*, vol.1, pp.207–9.

12 The B flat Piano Concerto is noted as previously owned by Mr G.E.J. Powell (this ownership is not listed in Kinsky-Halm [G. Kinsky and H. Halm, *Das Werk Beethovens*, Munich and Duisberg, 1955] which states that the MS only appeared in 1870s); a Beethoven letter to Broadwood (in French) is noted as owned by Mr M.M. Holloway and quoted in full; the Heiligenstadt Testament (of which Grove obtained a photograph) is noted as owned by Jenny Lind Goldschmidt: *Grove 1*, vol.1, pp.162–207; Karoline Unger-Sabatier's visit noted in *Grove 1*, vol.1, p.197. The British Library had also owned the autograph of the *12 Variations on a Folksong Theme*, op.105, since 1873. See Pamela J. Willetts, *Beethoven and England* (London, 1970); A.H. King, *Printed Music in the British Museum* (London, 1979).

13 Grove's Vienna recollections are quoted in Graves, *Life & Letters*, pp.144, 345–7; Grove knew the account of the reinterment of Beethoven and Schubert before his Vienna visit: *Actenmässige Darstellung der Ausgrabung und Wiederbeisetzung der irdischen Reste von Beethoven und Schubert* (Vienna, 1863); some material is slightly varied and shorter in the Beethoven article.

14 Eduard Hanslick, *Geschichte des Konzertswesens in Wien*, I (Vienna, 1869); Eduard Hanslick, *Aus dem Konzertsaal 1848–1868* (Vienna, 1870); C.F. Pohl, *Jahresbericht*

des Konservatorium (Vienna, 1870); George Hogarth, *The Philharmonic Society of London from its foundation 1813 to its Fiftieth year 1862* (London, 1862); the early history of the Leipzig Gewandhaus Orchestra, which he particularly valued: A. Dörfell, *Geschichte der Gewandhauskonzerte zu Leipzig* (Leipzig, 1884). On the basis of his preparatory work, *Grove 1* was able to publish some small works for the first time (though not in Grove's articles). Gehring's article on Schuppanzigh reproduces 'Lob auf den Dicken' (WoO 100) for three solo voices and choir (vol.3, p.424); A.J. Hipkins's article on the Mandlone has the *Two Pieces for Mandoline*, WoO 44 (vol.2, p.205).

15 *Beethoven and his Nine Symphonies*, pp.43, 228. Grove was on very close personal terms with Thayer, with whom he began his correspondence as early as 1864, remaining in regular contact till Thayer's death in 1892. One of Grove's unfulfilled projects was a Primer on Beethoven in collaboration with Thayer. Krehbiel later invited Grove to undertake the English edition of Thayer's biography, or at least a preface (in 1898), before undertaking the work himself. Graves, *Life & Letters*, pp. 224; 443.

16 Graves, *Life & Letters*, p.376; George Grove, 'A Few Words on the Successive Editions of Beethoven's Ninth Symphony'. *Proceedings of the Musical Association*, 17 (1895–96), pp.65–70.

17 W.A. Lampadius, *Felix Mendelssohn Bartholdy; ein Denkmal für seine Freunde* (Leipzig, 1848, trans. 1876); Julius Benedict, *A Sketch of the Life and Works of the late Felix Mendelssohn Bartholdy* (London, 1850; 2nd edn, 1853); E. Devrient, 'Meine Erinnerungen an Felix Mendelssohn Bartholdy' *Daheim* (Leipzig) 26 (1866), trans. London, 1869; Carl Mendelssohn Bartholdy, *Goethe and Felix Mendelssohn Bartholdy* (Leipzig, 1871, trans. 1872); Ferdinand Hiller, *Mendelssohn* (London, 1874; first published in English in *Macmillan's Magazine*, 1874); Elise Polko, *Erinnerungen an Felix Mendelssohn Bartholdy* (Leipzig, 1868, trans. Lady Wallace as *Reminiscences of Mendelssohn Bartholdy*, London, 1869); Sebastian Hensel, *Die Familie Mendelssohn 1729–1847, nach Briefen und Tagebüchern* (Berlin, 1897); George Hogarth, *The Philharmonic Society of London* (London, 1862); C. Moscheles, *Aus Moscheles Leben* (Leipzig, 1872–73, trans. London, 1873); J Schubring, *Erinnerungen an Felix Mendelssohn Bartholdy*, Daheim, II (1866, trans. *Musical World*, 31 [12, 19 May, 1866]); C.E. Horsley, 'Reminiscences of Mendelssohn', *Dwight's Journal of Music*, rept. in the *Choir* (11 January–15 February, 1873); Heinrich Dorn, 'Recollections of Mendelssohn and his Friends', *Temple Bar* (February 1872); H.F. Chorley, *Autobiography, Memoirs and Letters*, ed. H.G. Hewlett (London, 1873); A.B. Marx, *Erinnerungen* (Berlin, 1865); L. Rellstab, *Aus mein Leben*, 2 vols (Berlin, 1861) vol.2, ch.11; J.C. Lobe, *Fliegende Blaütter für Musik* (Leipzig, 1853). Of letters: F. Mendelssohn, *Reisebriefe aus den Jahren 1830 bis 1832*, ed. P. Mendelssohn Bartholdy (Leipzig, 1861, rept, 1870); *Briefe aus den Jahren 1832–1847* ed. Paul and Carl Mendelssohn Bartholdy (Leipzig, 1863, trans. of vol.2, 1863; 4th edn, 1864 by Lady Grace Wallace); subsequent editions of these works are listed in *The New Grove* (London, 1980, vol.12, p.157); for further items, see *Grove 1*, vol.2, pp.309–10.

18 *Vollständiges Verzeichnis im Druck erchienener Compositionen von Felix Mendlessohn Bartholdy* (Leipzig, 1841); *Thematisches Verzeichnis der im Druck erschienener Compositionen von Felix Mendelssohn Bartholdy* (Leipzig, 1846; new edn. 1853; 2nd edn, 1873); *Letters of Mendelssohn*, ed. Paul and Carl Mendelssohn, with catalogue of all his musical compositions by Dr Julius Rietz, trans. Lady Wallace (London, 1864, rept 1970).

19 British Museum holdings are listed in A. Hughes-Hughes, *Catalogue of Manuscript Music*, 3 vols (London, 1965); see also M.B. Forster, *The History of the Philharmonic Society* (London, 1912), pp.92–3, which includes a facsimile of page 1 of the autograph; the Mendelssohn holdings in the Bodleian are listed in *Catalogue of the Mendelssohn Papers in the Bodleian Library*, Oxford, 3 vols (Tutzing, 1980–89); The C major symphony is discussed by R. Larry Todd in 'An Unfinished Symphony by Mendelssohn', *Music and Letters*, 61 (1980), pp.293–309.

20 *Thematisches Verzeichnis der im Druck erschienen en Compositionen von Felix Mendelssohn Bartholdy, dritte Vervollständige Ausgabe* (Leipzig, 1882); The works are: String Quartet in E flat, 1823 (autograph in the British Museum), published 1879 and first performed in London 1880; the following works are given as listed, and identified through their dates where possible: '11 symphonies for strings [1821–23]; and one for full orchestra in C [incomplete: see below]; many fugues for strings; concertos for piano [a, 1822]; for violin [d, 1822]; for piano, violin and quartet [d, 1823]; concerto for 2 pianos and orchestra [E, 1823], trio for piano, violin, viola [c, 1820], 2 sonatas for piano and violin [F, 1820, d, 1820], one sonata for piano and viola [c, 1824]; sonata for piano and clarinet [1824]; 2 sonatas for piano solo; studies, fantasias (one a 4); fugues for organ, and the organ part to Handel's Solomon; 5 operas, music to Calderon's 'Steadfast Prince' ['*Der standhafte Prinz*', 1833]; one secular and three sacred cantatas, various motets, many songs and vocal pieces'; he also lists 'Mendelssohn's additional accompaniments and scorings of Handel's *Dettingen Te Deum* and *Acis and Galatea*; Bach's Chaconne for violin with piano accompaniment; an additional chorus to Mendelssohn's setting of Psalm 95 [see below]; Prelude for organ in C minor'.

21 Graves, *Life & Letters*, p.387; Young, *George Grove*, p.130.

22 'Mendelssohn's Unpublished Symphonies (From the programmes of the Crystal Palace Concerts)', *Monthly Musical Record* (1 December 1871) pp.159–60. Letter to *The Times* on the 'Trumpet Overture' of 21 February, 1865. Of other specific bodies of research, he includes in the *Grove 1* article a list of the revisions to *Elijah* made by the composer. The *Musical Times* printed several extended analyses of works by Mendelssohn, though without detailing their provenance in his output, in the decade after Grove's death. See the list of Grove's published writings in Appendix 1 of the present book.

23 Grove acknowledged the permission of Marie Benecke for access to the MS of the unpublished symphony, and permission to publish it; *Mendelssohn's Psalms* (in English with piano accompaniment), London (Novello), *c.* 1876. For a modern response to Grove's judgement in adding this piece to the ending see Wolfgang Dinglinger, 'Felix Mendelssohn Bartholdy: Der 95 Psalm', *Mendelssohn Studien*, 7, ed. C. Lowenthal Hensel and R. Elvers (Berlin, 1990), pp.262–93. Grove also stressed the first Crystal Palace performance of the Reformation Symphony on 6 December 1867 which was claimed as a world premiere, a year before publication in 1868, the work having been neglected after its German premiere in 1832.

24 Graves, *Life & Letters*, pp.128–9; to Lady Wallace, *Letters from Italy and Switzerland*; Elise Polko, *Reminiscences of Felix Mendelssohn Bartholdy*; Mendelssohn's poem is quoted by Eric Werner, *Mendelssohn. A New Image of the Composer and his Age*, trans. D. Newlin (New York, 1963), p.75.

25 Ferdinand Schubert, 'Aus Franz Schuberts Leben [four short papers] *Neue Zeitschrift für Musik*, 1839; Johann Mayrhofer, 'Erinnerungen', *Neues Archiv für Geschichte… Literature und Künst*, 23 February 1829; Eduard von Bauernfeld, 'Über Franz Schubert', *Wiener Zeitschrift für Kunst und Literatur*, 9, 11, 13 June 1829; Bauernfeld additionally published six letters and portion of letters in the *Neue Freie Presse*,

November 1869, rept in the *Signale*, 1869, and his *Gesammelte Schriften* of 1873. Schindler, in Bauerle's *Wiener Theater Zeitung*, 3 May 1831; The Diary of Sofie Müller (Vienna, 1832); H. von Chézy, *Unvergessenes of von Chézy* (Leipzig, 1858); Wilhelm von Chézy, *Aus meinem Leben* (Schaffhausen, 1863); Ferdinand Hiller, *Künstleben* (Cologne, 1880); L. von Köchel, *Nachruf an Joseph von Spaun* (Vienna, privately printed, 1866); J.C. von Zedlitz, 'Nachruf an Schubert' (*Wiener Zeitschrift für Kunst und Literatur*, 25 November, 1828); L. von Sonnleithner, 'Biographie des Franz Schuberts', *Monatsbericht der Gesellschaft der Musikfreunde des Österreichischen Kaiserstadts*, I, 2, 1829, p.19; C.G. von Leitner, *Anselm Hüttenbrenner* (Graz, 1868); Ludwig Rellstab, *Aus meinem Leben* (Berlin 1861).

26 Heinrich Kreissle von Hellborn, *Franz Schubert* (Vienna 1865); Edward W. Wilberforce, *Franz Schubert* (London, 1866); H. Kreissle von Hellborn, *The Life of Schubert*, translated by Arthur D. Coleridge, with appendix of unpublished works by George Grove (London 1868); H. Barbedette, *F. Schubert, sa vie* (Paris, 1866); A.Reissmann, *Franz Schubert* (Berlin 1873); C. von Wurzbach, 'Schubert', in *Biographisches Lexicon des Kaiserthums Österreich*, Pt. 32 (Vienna 1876), pp.30–110;. A. Niggli, *Franz Schuberts Leben und Werk* (Life and Works of F. Schubert), Sammlung Musikalischer Vorträge, 15 (Breitkopf und Härtel, 1879); Otto Gumprecht, *Musikalischer Charakterbilder* (Leipzig, 1869); La Mara (Maria Lipsius), *Musikalisch Gedanken Polyphonie* (Leipzig, 1873); *Musikalische Studienköpfe* (Leipzig, 1875), vol.3; 'Von Wiener Männergesangverein. Festschrift zur Enthüllung der Schubert Denkmals am 15 Mai 1872' (Vienna, 1872).

27 H. Kreissle von Hellborn, *The Life of Schubert*, pp.297–330. Grove elaborates early European reception in the article, but there was more than he realized: see further Maurice Brown, *Schubert. A Critical Biography* (London, 1958), pp.324–7; and F.G. Edwards, 'Schubert's Music in England', *Musical Times*, 38,646 (February, 1897), pp.81–4.

28 *Thematisches Verzeichnis der im Druck erschienenen Compositionen von Franz Schubert* (Vienna, 1852); Gustav Nottebohm, *Thematisches Verzeichnis der im Druck erschienenen Werke von Franz Schubert* (Vienna, 1874).

29 Grove also includes the following information: the circumstances of his visit to Vienna; the manuscript sources of Symphonies Nos 1–9 and the Arpeggione Sonata (D821); other works including the first part of *Lazarus* (D689), a Magnificat of 1815 (D486); a duet with orchestra 'Auguste jam coelestum' (D488), a string trio in B flat (D471 or 581); an 'entr'acte and Hirten melodie' to *Rosamunde* (D797); a march and chorus from *Fierrabras* (D796); many songs; the B flat Quartet, op.168, begun as a string trio (D112); a Stabat Mater to Klopstock's German version (D383); *Miriams Siegesgesang* (D942); and including the complete *Rosamunde* then available. Grove was not the only one to examine the first part of *Lazarus*, at least. Brahms had done so at around the same time and made a copy.

30 Grove did his best in London. The first footnote of the Schubert article reveals that Grove did his initial locational research on Vienna from a map of the city in the British Museum. The works of which MS copies were sent were all in press for their first publication in score in 1866 and 1867, the period of Grove's requests. (See Plate 12, which shows Spina's offering of them all in 1867 as frontispiece for the two *Rosamunde* 'Balletmusiks', Nos 2 and 9.) It is difficult to know which Manns performed, whether the overture to *Die Zäuberharfe* (in C major) or to *Alfonso und Estrella* (in D minor/major), Schubert having written no overture to the drama. Schubert had published them in duo form; although the parts for the latter were published in 1854, it is the former work which was known as the

Rosamunde overture. The work was published complete only in the Breitkopf und Härtel collected edition in 1891 (though with the *Zäuberharfe* overture in C as overture).

31 The score of No.7 was orchestrated by John Frances Barnett, who describes his difficulties in a paper to the Musical Association. John Frances Barnett, 'Some Details concerning the work done in connection with completing and instrumenting Schubert's Sketch Symphony in E', *Proceedings of the Musical Association*, 17 (1890–91), pp.177–90. These claims for world premieres ignore the probability of unrecorded early private performances through Schubert's circle. See Otto Biba, 'Schubert's Position in Viennese Musical Life', *19th Century Music*, 3, 2 (November 1979), pp.106–13.

32 Graves, *Life & Letters*, p.144; Geisler-Schubert is quoted in *ibid.* pp.208, 259–60.

33 The publication dates of Schubert's symphonies: Nos 1–4: 1884; Nos 5–6 1885; No.7 (in piano arrangement 1884, it was announced by Breitkopf und Härtel, but never released; orchestral realization, 1934, by Weingartner). An important Schubert contact was the German song scholar Max Friedländer. His connection with Grove has recently been illuminated through publication of their correspondence. Graves, *Life & Letters*, p.295. See note 48.

34 See the summary in Maurice Brown, *Schubert* (London, 1951), Appendix 1, pp.354–61; and in Otto Erich Deutsch, *Schubert. Memoirs by his Friends* (London, 1958), pp.456–7, which reproduces Grove's letters. Grove's letter to Squire is in Young, *George Grove*, p.159.

35 Otto Erich Deutsch, in collaboration with Donald E. Wakeling, *Schubert. Thematic Catalogue of all his Works* (2nd edn, London, 1951), p.xii; Brown, *Schubert*, p.344. More direct evidence of Deutsch's attitude has emerged from his posthumously published letter to Maurice Brown of 2 September 1950: 'Until a sketch is found of the last symphony, I shall stick to Grove's theory. But, again, I may be wrong.': *'Dear Brown', Letters from Otto Erich Deutsch to J.E. Brown. An Introduction by Paul Reed*, with a preface by Ditta Deutsch (Leeds: Schubert Institute, UK, 1997), p.10. Of other literature, Elaine Brody challenges Grove's specification of the setting of Psalm 112 as for baritone solo and four voices in her article on Sulzer: see 'Schubert and Sulzer revisited', *Schubert Studies. Problems of Style and Chronology*, ed. E. Badura Skoda and P. Branscombe (Cambridge, 1982), pp.47–60; 4; Robert Winter discusses op.99 in 'Paper Studies and the Future of Schubert Research', *Schubert Studies*, pp.209–76 on the date of op.99.

36 See Kinsky-Halm, *Das Werk Beethovens*, pp.79, 375, 604, 55; revisions in other literature have included datings and titles: see, for example, *The Beethoven Companion*, ed. Thomas K. Sherman and Louis Biancolli (Garden City, NY, 1972) which cautiously accepts Grove's dating of the Minuet in E flat for piano WoO 82 as 1783 (p.773); and queries the classification of the piano piece 'Für Elise' (WoO 49, listed by Grove as op.173) as a Bagatelle, favouring rather that of Albumblatt.

37 Werner, *Mendelssohn*, p.352; Peter Ward Jones, 'Felix Mendelssohn Bartholdys Tod. Der Bericht seiner Frau', *Mendelssohn Studien*, 12, ed. Rudolf Elvers and Günter Klein (Berlin, 2001); Wolfgang Dinglinger, 'Felix Mendelssohn Bartholdy. Der Psalm 95', *Mendelssohn Studien*, 7, ed. Hensel and Elvers, p.277.

38 Graves, *Life & Letters*, p.368.

39 Letter of Grove to Mrs Wodehouse, 18 March 1882, in Graves, *Life & Letters*, p.282. H. Kreissle von Hellborn, *The Life of Schubert*, trans. A.D. Coleridge, p.332. *Grove 1*, vol.3, p.362.

40 *Grove 1*, vol.3, pp.340, 362, 353.

41 Statham is cited in Graves, *Life & Letters*, pp.292–3, quoted from *Edinburgh Review*, October 1883, p.482; see also 'Schubert's Music in England', *Musical Times*, 38,646 (1897), pp.81–4, and more recently the important discussion by David Gramit, 'Constructing a Victorian Schubert', *19th Century Music*, 17, 1 (1993), pp.65–78.
42 'Is Mendelssohn in Danger?', *Musical Times*, 18 (1 May 1877), pp.209–11; Werner comments in 1963 that it is 'extremely valuable (up till now the most reliable article)': Werner, *Mendelssohn, a New Image of the Composer and His Age*, p.162; and John Michael Cooper that it is 'one of the finest achievements of Mendelssohn scholarship and of musical scholarship in general', *Felix Mendelssohn Bartholdy. A Guide to Research* (New York and London, 2001), p.5.
43 Preface to Ferdinand Hiller, *Mendelssohn, Letters and Recollections*, trans. M.E. von Glehn, (1874), p.xiv; see Chapter 1, p.18, for the full quote.
44 The comment was made with regard to the overture 'Calm Sea and Prosperous Voyage'; for Grove's article on the *Hebrides*, see Appendix 1 of the present book: Published Writings. *Grove 1*, vol.2, p.298; *ibid.*
45 'Beethoven', *Grove 1*, vol.1, p.173. This diagnosis has long been refuted.
46 *Grove 1*, vol.1, p.207; *ibid.*, vol.3, p.370. See Christopher Gibbs, 'Performances of Grief; Vienna's Response to the Death of Beethoven', *Beethoven and His World*, ed. Scott Burnham and Michael P. Steinberg (Princeton, 2000), pp.227–85.
47 Quoted in Young, *George Grove*, p.283.
48 George Grove, 'A Few Words on the Successive Editions of Beethoven's Ninth Symphony', *Proceedings of the Musical Association*, 21 (1894–5), p.65–75; Grove greatly admired Max Friedländer's careful comparison of the sources in his edition of the Schubert songs for Peters, see Graves, *Life & Letters*, p.295. See also Franz Krautwurst, *George Grove als Schubert-Forscher. Seine Briefe an Max Friedländer*, Veröffentlichungen des Internationalen Franz Schubert-Instituts, Band 13 (Tutzing, 2002).
49 For Manns's role in promoting accurate performance practice and his connections with Grove, see Michael Musgrave, 'Costa and Manns' Changing Values in Performance', in *Music and British Culture 1785–1914. Essays in Honour of Cyril Ehrlich*, ed. C. Bashford and L. Langley (Oxford, 2000); Graves, *Life & Letters*, pp.296, 347.

6
Not Just 'G.': Towards a History of the Programme Note

Christina Bashford

In December 1836, when George Grove was but 16, a letter from the musician C.H. Purday appeared in the newly established journal the *Musical World*. In it Purday called for reformed behaviour at concerts, including more musically attentive modes of listening; and to this end he put forward ideas for the introduction of what we have come to call the programme note, a type of nineteenth-century music writing that has become famously associated with Grove. Purday wrote:

> To effect the object which gave rise to this letter, I would propose that a prologue, if I may use the term, should preface every performance of the works of the great masters, giving a brief and pithy analysis of the composition to be performed, showing its relative character to the mind of the musician, the feelings by which he was actuated in the production of his work, and the circumstances (where known) under which it was brought out[.][1]

In its day, the letter had little significance; no further correspondence on the topic was published, and Purday's suggestion – as far as is known – had no direct impact on Grove or the other programme-note writers who came forward in the ensuing years. And yet with hindsight the letter seems a prophetic articulation of a cultural desire in Britain that was voiced increasingly as concerts and listening publics grew in the nineteenth century, like cheap print, with astonishing rapidity. Indeed, the programme note, and other related forms of music appreciation, lived on well into the twentieth century, in various transformations.

This chapter grew out of work on concert life and listening history, and an unabashed fascination with the programme note, arising from its potential usefulness as an index of musical consumption and a barometer of cultural attitudes in nineteenth-century Britain. My emphasis in what follows is on the programme note as cultural object rather than as music analysis, criticism, or even text for reception history (the main lines of enquiry to date), and I shall attempt to position the celebrated notes that Grove wrote for the Saturday Concerts at the Crystal Palace within the broader continuum of programme-note provision in the 'long' nineteenth century, up to the First World War, both in London and other British urban centres.[2] Then, having sketched a chronology for what might eventually become a full history of the programme note, I shall outline a number of key themes and historical challenges that lie in wait for anyone interested in contextualizing the programme note within nineteenth-century British culture.[3] Along the way the essay will suggest that programme notes (including those by Grove) made a significant contribution to the delineation of high musical culture, most notably through their role in developing music appreciation and in shaping listening practices for Classical and Romantic instrumental music in the nineteenth century. It will demonstrate the existence of a network of writers supplying a growing market for programme notes across Britain, and will show that by the end of the century the programme note had become a staple of 'serious' concert-giving, feeding the habits of concert publics whose listening experiences were necessarily constrained by limited access to performances. Nevertheless, the essay is no more than a first step towards a history and I hope it will stimulate further work.

There are many limitations to our current knowledge and understanding of the history of programme notes in general, not to mention Grove's place within that history. The existing secondary literature is thin, typically presenting a documentary history of the programme-note genre that is centred largely on Britain, particularly London. Most accounts link important developments, especially 'firsts', and the best exemplars of writing about music. That they tend to tell the same story reflects the fact that much of their material derives from two main sources. The first of these is the entry in *Grove 1* entitled 'Analysis' (a headword reflecting the common nineteenth-century designation 'analytical notes') by Grove himself, which continued under different headwords with accretions by H.C. Colles and others across the dictionary's next four editions.[4] The second is a historical essay by J.S. Shedlock (himself a note-writer) in the *Musical Times* of 1897, which was used for the first revisions of Grove's piece and for Percy Scholes's accounts of programme notes in his *Oxford Companion* and, fittingly, in *The Mirror of Music*.[5] Furthermore, since so much of the conventional wisdom comes from articles in the dictionaries that bear Grove's name, modern scholars might be prepared to question at least the view of Grove's own notes that emerges from them.

By the mid-twentieth century commentators such as Scholes had begun to chart the demise of the specifically analytical note at concerts (something we shall return to later); and in the *New Grove* of 1980 the entry did not appear, the musical significance of the programme note and Grove's writings in the genre being condensed into its 'Analysis' article. Since then, historical enquiry has been sparse, though the late 1990s have seen interest rekindled: the second edition of *New Grove* restores the topic in a general essay under

'Programme Note' by Nigel Simeone, while Catherine Dale's recent work on the analytical methods used in programme notes develops theoretical perspectives.[6] Crucially, with concert history now emerging as a growth area, the cultural dimension of the programme note firmly beckons.[7]

Historical perspectives

Programme notes – that is, printed words addressed to audiences at public concerts, sometimes (though not always) accompanied by thematic material printed in music type – were, as George Grove intimated in his original *Dictionary* article, a phenomenon born of the nineteenth century. Typically written to explicate textless orchestral or chamber pieces (symphonies, overtures, concertos, string quartets), they emerged initially in London, the dominant, pre-eminent locus for concerts, in the middle decades of the century,[8] and primarily at the meetings of a varied group of concert societies that promulgated serious musical values, beginning with John Ella's Musical Union (1845–81). Thereafter they were introduced at such institutions as the Quartett Association (1852–4), Chappell's 'Popular' Concerts (1859–1902),[9] the Philharmonic Society (in use from 1869), and the Crystal Palace Saturday Concerts, where they crept in gradually, appearing in earnest from the mid-1860s. While these examples are rightly emphasized in histories of the programme note *per se*, not only on account of the quality of their content but also because – with the exception of the Quartett Association – the institutions for which they were written all achieved permanence, we should not assume that note-writing henceforth was pervasive. In point of fact, for most of the nineteenth century and across most of the country what was provided at most concerts was either a simple printed programme order or the words to the songs being performed, between which the titles of the instrumental pieces were entered without comment. It was only during the century's last two decades or so that prose programme notes for instrumental items – the focus of this essay – became the norm.[10] Nevertheless, elucidation came at a price: both booklets of words and full-blown concert notes usually had to be paid for on top of a ticket or subscription, their cost dependent on several factors including basic economics and the extent and form of the literature.[11]

Of course, back at the time of Purday's letter to the *Musical World*, the performance of extended, symphonically conceived instrumental repertoire (of which Beethoven's works were the extreme example) in the still relatively young social institution of the 'public' concert was presenting performers and audiences with a number of new challenges, at the time when prevailing modes of social behaviour in public arenas were coming under scrutiny and a new reverence for the whole concept of the musical work was beginning to emerge.[12] Modern instrumental music, with its lengthy movements, was the central problem for listeners, many of whom neither knew what to follow nor how to approach such repertoire; and audience noise and inattentiveness frequently prevailed, to be railed against by a nascent generation of music critics in particular. Purday noted an 'inattention' in the conduct of his contemporary concert-goers, and diagnosed ignorance of how to listen to instrumental works – or rather, how to find anything other than sensual meaning in them – as the root of the problem.[13] This inattention was particularly acute during instrumental works. Vocal music, because of its text, he declared, made a 'direct appeal' to the 'reasoning faculties', an observation that raises many intriguing questions – not least because of the attendant issues of language and translation – which would benefit from scholarly scrutiny. Giving people something to read during instrumental music would, Purday reasoned, keep the mind alive and focused on tracing the composer's design through a work. (It might also, we should note, serve to quieten the audience.) And as such it accorded with the idea of intellectual engagement with music, something that was gathering new momentum around this time.[14]

It was certainly at the heart of John Ella's vision for the Musical Union, his erudite and long-lived chamber-music club. Programme notes – he termed them 'synopses analytiques' – were one of a series of measures Ella employed from 1845 to encourage his subscribers to develop skills in concentrated and musically informed listening, and to reform their concert-room behaviour. His notes included brief comments on individual works, accompanied by a few bars of the principal thematic material in music type and a rudimentary sign-posting in prose of important aural events and thematic development.[15] They formed part of a simple pamphlet, also containing musical information and news, that was distributed to subscribers ahead of performance, deliberately so they could prepare themselves in advance, presumably with the aid of a piano.[16] Ella's notes are significant for being the first sustained attempt at programme-note writing and usage, commencing some years before Grove's. They drew much attention from commentators, particularly foreign visitors: Mendelssohn, Onslow, Berlioz and Meyerbeer were among those who wrote in highly favourable terms about them. According to Meyerbeer the notes were

> written with equal science and fine observation; and they contain excellent criticisms. They must powerfully aid such of the audience as are not professional musicians to note instantly the severer beauties of the *morceaux*, which without that guide would probably have escaped them at a first hearing.[17]

Berlioz went further, commenting with ardour in a report of music in London published in the *Journal des débats*:

> Mr. Ella does not confine his attention to the performance of the masterpieces which figure in the programmes of these concerts; he also wants

> the public to understand them. . . . [I]n general it is a good analysis, appealing to the eye as well as the mind, by adding to the critical text musical extracts, the theme of each piece, the most important musical figure or the most striking harmonies or modulations. One could not do more.[18]

Whether Ella had a specific model for his notes and for their intended use is unclear: he later claimed the idea had come from one of the Musical Union's patrons, Clayton Freeling, son of the postal reformer and book collector Sir Francis Freeling, and a friend of Anthony Trollope.[19] On the other hand, the intellectual thrust of the Musical Union may have had roots in Ella's knowledge of the activities of the Literary and Philosophical Society in Leicester, his home town.[20]

The provision of programme notes by other mid-century London concert institutions may well have been stimulated by an awareness of Ella's innovations, which were much reported in the press. Their specific use at chamber music series in the 1850s may even have been fuelled by the social and professional tensions and rivalries that existed between Ella and others, notably G.A. Macfarren and J.W. Davison, who supplied the notes for the Quartett Association and Monday Pops respectively.[21] Grove himself was certainly aware of Ella's notes, and had attended occasional Musical Union concerts, presumably as a guest of his brother Edmund, who was a subscriber, 1852–4.[22] He was also familiar with the discursive notes, supported by musical examples, which were provided for the New Philharmonic Society, founded in 1852. Although these notes were unsigned, manuscript annotations to copies held at the Royal College of Music indicate that some of them were composed by the scholar William Pole who, like Grove, combined a serious interest in music with the profession of civil engineering; he later contributed articles (including that on 'Pitch') to Grove's *Dictionary*.[23] Indeed, in the letter printed by way of an introduction to the American edition of Grove's book on Beethoven's symphonies, itself developed from his concert notes, Grove intimated that he considered both Ella's and the New Philharmonic Society's notes important precedents for his own.[24]

The introduction of programme notes at the Crystal Palace Saturday Concerts was a gradual process rather than a sudden and self-conscious initiative, and was in keeping with the broader context of self-improvement and education evident at Sydenham. Moreover, the Saturday programme notes were accorded a special status within the Palace's music-making generally, since the numerous daily concerts were not so treated. Notes on instrumental pieces began to appear, alongside the words to the songs and often anonymously, at the Saturday Concerts from 1856, but only from the mid-1860s did they become a regular feature: and even then, not all works were guaranteed coverage. In the 1860s and early 1870s, first and – especially – last works in the programme, typically opera overtures, often received either cursory coverage or nothing at all, presumably on account of their position in the concert and the expectations for attendance and attentiveness that flowed from this. Surviving programme booklets indicate that for a few years (*c*.1867–71) the first and last items were often separated from the rest of the proceedings by a five-minute interval whose seeming purpose was to accommodate late comers and early goers, suggesting that the pieces were viewed largely as 'play-ins' and 'play-outs' rather than the afternoon's main business.[25] Virtuoso showpieces were likewise liable to be passed over, Reinecke's *Horn Notturno* (27 January 1872) and Molique's *Fandango* for violin and orchestra (28 October 1882) being two such. In fact, the provision of a programme note, plus the length of its coverage, were measures of the critical weight imparted to a work (the more structurally complex the work, the more words, generally speaking, were spun) and usually indicated its membership of the league of 'good' music.[26] At the same time, programme notes played a central role in explicating the new and unfamiliar, to such an extent that by the 1890s an apology was likely to be printed if analytical comments were not provided.[27]

Grove is the name most usually associated with the Crystal Palace programmes, but he was not the first, nor the only, regular writer of these notes. The very first signed notes were written by the conductor, August Manns, and were fairly straightforward, typically a mix of biography and compositional history with thumbnail characterizations of the music, and no music examples.[28] Grove, who had been secretary to the Crystal Palace Company since 1852, made his first signed contribution – using just the letter 'G.' – in December 1867; appropriately, from the man who so championed Schubert, it was on the composer's Ninth Symphony. Grove was certainly producing unsigned pieces earlier than this, however,[29] and Manns continued to contribute new notes, as 'A.M.', alongside him for at least two decades. Furthermore, from the early 1870s others joined in, to help cover the remarkably wide repertoire the concerts were embracing. The *Guardian* critic Charles Ainslie Barry ('C.A.B.') was the most prolific of the newcomers, followed by a handful of occasional contributors – many of them eminent voices – such as Edward Dannreuther, Ebenezer Prout, G.A. Macfarren, Joseph Bennett and Friedrich Niecks. Even so, unsigned notes on hundreds of works continued to be printed; who wrote them and why they were unattributed (was Grove involved, in his capacity as programme editor?) needs further research.[30] For a list of the Crystal Palace note-writers, and the works on which they wrote, see Appendix 2, pages 301–17.

In Grove's hands the Crystal Palace notes expanded to include narrative accounts of the pieces accompanied by copious music examples (as Ella and others had done before him), to become aural 'roadmaps' that highlighted important structural moments, often through details of orchestration. The notes frequently ran to several pages and, over time, Grove's writing became established as a tour de force of engaging readability, bibliographic accuracy and documentary precision (see Appendix 3 for Grove's note on Beethoven's

C minor symphony). In this respect, Grove's domination in the histories of programme notes is well deserved: his ability to find the right form of words and connect with the general reader was rarely matched or surpassed by any other British writer of his generation. Grove's integration of music examples set a new standard, and other Palace writers – including Manns – followed his lead. Examples include Manns's note on Schumann's Symphony No.4 (first issued 1869) and his much-reprinted account of the Bruch Violin Concerto (1870), as well as Dannreuther's note on Liszt's E flat Piano Concerto (1872).

Grove explained in a public speech in 1880 that he came to write his notes over a long period of time, initially at Manns's suggestion. The passage, though often quoted, bears repetition, not least because it breathes Grove's personal fervour for music and its elucidation:

> I tried it, and that gave me the initiation; and after that, as the Saturday Concerts progressed, I went on week by week. I wrote about the symphonies and concertos because I wished to try to make them clear to myself, and to discover the secret of the things that charmed me so; and then from that sprang a wish to make other amateurs see it in the same way.[31]

More tellingly, in a private letter to his sister-in-law a few years earlier he had stressed his belief in music's power as a cultivating agent, particularly when the mind was engaged, explaining he wrote as he did 'because it added so much to my own pleasure in listening to observe how the subjects came back and were treated, and were related to one another, or were like those in other pieces'.[32] It was a commitment to the idea that intellectual engagement could enhance understanding and deepen the enjoyment of listening: Purday would surely have approved. In addition, the comment reveals Grove's interest in the structural 'working-out' of sonata forms, which came to be a hallmark of his programme notes, and which at root suggests a curiosity stemming from his engineering mindset.

As Appendix 2, section 1 (pages 301–9) shows, the repertoire typically covered by Grove comprised most of the symphonies, overtures and concertos of Beethoven, Mendelssohn, Schubert and Schumann, some Haydn, Mozart and even Brahms. It was mostly left to others, notably Barry, Dannreuther or Manns (who as conductor had special acquaintance with the score), to navigate many of the modernisms of the late Romantics – the 'noxious flood' as Grove once wrote – essentially Liszt, Wagner, Dvořák, Smetana and Tchaikovsky: see sections 2–5 of Appendix 2.[33] Wagner's music, in particular, posed new challenges for listeners, and the selections that became prevalent in concerts towards the end of the century demanded a special type of explication involving the identification of leitmotifs, rather than just the sung texts in translation. Over time, the changing shape of the repertoire was reflected in a reduced number of works covered by Grove; nevertheless, the Classical heartland, and specifically Beethoven, bore frequent repetition, so even in 1901 Grove's name was only occasionally absent from a Crystal Palace programme booklet. Grove also made excursions into notes for vocal works. These presented historical information, rather than functioning as listening guides, and the songs and arias so treated were those of his faithful 'friends': Handel, Mozart, Schubert and so on. Stand-alone essays by Grove on musical topics, for instance 'English Dining and Dancing in 1790' (1871) and 'A Visit to the Grave of Mendelssohn' (1874), were sometimes included in the booklets, providing outlets for Grove's journalizing instincts, while systematic writing, as evidenced by the list of Beethoven's autograph manuscripts in the Imperial Library, Vienna (1869), typically expressed his bibliographic tendencies.

Grove's apparent reluctance to offer guidance on understanding the really new or unfamiliar is demonstrated by the fact that relatively few of the notes accompanying the first British performances of such works bear his signature. Even works by his heroes Schubert and Schumann were often allotted anonymous analyses at their premieres, although many of these notes, admittedly, may have come from Grove's pen. Several other premiere notes were signed by Manns (writing for example on Schumann's First Symphony and Liszt's *Mazeppa*) or by Barry (on Dvořák, Strauss, Rimsky-Korsakov and many others), for whose musical understanding, like that of Dannreuther, Grove had the highest admiration.[34] That said, one must point out that Grove did make some excursions into new music, providing notes to works by such composers as Goldmark, Raff, Saint-Saëns and Hamish MacCunn, and writing for some first performances – typically of works in perceptibly classical moulds (e.g. Saint-Saëns' Third Piano Concerto, Brahms's Second Symphony).[35] And in a working environment where the norm was for notes to be reprinted without amendment, Grove stood out because, unlike most of his journalist colleagues, he was driven constantly to seek new insights into the works he held so dear, and continued to revise and expand his notes accordingly. This makes an interesting study in itself, particularly since he was a man fascinated by the process of composition (often hinting at an awareness of the organic development of material, as in his note for Schubert's Ninth Symphony), and aware of the importance of manuscript sketches for gaining an understanding of musical creativity, especially Beethoven's. Grove's note on the 'Leonora Overture No.3' aptly demonstrates his fascination with the genesis of themes, in this case the reworkings of the overture, while also illustrating his enduring ability to communicate with the general reader, a skill that surely involved balancing the requirements of scholar and journalist. Besides, to compare any two versions of Grove's notes on the same work is to demonstrate that Grove's own working methods are worth detailed consideration.[36] The recent acquisition by the Royal College of Music Library of Grove's set of working copies of the Crystal Palace programmes, complete with annotations and corrections, offers new opportunities for work in this area; see Figure 6.1.[37]

Figure 6.1 Grove's handwritten annotations to a page of his programme note on Schubert's Symphony no.9. The annotations appear in the booklet for the Crystal Palace concert of 6 April 1872, now housed in the Royal College of Music Library. Copyright of the Royal College of Music.

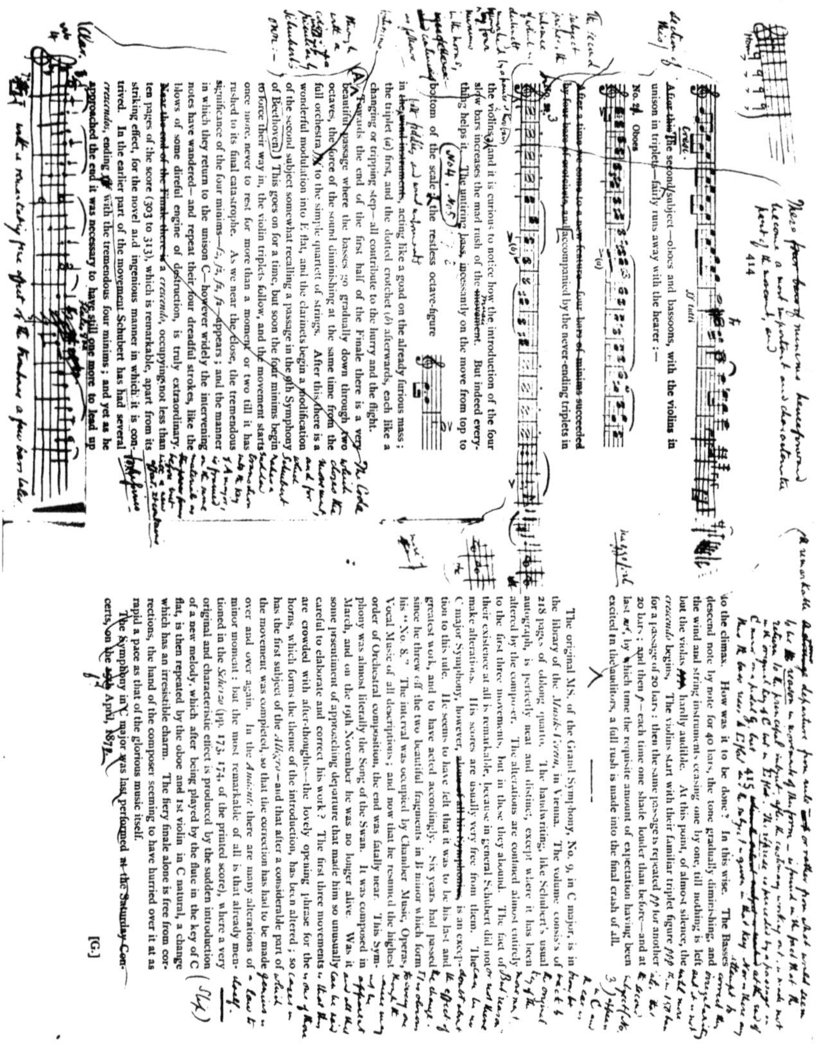

In the article on analytical notes for his *Dictionary* Grove made only passing reference to the Crystal Palace ones, played down their significance and made no mention of himself, seemingly in a burst of characteristic self-effacement. By the third edition H.C. Colles had tipped the scales in the other direction, with an addendum to the piece that made Grove's name synonymous with all the Crystal Palace notes – as if Barry's and others' somehow had never existed – and that also hailed Grove's notes as having 'more than any others, established the practice in the English concert-room'.[38] This phrase survived intact up to *Grove 5*, and thus the view was transferred to received opinion, reinforced by the weight and reputation Grove's name had acquired through Macmillan's formidable success in selling the *Dictionary*. What Colles did not explain was what his claim for the influence of Grove's notes was based on.

Looked at from a historical perspective, the bulk of the Crystal Palace notes, and Grove's contribution to them, seems to prefigure the first flowering of concert-note provision in Britain, which formed part of the huge commercial expansion in concerts from the 1890s up to the First World War. At this period, in London alone, notes were regularly provided for the Richter Concerts and the Queen's Hall Promenade Concerts, the orchestral Saturday (and Sunday) concerts at the Queen's Hall, the Sunday concerts at the Albert Hall and Covent Garden, the Broadwood chamber concerts at the Aeolian Hall, Tovey's chamber concerts, the South Place chamber concerts, and many more. Among the several prominent writers were Tovey himself, Percy Pitt, Alfred Kalisch, F. Gilbert Webb, Robin Legge and Rosa Newmarch. Much fresh work is needed here, but first impressions suggest that from the 1870s the provision of notes increased gradually, in tandem with the ever-rising tide of concerts, particularly at events given by institutions that aspired to serious musical values, and at occasional concerts organized by special-interest groups. These included the Philharmonic Society, which began to sell notes by Macfarren in 1869 and may even have been bounced into note provision by the example of Sydenham,[39] and Walter Bache's annual Liszt-centred concerts at St James's Hall, which provided detailed analyses of the composer's innovations (Bache was a devotee) by Dannreuther, Niecks and others.

The use of programme notes in the regions, and their relationship with those provided for London, also deserves detailed study.[40] From my work so far it appears that the provision of substantial notes was rare at concerts outside the capital until the 1890s, although there were clearly some honourable and understandable exceptions such as Manchester and Liverpool, two important, fast-growing Victorian cities with highly developed musical cultures.[41] In Manchester as early as 1849 Charles Hallé was providing the subscribers to his chamber concerts with programme notes, some of which derive from Ella's Musical Union ones.[42] This in itself points up the importance of social networks in British musical life – Hallé was a good friend of Ella's, and was for many years, from 1848, a regular player at the Musical Union.[43] Surprisingly, the audiences at Hallé's orchestral concerts, in contrast to his chamber ones, were usually provided simply with the words to the songs to be performed, and it was only after Hallé's death in 1895 that extensive analytical notes with music examples were introduced there. Their author was E.F. Jacques, *Observer* critic and erstwhile editor of the *Musical Times*; he was followed (from 1903) by Ernest Newman.[44]

Liverpool's Philharmonic Society had a strong programme-note tradition at its orchestral concerts by the mid-1870s, though for unfamiliar repertoire its programmes borrowed heavily from London notes, including those for Crystal Palace and the (London) Philharmonic Society. Reprinting some notes with (though sometimes without) acknowledgement seems to have become a standard practice in Britain's burgeoning concert world. Hence in 1882 the notes for Chappell's Pops turned up, with acknowledgement, at Huddersfield subscription concerts, and in 1897 one E. Gordon Cockrell, note-writer to the Beethoven Society in Manchester, acknowledged that his notes drew on ones for the Crystal Palace and Queen's Hall. It is interesting that Charles Hallé's sole excursion into programme-note provision at his orchestral concerts was in 1870, when, in conjunction with his presentation of all Beethoven's symphonies to celebrate the centenary of the composer's birth, he reprinted Grove's notes on those works. In the early twentieth century, with the number of touring artists (appearing courtesy of their agents) and ensembles growing, programme-note dissemination likewise increased; and in the years leading up to the 1911 Copyright Act note-writers became especially vociferous in claiming ownership of their prose in print. These practices are intriguing for what they might, with further work, eventually reveal about the networks, modes and economics of concert organization in Britain.[45]

Not that such activities were limited to the regions. London concerts inter-borrowed too, particularly in the final decades of the century when concerts were proliferating: Barry's and Dannreuther's Crystal Palace notes on Liszt, for instance, turned up in Bache's concerts; Philharmonic notes by Joseph Bennett appeared alongside Grove's and Barry's at the Crystal Palace; and Crystal Palace notes sat in Philharmonic booklets. Similarly, many Crystal Palace notes – especially Grove's on Beethoven and Barry's on Wagner, Liszt and Brahms – were taken wholesale into the Richter concert programmes at St James's Hall and Queen's Hall (1879–97), and thereafter into programmes for Richter's provincial tours. His autumn 1895 tour, for example, took Grove's and Barry's material to Brighton, Nottingham, Edinburgh, Glasgow, Manchester, Liverpool, Oxford, Birmingham, Sheffield and Bradford. What is interesting about this in regard to Grove is that it was through such recycling that his notes reached a wider audience than just those who travelled to Sydenham, and notably some years before the publication of his monograph on Beethoven's symphonies.[46] Potentially even more fascinating is the fact that in 1879 Grove was suggesting to Theodore Thomas in Cincinnati that he might like to reprint Grove's Crystal Palace notes in programmes for Cincinnati concerts free of charge, in return for some publicity for Macmillan's new dictionary and Grove's editorship of it.[47] Quite what came of this is unclear. Nevertheless, the widespread practice of reprinting notes, though by no means limited to Grove's or even Crystal Palace's, was quite possibly what Colles was getting at when he made such a strong claim for the impact of Grove's notes on concert life.

The story of programme-note provision is not a wholly nineteenth-century one. The practice continued right through the twentieth century, but with the truly analytical concert note eventually being displaced by new journalistic trends that emphasized the cult of personality and the magnetism of extra-musical themes, and reflected the demise of widespread musical literacy in most concert-going publics. This is not the place to embark on a comprehensive account of the programme note in the twentieth century, although a few developments may usefully be sketched in. In the first thirty years of the new century the pianola and later the gramophone spawned a new type of programme-note and music-appreciation writing, much of it by Percy Scholes, specifically linked to the new technologies and the special opportunities for close listening that they embodied.[48] It was not, however, until the 1950s that such material came to be packaged with the recordings, in the form of sleeve notes. Additional modes of listener education, alongside introductions to the musical avant-garde, were offered by the BBC through broadcast lectures and listening guides in the *Radio Times* and *Listener* magazines.[49] Programme notes in various guises continued to be provided for concerts, and new writers, for instance Ernest Newman, Edwin Evans and E.J. Dent, emerged; these materials were joined by repertoire guides such as Rosa Newmarch's *Concert-Goer's Library of Descriptive Notes* (1928–48), based largely on her own analyses for Queen's Hall concerts between 1908 and 1927. We should note at this juncture, too, that the template for the nineteenth-century programme note fitted poorly with the modernisms of Schoenberg and Stravinsky, and writers needed new strategies. As Newmarch wrote in her note for a performance of Schoenberg's *Five Orchestral Pieces* at the Queen's Hall Symphony Concerts in January 1914: '[a]ny attempt to analyze them in an ordinary way would be futile', falling back on trying to glimpse some sense of intended poetic content by citing the pieces' subtitles.[50] Eventually, however, concert notes adapted themselves to the demise in musical literacy and abandoned the use of printed music examples; the Hallé concert programmes were a long-standing and somewhat exceptional survivor, ceding their music examples only in the early 1990s.[51]

*

Much of the above has, of necessity, been approached with a broad brush, and lays down many challenges for refinement. Models for such work may be found in other disciplines, for just as literary historians have come to emphasize the diversity of the reading public and to question the usefulness of the term 'common reader',[52] so might music historians begin to try to unravel the complexity of what it means to talk about the 'listening audience'. In this spirit, an extended historical narrative might one day take account of the variety of note-writing and writers in Britain, pinning the supply and use of programme notes closely to the richness and diversity of concerts and audiences, and revealing the subtleties that will inevitably be found in a story based on individuals and on localized social practices. With this in mind, I now turn to the programme note as cultural object, and flag a few themes and questions that might usefully be explored in conjunction with any set of notes.

Cultural dimensions

The cultural significance of the nineteenth-century programme note is most commonly linked to its undisputed educational function as an aid to music appreciation, in an age when self-improvement was, for many, virtually a way of life. But as Purday's letter of 1836 suggests,[53] the matter goes deeper than this, not least in the paradigms for concert-listening that may be implicit in different types of programme note. Broadly speaking, behind the type of analytical programme associated with Ella, Macfarren, Grove and Barry was a belief in the importance of encouraging an intellectual engagement with the structure of music, and an attentive, musically-informed mode of listening as a path to understanding. There were, self-evidently, different ways of achieving this, starting with the prose itself; and behind the words were many embedded assumptions of cultural norms. Indeed, it is worth stressing at the outset that programme notes – however 'analytical' their cast – were aimed, first and foremost, at 'amateurs', that is, interested lay men and women, and, as one contemporary voice put it, were 'not primarily intended for musicians in the strict sense of the word' (i.e. professional musicians).[54]

Responses to the question of how to find the right form of words inevitably varied, depending not only on the type of work described (programmatic; purely symphonic; impressionistic; and so on) but also on the writer's sensitivity to audience 'level' and the idiosyncrasies of his/her literary style. One has only to compare Grove's 'common-touch' approach with the drier analyses of, say, Macfarren to see this (Figures 6.2 and 6.3). Both give 'analytical' accounts, but Grove's description of the second subject of the first movement of Beethoven's Symphony No.8 is easy for the lay music-lover to follow and built around the obvious aural features, whereas Macfarren's prose is often awkward, its 'knowing' style at times more reminiscent of a harmony lesson than a listener's guide. Compare these two extracts:

> [A]fter a bar's rest, and a very sudden change of key (from F to D), the second subject is brought in, preceded by a bar's rest and by a most comical exclamation by the Bassoon in its highest register. . . .The very fact of beginning this theme in D and ending it in C is a stroke of humour, which is brought out still more by the *ritardando* [see Figure 6.2].

Figure 6.2 Part of Grove's note on Beethoven's Symphony No.8, from the programme book for the Richter Concerts, London, 4 November 1895 (Private Collection).

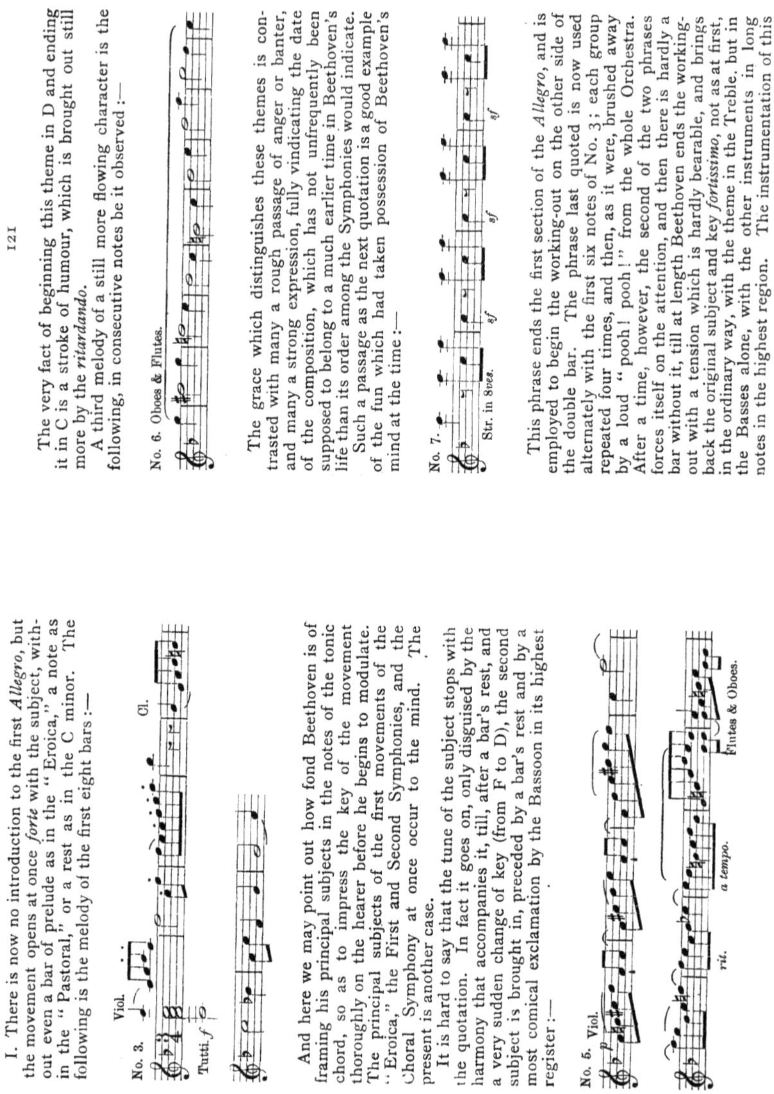

120

I. There is now no introduction to the first *Allegro*, but the movement opens at once *forte* with the subject, without even a bar of prelude as in the "Eroica," a note as in the "Pastoral," or a rest as in the C minor. The following is the melody of the first eight bars :—

And here we may point out how fond Beethoven is of framing his principal subjects in the notes of the tonic chord, so as to impress the key of the movement thoroughly on the hearer before he begins to modulate. The principal subjects of the first movements of the "Eroica," the First and Second Symphonies, and the Choral Symphony at once occur to the mind. The present is another case.

It is hard to say that the tune of the subject stops with the quotation. In fact it goes on, only disguised by the harmony that accompanies it, till, after a bar's rest, and a very sudden change of key (from F to D), the second subject is brought in, preceded by a bar's rest and by a most comical exclamation by the Bassoon in its highest register :—

121

The very fact of beginning this theme in D and ending it in C is a stroke of humour, which is brought out still more by the *ritardando*.

A third melody of a still more flowing character is the following, in consecutive notes be it observed :—

The grace which distinguishes these themes is contrasted with many a rough passage of anger or banter, and many a strong expression, fully vindicating the date of the composition, which has not unfrequently been supposed to belong to a much earlier time in Beethoven's life than its order among the Symphonies would indicate.

Such a passage as the next quotation is a good example of the fun which had taken possession of Beethoven's mind at the time :—

This phrase ends the first section of the *Allegro*, and is employed to begin the working-out on the other side of the double bar. The phrase last quoted is now used alternately with the first six notes of No. 3; each group repeated four times, and then, as it were, brushed away by a loud "pooh! pooh!" from the whole Orchestra. After a time, however, the second of the two phrases forces itself on the attention, and then there is hardly a bar without it, till at length Beethoven ends the working-out with a tension which is hardly bearable, and brings back the original subject and key *fortissimo*, not as at first, in the ordinary way, with the theme in the Treble, but in the Basses alone, with the other instruments in long notes in the highest region. The instrumentation of this

> A modulation as novel as it is unexpected, is a device to give a most peculiar colouring to the second subject,. . . which, after its announcement in this unwonted key of the 6th, instead of the customary 5th, of the original tonic, winds its rhythmical course into the more usual key of C, and completes itself then, a tone lower than its commencement [see Figure 6.3].

In most analytical notes, musical literacy – in terms of an ability to read treble and bass clefs – was taken for granted, something that links up well with what we know of the proliferation of domestic pianos and piano-playing during the late nineteenth and early twentieth centuries.[55] What we know far less about are the assumptions made about other types of technical knowledge and understanding embodied in each piece of written prose. On the one hand, most note-writers were journalists, well used to addressing an imagined readership and pitching content accordingly, so that the presence of a technical vocabulary, with terms such as first and second subjects, augmentation or double counterpoint, would suggest an audience broadly familiar with such terminology, or would at least imply that the meaning of the vocabulary, through pertinent and well-positioned music examples, was self-evident to intelligent readers. On the other hand, by the end of the century, when concerts and programme notes were proliferating, there is evidence that some analytical notes were considered, to quote comment from the *Musical Times* in 1881, 'too technical for the general reader'.[56] It was a sentiment famously crystallized by George Bernard Shaw, who in the *World* in 1893 sarcastically parodied the overly knowing, technical analysis of music by beginning a grammatical and syntactical piecemeal account of Hamlet's famous soliloquy.[57] In Shaw's estimation Grove was the doyen of programme-note writing because of his simplicity of style and avoidance of technical affectation. In his review of Grove's book on the Beethoven symphonies, Shaw spelt things out forcefully:

> I leave it to his [Grove's] old readers whether his huge success as a program writer was not due to the perfect simplicity with which he seized and followed up this clue to the intention of Beethoven's symphonies. He seeks always for the mood, and is not only delighted at every step by the result of his search, but escapes quite easily and unconsciously from the boggling and blundering of the men who are always wondering why Beethoven did not do what any professor would have done.[58]

Of course, concert-goers unfamiliar with the technical language could always engage in 'self-help' after the concert, by reference to those terminological dictionaries or primers that gave basic definitions of such terms, and/or by tinklings at the piano. We need to know a lot more about these sources, their availability and dissemination among concert-goers across the

Figure 6.3 Part of MacFarteu's programme note on Beethoven's symphony No.8, for the Philharmonic Society concert, London, 5 April 1869. (© Royal college of Music)

13

Analytical and Historical Programme.

A modulation as novel as it is unexpected, is a device to give a most peculiar colouring to the second subject,

which, after its announcement in this unwonted key of the 6th, instead of the customary 5th, of the original tonic, winds its rhythmical course into the more usual key of C, and completes itself then, a tone lower than its commencement; or rather, it is broken off incomplete, and its playful sweetness takes an air of mischief from this interruption, which varies but breaks not the character of the whole piece. Exultation marks the first bars of the following, which are the summit of a crescendo passage,

century. Grove's own *Dictionary*, as its preface and entries on theoretical terms such as 'Form' and 'Working-out' indicate, was partly addressing the growing demand for this sort of information among note-buying concert-goers. Likewise, one of the aims of Stainer and Barrett's *Dictionary of Musical Terms* of 1876 was to define the 'chief musical terms met with in the more common annotated programmes and newspaper criticisms'.[59] At the same time, some note-writers delivered minimal technical sign-posting, and mixed in biography, compositional history and simple characterization of the music.[60] Certainly it would be instructive eventually to map programme-note content (including advertising, which became a significant presence from the end of the century) against concert type, audience and other factors.

The sheer length of some notes, for instance Grove's on Beethoven, can seem quite astonishing to modern readers, but one has to remember not only that music, quite simply, mattered in people's lives, but also that this was the great age of print communication, and that, for the literate classes, reading large quantities of material was nothing out of the ordinary. Similarly, from the perspective of today's throw-away society, it might seem strange for programme notes to have been accorded a sense of permanence and value; but many of the concerts mentioned, including Crystal Palace's and the Hallé orchestral concerts from 1897, issued their seasons' programmes with a continuous pagination and even with running heads, implying they would be collected, kept and bound for future reference – not to mention a spot of reverence born of what they symbolized – by regular concert-goers.[61] Respect for knowledge, critical authority and the best music were, after all, significant cultural values.

Yet even the fullest notes were not magical routes to understanding. Arguably one of the biggest difficulties hampering nineteenth-century reader-listeners was the attainment of real familiarity with repertoire. Concert performances at which notes were provided were – we must not forget – special and relatively rare events. Grove, for example, writing to Richter in 1897 after listening to Tchaikovsky's *Pathétique* and waking at last to its beauties, admitted he would 'have given *anything* to be able to hear it once again'.[62] And although renditions in the home of piano transcriptions of concert works (typically piano duets) offered genuine routes to familiarity, they were often compromised in quality. Repeated hearings of good performances, in addition to study, were essential to proper familiarity and understanding, as the more enlightened critics of new music had always pointed out.[63] Moreover, as the pianola, gramophone and radio were to show, the innovations of technology could transform the listening and learning experience by providing easy access to repetition and reinforcement.[64] In the days when such marvels were unimaginable, programme notes could of course help the reader recall some of the music in tranquillity.

Equally high on the list of prerequisites for 'good' understanding through listening was quiet in the concert hall – a vexed issue and overriding concern throughout the century, tied as it was to shifting social and aesthetic attitudes – without which the listening experience itself was clearly compromised. Programme notes may well have accelerated the shift to quiet listening, since they stood to introduce the atmosphere of the library reading-room to concerts.[65] However, opinions differed as to how notes should be used, and, more to the point, in practice there must surely have been much diversity, not just between audiences but within any one group of listeners. This was not just a matter of differences of repertoire knowledge and familiarity (or of new listeners versus old), but also of a kaleidoscope of varying modes of listening, even at the level of the one individual.[66]

For some concerts, audiences were expected to read the notes ahead of performance – for instance at home beforehand, or in the intervals (as was apparently Grove's intention for his Crystal Palace notes)[67] – rather than during the performance itself. And as far as one can tell, a good number of people did read the notes while the music was played – just as gramophone listeners would later do in their own homes – and some followed (or attempted to follow) scores.[68] Nevertheless, reading during concerts presented several problems. In 1886 a writer for the *Musical Times* lamented that programme notes had become so long that 'unfortunate amateurs may often be seen, with eyes glued to the book, struggling to keep pace with the orchestra, and deriving more bewilderment than enlightenment from the comments and musical illustrations of the analyst',[69] and by the early twentieth century, it seems, there was mounting opposition. The dilemmas were many and complex. Even the best reader-listeners were capable of causing annoyance to others, as Tovey reminded his own audiences in prefaces to his programme notes for his London chamber concerts of 1900. Here he compares, with a touch of hyperbole, the noise of the St James's Hall audience turning pages simultaneously to the sound of a thousand muskets striking the ground together:

> Berlioz remarks in his *Traité d'instrumentation* that a sound, insignificant when heard singly, such as the thud when the butt-end of a musket strikes the ground at 'ground-arms,' becomes brilliant and attractive, if performed by a thousand men simultaneously. I am sure that the public will forgive me for reminding them that the truth of this is positively venomous in the case of an audience turning over the leaves of programmes with smartness and precision in St. James's Hall.[70]

Perhaps more significantly, he goes on to accept that some people query the feasibility of listening to a work properly if trying to read about it at the same time. To this end, like some note-writers before him (such as Davison and Dannreuther), Tovey produced programmes that were little more than a sequence of carefully chosen passages in music type, with a minimal connecting tissue of prose, and had them printed on soft, vellum-like paper. The suggestion was that attention should not (and could not) be divided between reading words and listening to sounds; that following notation was quite enough; and – implicitly – that silence during performance was a precondition at all times.[71]

Yet even for those who accepted this sort of edict and read beforehand, there are still many questions about how they actually listened. In the analytical note, for example, listeners were encouraged to follow the linear flow of the music, and grasp its shape and structure in those terms. But to what extent did people consciously follow the note-writers' delineation of structure, modulation and so forth – what Purday had called tracing the design of the work – and engage with music in a linear way? And how frequently did they connect with the expressive essence of the music, or just bathe in its sensual pleasure? Clearly we will never be able to provide adequate answers to these questions – though we may usefully remind ourselves of listeners' tendencies and abilities to switch between different modes of listening and attentiveness during any one piece of music. And we might, too, consider whether our assumptions about listeners and listening in the past are overly conditioned by our personal listening habits and experiences. Caveats aside, the fact remains that listeners were being encouraged to listen to Classical and Romantic instrumental music in specific ways – one might even say nineteenth-century ways, since these can seem quite alien to early twenty-first-century listeners who are used to having music as a ubiquitous background presence, and who, even when they listen closely, know they have the luxury and security of the replay button. What is more, the nineteenth-century programme-note writer had at least the potential to mould a group listening experience, and to shape audience responses to music (and those note-writers who were also journalists, producing regular concert criticism, presumably had two sites for shaping taste and understanding). If nothing else, the notion of nineteenth-century listening paradigms might need to be taken into account in any consideration of reactions provoked by early twentieth-century performances of Schoenberg, Stravinsky and others.

Here, then, are some indications of the cultural significance of the programme note, and a clear suggestion as to why the topic is ripe for broad-based historical enquiry. Among other avenues waiting to be explored are the economics of programme-note provision, a study of which could place the phenomenon more squarely in the context of the commercially-driven musical world that was nineteenth-century Britain, and establish the extent to which the programme note was supply– and/or demand-led. And then there is the issue of whether the programme note really was, as many writers (Grove among them) have implied, a uniquely

British phenomenon for most of the nineteenth century, and, if so, why this should have been so.

*

Come the day when a full history of the programme note in Britain is written, Grove's notes will certainly appear prominently, not only on account of their musical, scholarly and literary merit, but also because they were disseminated over a wide domain, both as concert notes and, in the case of his lengthy accounts of Beethoven's symphonies, in book form. Grove had, indisputably, special and remarkable gifts of communication, but, as we have seen, there were many other note-writers, and an almost inexhaustible supply of concerts requiring their services, on the nineteenth-century scene, and they will also need to figure in the story. In fact, it is arguably only through their proper contextualization that the significance of Grove's notes and his ideas about their social and musical function will fully emerge. In the meantime, Grove's close identification with the Victorian concert-goer and his deep-felt desire to help others in their quests for musical appreciation give us many telling insights into the place of music in people's lives and into the ways in which they aspired to listen to it. So it should come as no surprise that it was the very abundance of concerts in Britain, and the widespread thirst for music and its elucidation, that gave Grove the audience and justification for yet another of his celebrated writing projects, the *Dictionary of Music and Musicians*. In this respect, as in many others, the history of the programme note is inevitably entwined with other aspects of British cultural life.

Notes

1 *Musical World*, 3, 38 (2 December 1836), p.191. Letter dated 11 November 1836.
2 The main studies of Grove's programme notes are in Percy M. Young, *George Grove, 1820–1900. A Biography* (London, 1980) and Michael Musgrave, *The Musical Life of the Crystal Palace* (Cambridge, 1995).
3 The problems of defining culture and cultural history have, of course, been the subject of much discussion. For a useful introduction up to *c.*1988 see the collected views in Juliet Gardiner, ed., *What is History Today. . . ?* (London, 1988), pp.120–30. The programme note, allied as it is to art music traditions, clearly demands treatment as part of a history of culture in terms of the civilized pursuit of the arts and learning. But it also invites broad-based investigations of how that tool of 'high' culture worked in practice, and how, as a musical phenomenon, it fits into patterns of ideas, values and social behaviour in nineteenth-century Britain more generally. This chapter seeks to trigger both types of historical enquiry.
4 The Grove articles carry the following titles: 'Analysis' (*Grove 1, Grove 2*), 'Analytical Notes' (*Grove 3, Grove 4*) and 'Programme Notes' (*Grove 5*).
5 J.S.S[hedlock]: 'Analytical Programmes', *Musical Times*, 38, 655 (1897), pp.593–6; see also his Letter to the Editor, *ibid.*, 38, 657, p.760; Percy A. Scholes: 'Annotated Programmes', *The Oxford Companion to Music* (London, 1938), pp.36–7; *idem*: 'The Annotated Programme', *The Mirror of Music, 1844–1944: a Century of Musical*

Life in Britain as Reflected in the Pages of the Musical Times (London, 1947), pp.216–18. Shedlock appears to have been the first to cite Purday's letter of 1836.

6 See Catherine Dale, 'Towards a Tradition of Music Analysis in Britain in the Nineteenth Century', *Nineteenth-Century British Music Studies*, vol.1, ed. Bennett Zon (Aldershot, 1999), pp.269–302. Broad-based histories of programme notes are few, with the work of the historian Leon Botstein, who has written on the Viennese context for programme notes at the *fin de siècle*, an important exception: see his 'Music and its Public: Habits of Listening and the Crisis of Musical Modernism in Vienna, 1870–1914' (PhD. diss., Harvard University, 1985), pp.927–1017.

7 One of the deterrents to sustained work on programme notes has been the lack of a union catalogue of library holdings of concert programmes. This chapter draws primarily on collections at the British Library, London; the Royal College of Music, London (Department of Portraits and Performance History, and the Library); Manchester Central Library (Henry Watson Library); the Bodleian Library, Oxford (John Johnson Collection); Huddersfield Public Library (Local Studies Library); and Birmingham Central Library (Local Studies and History Department).

8 For the historical record it should be noted that the very first printed programme notes in Britain are usually considered to have appeared not in London but in Edinburgh, at the Professional Society Concerts in the late 1830s: see J.S. Shedlock, Letter to the Editor of the *Musical Times* (38, 655 [1897]), p.760. These were written by John Thomson, later Reid Professor of Music in Edinburgh, who followed this initiative with notes for the Reid memorial concert of 1841. London is nevertheless emphasized in the present essay, because it was the place where the phenomenon of programme notes first became firmly rooted. For examples of even earlier precedents see Scholes, 'Annotated Programmes'.

9 At the 'Pops', discursive analytical notes began to be printed from the fourth season of concerts (1861–2) onwards. Before that, the notes were often more cursory, and largely historical in orientation.

10 For most of the 1800s programme notes for vocal items (songs, arias, duets and so forth) were rare. Among exceptions were the occasional notes on songs by Schubert and others in the Crystal Palace programmes. The situation altered towards the end of the century, when programme notes began regularly to be supplied for the substantial Wagner selections that were entering the concert repertoire.

11 The provision of extracts in music type would have increased production costs. At the end of the century programme prices typically ranged from 6d for a 32-page booklet with music examples at the Crystal Palace to 1d for one sheet of notes (and no music type) at the South Place Sunday Concerts. The number of programme booklets typically sold at concerts, and the economics of providing them for audiences, awaits investigation.

12 On changes in attitudes towards the musical work, and shifting modes of social behaviour, see the discussions of the Italian Opera in Jennifer L. Hall-Witt, 'Representing the Audience in the Age of Reform: Critics and the Elite at the Italian Opera in London', *Music and British Culture, 1785–1914: Essays in Honour of Cyril Ehrlich*, ed. Christina Bashford and Leanne Langley (Oxford, 2000), pp.121–44; see also my explorations of listening and programme-note provision at London chamber music concerts in 'Learning to Listen: Audiences for Chamber Music in Early-Victorian London', *Journal of Victorian Culture*, 4 (1999), pp.25–51.

13 'Surely the most delightful art in the world was never intended merely to please the senses and gratify the ear. But such seems to be the principal object which the majority who frequent our concerts and music meetings have in view, if we may judge from the inattention observable in their conduct.' Purday's criticisms are levelled at concerts generally, but presumably at those in London (where he worked) in particular. Remarks towards the end of the letter suggest he was familiar with audiences of the Choral Harmonists' and Classical Harmonists' societies in London (though he would almost certainly have known others), as well as those at provincial concerts.

14 Purday's advocacy of intellectual engagement with musical structure was by no means new. In 1818 for instance, William Crotch, in one of his lectures at the Surrey Institution, had adumbrated the need to engage the mind when listening to modern instrumental music, pointing up its different listening demands compared with vocal music, while also castigating fashionable instrumental pieces that left 'so little for the mind to dwell upon' (Lecture II, 1818). For the text of the lecture in question and a useful summary of Crotch's stance, see Howard Irving, *Ancients and Moderns: William Crotch and the Development of Classical Music* (Aldershot, 1999), pp.219–23 and pp.202–6.

15 The notes typically began with Ella 'evangelizing' to his readers about the aesthetic qualities of the work in question; the length of the notes for any one work ranged between *c.*200 and *c.*1000 words. Some of Ella's theoretical bearings appear to have come from Antoine Reicha, whose *Traité de mélodie* (1814) and *Cours de composition musicale* (1818, English translation published by Robert Cocks & Co., *c.*1860) were in Ella's private library. For a discussion of contemporary analytical methods, and examples from Reicha's treatises, see Ian Bent (ed.), *Music Analysis in the Nineteenth Century*, Vol.I: Fugue, Form and Style (Cambridge, 1994).

16 At the end of each season Ella had the programmes bound up and sold as an annual compilation, the *Record of the Musical Union*.

17 For Mendelssohn's, Berlioz's and Meyerbeer's remarks, as well as many other anonymous favourable comments from foreign and British papers, see the preliminary matter to the 1875 *Record of the Musical Union*. Onslow's remarks, taken from a letter to Ella, appeared in the *Musical World*, XXI, 21 (23 May 1846), pp.245–6.

18 The article was originally published in the *Journal des débats* (31 May 1851) and formed part of an account of London music during Great Exhibition year. The translation is from A.W. Ganz, *Berlioz in London* (London, 1951), p.92.

19 The claim is in the *Record of the Musical Union* (1854), 1, p.4. The Freelings are mentioned in Anthony Trollope, *An Autobiography*, ed. Bradford Allen Booth (Berkeley, CA and London, 1947), pp.26, 30–1, 37–8.

20 In his youth, Ella (b.1802) almost certainly knew William Gardiner, a founder member of the Leicester Literary and Philosophical Society, on which see Jonathan Wilshere, *William Gardiner of Leicester (1770–1853): Hosiery Manufacturer, Musician and Dilettante* (Leicester: Leicester Research Services, 1970), pp.19–20. The work of F.-J. Fétis, who had given Ella a series of counterpoint lessons in the 1820s, may have also been influential. His *Music Explained to the World: or, How to Understand Music and Enjoy its Performance* (published London, 1844, and also Boston, MA, in 1842), which foreshadowed the flood of music appreciation literature by at least half a century, contains a number of passages that resonate with Ella's ideals, and was recommended by Ella to amateurs; see John Ella, *Musical Sketches, Abroad, and at Home* (London, 1869), p.305. Fétis's

book was originally published as *La musique mise à la portée de tout le monde* in 1830; the English translation was made from the second edition (1834).

21 On Ella's europhilia and the tensions between him and British musicians, see Christina Bashford, 'John Ella and the Making of the Musical Union', in Bashford and Langley, *Music and British Culture*, pp.193–214 (at 212–14). On the British music lobby more generally see Simon McVeigh, 'The Society of British Musicians (1834–1865) and the Campaign for Native Talent', ibid., pp.145–68.

22 Evidence for Grove attending Musical Union concerts (a letter to the *Spectator*, 11 June 1853) is cited in Charles L. Graves, *The Life & Letters of Sir George Grove, C.B.* (London, 1903), pp.44, 51. George Grove himself was not a subscriber. Edmund subscribed to both the Musical Union and another of Ella's initiatives, the Musical Winter Evenings, 1852–4; the latter's audiences were also supplied with Ella's notes.

23 New Philharmonic Society notes tended to be longer than Ella's, typically 1000 words or more. Writers' identities are indicated by annotations in an unknown hand in the margins of the programmes at the RCM. One note is attributed to Grove: that for Mendelssohn's overture 'Die schöne Melusine', op.32 (fourth concert, 1855).

24 George Grove, *Beethoven's Nine Symphonies: Analytical Essays*, with a preface by Georg Henschel (Boston, 1884), p.viii. The letter is from Grove to Henschel, and is dated 'Sept. 6, 1883'.

25 Coverage of overtures gradually increased, and by 1890 the norm was for them almost always to be accorded notes. In the 1860s and early 1870s the overtures in question ranged from Mozart's 'Le Nozze di Figaro' and Weber's 'Oberon' to Sullivan's 'In Memoriam' and Austen Pearce's Concert Overture.

26 In the 1880–81 season, for example, Grove's note on Schubert's Ninth Symphony stretched to more than 3250 words and included copious music examples, while that for Spohr's Sixth Violin Concerto was little more than 300 words plus musical exemplification.

27 For example, the programme of the first concert of the 1891–2 season noted 'As the score [of Popper's cello concerto]. . . was not received till Friday morning, it is impossible to give the usual analysis'.

28 Signed notes by Manns began to appear from 1859. Notable contributions from this period include his pieces on Schumann's Symphony No.1 (10 March 1860; *c.*500 words) and Beethoven's Symphony No.3 (9 March 1861; *c.*850 words).

29 For example, the unsigned notes for the Beethoven and Schubert works performed the previous season bear Grove's literary hallmarks. Grove himself claimed to have written the note for the Mozart centenary concert in 1856 (speech of 1880, cited in Graves, *Life & Letters*, p.52); but how frequently Grove wrote unsigned notes in the period up to 1867 (and beyond) is unclear, and could only be ascertained by a stylistic study.

30 Graves, *Life & Letters*, p.208, suggests that Grove was still editor of the programmes, even after resigning the secretaryship of the Crystal Palace Company (in 1873). One possible reason for the notes' anonymity may simply be editorial, reflecting their 'confection' from the work of others. A partial precedent for this practice may be found in Grove's paraphrase of material by Sullivan in a note on Schubert's Overture 'In the Italian Style'; the note is signed, but the debt unacknowledged. The reworking is uncovered in Richard Sherr, 'Schubert, Sullivan and Grove', *Musical Times*, 121, 1650 (August 1980), pp.499–500. Grove's lack of confidence in his own writing may have also led him to omit his signature from time to time: see also note 29.

31 Graves, *Life & Letters*, p.52.
32 Graves, *Life & Letters*, pp.216–17.
33 '[T]he flood may be noxious, but one can't stop it; we can't dam everything back to Schumann or even to Brahms'; from a letter to Edith Oldham, dated 17 October [1889], cited in Young, *George Grove*, pp.204–6.
34 According to Graves (*Life & Letters*, pp.208, 453, 458), Grove 'constantly consulted' Dannreuther, Barry and others on technical matters, was 'fully conscious' of his limitations, never making 'the slightest secret of his reliance on the technical knowledge of others to eke out the imperfections of his equipment', and considering Barry's and Macfarren's notes (for example) far superior to his own. Grove's attitude to programme-note writing , as well as his perceptions of his own limitations as a writer, are further suggested by a letter of his, dating from the mid-1880s, to William Barclay Squire (London, BL Add. MS 39679, ff.119–120). I am grateful to Leanne Langley for drawing this correspondence to my attention.
35 A database of Grove's signed programme notes is held in the Portraits Collection at the Royal College of Music. I am grateful to Oliver Davies (curator) and Augustine Ford for allowing me access to this useful resource.
36 Such is the approach of Percy Young in his biography of Grove, in which he compares an 1867 programme note on the Pastoral Symphony with Grove's later, more reflective, account of the same work in his book *Beethoven and his Nine Symphonies* (London and New York, 1896); see Young, *George Grove*, pp.278–80.
37 The programmes (RCM Library, MS 7328) were acquired through a Sotheby's sale in May 2000, and seem previously to have been owned by F.G. Edwards. How and when they came into Edwards's possession is unclear, though the transfer may have occurred in the 1890s when Grove passed some of his Mendelssohn material to Edwards. I am grateful to Peter Horton of the Royal College of Music Library for this suggestion. In correspondence with William Barclay Squire in the mid-1880s, Grove discussed ways for the British Museum to obtain copies of Crystal Palace programmes, and indicated his intention – for some reason, not carried out – to give his own set to the RCM; see the letter in London, BL Add. MS 39679, ff.136–7.
38 Colles's remarks are reminiscent of Graves's account and appraisal of the notes in his biography of Grove. Graves states, for example, that '[f]or upwards of forty seasons Grove contributed the lion's share of the analyses' (p.53) and relates (as quoted in Chapter 5 of this volume, page 86) what he claims Richter told him personally, that 'the services rendered by Grove in his picturesque and genial analysis of the symphonies of Beethoven, Schubert, Brahms, &c. were of incalculable value in educating the public' (*Life & Letters*, p.454). Graves's use of the term 'the public' demands qualification: the audiences for the Crystal Palace and Richter concerts were constrained socially, to say the least, since the concerts were not, as Bernard Shaw trenchantly pointed out in 1885, 'cheap enough for the people' (Shaw's comments are cited in full in Musgrave, *The Musical Life of the Crystal Palace*, p.124).
39 Documentation of the Philharmonic Society's decision to provide programme notes is in the Philharmonic Directors' Minute Book for 1869 (BL MS Loan 48.2/6). Programme note provision also coincided with the Society's move to St James's Hall; for further discussion see Cyril Ehrlich, *First Philharmonic: a History of the Royal Philharmonic Society* (Oxford, 1995), pp.121–2. In 1881 the position of official note-writer had passed to Francis Hueffer, and by the mid-1880s had been taken over by Joseph Bennett (see Robert Elkin, *Royal Philharmonic: the Annals of the Royal Philharmonic Society* (London, [1946]), p.76.

40 Scottish institutions do not form a large part of the analysis that follows, though they were not deliberately excluded; the Choral Unions of Edinburgh (established 1858) and Glasgow (1855) issued analytical programme notes and are ripe for further work.

41 Stimulating discussions of musical culture in nineteenth-century Manchester include Simon Gunn, 'The Sublime and the Vulgar: the Hallé Concerts and the Constitution of "High Culture" in Manchester c. 1850–1880', *Journal of Victorian Culture*, 2 (1997), pp.208–28, and Dave Russell, 'Musicians in the English Provincial City: Manchester, *c.* 1860–1914', in Bashford and Langley, *Music and British Culture*, pp.233–53. Information on Liverpool may be found in Ruby M. Lewis, 'The Educational Functions of the Royal Liverpool Philharmonic Society, 1840–1990' (PhD diss., University of Liverpool, 1998).

42 A set of notes for Hallé's chamber concerts, 1852–8, is preserved in the Henry Watson Library, Manchester Central Library. The Musical Union notes, on which they were based, were judiciously edited to remove some of Ella's literary excesses. The programmes also include a few notes signed by Macfarren; he, it should be remembered, wrote notes for the London Quartett Association (1852–4), at which Hallé sometimes performed.

43 His regular association with the Musical Union ended in the mid-1860s for reasons that are not entirely clear, but are possibly bound up with stipulations imposed by his agent, Chappell.

44 The lack of programme notes for Hallé's orchestral concerts may have been compensated for by the provision of concert notes in the morning newspapers (see, for example, the *Manchester Examiner and Times* for 12 December 1889, which included notes for that evening's concert). Whether this was regular practice in Manchester or elsewhere requires further investigation. After Hallé's death, the conductorship passed temporarily to Frederic Cowen, and then to Hans Richter, and the printed programmes introduced analytical notes in the London tradition, though initially (1897–98) without music examples. Richter's role in the adoption of notes in Manchester is unclear; but having worked not only in London but also in Vienna, he was well used to audiences being provided with reading matter.

45 Some centres may nevertheless have relied heavily on local music writers. The large collection of concert programmes in the Local Studies and History Department of Birmingham Central Library shows, for example, that the music critics Andrew Deakin, Stephen Stratton and Sydney Grew provided many of the programme notes for the city's concerts, *c.*1890–1910.

46 The inter-borrowing and circulation of programme notes is explored further in Christina Bashford, 'Educating England: Networks of Programme-Note Provision in the Nineteenth Century', in *Music in the English Provinces, 1700–1900*, ed. Rachel Cowgill and Peter Holman (Aldershot: Ashgate, forthcoming).

47 Letter from Grove to Theodore Thomas dated 1 November [1878] in the Newberry Library, Chicago (Special Collections, Papers of Theodore Thomas). I am grateful to Celia Clarke of the Royal College of Music for alerting me to this reference, and for providing me with a transcription of the letter.

48 A wealth of literature for the pianola player and gramophone listener quickly emerged, such as Percy Scholes's *The Appreciation of Music by Means of the 'Pianola' and 'Duo-Art'* (London, 1925) and *The Columbia History of Music through Ear and Eye* (London, 1930–38), which he edited. On Scholes see Megan Prictor's essay, 'To Catch the World: Percy Scholes and the English Musical Appreciation

Movement, 1918–1939', *Context: a Journal of Music Research*, 15–16 (1998), pp.61–71.

49 New repertoire in particular was given impetus by the inroads into music appreciation that were made by the BBC, and Scholes played his part here too: see Jennifer Doctor, *The BBC and Ultra-Modern Music, 1922–1936: Shaping a Nation's Tastes* (Cambridge, 1999), pp.66–79.

50 Quoted in Nigel Simeone's exhibition handlist, 'The Analytical Programme Note' (Faculty of Music, University of Cambridge, 26–29 September 1986).

51 Before the move to more populist programme notes in the 1992–93 season, Hallé notes were regularly provided by such writers as Michael Kennedy and Leonard Duck.

52 See for example the introduction to James Raven, Helen Small and Naomi Tadmor, eds., *The Practice and Representation of Reading in England* (Cambridge: Cambridge University Press, 1996), pp.1–21.

53 See note 1 (page 134).

54 'Orchestral Music and the Amateur', *Musical Times*, 27, 515 (January 1886), p.11–13.

55 For discussion of the piano culture in Britain during this period see Cyril Ehrlich, *The Piano: a History* (rev. edn, Oxford, 1990).

56 *Musical Times*, 22, 459 (May 1881), p.241. But see also the letter to the *St James's Gazette* (7 June 1886), signed 'T.' and attributed to Grove by Percy Young (*George Grove*, p.302), which appears to send up the overly populist, non-technical style of writing.

57 The celebrated passage is reprinted in the compilation of Shaw's writings, *Music in London, 1890–94*, 3 vols (London, 1932), vol.2, p.321.

58 From a review of Grove's *Beethoven and his Nine Symphonies* in the *Saturday Review* (14 November 1896); the text is reproduced in full in Young, *George Grove*, pp.295–8.

59 *Grove 1*, p.v, and J. Stainer and W.A. Barrett, eds, *A Dictionary of Musical Terms* (London, 1876), p.iii. These dictionaries seem to have been the first in Britain to define the vocabulary of sonata form. Stainer and Barrett have entries on 'Form', 'Sonata' and 'Subject', as does Grove, but his dictionary's entries, written by Parry, have the more learned and extensive discussions. Parry also wrote 'Development' and 'Working-out' for *Grove 1*.

60 See, for example, the notes on Beethoven's op.18 no.4 string quartet by Robin Legge for the Broadwood Concerts at the Aeolian Hall, London, 17 December 1908 (John Johnson Collection, Bodleian Library, Oxford).

61 In his 1938 *Oxford Companion* article, Percy Scholes noted that the Crystal Palace programmes were 'stored up by many regular attendants at the concerts, so that sets of them occasionally come into the market today'. Surviving programme sets show that some owners compiled their own indexes to the works covered in each of the volumes they had bound.

62 Letter cited in Christopher Fifield, *True Artist and True Friend: a Biography of Hans Richter* (Oxford, 1993), p.329. Twenty years later the work had become a 'classic', and was much heard.

63 Such were the remarks made by Edward Holmes on the challenging 'late-period' works of Beethoven in the 1830s and 1840s; see Christina Bashford, 'The Late Beethoven Quartets and the London Press, 1836-ca.1850', *Musical Quarterly*, 84, 1 (2000), pp.84–122 (at 110–11). See also William Crotch's remarks on the need for repeated hearings to appreciate fully Haydn's Symphony No.73 (cited and discussed in Irving, *Ancients and Moderns*, pp.202–4, 234–5).

64 New arguments nevertheless emerged. For instance, the shift from 78 rpm recordings to LPs was not welcomed by Compton Mackenzie (editor of *Gramophone* magazine), who argued that the earlier technology actually encouraged 'active' listening; his reasoning is recounted in Simon Frith, *Performing Rites: Evaluating Popular Music* (Oxford, 1998), p.25.

65 There is no full account of the history of silence in libraries, though the norm was for particular areas to be designated as quiet ones. The role of such spaces and the encouragement of 'concentrated reading' in eighteenth-century libraries is discussed in James Raven, 'From Promotion to Proscription: Arrangements for Reading and Eighteenth-Century Libraries', in Raven et al., *Practice and Representation of Reading*, pp.175–201. In the Victorian public library the reference department and the reading room were deemed silent areas, though transgressions occurred occasionally, as Alistair Black notes in his stimulating discussion of libraries as places of 'social control': *A New History of the English Public Library: Social and Intellectual Contexts, 1850–1914* (London and New York, 1996), p.190. For contemporary ideals on the expected behaviour in the reference department, see Thomas Greenwood, *Public Libraries: a History of the Movement, and a Manual for the Organization and Management of Rate-Supported Libraries* (4th edn, London, 1894; reprinted by University Microfilms Limited, 1971), p.35. I am grateful to Robert Snape of Myerscough College, Preston, for alerting me to these sources, and for much fruitful discussion.

66 This point is well encapsulated by the multiple characterizations of listeners among the Queen's Hall concert audience in Chapter 5 of E.M. Forster's novel *Howards End* (1910), and in his essay 'From the Audience', which appeared in a book on the National Gallery (chamber music) concerts; see *National Gallery Concerts... 10th October 1939–10th October 1944* (London: Trustees of the National Gallery, 1944), pp.6–7; repr. in *Musical Times*, 110, 1516 (June 1969), p.582. I am grateful to Stanley Sadie for alerting me to the latter.

67 Georg Henschel's preface to Grove's *Beethoven's Nine Symphonies* of 1884 suggests that this was Grove's intended purpose for the notes on which his book was later based. Celia Clarke kindly drew this (rare) edition of the book to my attention. Remarks in the *Musical Times* article 'Orchestral Music and the Amateur', p.13, support the idea that the Crystal Palace programmes were sold on the day of the concert and not before.

68 Concert audiences were frequently represented in journalistic images and prose of the time as avidly consulting printed material during performances, though there may be numerous reasons why particular papers chose to depict listeners in such a way. See the illustration of two people reading scores ('A Pair of Enthusiasts') at the 1874 Handel Festival at the Crystal Palace in the *Graphic* (27 June 1874; the issue contains depictions of other listener types, both as images and in prose, the latter on p.608), or see the remarks of the *Athenaeum* (20 April 1872) regarding women at Musical Union concerts 'sitting round. . . with books in their hands, and if a glance be obtained of their pages, it will be seen that the books are scores of the music to be executed'. A search for why such documents carried messages of listener absorption might well be fruitful, and would help to contextualize the occasional contradictory pictures of sections of the audience that can also emerge from primary documents. Berlioz, for instance, visiting the Beethoven Quartett Society in 1851, noted some enthusiasts getting 'lost' while trying to follow scores during concerts (see Ganz, *Berlioz in London*, pp.92–3).

69 'Orchestral Music and the Amateur', p.13.

70 'Analytical Programmes to Mr. D.F. Tovey's First Concert in St. James's Hall, Thursday Afternoon, November 1st, 1900', introduction; programmes held in the British Library, London (shelfmark d.490).

71 See the introduction to the third of Tovey's 1900 programmes, which contains a significant discussion of the difficulties of reading programme notes while listening, and of the form the notes should take on the page. The notes themselves were published after Tovey's death as *Essays in Musical Analysis: Chamber Music*, ed. Hubert J. Foss (London, 1944).

Part 3

At Macmillan

7
Grove as Editor of *Macmillan's Magazine*, 1868–83

Rosemary T. VanArsdel

George Grove, 1820–1900

When George Grove, at the age of 48, slipped into the editor's chair of *Macmillan's Magazine* in May 1868, he brought with him a breadth and variety of experience and knowledge of the world, as well as his dedication to the arts, which would shape and define his 15 years as editor. Although it causes one to digress slightly at the outset, it is imperative to recall the scope and variety of Grove's intellectual activities up to and at the same time that he was editing *Macmillan*'s, for which he supervised publication of 30 volumes, 180 issues, and 1,387 articles, 223 selections of poetry, and 23 novels, plus the odd short narrative, over 15 years.

To begin with, he was the product of an enlightened school and headmaster, Charles Pritchard, whose philosophy of education embraced not only the traditional classical foundation, with English literature, Bible study, history and languages, including Hebrew, but also instruction, unusual for its time, in mathematics, chemistry, astronomy, geography, and map-making. Finally, music appreciation was added, thus augmenting his musical tastes for Handel, Bach and sacred music, which were part of his family life. Pritchard also imbued his charges with the original idea of using their leisure time in creative and useful ways, which was his method for encouraging free enquiry. Grove received an unusually progressive Victorian education, one in which 'the enthusiasms of Pritchard . . . [would be] mirrored in Grove's career at almost every turn'.[1]

Upon leaving school to pursue a career in Engineering, 'one of the most colorful and highly esteemed new professions' to come to maturity during the Victorian era, and with much subsequent travel on civil engineering projects, he gained a wide outlook, whilst at the same time 'developing an attraction to and appreciation of poetry and the art of literature, beginning with interest in Coleridge and various memorabilia associated with the poet . . . .' Grove began to feel himself within the tradition of English poetry, for which his affection was to be deepened by experience. In later periods of isolation he would often turn back to the poetry he had read in youth . . . and find in its recollection a form of therapy'.[2]

Seeking a career change, his appointment to the Society of Arts and the Crystal Palace provided a stepping stone into arts management which was then developed extensively for 20 years. George Grove was not a man who was ever satisfied to do one thing at a time. During his years as an engineer, he used his spare time to study and investigate music and literature in the various areas where he worked, and to this was added at the Society of Arts and Crystal Palace, biblical study and the work with Dr William Smith and the Palestine Exploration Fund. His years at Macmillan would be in counterpoint with his work in the *Dictionary of Music and Musicians* and involvement in the debate around a new College of Music and its foundation as the Royal College in 1882. Grove became editor of *Macmillan's Magazine* in 1868 whilst still in his post at Sydenham, where he remained till 1873. He was thus unusually well prepared for the range of activity he would find at Macmillan.[3]

Alexander Macmillan, 1818–96

When George Grove went to work as editor of *Macmillan*'s he entered into a partnership of sorts with another most unusual self-made man, the owner and publisher Alexander Macmillan, just two years his senior. With no schooling beyond four or five years in his Scottish village school, he certainly had no chance at a university education, yet through sheer determination and perseverance he and his elder brother Daniel pursued a course of self-education through voluminous reading of the classics. Daniel left Scotland, moving first to Glasgow in 1841, then to Cambridge (when London proved to be inhospitable), but finally to a post at Seeley's Bookshop in Fleet Street, London. Alexander was not long in following in his brother's footsteps. The pay was low but the work was honourable and offered the additional benefit of unlimited educational reading. Not the least of their troubles as provincial newcomers were their efforts to overcome their heavy Scottish brogue and their country clothing and customs. Nevertheless, they were persistent, and together the brothers went on to establish a profitable and respected publishing business which, after Daniel's death in 1857, allowed Alexander to found *Macmillan's Magazine* in 1859, the first of the popular 'shilling monthlies'.[4]

While Grove brought with him the obvious breadth and diversity of his contacts in the Victorian world, Macmillan, through his publishing business, was equally well connected in academic circles and the literary world. The Thursday evening 'Tobacco Parliaments' held at his headquarters in London brought together such leading figures as Alfred Tennyson, Herbert Spencer, Thomas Henry Huxley, Francis Turner Palgrave, Coventry Patmore, F.D. Maurice, Charles Kingsley and Thomas Hughes. The Macmillan firm

1. George Grove as photographed in 1890 (Royal College of Music).

2. Grove's portrait in oils by Charles W. Furse of 1895 commissioned by the RCM (Royal College of Music).

3. Grove at the laying of the foundation stone of the new RCM building on 8 July 1890. Grove is seated at the centre back with arms folded (Royal College of Music).

4. The first RCM building in Kensington Gore, formerly the National Training School for Music, later the Royal College of Organists (Royal College of Music).

5. The present RCM building designed by Sir Arthur Blomfield and opened on 2 May 1894 (Royal College of Music).

6. The Floating of the Second Tube of the Britannia Bridge, July 1850, By G. Hawkins (National Library of Wales).

7. The Building for the Great Exhibition in Hyde Park as pictured in the year of the Exhibition, 1851 (Guildhall Library, Corporation of London).

8. 'Bird's Eye View' of the Crystal Palace by James Duffield Harding (RIBA Library Drawings Collection).

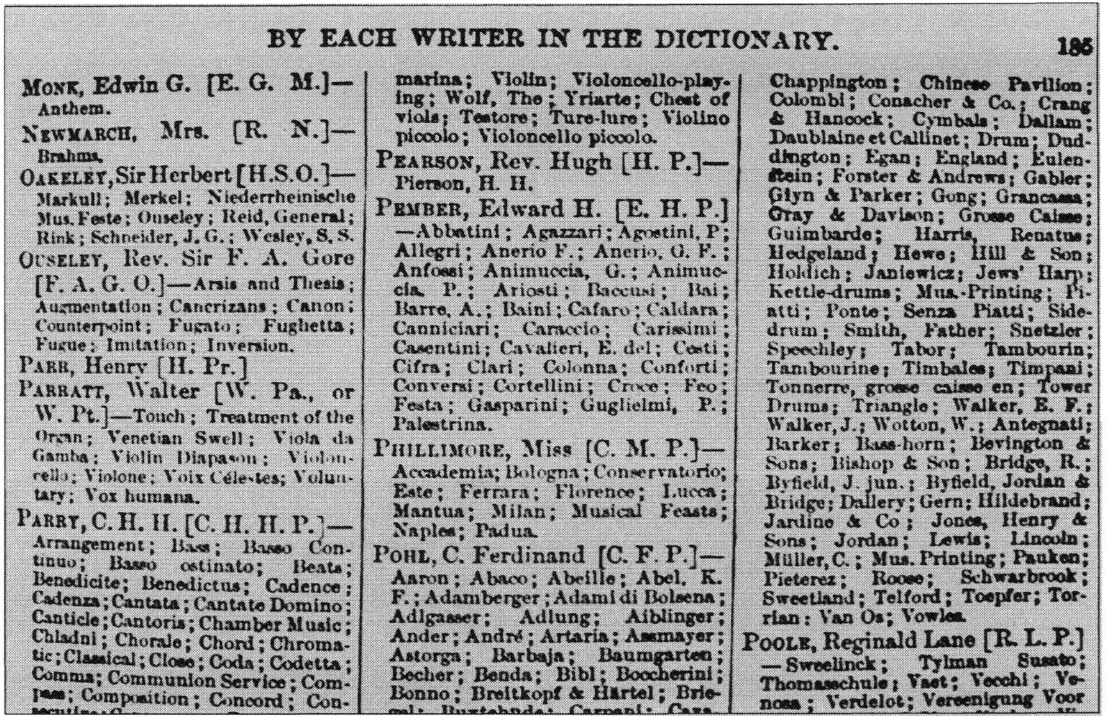

BY EACH WRITER IN THE DICTIONARY. 185

MONK, Edwin G. [E. G. M.]—Anthem.

NEWMARCH, Mrs. [R. N.]—Brahms.

OAKELEY, Sir Herbert [H.S.O.]—Markull; Merkel; Niederrheinische Mus. Feste; Ouseley; Reid, General; Rink; Schneider, J. G.; Wesley, S. S.

OUSELEY, Rev. Sir F. A. Gore [F. A. G. O.]—Arsis and Thesis; Augmentation; Cancrizans; Canon; Counterpoint; Fugato; Fughetta; Fugue; Imitation; Inversion.

PARR, Henry [H. Pr.]

PARRATT, Walter [W. Pa., or W. Pt.]—Touch; Treatment of the Organ; Venetian Swell; Viola da Gamba; Violin Diapason; Violoncello; Violone; Voix Célestes; Voluntary; Vox humana.

PARRY, C. H. H. [C. H. H. P.]—Arrangement; Bass; Basso Continuo; Basso ostinato; Beats; Benedicite; Benedictus; Cadence; Cadenza; Cantata; Cantate Domino; Canticle; Cantoris; Chamber Music; Chladni; Chorale; Chord; Chromatic; Classical; Close; Coda; Codetta; Comma; Communion Service; Compass; Composition; Concord; Con-

marina; Violin; Violoncello-playing; Wolf, The; Yriarte; Chest of viols; Testore; Ture-lure; Violino piccolo; Violoncello piccolo.

PEARSON, Rev. Hugh [H. P.]—Pierson, H. H.

PEMBER, Edward H. [E. H. P.]—Abbatini; Agazzari; Agostini, P; Allegri; Anerio F.; Anerio, G. F.; Anfossi; Animuccia, G.; Animuccia, P.; Ariosti; Baccusi; Bai; Barre, A.; Baini; Cafaro; Caldara; Canniciari; Caraccio; Carissimi; Casentini; Cavalieri, E. del; Cesti; Cifra; Clari; Colonna; Conforti; Conversi; Cortellini; Croce; Feo; Festa; Gasparini; Guglielmi, P.; Palestrina.

PHILLIMORE, Miss [C. M. P.]—Accademia; Bologna; Conservatorio; Este; Ferrara; Florence; Lucca; Mantua; Milan; Musical Feasts; Naples; Padua.

POHL, C. Ferdinand [C. F. P.]—Aaron; Abaco; Abeille; Abel, K. F.; Adamberger; Adami di Bolsena; Adlgasser; Adlung; Aiblinger; Ander; André; Artaria; Assmayer; Astorga; Barbaja; Baumgarten; Becher; Benda; Bibl; Boccherini; Bonno; Breitkopf & Härtel; Brie-

Chappington; Chinese Pavilion; Colombi; Conacher & Co.; Crang & Hancock; Cymbals; Dallam; Daublaine et Callinet; Drum; Duddington; Egan; England; Eulenstein; Forster & Andrews; Gabler; Glyn & Parker; Gong; Grancassa; Gray & Davison; Grosse Caisse; Guimbarde; Harris, Renatus; Hedgeland; Hewe; Hill & Son; Holdich; Janiewicz; Jews' Harp; Kettle-drums; Mus.-Printing; Piatti; Ponte; Senza Piatti; Side-drum; Smith, Father; Snetzler; Speechley; Tabor; Tambourin; Tambourine; Timbales; Timpani; Tonnerre, grosse caisse en; Tower Drums; Triangle; Walker, E. F.; Walker, J.; Wotton, W.; Antegnati; Barker; Bass-horn; Bevington & Sons; Bishop & Son; Bridge, R.; Byfield, J. jun.; Byfield, Jordan & Bridge; Dallery; Gern; Hildebrand; Jardine & Co; Jones, Henry & Sons; Jordan; Lewis; Lincoln; Müller, C.; Mus. Printing; Pauken; Pieterez; Roose; Schwarbrook; Sweetland; Telford; Toepfer; Torrian; Van Os; Vowles.

POOLE, Reginald Lane [R. L. P.]—Sweelinck; Tylman Susato; Thomasschule; Vaet; Vecchi; Venosa; Verdelot; Vereenigung Voor

9. Detail from *A Dictionary of Music and Musicians*, 'Catalogue of the Articles Contributed by Each Writer in the Dictionary' (1890) (Leanne Langley).

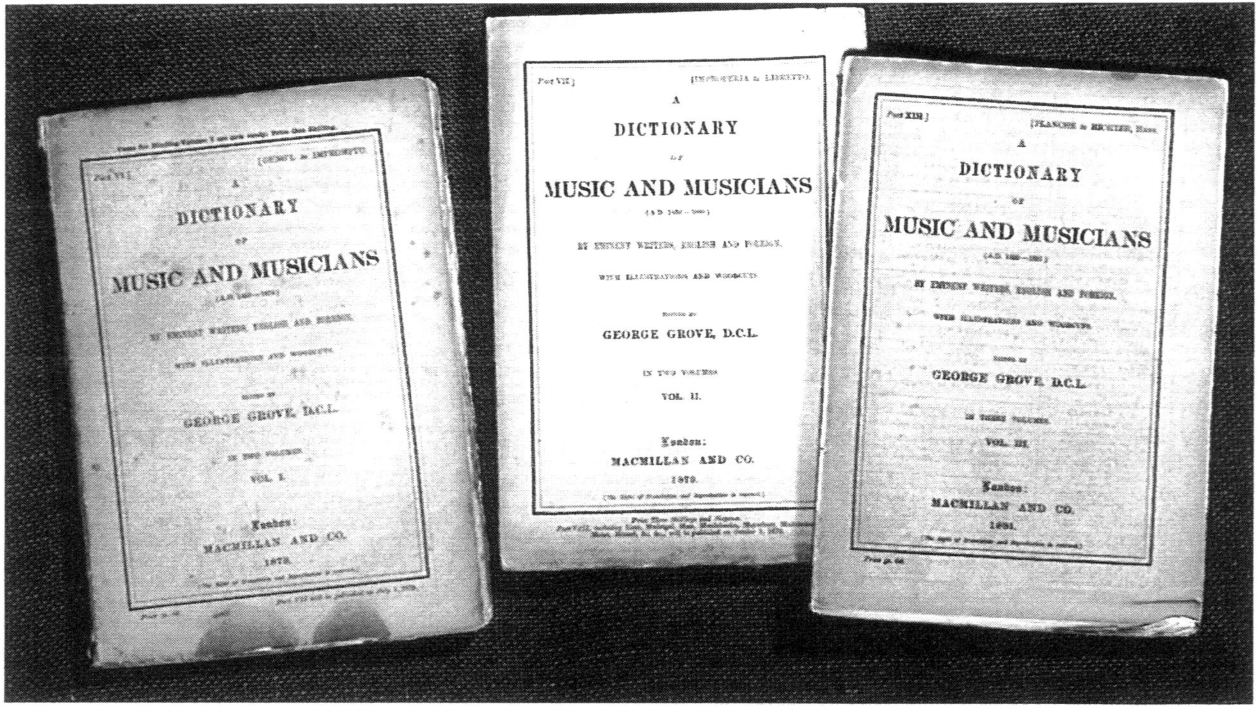

10. Three original fascicles of *A Dictionary of Music and Musicians:* part 6 (1879), part 7 (1879) and part 13 (1881) (Royal College of Music).

11. The opening bars of the autograph score of Schubert's Symphony No. 7 in E major D729 (the 'Sketch' Symphony) (Royal College of Music).

OUVERTUREN

und

Entr'actes

für das ORCHESTER componirt

von

Franz Schubert.

Partiturausgabe.

Nº 1.	Rosamunde, Op. 26	Fl. 3.15 Nkr. / R. 2.
Nº 2.	Zwei Entr'actes aus Rosamunde	Fl. 3.15 Ngr. / R. 2.
Nº 3.	Alphonso und Estrella, Op. 69	Fl. 2. / R. 1. 7½ Ngr.
Nº 4.	Fierrabras, Op. 76	Fl. 2.24 Nkr. / R. 1.12½ Ngr.
Nº 5.	Ouverture im italienischen Style, Op. 170	Fl. 2.40 Nkr. / R. 1. [illegible]5 Ngr.
Nº 6.	Ballet-Musik aus Rosamunde Nº 1 u 2. [illegible]	Fl. 2.70 Nkr. / R. 2.10 Ngr.

1867

England, Frankreich, Belgien, Russland, etc. Eigenthum des Verlegers

Eingetragen in das Vereinsarchiv

WIEN, C. A. SPINA

k. k. Hof-u. pr. Kunst-u. Musikalienhandlung

Med. 1 Cl. der Pariser Welt Ind.-Ausstellung

12. Schubert in 1867: Spina's new publications of orchestral music (Editor).

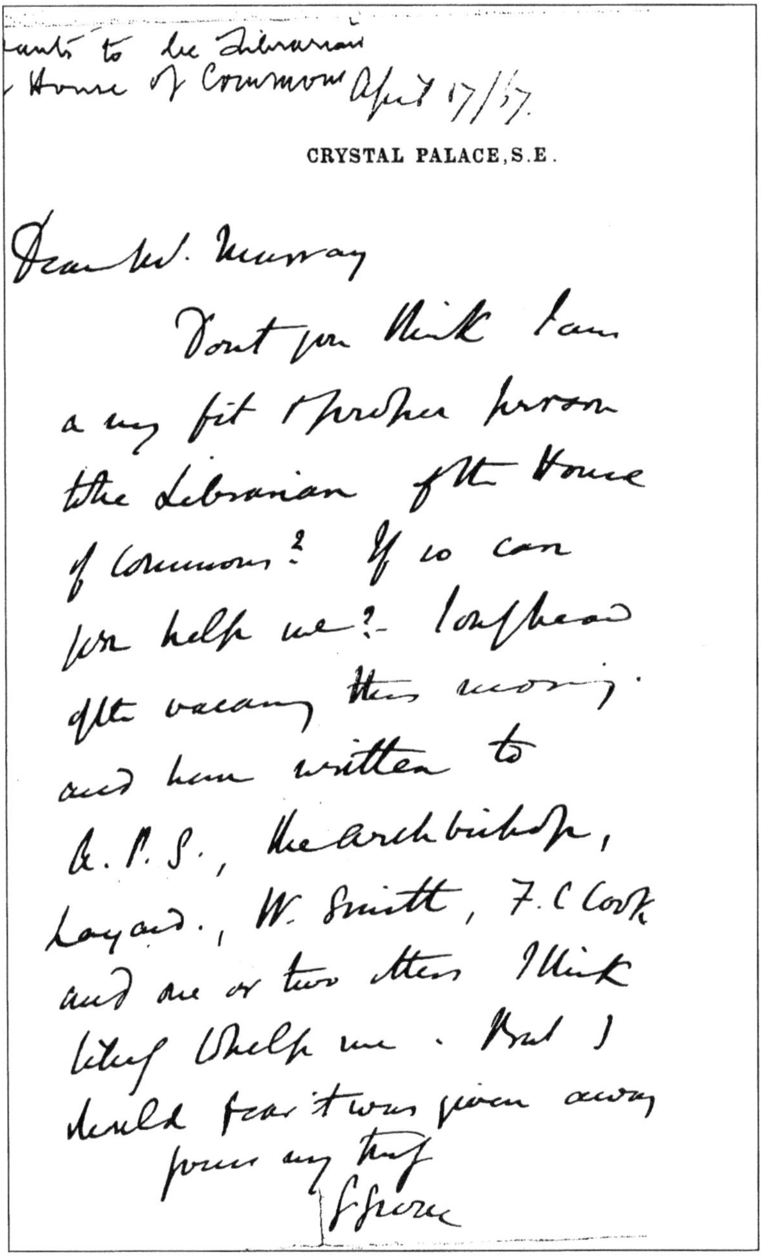

wants to be Librarian
House of Commons April 17/57.

CRYSTAL PALACE, S.E.

Dear Mr. Murray

Dont you think I am a very fit & proper person for the Librarian of the House of Commons? If so can you help me? – I only heard of the vacancy this morning and have written to A.P.S., the Archbishop, Layard, W. Smith, F.C. Cook and one or two others I think likely to help me. But I should fear it was given away

Yours very truly
G Grove

13. Grove seeks the support of John Murray for the post of Librarian at the House of Commons (John Murray Archive).

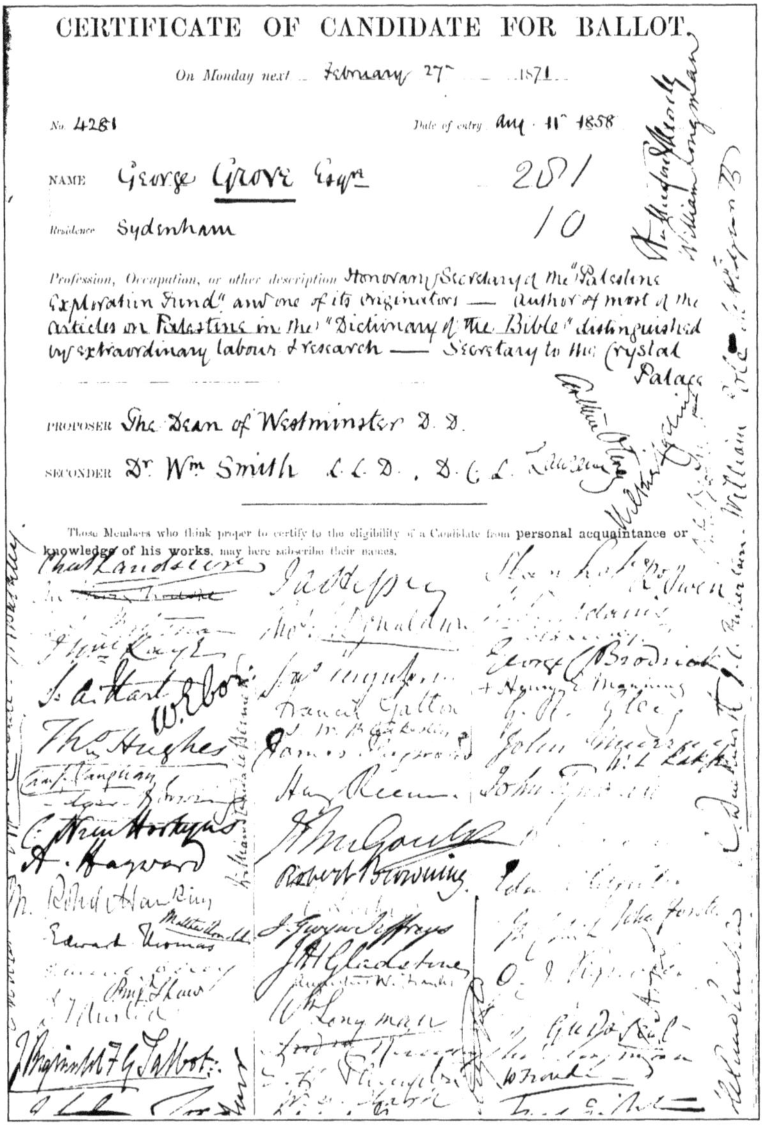

CERTIFICATE OF CANDIDATE FOR BALLOT.

On Monday next February 27th 1871.

No. 4281 *Date of entry* Aug. 11th 1858

NAME George Grove Esqre 281

Residence Sydenham 10

Profession, Occupation, or other description Honorary Secretary of the "Palestine Exploration Fund" and one of its originators — Author of most of the articles on Palestine in the "Dictionary of the Bible" distinguished by extraordinary labour & research — Secretary to the Crystal Palace

PROPOSER The Dean of Westminster D.D.

SECONDER Dr. Wm Smith LL.D., D.C.L.

Those Members who think proper to certify to the eligibility of a Candidate from personal acquaintance or knowledge of his works, may here subscribe their names.

Chas Landseer

Thos Hughes

A. Hayward

Francis Galton

Robert Browning

J.H. Gladstone

Wm Longman

George C. Brodrick

William Longman

14. Election to The Athenaeum in 1871: Grove was supported by an unusually large number of members (The Athenaeum).

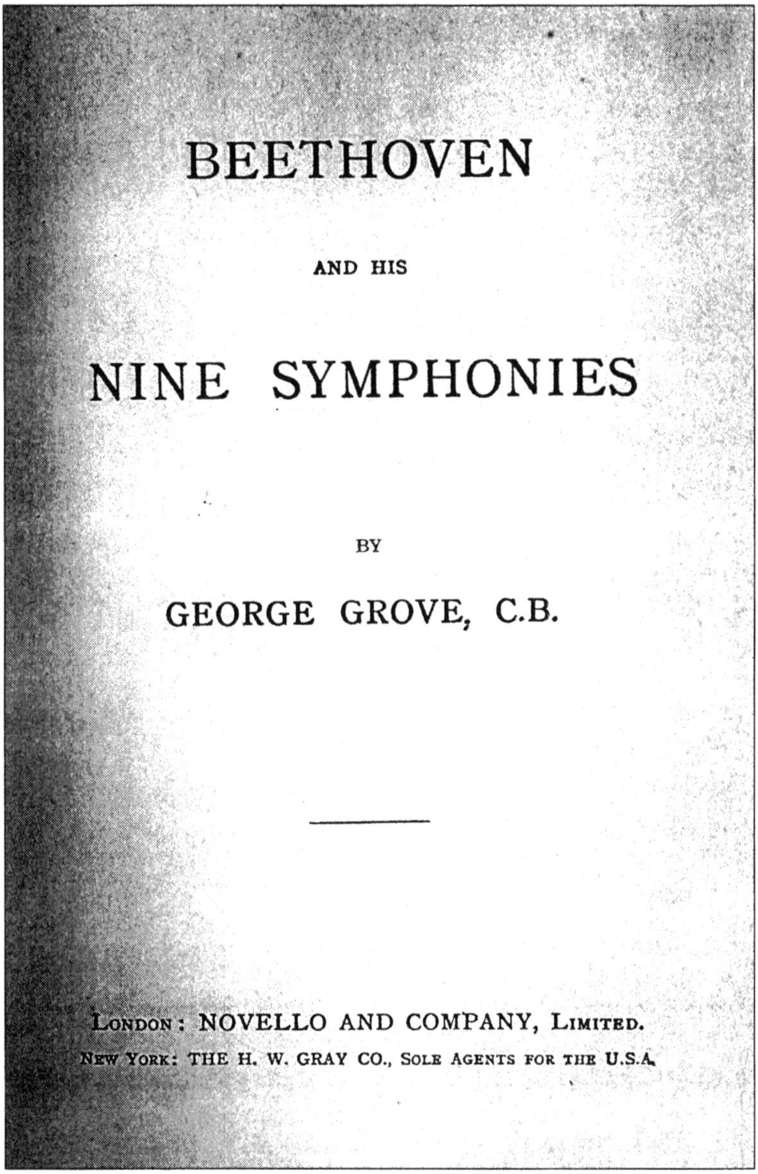

BEETHOVEN

AND HIS

NINE SYMPHONIES

BY

GEORGE GROVE, C.B.

LONDON: NOVELLO AND COMPANY, LIMITED.
NEW YORK: THE H. W. GRAY CO., SOLE AGENTS FOR THE U.S.A.

15. A lifetime's work: Grove's *Beethoven and His Nine Symphonies* of 1896 (Editor).

16. The plaque commemorating Grove outside the site of his former house in Sydenham High Road (Photo by Editor).

itself never forgot its original commitments to publish religious, educational and scientific work on a broad scale, thus keeping in touch with development of current Victorian thought. Many authors, who were already acquainted with Macmillan as a publisher, and now seeking to contribute to the *Magazine*, found it easier to make first communication with him, and only later with Grove, which could have undermined the latter's authority and created tension. That the two were able to share responsibility and work together seamlessly for many years was a credit to the tact and innate courtesy of both men.

Grove's editorship

Grove entered upon his editorship in May, 1868, after a period of interregnum in the editorial hierarchy. David Masson, the first editor of *Macmillan's*, was Professor of English Literature at University College, London, from 1853 to 1865, when he assumed a similar post in his native Scotland, at the University of Edinburgh. A scholar of honour and dedication, he attempted manfully to continue his duties as editor from the northern city, relying heavily on the newly perfected telegraphic system, but inevitably much of the day-to-day detail fell increasingly on Macmillan, and sometimes even on George Craik, Alexander's business partner, who was often tactless and whose duties were usually restricted to business matters. A good example of the confusion which could result from this cumbersome system occurred when Caroline Norton, whose novel *Old Sir Douglas* was being serialized in *Macmillan's* during 1866 and 1867, fell into a controversy with both Macmillan and Masson over a chapter to which they objected. Macmillan wrote to her explaining why the chapter was omitted from the current issue; she wrote back to him; Macmillan replied; Norton wrote again; Masson wrote to her from Edinburgh, a placating letter; she replied to Masson; Macmillan and Masson wrote to each other. The air was blue with correspondence over a matter which should have been easily resolved by the editor making a simple afternoon call on Mrs. Norton.[5]

When Macmillan began to look about for a successor to Masson his eye naturally fell upon Grove, who had been informally involved with the *Magazine* and with the publishing house for several years. Precise details of the editorial transition have not been preserved, but it appears to have been gradual. He was offered the job of editor at a salary of £250 a year, for the present, but there was some confusion on Craik's part who misfigured the second cheque. Grove wrote on 6 March, 1868: 'The twelfth part of £250 is £20.16.8. This you paid me for January (or rather £20.13.4. . .) Why should you give me less for February?'[6] Later correspondence shows that Craik corrected the error.

Grove's first important task as editor was to negotiate late in 1867 with Alfred, Lord Tennyson, friend to both Grove and Macmillan, to publish his new work 'Lucretius'. In this he was successful at first, and then ran into difficulties when he, Macmillan and Masson all objected to some lines they considered too sexually explicit and suggestive for a family magazine. Tennyson, easily irritated, was on the point of withdrawing his work, when Grove effected a compromise and publication went forward, in the first issue for which Grove was responsible, May 1868. Peaceful settlement of this dilemma was important to Grove because Tennyson, as Poet Laureate, would attract readers and favourable comment on the journal and because he hoped to publish future selections from the poet's pen.

Poetry and *Macmillan's Magazine*

Poetry published in Victorian periodicals has received scant attention from scholars. There are several reasons for this. First, a good deal of poetry was published anonymously, or using initials or pseudonyms, and even with the aid of dictionaries of pseudonyms these symbols remain obscure. Second, although in his pioneering work, *The Wellesley Index to Victorian Periodicals, 1824–1900*, Walter Houghton unmasked the identity of writers in 43 major quarterlies and monthlies, in order to keep his project within achievable limits he was obliged to omit all attention to poetry, thus depriving the modern researcher of a valuable tool. And third, research into the prose to be found in Victorian periodicals is such a vast topic that there has been little time or energy left for poetry.[7]

It appears that Grove took the chief editorial responsibility for poetry, and any journal which could number among its contributors such names as Christina Rossetti, Tennyson, Matthew Arnold, Caroline Norton, George Eliot, Charles Kingsley, William Ernest Henley, and George Meredith, as *Macmillan's* did during Grove's editorship, certainly can be said to have taken poetry seriously. Other poets, not so well known today, also made substantial contributions, such as Frederick W.H. Myers, Francis Turner Palgrave, of *Golden Treasury* fame, Walter Herries Pollock, and Arthur Penrhyn Stanley, Dean of Westminster.

The 223 items of poetry published by Grove represent the work of 76 identified poets, and 64 others who published anonymously or used a pseudonym (an unusually high number for a journal which prided itself on its editorial policy of signed articles); 24 of the identified poets were women. This latter figure was in keeping with the policy of *Macmillan's Magazine* from its very first issues to publish freely the work of women.[8] Among those poets who are better known today, Christina Rossetti first came to *Macmillan's* on her own initiative, publishing 'Up-Hill' in February, 1861, followed by 16 additional lyrics up to the March, 1868 issue.[9] Under Grove's editorship she appeared in May 1868, with 'A Smile and a Sigh' and 'Dead Hope' followed by 'Autumn Violets' (November 1868), 'They Desire a Better Country' (March 1869) and then, because of ill health, not again until

April, 1883 with 'A Wintry Sonnet', thus aptly punctuating Grove's opening and closing issues.

Tennyson, whose 'Sea Dreams' was published in January 1860, made his final appearance with 'Charge of the Heavy Brigade' in May 1882. Caroline Norton, who had published six lyrics in the early years of *Macmillan's*,[10] returned to its pages briefly with 'St. Andrew's Links' (July 1875), 'Haunting Eyes' (August 1875) and 'April Days' (May, 1876). George Eliot, always more noted for her fiction than her poetry, nevertheless chose *Macmillan's* for three of her longer pieces: 'The Legend of Jubal' (June 1870); 'Armgart' (July, 1871); and 'A College Breakfast-Party' (July 1878), which grew from conversation with young Trinity men on her first visit to Cambridge in May, 1873, and for which she was paid the unusual sum of £250.[11] Charles Kingsley, who was one of the earliest and most successful of the Macmillan authors, appeared five times, the last two posthumously.[12] Well-known poets who made fewer contributions included: Matthew Arnold, 'The New Sirens' (December 1876 reprinted from his 1849 volume at the express request of A.C. Swinburne), and 'Poor Matthias' (December 1882); George Meredith 'Love in the Valley' (October 1878); 'Phoebus with Admetus', (December 1880); and William Ernest Henley, 'Notes on the Firth' (in 10 parts, October 1875).

Arthur Penrhyn Stanley (1815–1881), who would later be called to high Anglican preferment as Dean of Westminster (1864–1881), and George Grove enjoyed a warm friendship from 1854 onward, which allowed Grove the editor to publish a poetic sequence of 14 of Stanley's devotional poems, quite remarkable for their depth and intensity of faith. The tone was didactic, in the sense of a pastor instructing his flock, as indeed, he was instructing his readers. He employed the technique of a prose preface explaining the history of his 'hymns' through the ages, for which he then supplied his own translation or adaptation. Often the question and answer method was invoked, as in the case of 'The Traveller's Hymn for All Saints' Day' (November 1872); 'Where is the Christian's Fatherland?' he asked and replied, 'Where round God's throne His just ones stand/There, Christian, is thy Fatherland.' Sometimes Stanley used the refrain, as in 'Hymn for Advent' (December 1872) where 'The Lord is come!' introduces each of the 6 stanzas. He also wrote poetry of thanksgiving, such as 'Hymn on the Accession [of Victoria to the throne]' (June 1873) or 'The Untravelled Traveller' for the recovery of Prince Leopold from an attack of hemophilia. As he grew older Stanley reflected on 'The Divine Life' and 'The Perfect Death' (both in March 1880) and concluded both were at the Throne of God, of course.[13]

Poetry in *Macmillan's* during Grove's tenure was by no means confined to lyric verse but enjoyed a rich diversity of genre. There was the 'lament' – for things lost such as youth, springtime, or the two dead children in 'Christingles' (January 1869) by the unknown author B.B.B.; the elegy – of various kinds; the ballad as in 'The Sprightly Ballad of Minikeena' (January 1875); there was long narrative poetry such as 'Betsy Lee: a Fo'c's'le Yarn' (April, May 1873) which was so long it appeared in two successive issues and covered 34 pages with rhymed couplets; verse based on classical lore such as 'The Prayer of Hercules' (November 1869) by R.C. Jebb, and 'Timoleon' (June 1881) by R.C. Dublin, based upon Plutarch's *Lives*; and there was poetry dealing with topical subjects, such as J.C. Shairp's 'Balliol Scholars, 1840–43: A Remembrance' (March 1873). Many contributed sonnets, both Elizabethan and Petrarchan, while Frances Martin published a sonnet sequence in 12 parts (October 1876). To compete the roster, there was even a saga, 'The Saga of King Hjorward's Death' (September 1880) by M.L. Ward.

Although there are many instances where Grove revealed his sharp eye as a critic, one in particular stands out for its international implications. Evidently J.T. Fields, American journalist and editor of the *Atlantic Monthly* 1862–70, proposed that a poem by James Russell Lowell, the American poet, be published in *Macmillan's*, but Grove protested to Alexander (7 December 1869):

> I can't take Lowell's poem if Fields paid us 40 guineas to do so. It is as dreary, affected and uninteresting a piece of goods as I have read for a long time . . . but besides that the man does not know fact. What cathedral in Catholic countries ever rang great bells before ordinary daily service as Westminster Abbey does? Why he can't even quote his Milton right, but must turn sunbowed into embowered![14]

Thus, one editor's judgment against another's.

Because of Grove's close personal supervision and selectivity the Victorian reader of *Macmillan's Magazine* would have gained a good sense of the variety and vitality of contemporary nineteenth century poetry.

Fiction and *Macmillan's Magazine*

Every editor of a 'shilling magazine' knew that the economic success of his journal was tied to the quality of its fiction and Grove was no exception. Earlier in the century novels had often been published in monthly parts, at one shilling per part, because the cost of the entire three-volume edition would have been beyond the purse of all but the wealthy. This was one reason for the enormous popularity of Mudie's Lending Library, established in 1842, where patrons might borrow novels, for a fee, one part at a time.[15] Under this new scheme, by purchasing the magazine it would now be possible to have the monthly part of the novel at the same price, plus half a dozen or more articles on timely topics, plus some poetry, at no extra charge. This had the further virtue of securing the circulation, playing, as it did, on the very human need to know 'what came next' in the serial. And circulation was always uppermost in the mind of the editor, as Grove wrote to Macmillan early in 1868: 'Cheer up old man, we shall beat the *Spectator*, and all the other 'ators and get up to 20,000 a month yet, and that by fair means'[16] Since *Macmillan's* was the first of these monthlies, it was the first to set the pattern by starting off, in November 1859, with what would be a popular novel, *Tom Brown at Oxford*, by a popular novelist, Thomas Hughes.

The *Cornhill*, the second shilling monthly, inaugurated just two months later, in January 1860, would prove to be a formidable competitor in this field, because Thackeray was its first editor and through the years it attracted many well-known novelists such as Anthony Trollope, Charles Lever, George Eliot, Elizabeth Gaskell, Wilkie Collins, Charles Reade, Thomas Hardy and Henry James, although Trollope, Hardy and James also wrote for *Macmillan's*. However, a case can be made for the proposition that while the Macmillan fiction writers may not have come down to posterity with as much acclaim as those of the *Cornhill*, in their own time they were, almost without exception, popular, well known, and successful authors. Gender-bias may also have played a role in this because nearly two-thirds of Macmillan serial writers were women, whose work was apt to be taken less seriously.

When Grove became editor, two novels were then in progress: *Realmah* by Arthur Helps, who was not a prolific novelist; and *The Chaplet of Pearls* by Charlotte Yonge, who was, each serial being about half-way to completion. Grove was clearly intent on improving the quality of novels offered, writing to Craik: 'Miss Yonge's is a very poor production and *Realmah* can never be popular'.[17] He was also conscious of the need to meet the *Cornhill*'s competition, saying in the same letter, 'I thought we had settled . . . to give 6 sheets on the faith of an increased sale. The *Cornhill* contains 8 sheets and though each sheet is rather less full than ours the whole result is more . . . .' Incidentally, the fact that the two titles were running together illustrates another economic fact about serial publication: novels frequently overlapped and often one was begun before its predecessor was finished, thus ensuring uninterrupted suspense for the reader.

Grove and Macmillan shared the responsibility for selecting novels to be published, chiefly for economic reasons. After serial publication titles were often picked up by the firm to be published in either two or three volume editions, so the choice had to be a careful one. With the enthusiasm of a new editor Grove initially was active in seeking new talent. Thus, he wrote to Macmillan early in 1868, 'Miss Thackeray writes me a pleasant note . . . She tells me that Mrs. Brotherton (author of *Monsieur Babou* [March, 1865] and other charming stories in *Cornhill*) is probably open, so don't decide about Keary or Olney just yet'.[18] Later, in June 1868, he wrote: 'Miss Olney's *Estelle* will do' and then speaking like the experienced editor he was, added, 'It will want a little care in going through the press, some ventures putting straight, but this I am sure the accomplished and spirited authoress will see at once, when she looks at her work in type, without any prompting from me'.[19]

As it happened, these were the novelists Grove chose to appear first during his tenure. Mary Allan Olney's *Estelle Russell*, in 14 parts, came on the heels of Charlotte Yonge, and ran from January, 1869 to February 1870. However, later in 1868 Grove was dissatisfied with *Estelle* and vacillating between Annie Keary and Mary Brotherton as replacements. He wrote to Macmillan: 'Remember I have yet to use Miss Keary's story and *Mlle. Estelle* though bright and sweet is in my judgement far below the *Cornhill* standard. Read *Monsieur Babou*. . . (by the lady on whom I have my eye) and you will I think agree with me'.[20] (During the same period Mary Brotherton's *Captain George and the Little Maid* appeared in two parts, February and March 1869, which was followed by Dinah Mulock's *A Brave Lady* in 12 parts, May 1869 to April 1870. Virtually nothing is known today about Mary Allan Olney; even that reliable source, the *Wellesley Index*, is unable to supply her dates, yet Grove, and obviously Macmillan, originally thought highly of her work. About Mary Brotherton (1819/1820–1910), more is known; she was married to landscape painter Augustus Henry Brotherton, and had written several novels and some poetry. Dinah Mulock Craik (married to Macmillan's business partner in 1865) on the other hand, was a long-time personal friend of Macmillan and an intimate of his family, who had been one of his early and steady contributors to *Macmillan's Magazine* from its launch. She had begun her career writing children's stories and poems, had had modest success with her early novels, and then produced a highly successful bestseller in *John Halifax Gentleman* (1856) which made her a wealthy woman. During the 1860s she had contributed 16 articles and 12 poems to *Macmillan*'s, so would have been well known, and appreciated by, its readers.[21]

When Olney's novel concluded in February 1870 and Mulock's in April 1870, the stage was set for Anthony Trollope to begin *Sir Harry Hotspur of Hunblethwaite* in eight parts, beginning in May, and in June he was joined by Katherine Macquoid's *Fifine*, which lasted for only eight chapters. Trollope, extremely well known to the public, received excellent reviews; 'the *Athenaeum* and the *Spectator* judged it to be among the most successful of [his] short fiction'.[22] Macquoid, a novelist whose contemporary following was legion, particularly among women, began to serialize *Patty*, very possibly her most successful work, between January 1871 and November 1871, immediately after Trollope's last issue.[23] When *Patty* concluded Eleanor Towle was introduced with *Christina North*, from December 1871 to July 1872, which would run in tandem with *The Strange Adventures of a Phaeton* by William Black, from January to November, 1872. Towle is unknown today (gender bias?) while Black is known as a Scottish migrant from Glasgow to London in 1864, who made his name first as a newspaper man, rising to assistant editor of the *Daily News*, and then by being sent to cover the Franco-Prussian War. *Phaeton*, story of a coaching expedition between London and Edinburgh, relied heavily on Black's talent for describing beautiful Scottish landscape and was both a financial and a critical success.

Macmillan appears to have taken an interest in the career of his fellow Scotsman and Black visited freely in the Macmillan home at Tooting. Correspondence shows him confiding in the older man: 'I have a profound project to talk to you about some Sunday when I can get a chance to walk down your way' (1871); and also appreciating his confidence; 'I am very glad you continue to like *Phaeton*. I wish [you could know] the favourable opinions I hear of it in many quarters' (1872).[24]

Grove's correspondence shows him exercising admirable editorial prudence with regard to Black as an author new to the *Magazine*. During a meeting late in 1871 where Black first proposed the idea for the book, as yet unwritten, and promised to have a 'good bit' finished by January 1872, Grove, in a letter to Macmillan, reported telling Black, 'I should prefer to have the first two-thirds of the MSS. in our hands before beginning publication.'[25] At the same time, emphasizing the inter-relationship between editor and management, he reminded Macmillan that Black 'would be glad to hear from you [Macmillan] on the business part of the matter.' In fact, Black was paid £200 specifically to publish *Phaeton* in the *Magazine* and another £200 for the absolute copyright. The publisher was then free to issue the novel himself or to sell the copyright to another house, as Macmillan did with Trollope's novel when they sold the book rights of *Sir Harry* to Hurst and Blackett.[26] Incidentally, Macmillan paid Trollope £750 for the copyright and the right to serialize in the periodical, an indication of how wide the spread could be depending on the eminence of the author. At their meeting, Black told Grove that although he had a favourable offer from a rival publisher 'he said that he very much preferred our magazine', showing that 'eminence' could work both ways.

The foregoing paragraphs give a good indication of how serial publications were interwoven to heighten public interest and suspense. To continue to list and date novels published by *Macmillan's* would be counterproductive when anyone who wishes may consult the periodical itself, a microfilm copy, or the *Wellesley Index*, to follow the procedure for the balance of Grove's editorship. Suffice it to say, that Grove and Macmillan chose to publish two more of Black's novels: *The Princess of Thule* (March–December 1873) and *Madcap Violet* (January–December 1876), on the same terms except that the copyright would revert to Black after five years. Other fictional highlights during Grove's tenure included two novels by Annie Keary: *Castle Daly* (January 1874–July 1875); and *A Doubting Heart* (June 1878–December 1879). Both Grove and Macmillan were fond of Keary, a semi-invalid living in France while writing primarily domestic fiction. When she died (3 March 1879), half-way through her last book, Grove wrote in remembrance of her (April 1879, p.559): 'Her novels showed a great power of observation, spontaneity of expression, and sweetness and delicacy of tone . . . They were emphatically the work of a delicate and high-souled woman and will inevitably take their place in English literature' Although some sources have mistakenly stated that her novel was finished by Katherine Macquoid, Grove remarked: 'The Mss. of *A Doubting Heart* was completed by Miss Keary some time before her death.' (*ibid*.)

If one novelist more than any other could be said to have had a dominant place in *Macmillan's* it would have to be that redoubtable veteran of novels and periodicals, Margaret Oliphant, 'Who contrived to combine mass production with a high degree of artistry.'[27] As a fellow Scot she was, of course, known to Macmillan, and the firm published many of her works, including the four serials which appeared during Grove's editorship: *The Curate in Charge* (August 1875–January 1876); *The Young Musgrave* (January–December 1877); *He Who Would Not When He Could* (October 1879–November 1880); and *The Wizard's Son* (November 1882–March 1884).

It should also be noted that Henry James' *The Portrait of a Lady* (October 1880–November 1881) first appeared in *Macmillan's Magazine* and was published by the firm; and Nathaniel Hawthorne's son Julian contributed *Fortune's Fool* (December 1881–September 1882).[28]

Later critics may have considered fiction in the *Cornhill* to be more sparkling and attractive than that found in *Macmillan's*, but it should be remembered that those who wrote for the latter journal were well regarded by the contemporary audience, and also that the editorial objectives of *Macmillan's*, while recognizing the need for fiction, also attempted to give its readers a well-rounded view of current thinking in education, science, religion, philosophy and classical *belles lettres*.

Women authors and *Macmillan's Magazine*

Novelists

As has been shown, women novelists carried the burden of fiction during Grove's editorship, contributing 16 titles as opposed to seven for male authors. The prodigiously prolific Oliphant contributed four; Macquoid, three; Annie Keary, two; plus one each from Mary Brotherton, Frances Hodgson Burnett (soon to be the famed author of *Little Lord Fauntleroy*, 1886), Katharine Cooper, Dinah Mulock (Mrs Craik), Mary Allan Olney, Jane Sexey, Eleanor Towle and Charlotte Yonge. While their names may not be as familiar to the modern reader as some of the more 'classic' novelists, in their own day the women's work sold well and they were popular with the public. Of the eleven women contributors, six of them went on to commercial success by having one or more of their titles published by the Macmillan Company (Burnett, Cooper, Keary, Macquoid, Oliphant and Yonge); Mulock was a long-time established member of the Macmillan family of authors, although *A Brave Lady* was not published by Macmillan.

Grove and Macmillan together found women's fiction entirely compatible with operating a successful shilling monthly.

Poets

Little attention has been paid to *Macmillan's* women poets although 24 women contributed 54 signed selections during Grove's tenure. There is no way of knowing, of course, how many more may have contributed anonymously. That he was a demanding editor is shown again in his letter to Macmillan of June or July 1868 (the date is uncertain) concerning Emily Henrietta Hickey (1845–1924), a poet and English lecturer, whose work had appeared frequently during Masson's editorship.[29] However, a new editor brought new critical standards and Grove was not pleased, as he wrote to Macmillan:

> You know Miss Hickey and I do not, so you had better reply to her. I send you her poem and if you read it carefully as I have just done, I am sure you will come to the same conclusion. Spirit and lofty intention, and a certain amount of poetic faculty, and vast fluency – these she has – but these things don't make poetry – She ought to work and work, condense and compress and never let a bad line pass her – (what a lot of bad lines there are here). The piece would be no use to us and I therefore return it.[30]

Thus, early in his editorship Grove served notice that only the highest quality would be acceptable, in women's work as well as men's. Thereafter, Hickey appeared only twice during Grove's 15 years as editor: 'Restitution', (August 1870); and 'Mopsa's Tale' (January 1881).

Grove's most prolific contributor was Mary Brotherton who wrote a series of chiefly domestic and devotional lyrics, such as 'Birthday Songs to an Old Friend', (February 1872). She appeared five more times between 1872 and 1875, suggesting that her simple verses were popular with readers.[31] Grove's second most prolific writer was Jane Ellice Hopkins (1835–1904), a social reformer, whose verse 'Life's Lost', (February 1875) is a reflection on the debt owed to others for one's comforts: 'I cannot sure be warmed or lit/ But men must crouch and toil in tortuous caves: [miners]', or 'The sheep must shiver in the April cloud/ Yielding his one white coat to keep me warm.' Her other contributions contained similar reflections.[32]

Mention has been made of the four lyrics by Christina Rossetti published during Grove's years and of George Eliot's three longer poems; the aging Caroline Norton also offered three selections.[33] Also of interest are two long narrative poems by Eliza Keary (sister of the novelist Annie Keary): 'Little Seal-Skin' (November 1868), a tale in which she gives her own imaginative twist to the ancient Scottish legend about 'selkies', beings believed to be human who don seal skins in order to live in water. The poem tells of a sea-woman who slipped out of her sealskin, married a fisherman, had children, then found her sealskin again and, answering to the irresistible call of her origins, left them all to go back to dwell in the sea. 'The Little Goose-Girl: a Tale of the Year 2099', is a delightful and imaginative pastoral fantasy, where the Goose-Girl represents the life of the free spirit – 'Sweet May, Oh! The long sweet day', and 'Idleness, sweet idleness.' She encounters the high priests of the year 2099 who represent the life of the pragmatic and static mind, where

> Everything was made as plain as could be
> Not the ghost of a doubt even left to roam about free;
> Everybody's concern
> Being just to learn, learn, learn.

In the ensuing struggle between the two forces the conclusion is ambiguous: 'Neither No, nor Yes,/ But come unto God and see.'

Many of the women poets who wrote for *Macmillan's* are difficult to trace today, even through the *British Biographical Index* with its wide-ranging references. This is partly due to female exclusion from primarily male-oriented contemporary biographical dictionaries, and partly to the ephemeral nature of occasional poetry. But it is clear that the pages of Grove's journal were open to women who the editor felt offered poetry of a high quality, or something emphatically better than just 'good – for a woman.'

Prose writers

During Grove's editorship, women prose essayists were generously represented in the pages of *Macmillan's Magazine*; excluding poets and novelists, 73 signed authors published 142 articles on the widest possible range of subjects. The list forms an interesting commentary on the subjects women were willing to tackle and on the broadmindedness of Grove's editorship. As with the poetry, many women appeared once and these single pieces are too numerous to be noticed individually here, but a number produced a series of articles, while sometimes several women contributed on related subjects, thus forming a series of sorts.

Octavia Hill, the great social reformer and philanthropist, contributed seven articles between 1869 and 1876, which examined the plight of the poor. She wrote on such things as organized work among the poor, landlords and tenants, the homes of the poor, and volunteers for charity. Through the early influence of her grandfather, Dr Thomas Southwood Smith, a leading authority on fever, epidemics, and sanitation, she had been alerted to the wretched living conditions of the poor. After practical experience with social work as a young woman, in 1865, through the generosity of her friend John Ruskin, she was able to purchase three houses in a court, and to begin her pioneering work. Her articles in *Macmillan's* laid down the principles according to which she worked and advanced a powerful plea for greater understanding on the part of the public. One of her ideas, original to her, was to put aside space for a common room in her courts, a place where the poor could come together for meetings, social events or instruction; landlords, generally, were loth to give up space which might be earning rent for such philanthropic purposes.[34]

Ancillary to Octavia Hill's work were a number of other pieces dealing with allied subjects. Joanna Hill (no relation), daughter of Matthew Davenport Hill, the influential criminal law reformer, wrote a moving article on 'Workhouse Girls: What they are and how to help them' (June 1873) and another, entitled 'Homes for the Homeless' (June 1875). Menella Bute Smedley submitted 'Workhouse Schools for Girls' (November 1874) and Henrietta O. Barnett contributed 'The Young Women in Our Workhouses' (June 1879).

Grove was a courtly man and had many sincere friendships among his women writers. He accepted articles of remarkable intellectual sophistication from a youthful Millicent Garrett Fawcett (later the famous suffragist) on parliamentary representation and the national debt.[35] Frances Martin, whose correspondence shows her to have been headstrong and long-winded, nevertheless found a warm friend in Grove. She was involved in founding a College for Working Women and wrote an article about this for *Macmillan's*; when they could not find a location for the classes she pleaded time and again for postponement of the announcement of the school in his publication. Grove patiently indulged her whims despite any inconvenience it may have caused to his monthly page make-up.[36] Jane Chesney was convinced she had found the solution to women's need for gainful employment in poultry-keeping and Grove accepted her work.[37] In Catherine Mary Phillimore, unfortunately a shadowy figure today, he found a truly distinguished critic of Italian politics, literature, and fine arts who sent him a series of six articles consisting of 12 parts, on such varied subjects as Manzoni, Petrarch, Tasso, and the Italian drama, both classical and contemporary.[38]

Prose writers and *Macmillan's Magazine*

Literally tens of thousands of periodicals were published during the Victorian period, some catering to specialist or professional interests, such as architecture, engineering, or the law;[39] others were targeted to a generalist audience. *Macmillan's* fell into the latter category, appealing to a middle-to-upper-class, educated readership. As editor, Grove sought to adjust his pages to shifting contemporary thought, but also to guide and educate public opinion by seeking out reigning authorities on a wide variety of topics. Education, science, religion, politics, history, literature, social concerns, the arts, music, women and foreign/military topics all found places on his pages, with varying frequency. Because there is no really adequate subject index to Victorian periodicals perhaps the most accurate way to judge the personality of a journal as diverse as *Macmillan's* is to note the work of its most prominent and prolific contributors.

Arthur Penryhn Stanley

Grove's old and dear friend, Arthur Penryhn Stanley was a stalwart contributor on Church of England matters and on religious thought in general. During Grove's editorship, which encompassed the last thirteen years of the Dean's life, Stanley submitted 14 major articles on a wide variety of ecclesiastical subjects. In a ten-page, lead article for January 1869, he memorialized 'The Late Dean of St. Paul's, Henry Hart Milman, DD', pointing out his matchless literary scholarship; his courage under fire from fellow churchmen following publication of his *History of the Jews* (1829), which Stanley called 'the first decisive inroad of German theology' and the 'first palpable indication that the Bible could be studied like another book' (p.179). By chance it fell to Stanley, just two months later, to review a *Memoir* by J.F. Coleridge of another churchman, John Keble, late leader of the Oxford Movement, and author of the influential book of sacred verse, *The Christian Year* (1827). In another ten-page article Stanley pleaded for ecclesiastical tolerance and forbearance in judging Keble, and called on the church to rise above men's petty squabbles.

As a Macmillan author, Stanley exhibited a high order of scholarship, as well as his natural tendency to teach and illuminate his flock on church issues. 'The Pope's Posture in Communion' (July 1869) is a learned disquisition on the history, from the days of Christ, of the posture adopted by the celebrant, later the Pope (recumbent, sitting, kneeling or standing) as well as the communicant, during administration of the sacrament of holy communion. Grove's readers, as active members of the national church, would naturally have had a real interest in this historical commentary.

In all that he wrote for *Macmillan's*, Stanley's style was clear, direct, and precise in his presentation of fact, and meticulous in recreating history. It was also bolstered by his immense knowledge of classical languages and skill at translation. Grove demonstrated his confidence in Stanley's popularity with readers by according Stanley the lead article of the month in five of the 14 instances.

Of particular interest is Stanley's article 'The Historical Aspect of the American Churches' (June 1879), written after his tour of America with Grove. In it he pointed out the error often committed by English churchmen of speaking of 'the American church' as though it were somehow a branch of the Church of England. Instead, he explained, there are many church organizations in America (indeed, when he was finally able to cross the Atlantic 'he went with invitations to address not only Episcopalians, but also Presbyterians, Congregationalists, Baptists, Methodists and secular meetings'.[40] He stated, 'it would be as absurd to speak of the 'Church of America' as it would be to speak of the Church of Europe' (p.97).

Stanley's final essay for *Macmillan's* was published posthumously in the August 1881 number (he had died on 18 July) with an introductory note by Grove, expressing his personal and profound grief at the loss. He noted

Stanley's long association with the journal, beginning with his description of 'The Ammergau Mystery in 1860' (October 1860 – when the magazine was less than a year old) and said the Dean had insisted on correcting the final proof of his last article during his fatal illness. The title was 'The Westminster Confession of Faith', and it was an analysis of the origin, history and contemporary relevance of this as a church document. Grove noted that this was Stanley's final plea for 'tolerance, comprehensiveness, and liberty of conscience' for all peoples, and concluded mournfully 'we . . . are left 'To wander on a darken'd earth/Where all things round us breathe of Him.'[41]

Mandell Creighton

Another of Grove's long-time clerical friends was Mandell Creighton (1843–1901) who achieved high preferment in the church, completing his career as Bishop of London (1897–1901). Grove first knew Creighton through his wife, Louise, who was a member of the von Glehn family, neighbours of Grove's in Sydenham. Indeed, Louise's memories of Grove dated from her girlhood when 'he used to call every morning on his way to the Crystal Palace and sometimes in the evening also, and would often stay for a long talk'.[42] Mandell, an Oxford scholar, dedicated historian and ordained priest, and Louise married in 1872, and in 1874 he accepted a living in the gift of Merton, his Oxford college, in Embleton, a remote and tiny village in Northumberland. Here he hoped for the leisure to devote himself to what would be the defining work of his career, the five-volume history of the papacy during the Reformation.[43] During this ten-year stay in the North he published portions of his scholarship in *Macmillan's Magazine*, on such topics as 'Pope Pious II', 'Dante', and 'A Schoolmaster of the Renaissance', for a total of six learned essays (the Dante was in two parts).[44] Creighton's work was an interesting complement to that of Catherine Mary Phillimore.

Education

Education was always a prominent topic in *Macmillan's* during Grove's editorship, particularly in the years before and after passage of the Education Act of 1870. One finds John Morley examining the question of 'Leisure and the Scholar' in May 1868, followed by E.A. Abbott's 'The Teaching of English' in the same issue, and 'A New College for Women' by J. Llewelyn Davies in June. The pen of a truly distinguished woman, Anne Jemima Clough, first principal of Newnham College for women at Cambridge University, was brought to bear on 'Suggestions on Primary Education' while Frederick W.H. Myers, poet and Cambridge fellow, wrote on 'Local Lectures for Women', both in December 1868. James Bryce examined 'The Worth of Educational Endowments' (April 1869), and F.W. Farrar, dean of Canterbury, commented on 'Learning to Read' (March 1870).

Science

The considerable attention paid to science reflected the very real increase in interest, among the general public, in the advancement of knowledge in this field during the nineteenth century. J. Norman Lockyer, British astronomer, and founding and long-time editor of the Macmillan publication *Nature*, wrote on 'The Sun's Distance' (November 1868); 'Recent Solar Discoveries' (January 1869); and 'Ears and Eyes' (January 1878). T.H. Huxley offered seven contributions during Grove's term, beginning with 'A Piece of Chalk' (September 1868), which the editor anticipated eagerly, writing to Macmillan (23 July 1868): 'Huxley has promised me a paper on a 'Lump of Chalk' and all that hangs on it – which is sure to be very good'.[45] He spanned both education and science with his thoughts on 'Scientific Education' (January 1869). F.W. Farrar reported on 'Philology Is One of the Sciences' (January 1869), and C.C. Chesney, military critic, on 'The Advance of Science in Military Organization' (May 1872).

History

Anchoring the coverage of history in *Macmillan's* was a trio of truly distinguished historians, authors who were willing to write for a popular audience. Edward Augustus Freeman (1823–92), Regius Professor of Modern History at Oxford 1889–1892, was the most prolific contributor, submitting 19 articles during Grove's tenure, including one in three parts and one in five, for a total of 25 exposures to which his name was signed. John Robert Seeley (1834–95) came a close second, contributing 13 articles, including two in three parts, and one, 'Natural Religion', in ten parts, for a total of 24 exposures. John Richard Green (1837–83), famous for his *Short History of the English People* (1874) was the first historian to focus on the actual history of people as opposed to documenting their wars and conquests. In featuring these men, who were pre-eminent in their fields, Grove was certainly committing a great deal of space to the subject of history – 62 separate exposures from these three alone - but as editor he knew his audience and their interests.[46]

Music in *Macmillan's Magazine*

Finally, Grove himself was, of course, uniquely positioned to keep his readers abreast of the developing musical culture of nineteenth-century Britain. With his popular Saturday programs at the Crystal Palace, and his rapidly developing plans for his unique *Dictionary of Music and Musicians* Grove was well aware of what was new and important in musical scholarship. In his time at the Crystal Palace he saw his mission as one of educating the British public in the joys and delights of orchestral music. In the past musical experience had been largely confined to choral offerings in halls restricted in size;

the expansiveness of the Sydenham facility added a new orchestral dimension to the public's musical enjoyment.

In much the same way, Grove saw an opportunity, through the pages of *Macmillan's Magazine*, to educate people in music history, musical form, composers, both European and British, and music criticism. That this was an unusual and original topic among generalist periodicals is illustrated by a glance at the contents of the *Cornhill* and *Blackwood's*, the journals most often compared with *Macmillan's*; their editors, John Blackwood and Leslie Stephen (the latter's term was roughly concurrent with Grove's), were literary men, not musicians, and hence the former carried only three articles on music in 15 years, while *Blackwood's* had none.

In a remarkable series of 21 articles during Grove's editorship he offered a rare banquet of musical thought. Almost immediately after assuming the editor's chair he turned to his old friend John Hullah (musician, composer, teacher, known for being the first to teach singing classes using the Wilhelm, or 'tonic sol-fa' [fixed doh] method) for a travel article about a journey to the Nevers-Dijon region in France. Characteristically, Hullah managed to include a section on a peasant demonstrating a native instrument, the *coremuse*, a type of pipe on which he played local airs, both 'vague and lugubrious' and 'spritely . . . dance tunes'. ('Ten Days in the Nivernais', July 1868, p.224). In this article, for the first time, the pages of *Macmillan*'s printed a musical score which readers, if so inclined, could play for themselves, a practice which was to be repeated many times in the years ahead.

The following month a most unusual article appeared, by Joseph Bennett, a music critic, and another old friend. 'The Autograph of Handel's 'Messiah' (August 1868) described the successful efforts of the Sacred Harmonic Society to 'photo-lithograph' the manuscript of *Messiah*, a work of 270 pages which the composer completed in 23 days. Bennett was ecstatic at the prospect of using this technique to preserve the manuscripts of other great musicians - Beethoven, Mozart, Mendelssohn, and so on, – so that 'the least curious of men [might] pry into the creative processes' (p.328). Bennett, who was a strong and forceful writer, also described the history of the other 87 volumes of Handel's manuscripts: the composer had first left them to a favorite pupil, J.C. Smith; on his death-bed he recanted and left them to Oxford University, but Smith refused to give them up. Eventually, in some unexplained way, they came into the possession of George III, and so to Victoria, and Bennett was outraged to know that they were still uncatalogued and just loosely stored in Buckingham Palace. Again, this article contains many excerpts from musical scores.

Several contributors wrote on opera. Bennett brought his passionate pen to bear on it with 'The Condition of Opera in England' (July 1869) in which he did not attempt to hide his displeasure, saying, 'The subject is so out of proportion to the limits of a magazine article' and again that 'opera in England has always been regarded . . . as expensive and fashionable,' and 'of little artistic worth' (p.260). He went on to attack the exclusivism of the opera patron, the evils of disreputable opera managers, abject worship of the singers, the high prices, and regulation of dress among the audience. The only solution was to popularize, to give the people 'a temple of art as distinct from a temple of fashion' (p.265).

Edward Dannreuther, the brilliant German pianist, who had made his professional debut at the Crystal Palace playing Chopin and Greig, elaborated on opera in two very scholarly articles offering historical perspective on the form. 'It sprang from a mistaken attempt at resuscitating Greek music and Greek drama' ('The Opera's Growth and Decay', May, 1875, p.64), but music of the fourteenth, fifteenth and sixteenth centuries, being religious, 'was entirely unfit for any dramatic purpose' (p.64). Its development belonged to Italy and France from the mid-seventeenth century on, but in England 'opera has always been an exotic' (p.65). His second study, 'The Musical Drama', (November 1875) boldly proclaimed that opera – the musical drama – was 'rescued' by Wagner. There was also a good bit about opera in 'Cherubini' (July 1875) by Ferdinand Hiller, the German composer and conductor, who wrote a memoir and assessment based on his personal knowledge and acquaintance. He described him as 'a composer whom every cultivated musician must look up to with reverence' (p.272).

Should a *Macmillan's* reader prefer a lighter approach to musical enjoyment, Grove provided several selections: 'Popular Songs of the Last Half-Century' (December 1869) which provided an interesting historical review of composers, singers and fluctuation of tastes in the vocal solo; 'Current Street Ballads of Ireland' (June 1872) a cultural review and analysis; and two rollicking pieces by John Oxenford (dramatist, translator, and music critic for *The Times* for 25 years), celebrated folk music of Bulgaria, 'The Brigands of Bulgarian Song' (August 1876) and 'The Bogies of Bulgarian Song' (October 1876). The Bulgarian brigand was described in their own folklore as 'a ruffian so thoroughly atrocious and ignoble that it would be hard to find his parallel' (p.302). The Bulgarian bogie, on the other hand, was derived more from fairy tale; they were 'perhaps not so original in their badness, but every malignant quality recorded in faery lore they have taken good care to secure' (p.547).

Other occasional articles included: 'Music in England' (July 1872) by Henry David Leslie (musician and revered choir director) – a learned and humane discussion of the therapeutic role of music in the lives of the people, the good that regional choral societies have accomplished, and the need to rescue the Royal Academy of Music from the desuetude into which it had fallen. C. Halford Hawkins, an official of Winchester College, wrote on 'The Wagner Festival at Bayreuth' (August 1876) and Edmund Gurney, a miscellaneous writer, on 'Schumann on Music and Musicians' (September 1878), a review of a recently published book by Schumann on this subject. Pieces of only passing interest include: Julian Marshall's 'Some Traits of Composers'

(February 1876) and H. Sutherland Edwards 'The Literary Maltreatment of Music' (April 1876).

By far the most substantial music criticism in *Macmillan's* occurred in connection with the work of Mendelssohn and Beethoven, both favourites of Grove. In a decision that was partly personal and partly economic, and no doubt closely involved Alexander Macmillan, Grove in 1874 devoted an uncommonly large amount of space to publication of Ferdinand Hiller's book *Mendelssohn*, in parts, between January and May. It was translated by Mary Emilie von Glehn, a friend of Grove's, and Grove wrote the Preface to the hardback edition published by Macmillan and Company in June. The book was based on Hiller's personal friendship with the composer from age 11 to his death and filled with memories of making music together, socializing together, and of the rich musical life of Germany early in the nineteenth century. An earlier article on Mendelssohn (June 1871) published a series of eight uncollected letters by the composer, dating mainly from 1834 and 1835, during his time in Düsseldorf.

Edward Dannreuther returned to *Macmillan's* pages with the long, lead article for July 1876, a lyrical appreciation of the genius of Ludwig von Beethoven. It was intended as a definitive statement of the crucial importance of the composer's work and was densely packed with excerpts from the musical scores. Dannreuther agreed with those who would divide Beethoven's professional life into three sections: the first, his youth when searching for a style; the second 'when he expresses the passionate strivings of a strong man;' and third, in his full maturity, when 'he touches upon the domain of the seer and the prophet' (p.197). While many composers may be good and successful, Dannreuther avers, only a few 'both spiritually and mechanically, enriched and enlarged the entire domain of musical art.' As a result 'By virtue of Beethoven, music has become THE modern art. His works are the only adequate artistic expression of the eager impulse and enhanced aspirations of modern life' (p.193).

The final three articles on music to appear during Grove's editorship have an almost symbolic importance. During his years of planning the popular Saturday concerts at the Crystal Palace it was Grove's objective to introduce the people of Britain to the joys of musical performance and to the many forms of music, both British and European, beyond the great choral festivals which had formerly seemed the only way to reach the people musically. In a way, he was trying to give music to the populace. Each of the final three articles suggests methods to achieve a greater involvement by people in the production of music. Francis Hueffer (1843–80), music critic and editor of the *New Quarterly Magazine*, asked questions about 'The Chances of English Opera' (May 1879); Charles Sumner Maine (1856–88), a lawyer, suggested 'A Conservatoire of Music for England' (December 1879); and Florence Ashton Marshall (1843–1922), composer and conductor, wondered about 'The People's Concert Society' (April 1881).[47]

Inasmuch as Grove's editorship of *Macmillan's Magazine* provided an opportunity for more advanced thinking about, and enjoyment of, music he may very well have achieved more than he realized. It was possibly his most important contribution as editor.

Conclusion

Early in 1874 Grove's business arrangement with Macmillan and Co. changed. He entered into a 'Memorandum of Agreement', between Alexander Macmillan and G.L. Craik of 29 Bedford Street, Covent Garden, and George Grove of Sydenham in the County of Kent, whereby he would 'devote the ordinary hours of business in assisting the said Mssrs. Macmillan in their business establishment . . . . The said George Grove is not to engage in any other business or employment . . . .'[48] For this he was to be paid £300 for editing *Macmillan's*, £600 a year for assistance in managing the literary department, and any royalties earned per annum not to exceed £400. The agreement was for seven years, excepting illness or incapacity. Grove was to give up his secretaryship at the Crystal Palace, although he continued to sit on the Board of Directors. This was a generous agreement on Alexander Macmillan's part, leaving Grove as editor, a job for which he was talented and experienced, and yet freeing his time for unspecified duties, which might well, and *did*, include working on his *Dictionary of Music*.

But, by 1883 the time had come for Grove to go, to relinquish his editorship and to move on to as yet unsuspected glories. He had given 15 years of faithful service. His sharp editorial eye, his critical skills, his insistence on quality, and his fearlessness in rejecting what he considered less than the best, had succeeded in establishing a 'character' for *Macmillan's Magazine*, one that led Walter Houghton to observe, almost one hundred years later, 'its serious articles seem more impressive than those of its rivals'.[49] The modern reader pales at the thought of the labour involved in reading those thousands of articles, novels, and poems, some to accept and some to reject; the thousands of letters written; the oceans of ink dispensed; the record-keeping; the taxing diplomacy needed to soothe contributors. Through it all, Grove forged ahead, clear in his goals and steadfast in his principles. If, indeed, the end is contained in the beginning, one turns back to Grove's progressive education, where he was exposed to mathematics, chemistry, astronomy, literature, Bible study, geography, languages, and music, subjects which all appeared in his journal at one time or another, to see what gave him the intellectual power and background to supervise and to shape such a diverse Victorian periodical. Surely, the enthusiasms of Pritchard (his schoolmaster) were, in fact, 'mirrored in Grove's career [at Macmillan's] at almost every turn'.[50]

Notes

1 Percy M.Young, *George Grove. A Biography* (London, 1980), p.22.
2 *Victorian Britain. An Encyclopedia*, ed. Sally Mitchell (New York and London, 1988), p.266; Young, *George Grove*, p.38.
3 The chief biographical sources for George Grove are: C.L. Graves, *The Life & Letters of Sir George Grove, C.B.* (London, 1903); Michael Musgrave, *The Musical Life of the Crystal Palace* (Cambridge, 1995); Young, *George Grove*.
4 The chief biographical sources for Alexander Macmillan are: C.L. Graves, *The Life and Letters of Alexander Macmillan* (London, 1910); *The Letters of Alexander Macmillan*, ed. George Macmillan (London, 1908); R.T. VanArsdel, 'Macmillan and Company', *British Literary Publishing Houses, 1820–1880* (London and Detroit, 1991).
5 BL Add. Mss 54964.
6 BL Add. Mss 54793, f. 43.
7 See Eileen M. Curran, 'Verse in Bentley's Miscellany, Vols. 1–36', *Victorian Periodicals Review*, 32, 2 (Summer 1999), pp.103–59. Rosemary Scott, 'Poetry in the Cornhill Magazine: Thackeray's Influence', *Victorian Periodicals Review*, 32, 40 (Fall 1999), pp.269–74; *Wellesley Index to Victorian Periodicals, 11824–1900*, ed. Walter E. Houghton, 5 vols (Toronto, 1966–89).
8 See R.T. VanArsdel, '*Macmillan's Magazine* and the Fair Sex, 1859–1873', *Victorian Periodicals Review*, 33, 4 (Winter 2000), pp.374–96 (Part One); *ibid.* 34, 1 (Spring, 2001) pp.2–15 (Part Two).
9 'A Birthday', April 1861; 'An Apple-Gathering', August 1861; 'Light Love', February 1863; 'The Bourne', March 1863; 'The Fairy Prince Who Arrived Too Late', May, 1863; 'A Bird's-Eye View', July, 1863; 'The Queen of Hearts', October 1863; 'One Day', December 1863; 'Sit Down in the Lowest Room', March 1864; 'My Friend', December 1864; 'Spring Fancies', April 1865; 'Last Night', May, 1865; 'Consider', January 1866; 'Helen Grey', March 1866; 'By the Waters of Babylon. B.C. 570', October 1866; 'Seasons', December 1866; 'Mother Country', March 1868.
10 'The Herald Star: a Christmas Poem', 'January, 1861'; 'Gone!', 'February, 1862'; 'The Chance Blessing', 'May, 1862'; 'Helen's Tower', 'June, 1863'; 'The Great Chestnut Tree at Keir. To Its Owner', 'September, 1866'; 'Autumn Musings', 'October, 1866'.
11 Gordon S. Haight, *George Eliot. A Biography* (Oxford, 1968), pp.506–7; Rosemary Ashton, *George Eliot. A Life* (London, 1996), pp.333–4.
12 'The Legend of La Brea', June, 1870; 'The Mango-Tree', June, 1871; 'The Priest's Heart', October 1873; 'Valentine's Day', December 1877; 'The Poetry of a Root Crop', April 1880.
13 'Dies Irae', December 1868; 'Hymn on the Transfiguration', April 1870; 'The Traveller's Hymn for All Saints' Day', November 1872; 'Hymn for Advent', December 1872; 'Hymn for Whitsunday', and 'Hymn on the Accession: For National Blessings', June, 1873; 'This Do in Remembrance of Me', November 1874; 'The Untravelled Traveller' and 'Lines Written on the Recovery of Prince Leopold', March 1875; 'Our Future Hope', May, 1878; 'Manzoni's Hymn for Whitsunday', May, 1879; 'Hymn for St. John the Baptist's Day (June 24)', July, 1879; 'The Divine Life', March 1880; 'The Perfect Death', March 1880; 'Death and Life. In Memorium', August 1882.
14 BL Add. Mss 54793, f.57.
15 Guinevere L. Griest, *Mudie's Circulating Library and the Victorian Novel* (Bloomington, 1970).

16 BL Add. Mss 54793, f.30.
17 *Ibid.*, f.40.
18 BL Add. Mss 54796, f.30.
19 BL Add. Mss 54793, f.44.
20 *Ibid.*, f.48. Grove was referring to Mary Brotherton.
21 See R.T. VanArsdel, '*Macmillan's Magazine* and the Fair Sex, 1859–1873', *Victorian Periodicals Review*, 33, 4 (Winter 2000), pp.374–96 (Part One) and 34, 1, (Spring 2001), pp.2–15 (Part Two).
22 R.C. Terry (ed.), *Oxford Reader's Companion to Trollope* (Oxford, 1999), p.94.
23 In 1878 Trollope offered *Macmillan's* a second title, *Ayala's Angel*, but Grove answered him as follows: 'Dear Mr. Trollope: Mr. Macmillan has told me of your offer of a new story. I wish I had had the chance of considering it six months earlier, but I have now gone too far with another author for a story to follow that which begins in the *Magazine* in June to allow me to [re]treat' (BL Add. Mss 54793). The novel which began in June, 1878 was Annie Keary's *A Doubting Heart*, which ran until December 1879. During that period, however, two other novels were begun: Frances Hodgson Burnett's '*Haworth's*' (October 1878) and Margaret Oliphant's *He Who Will Not When He May* (November 1879). It is unclear which Grove was referring to, or he may have intended Henry James' *The Portrait of a Lady* (October 1880) which technically was the next novel to begin after the conclusion of Keary's. In any case, Macmillan's had no shortage of fiction during this period.
24 BL Add. Mss 54929, ff.4, 15.
25 BL Add. Mss 54793, f.67.
26 Terry, *Oxford Reader's Companion to Trollope*, p.493.
27 John Sutherland, *Stanford Companion to Victorian Fiction* (Stanford, 1989), p.476.
28 Other novelists who contributed fiction during Grove's editorship, but not mentioned in the text included: Jane Sexey, *A Slip in the Fens*; F.C. Burnand, *My Time and What I've Done With It*; and Katherine Cooper, *Sebastian*.
29 See note 8, where her works are listed.
30 BL Add. Mss 54793, f.47.
31 See note 8.
32 *Ibid.*
33 *Ibid.*
34 *Wellesley Index*, V, p.364.
35 *Ibid.*, p.257.
36 *Ibid.*, p.518
37 *Ibid.*, p.150
38 'Manzoni', Jul. 1873; 'Petrarch' (2), September, October 1873; 'The Prince Printers, Italy' (2) February, March 1874; 'Torquato Tasso, 1525–1536' (2), September, October 1875; 'The Italian Drama, 1621–1723,' (4), August 1876–September 1877; 'Il Teatro Italiano Contemporaneo, 1835', January 1879.
39 *Victorian Periodicals and Victorian Society*, ed. J. Don Vann, and Rosemary T. VanArsdel (Toronto, 1994).
40 Young, *George Grove*, p.144.
41 *Wellesley Index*, V, p.737.
42 Louise Creighton, *Memoir of a Victorian Woman*, ed. James Thayne Covert (Bloomington, 1994), p.7
43 *History of the Papacy during the Reformation Period*, 5 vols, 1882–94.
44 *Wellesley Index*, V, p.190.

45 BL Add. Mss 54793, f.51.
46 The reader is reminded that in a survey such as this only the briefest mention can be made of each of the above categories. Any one of them could easily be the subject of a journal article or even a master's essay.
47 The following list of 21 articles pertaining to music published during the years of Grove's editorship shows clearly what a steady effort he was making at educating his readers: July 1868, 'Ten Days in the Niverrnais', John Hullah; August 1868, 'The Autograph of Handel's Messiah', Joseph Bennett; July 1869, 'On the Condition of Opera in England', Joseph Bennett; December 1869, 'Popular Songs of the Last Half Century', John Hullah; June, 1871, 'Letters of Mendelssohn', Introduction by G. Grove; January 1872, 'The Current Street Ballads of Ireland', William Barry; July 1872, 'Music in England', Henry Leslie; January, 1874, 'Mendelssohn' (Chapters 1–3), Ferdinand Hiller (this biography was continued February through May); May 1875, 'The Opera: its Growth and Decay', Edward Dannreuther; July 1875, 'Cherubini', Ferdinand Hiller; November 1875, 'The Musical Drama', Edward Dannreuther; February 1876, 'Some Traits of Composers', Julian Marshall; April 1876, 'The Literary Maltreatment of Music', H. Sutherland Edwards; July 1876, 'Beethoven and His Works: a study', Edward Dannreuther; August 1876, 'The Brigands of Bulgarian Song', John Oxenford; October 1876, 'The Bogies of Bulgarian Son', John Oxenford; November 1876, 'The Wagner Festival at Bayreuth', C. Halford Hawkins; September 1878, 'Schumann on Music and Musicians', Edmund Gurney; May 1879, 'The Chances of English Opera', Francis Hueffer; December 1879, 'A Conservatoire of Music for England', Charles Sumner Maine; April 1881, 'The People's Concert Society', Florence A. Marshall.
48 BL Add. Mss 54793, f.75.
49 *Wellesley Index*, vol. I, p.555.
50 Young, *George Grove*, p.22.

8

Roots of a Tradition: the First *Dictionary of Music and Musicians*

Leanne Langley

When completed in 1889, George Grove's *Dictionary of Music and Musicians* was twice its projected length and nearly a decade behind schedule. Compilation had been a hard slog, editing at times a torture ('...it has given me a world of worry and upon my word I am almost ill from it').[1] Dripped out in alphabetical fascicles over a 12-year period, the end product was unbalanced and by no means uniformly admired. Even the publisher, Alexander Macmillan, had little hope for its commercial success – a bitter disappointment to the founding editor. Grove was a literary professional with an eye on the reading public, as well as an enthusiast hoping to foster musical understanding among a wide audience. That he worked nine years beyond his contract to complete the project is a telling detail, and a further layer of the story not widely known. In fact the background to this celebrated *Dictionary*, how it was assembled and what it represented, has never really been investigated. There seems to have been little need, given the book's canonic status in more recent times. Why should it matter how such a work was created when its impact in professional, practical and economic terms through six further editions and related specialist works, across the twentieth century and into the twenty-first, has plainly been phenomenal?[2]

It matters for two reasons. How Grove conceived and executed his book is part of a bigger cultural picture in nineteenth-century Britain, indeed in Europe and North America, which has barely been taken in by historians. Broad theoretical questions about how serious music was perceived and discussed, categorized and explained – even what counted as serious and why – are directly relevant to what George Grove and his predecessors in dictionary-making were up to. Many of these questions have only recently begun to be asked. At the same time, any modern narrative that seeks to position this dictionary without understanding its particular history may mislead. That is because, paradoxically, the *Dictionary*'s later repute, paralleling the sophistication of twentieth-century readers and contributors (and of British composers and performers), has tended to obscure Grove's original aim. The book started to become something he never envisaged even before it was finished, while his name, soon synonymous with the book, accrued an almost religious authority he never sought. Projected to the top of a field in which he always doubted or disclaimed his own expertise, he has since become easy prey to revisionist theories about culture formation in the nineteenth century, and about the value of 'facts' in general.[3]

So the time seems ripe now, a hundred years after the founder's death, for a closer look at details. My purpose is not to tarnish our received image of the Grove achievement – great man, great idea, great publisher, great book – but to open the curtains and let in some fresh, nineteenth-century light, revealing new angles and exposing old cobwebs. I hope to show that what is loosely called the 'Grove tradition' has both a longer pedigree and a more empirical basis than some readers may have thought. The editor's practical choices in conducting the *Dictionary*, and the problems inherent in it, may in turn spark a more informed view of what he and his colleagues really did, at a time of enormous change in British musical and social life. I shall divide the discussion into four parts: lexical traditions behind the *Dictionary of Music and Musicians*, the concept and design of Grove's project, editorial processes and challenges, and finally, the *Dictionary*'s publication and reception.

'There is no one work in English...' (March 1874)

Early in 1874 Macmillan & Co. issued a brief prospectus describing what 'The Dictionary of Music' would contain and why such a work was needed. By that time George Grove had not only signed up a group of 'eminent and efficient writers' (32 are listed on the prospectus), he had also done his homework on other books in the field. In English there were not many, and all were out of date, incomplete, too specialized or 'inaccessible to the non-professional reader'. The key paragraph is this:

> There is no one work in English from which an intelligent inquirer can learn, in small compass and in untechnical language, what is meant by a Symphony or Sonata, a Fugue, a Stretto, a Coda, or any other of the terms which necessarily occur in every description or analysis of a Concert or a piece of Music; or from which he can gain a readable and succinct account of the history of the various branches of the art, or of the rise and progress of the Pianoforte and other instruments, or the main facts and characteristics of the lives of eminent Musicians.[4]

'Small compass', 'untechnical language', 'readable and succinct' and 'main facts and characteristics' say it all. (We might ask whether eminent writers were likely to achieve succinctness, but that is a different matter; if Grove lacked confidence in his troops, he had plenty in his own editing skill.) Indeed, tone and focus were to emerge continually as Grove's primary concerns in the project, not because, like Charles Burney, he felt he had to entertain his readers, but because as an amateur himself he valued technical clarity about music, and insight into its human associations.[5] To be sure, he was not a born lexicographer, still less a 'musicologist', a term not anyway in use at the time. He was curious and enquiring, but not semantically compulsive or systematic. He did not wish to understand and organize whole branches of musical knowledge and thereby control them, as we might say of Sébastien de Brossard, J.G. Walther and E.L. Gerber, Gustav Schilling and F.-J. Fétis, Hugo Riemann and Robert Eitner, the great names in modern music lexicography.[6] Nor did he find value in what he called the 'mere archaeology' of music,[7] despite his enthusiasm for biblical archaeology. Grove was instead a shrewd analyst, critic and biographer, an autodidact keen to win new converts, and a deeply responsive listener to the music of his own time. The *Dictionary* as he first imagined it was almost certainly a reference book he wanted to own – one he could pull down from the shelf and use rather than a lexicon of things he would never look up.

He says as much in the Preface to the first volume (1879), describing practical music as the book's main impetus ('the great spread of concerts, musical publications, private practice and interest in the subject'), and referring to his target in the broadest possible terms ('Professional musicians and Amateurs alike'). Excitement, confidence about musical progress, commonsense language and a welcoming voice pervade the *Dictionary*. Even its range of topics reflects the mind of someone sitting in a modern concert hall, not grubbing around in a medieval library. The pages are packed with entries on familiar technical terms, forms and devices, lives of composers and performers, individual work titles (remarkably, as headwords), collections of music and their repositories, societies and institutions, publications and publishers, instruments and their makers, a history of national schools – all dealing with Western European art music, no further back than the mid-fifteenth century. This was territory within the grasp of that 'increasing section of the public', musically active, who might well wish to learn more and, crucially, who could afford to.

In the same Preface, the editor excludes earlier and ethnic musics, and abstruse topics in theory, acoustics and human anatomy. Though not denying their importance, he omits them to suit the book's focus and chosen market. And he is direct about the English bias in an English dictionary. By his day, a degree of chauvinist coverage was not only standard in most dictionaries, it was expected.[8] Slighting his own nationals, or pretending a perfect balance, would have been unacceptable both to British and to international users. He rounds off the Preface with allusions to independent sources, the 'actual research of the writers', new and interesting information, 'ancient mistakes corrected', and of course his contributors, whose 'names ...guarantee...the value of their contributions' – all of it an impressive salvo meant to promote the book's novelty and appeal. On reflection, the scope is indeed almost unbelievable. Contemporary British readers might have wondered how the two subjects – music and musicians' lives, traditionally treated in separate dictionaries – could be handled meaningfully in one sequence.[9] The most fastidious probably wondered why the work was not called what it actually was, an encyclopedia. Grove's book was the first general music encyclopedia in English.

Here we might pause to ask just how significant the *Dictionary of Music and Musicians* was in historical terms, and how original. For surely the centuries of dictionary-making before 1870 had produced solid precedents, English and foreign. Since every reference work builds to some extent on earlier ones, Grove must have been indebted to existing conventions if not specific books. In fact, the history of knowledge compendiums starts in the fourth century BC, and for music as early as the first century BC. Grove did not look back that far. But for present purposes, a few landmarks should help put the character of his *Dictionary* in perspective.

General encyclopedias are the taproot of the Grove tradition, as much in their aim of providing a rounded education within one book (hence the address to a wide readership) as in their inclusion, from the twelfth century and especially in the nineteenth, of practical descriptions of crafts, or how everyday things were made.[10] The Great Exhibition in particular made mechanical processes intellectually respectable, and tantalizing to encyclopedia users in Grove's day. For some, music was one of those crafts or processes, and its tools and methods rightly belonged in a reference work for general readers. In addition, encyclopedia-makers had been among the first bookmen to devise ways of presenting complex information on the page: cross-referencing came into its own in the fifteenth century, italic type for quoted book titles by the early eighteenth. Although it was Francis Bacon who had set out the modern principles of encyclopedia-making in the early seventeenth century, the first English one appeared only in 1704. Thereafter the British contribution is remarkable. Ephraim Chambers's *Cyclopaedia* of 1728 was the prototype for Diderot and D'Alembert's great *Encyclopédie* as well as for the *Encyclopaedia Britannica* in the mid- and later eighteenth century. The success of those two in turn, among middle-class buyers, led to a boom in encyclopedia publishing in the early nineteenth century. Abraham Rees's scholarly *Cyclopaedia; or Universal Dictionary of Arts, Sciences, and Literature* (London, 1802–20), for which Burney himself wrote hundreds of music entries, was followed shortly by the Leipzig *Conversations-Lexikon* of Friedrich Brockhaus, a pioneering 'popular encylopedia', simply arranged, compellingly easy to use.

Competition increased as more new titles, revised editions of old ones, and specialist dictionaries to amplify the encyclopedias flooded the market. For a while the tactics of Grub Street reigned. In London particularly, publishers and other speculators hired hacks to copy, translate, cut and paste, mostly to rival the bookseller next door, sometimes to promote private causes. By the mid-nineteenth century, however, to ensure a lasting profit, a big reference work had to be thorough, well written, informative, up to date and neither too small nor too large. Getting the balance right required a partnership between a man of business, providing the necessary finance and sales organization, and a genuine scholar, who could write many of the articles himself. The lack of one or the other could be disastrous since huge financial outlay was needed at the beginning with no return for years, yet there was little chance of ongoing sale unless the product was 'authoritative'. Into this picture enter John Murray and Dr William Smith, producing a series of important classical and biblical reference works from the 1840s – in some of which the young George Grove had a hand[11] – and a few years later, Alexander Macmillan and the same George Grove, who by the mid-1870s was Macmillan's salaried literary adviser.

Meanwhile, there had been a separate line of music-reference works. Single-subject dictionaries appeared from the sixteenth century in theology, mathematics and chemistry, medicine, the law and military. Their purpose was not education so much as clarification, and standardization, in professions where precise meanings were increasingly required.[12] Lists of terms predominated. Johannes Tinctoris's *Terminorum musicae diffinitorium*, published in Treviso in the late fifteenth century, set the precedent in music.[13] By contrast, music biography had received only sporadic attention until J.G. Walther joined it with terminology in his famous *Lexicon* of 1732, and Ernst Ludwig Gerber produced the first international dictionary of musicians' lives in 1790.[14] In Britain, music-reference traditions had always been more pragmatic. Technical terms were appended to music treatises and tutors, helping performers with 'foreign' words, while lists of terms and topics featured in eighteenth- and early nineteenth-century music magazines.[15] English books of musical terms or of biography tended to be culled from earlier sources, English and foreign, repackaged for newer readers.[16] It seems that in London generally, publishing opportunity 'created' the lexical urge rather than the other way round – the most famous case being Samuel Johnson's *Dictionary*, first suggested to Johnson by the bookseller Robert Dodsley in the 1740s, underwritten by a conger of publishers and printers, and completed in two volumes by 1755.[17]

Opportunity allied to education is no bad thing, of course. In publishing and music it opened a vast cultural arena in nineteenth-century Britain – cheaper print, more readers, flourishing concerts, piano culture, the Great Exhibition, the Education Act. Grove was not wrong to have sensed the possibilities. He brought music articles into *Macmillan's Magazine* with the first issue he edited, in 1868, essentially testing the market for music books.[18] Later he started a series of school music primers, in competition with what John Stainer was doing for Novello.[19] And as we have seen, he hit on the lack of a substantial music-reference work in English, such as the French now had with Fétis and the Germans with Schilling, both begun in 1835.[20] Hermann Mendel's *Musikalisches Conversations-Lexikon*, begun in 1870, may have driven the point home[21] – there was not an English music-reference book comparable with the best European ones and never had been – but the local market was now crystal clear. Grove's choice of the title 'Dictionary', suitably modest, was probably the only one he ever considered for his projected work, issued in serial parts to help the finance, just like a magazine.[22] It would be broad but not exhaustive, relevant and interesting to non-specialists, and above all saleable – nothing so grand as a major encyclopedia.

'We are not a Dict'y of ancient music...' (May 1879)

Let us turn now to the project itself, its genesis and design. Records of George Grove's earliest discussions with Macmillan are not extant, nor is there any great cache of original editorial materials. We have to trace the *Dictionary*'s making through scattered references in company files and personal letters, memoirs, reviews and the book itself. Some elements are clear, such as the basic plan of alphabetical part-issue, making two octavo volumes of about 600 pages each, with music examples and woodcut illustrations. But working processes are more elusive, including the stimulus for the whole project. Near the end of his life, in an interview with F.G. Edwards for the *Musical Times*, Grove confirmed that the idea of the dictionary had been 'entirely his own'.[23] What he never stated is when or how the idea occurred to him.

Certainly Grove had the contacts, skills and sense of mission for a music dictionary, and we know that in 1873 he was seeking new professional pastures – a change from his Crystal Palace job to one with more autonomy and income.[24] Perhaps the immediate spark was, again, opportunity and more than a little careerism. As his work on Dr Smith's *Atlas of Ancient Geography, Biblical and Classical* was ending (it was published by Murray in 1875), that for *Macmillan's Magazine* was moving ahead. Alexander Macmillan approved his editor's innovations here, as well as the suggestion – possibly Grove's own, in mid-1873 – that he work more for the firm in an enhanced capacity, as a kind of commissioning editor. His experience in geography, music, technical subjects, religion and biblical criticism might be specially valuable in building a list of academic and school books. The *Magazine* required only part-time work, yet Grove had proved his worth by increasing the journal's circulation and cultivating a range of authors.[25] He could easily continue with that job (one imagines him saying) and at the same time generate new titles for the growing educational market, editing or even writing some of them himself. In the event, the company offered, and Grove signed, a formal contract specifying two literary roles and three payment streams. He would receive £300 a year as editor of *Macmillan's Magazine* (a rise of £50 over his initial salary there in 1868); £600 for managing the literary side of the business; and a guaranteed £400 in the event of profit from the sale of books or series of which he was editor or compiler. The contract, dated 26 February 1874 and signed by both Macmillan and George Lillie Craik,

Macmillan's partner and business manager, was to run from January 1874 to the end of 1880.[26]

A large-scale dictionary project is nowhere mentioned in this document, perhaps a deliberate precaution on both sides. But from subsequent correspondence in the Macmillan archives, it is clear the firm had discussed Grove's music dictionary scheme and allowed him to pursue it – expecting, however, that in the shorter term he would also produce school primers and other books likely to yield more immediate profit in which Grove himself would have a share. His dictionary work, on the other hand, was silently subsumed under the literary management clause, and on its completion, that book's copyright was to remain entirely Macmillan's property.[27] Despite the slight vagueness of this contract, in essence both parties understood that Grove would be paid £1,300 a year for seven years, working full-time as editor of *Macmillan's Magazine*, editor of the Music Dictionary, and projector and editor of possibly several new book series; profits were expected. It was a tall order, but also an exciting opportunity in a prestigious firm, a real literary position. We might even speculate that, once formed in his mind and discussed with close friends, his dictionary idea became the main lever in Grove's latest bid to do something notable in the world, through Macmillan's, and in his mid-50s to gain the rank and authority he felt he deserved.

Career drive may well explain a certain personal impetus behind the *Dictionary*. Yet we would be naive to ignore the ferment of the early 1870s in British music-educational and professional circles as a potent factor in Grove's thinking. He was saying no more than the truth when he described in the 1874 prospectus a marked broadening of intellectual interest in music since 1850:

> Within [this] period Music in England has made immense progress, and the number of persons who attend Concerts and practise Music has very largely increased. It is no longer regarded as a mere idle amusement, but has taken, or is taking, its right place beside the other Arts, as an object of study and investigation.

He knew what he was talking about, and not only from frequent attendance at St James's Hall and his closeness to the Crystal Palace operation, which included a library, arts courses and other educational opportunities open to the public.[28] By the time this statement was written, four years after the 1870 Education Act, formal music education was in the air at two levels – for school children in general education, and for aspiring musicians and music teachers. A tangible outcome was the founding in 1873 of the National Training School for Music, later to form the basis of the Royal College of Music. Another was the rush by music and general publishers to provide teaching materials for this very market – tutors and textbooks on a range of musical subjects. Meanwhile, partly mixed up with the ongoing national discussions about music training,[29] there was a more private move by some higher academics and research-minded professionals, chiefly scientists, to form a learned musical society in Britain. Spearheaded by John Stainer and William Pole, its outcome was the founding of the Musical Association, 'for the investigation and discussion of subjects connected with the art and science of music', in April 1874.[30] Grove and a number of his earliest *Dictionary* colleagues, William Chappell, John Hullah, Sir F.A. Gore Ouseley and others, were directly involved in all these initiatives, and would have readily spotted the need for a solid English reference work addressed to music students.

They were not the only ones. At almost exactly the same time, Stainer, together with a colleague from Oxford and more recently St Paul's Cathedral, W.A. Barrett, began work on the rather more specialized, one-volume *Dictionary of Musical Terms*. Published by Novello in 1876 and aimed at a narrower academic market than Grove's book, it acknowledged the assistance of more than a dozen British experts (including Chappell, Hullah, a barrister and a medical doctor), and laid stress on technical terms found in 'scientific, theoretical, and practical treatises'.[31] Some of the entries – most spectacularly 'Larynx', at 32 columns – went into extraordinary detail.[32] Moreover, even before Stainer's project, yet a bigger one in the general reference field embraced music with much else – the new, ninth edition of the *Encyclopaedia Britannica*, soon celebrated for its modern spirit and scholarly summation of so much recent work in the sciences, history, religion, philosophy, literature and the arts.[33] Among its many distinguished contributors were T.H. Huxley and Charles Swinburne; Francis Hueffer, the *Times* music critic; A.J. Hipkins, the organologist (who also assisted Stainer and Barrett, and was an early and valuable hand on Grove's team); E.A. Freeman, the Oxford historian (with whom Grove had had a run-in over a *Macmillan's Magazine* submission);[34] and Lord Rayleigh, the physicist (a founding member of the Musical Association and later to win the Nobel Prize for physics). Work had begun on this 'EB' in Scotland in 1871, the first volume appearing in 1875. Before long, still other groups would be immersed in major dictionary schemes. By the later 1870s a mammoth new English-language dictionary under Dr James Murray was underway at Oxford (helped partly by Macmillan), and in 1882 George Smith of Smith, Elder founded the *Dictionary of National Biography* with Leslie Stephen in the editorial chair.[35] Grove was in good company.

Still, while shrewd enough to detect both marketing and collaborating potential in this climate, Grove had strong views about what his own book should, and should not, contain. He remained skeptical about the direction and value of some of the new music research, and the divide it symbolized between what he saw as the music-loving British public and the largely insensible British music establishment. More to the point, Grove personally identified with the former group, not himself being interested in much music before about 1700, nor in organs, acoustics, cathedral choirs, vocal technique, theories of pitch notation and so on, which seemed to occupy rather a lot of British 'professors'. Stainer he thought knowledgeable but boring; Ebenezer Prout had ability but was a snob; Herbert Oakeley was aloof as well as limited.[36] These were private opinions, of course, yet they are expressed clearly enough in letters to indicate Grove's general irritation with the slender enthusiasms of English music academics. By contrast, he was a Europhile, full of admiration for the Austro-Germanic musical heritage, and constantly aware of new literary and musical trends on the Continent. He obviously had to consult a range of British authorities on past and present music – and benefited from their expertise – but he also took care to distinguish his book by bringing in foreign contributors at the outset (most notably Franz Gehring and C.F. Pohl), and by trying to ensure that all his collaborators wore their learning lightly. Mindless detail, especially about forgotten music or subsidiary topics, should have no place in his dictionary, a point he was at pains to reiterate when well-meaning but misguided contributors sent unusable entries. The following instruction to a new sub-editor, the young William Barclay Squire, gives the feel of Grove's approach, on the entry 'Lyre' by his friend Alfred Hipkins:

> My dear Squire
>
> You would do me a very great favour if you would take the enclosed in hand and cut it down, tear it down, boil it down into not more than half a column.
>
> We are not a Dict'y of ancient music and the Lyre which we can deal with is the instrument...that was so called in the last century. If left to my own unaided wisdom I should have begun the article by referring the reader for the antient Lyre to the Dictionaries of Dr. Smith or others[,] going on to say what the modern lyre had in common with it. But as poor Hipkins has in error taken the enormous pain to write all this dissertation I must...just describe the mere outward characteristics of the old instrument, referring to the wood cut which he has had made. This may be all done out of his description in a very small compass. [...]
>
> Yours ever G. Grove
>
> [PS] I should suppress all the facts about its history, scale, &c especially the scale because it can have nothing to do with us.[37]

Poor Hipkins indeed. A leading authority on musical instruments and a devoted contributor, like most scholars he was only trying to be thorough. Squire duly suppressed the scale, but half a column was too optimistic.

This letter was written in 1879, six years into the project. Without doubt it represented not only Grove's exasperation but that of his employers too, for whom space in the *Dictionary*, editorial time, and appeal to the average reader were paramount. In the same year, it might be noted, Grove deliberately avoided any entry at all on 'Larynx', and Alexander Macmillan coolly pointed out to Oxford University Press, for whom he was London selling agent, the limited readership for their new title *Certain Variations in the Vocal Organs of Passerine Birds (that have hitherto escaped notice)* : 'If there are musicians who add physiological considerations to their studies they will certainly value such a book, or on the other hand physiologists who care about the musical result of voice organs. ... How many people in each quarter are likely to buy such a book?' Macmillan was on to something: after 25 years *Passerine Birds* had sold only 21 copies, despite having been warmly recommended by Charles Darwin.[38] Though his instinct in this case seems hardly remarkable, it was indeed Macmillan's sense of the book market, and his firm's success through cautious husbanding of people and resources, that had attracted the OUP delegates in the first place.[39] George Grove picked up that caution, and knew he was responsible for shaping and controlling his biggest project to keep his publisher's support, never entirely secure. By 1879, in any case, work was again about to slip behind schedule.

To clarify the degree of risk the *Dictionary* entailed, as well as the conflicting pressures Grove began to face in its design and editing, it is important to recount here an episode of 1877 in which the book's viability was seriously challenged. In late June of that year, at the halfway point of Grove's contract (when editorial work had reached only the letter 'C'), George Craik confronted the editor about progress and put to him frankly the company's position. Nothing of the vaunted 'Dictionary of Music' had yet been published, expenses had grown alarmingly, attempts to get an American co-publisher had failed, and the prospect of financial return was receding by the hour. Once before the firm had considered dropping the project.[40] Now they were doing it again, urging their £1,000-a-year literary adviser to turn his attention instead to school books, where profits undoubtedly lay. Grove considered the problem for a month and worked feverishly on dictionary articles. Devising a shrewd counter proposal – linked with fewer demands on him elsewhere in the company – he thus entered negotiations to rescue the project he cared most about. Craik extracted his assent to the following statement:

> After careful calculation Mr Grove sees his way to complete the dictionary of Music for publication by Dec. 31. 1880, and in the event which he believes extremely improbable of its not being then completed, he engages to complete it, with all possible despatch, without Messrs. Macmillan & Co. making any further payment to him in respect of it. Messrs. Macmillan agree to postpone the Class book of Geography, and they do not ask him to attend in Bedford Street, except during such times as may be necessary or convenient for him to enable him to conduct the Magazine and the Dictionary.[41]

The company was both impatient and nervous, perhaps rightly so given Grove's responsibilities. He had a lot on his plate. The *Magazine* enjoyed considerable repute and 15,000 readers, and his proposed geography class-book was barely begun. But by any standard, this new agreement was driving a hard bargain, binding Grove to a possibly unrealistic target and months or years of work without pay. How far he realized this is a matter for speculation. Certainly no one could have foreseen that the project would gradually double in size and take not three but a dozen more years to complete. Indeed at the time, Grove found this agreement a relief – the dictionary was saved and his attention refocused ('It is perhaps as well for me to be bound down').[42] He attacked his work with new vigour, having just promised Craik the following 'careful calculation' for the book's two volumes, 1,500 pages in all:[43]

A–D	Aug. 31	1877
E–G	Dec. 31	"
H–J	June 30	78
K–M	Oct. 31	"
N–P	June 30	79
Q–S	Dec. 31	"
T–V	June 30	80
W–Z	Dec. 31	"

These were putative completion dates for the main commissioning and editorial work rather than publication dates. Although the scheme may look like some back-of-the-envelope plan to squeeze all 26 letters into the available time, in fact Grove and his team were to be remarkably successful, for a while, at keeping up the pace. It was rather the extent of each letter, and the scope and depth of the whole *Dictionary*, that stymied them. The seed of Grove's idea had fallen on richer ground than he knew.

'I am afraid that I am in a horrid fix…' (September 1885)

As we can now see, sixteen years elapsed between the project's start and its finish. During that time a number of processes were going on almost continuously – consultation and publicity, commissioning, research, writing, working on the copy (sometimes re-commissioning), checking sources, typesetting and proofing, assembling page proofs for each alphabet letter, inserting late corrections, publishing the fascicles, noting errors and omissions, dealing with reviews and other feedback, compiling the appendix. Each of these was a necessary task, interlinked with others and affecting subsequent work down the line – which is to say nothing of the politicking, cajoling and letter-writing that accompanied such activity, and the drain on Grove of doing or overseeing most of it himself, often at times of great stress unrelated to the *Dictionary* and without a ready-made template for how to do a music encyclopedia. There were bound to be problems and delays. That the book was completed at all seems a minor miracle. But it is not so much a miracle that needs explaining, as the day-to-day solutions Grove adopted, the phases of work he and his colleagues went through, and the gradual shifts in coverage that occurred over the course of the book. There were three main periods of work – roughly 1874–79, 1880–84 and 1885–89 – distinguishable by Grove's focus and associates in each one. What comes through in all of them is a genuinely frutiful tension between his professionalism as an editor and his utter fascination with music, and increasingly, music research. It is hard to think of anyone else, in any country, who could have achieved the same mix, rolling with the punches and still keeping his sanity.

In 1874 Grove's first assistant was the young George A. Macmillan, Alexander's son, fresh from Eton and a music enthusiast himself. The two Georges shared an office, young George helping the senior editor draw up lists of subjects and authors.[44] A fascinating glimpse of what must be among the earliest of these – lists of headwords organized under broad subjects (what would now be called 'area lists') – can be seen in a copy of the 'General Directions for Contributors' that once belonged to Hipkins, now in the Royal College of Music.[45] The first 30 areas were terminological and topical, from Violin Tribe ('Baryton', 'Belly' etc) and Personal ('Choragus', 'Conductor' etc) to Aesthetical Words and Rhythm and Measure. A further 11 areas were biographical: composers were categorized by nationality, performers by their instrument. At this stage, the lists were understandably fullest where Grove had the readiest advice, as in English School and Violin Players.[46] But he was also fortunate in finding specialists to take on and construct whole areas of their own (the first 'area advisers'), including J.R. Sterndale-Bennett (the Flemish school), C.F. Pohl (Austro-German school), Julian Marshall (singers), Edward Dannreuther (modern European school), and the rather less well-known T. Percy Hudson (violoncellists, gambists, contrabassists).[47] These and other early contributors named in the prospectus, including Franz Gehring, Hipkins, W.H. Husk, Prout (for a time), W.H. Stone and Franklin Taylor, made up a team of willing experts nearly all the way through the project, and were soon joined by others such as the 'excellent' Mrs Carr and the helpful French music historian Gustave Chouquet.[48] A few assistants touted in the beginning would actually contribute very little by the end – J.W. Davison, Ferdinand Hiller, Henry Lincoln – but their names added weight and they did at least write an article or two. Julius Benedict and Joseph Bennett appear as contributors on the prospectus and in the prelims to three published volumes, yet never wrote a word!

In fact, since considerable flexibility was required to get what was wanted out of the best available writers, on time and in alphabetical order – A's and B's had to be written and processed before C's and D's and so on –

contributors and headwords alike came and went as the *Dictionary* proceeded. The first lists show, for example, that a few imagined entries turned out to be superfluous ('Accompanist', 'Composer', 'Concert grand piano') or impracticable ('Unity', 'Variety'), and that others, appearing under more than one geographical area ('Billington, Mrs Elizabeth', 'Caldara, Antonio') or possible heading ('Band, military', 'Military music', 'Call (military)', 'Signal (military)') – still had to be decided on and assigned. Some were at first wrongly listed or categorized ('Cimbalum'), and obvious omissions had to be rectified ('Brambilla', 'Chickering', 'Senesino'). Meanwhile, good advice was not always easy to find and contributors varied in quality. A few old hands got older during the project and new experts came along, while some early writers proved less congenial, or less accommodating, than expected. Among solid acquisitions later in the work were Alexis Chitty, F.H. Jenks (an American writer), Florence Marshall, Rosa Newmarch (who rescued Brahms in the Appendix), and Philipp Spitta (who did the same for Bach, besides writing 'Schumann' and 'Weber').

The best way to see at a glance how the final authorship of the *Dictionary* came out – 118 contributors, roughly 80 per cent of them British – is to examine Adela Wodehouse's revealing 'Catalogue of the Articles Contributed by Each Writer in the Dictionary', appended to the Index volume of 1890 (see Plate 9). When this information is mapped against correspondence and fascicle dates we can begin to follow the project's development over time. This in turn helps explain some of the book's problems as well as its strengths. In terms of bulk, for example, Grove did write most of the *Dictionary* himself (though a large number of his entries were brief). Following closely behind were the indefatigable Husk, who made it to 'W' in his English composers before he died in August 1887;[49] W.S. Rockstro, who came in only at 'G' but covered a huge amount of early and ecclesiastical material, better than the Rev. Thomas Helmore whom he replaced; and of course William Barclay Squire and J.A. Fuller Maitland, the young Cambridge graduates who joined the project in the late 1870s. Squire and Maitland, who were friends, both of them recommended by C.V. Stanford, started by helping with a few troublesome articles in 'F' and 'M', respectively, but soon proved indispensable. Squire's articles for the *Dictionary* made his reputation, while Maitland (as Grove always called him) took charge of the Appendix, as well as, later, the entire second edition.[50] It is chiefly in their personal correspondence with the editor, together with that of C. Hubert H. Parry, at 27 Grove's first sub-editor,[51] that we find concrete details about how the work was done.

For articles other than those on the advisers' lists, commissioning appears to have been undertaken personally by Grove, a few entries at a time, through friendly letter-writing. Never was there anything like a proforma commission, stating length, copy date, rate of pay,[52] or prescriptive rules about content (the 'Directions for Contributors' contained only five points about presentation). He first sounded out a potential writer, gently explaining what was needed, perhaps with suggestions about sources or examples. Then, after leaving the way open for reaction, he tended to close with encouragement and solicitation. Grove was, after all, trying to coax the best efforts out of people who had probably never had quite this sort of assignment. To Parry, whose musical and literary taste he respected, he wrote cautiously with ideas for an entry on 'Arrangement' in July 1875, adding 'You may have what length you like – within reasonable bounds – and what number of music illustrations you require'.[53] These were words meant to inspire, no doubt, but they were also asking for trouble. A few years later, with less time and greater experience, the editor was more direct, especially with younger colleagues he could mould. He dashed off a note to Squire in May 1879, unhappy with the way a senior contributor was handling various dance entries; that writer happened to be Prout ('a man who never danced a step'):

> ...I don't only want them to be looked at musically though that of course is the great consideration – but there should be some idea given of what the dance is, and...there seems to be endless interesting information. ...Will you take Ländler, Lancers and Mazurka to try your hand. Lancers is probably a modification of Quadrille and could be diversified with a few words, but Ländler wants doing – also it is rather urgent so what thou doest do quickly. Pray don't refuse. You may quote an example or two (melody only unless the accompaniment is really necessary).[54]

The hint is not only about getting on with things, since the L's were in hand, but about putting some life into the content, cogently. Grove made further suggestions about Squire's 'Ländler' when it came, sharpening his reference points, querying the examples, trimming the speculation, and sending him back to sources – in short, teaching his young protégé how to research and write up what was required.[55] The method bore fruit. Squire's next assignment, 'Luther', was made in late June and completed within a month, engaging both editor and assistant in a process of discovery.[56] The finished article, nearly four columns, has an admirably clear focus, with pertinent work-list and bibliography. Meanwhile Squire polished off several more dances, pinpointing on a list of 45 others ('Matacin' to 'Varsoviana') those that could be omitted.[57] By September he was putting together the joint entry on 'Musical Libraries', a strikingly informative piece that grew from Grove's curiosity about manuscript collections and his flair for thinking laterally.[58]

All three of the *Dictionary*'s sub-editors, Parry (1875 to about 1880), Squire (1878 to 1885) and Fuller Maitland (1879 to 1889), assisted with research, original writing, structural editing, proof-reading and correction. From the letters that survive, Squire seems to have been the closest to Grove personally, or perhaps the most useful during an intensive period of work. Grove certainly admired his linguistic skills, and trusted his judgment about historical and documentary matters.[59] When consulted by Leslie Stephen about musicians to be included in the *DNB*, Grove put Squire up for that advisory job instead.[60] Two years later he encouraged and actively supported Squire's application for an assistant keeper's post at the British Museum, admitting that in Britain 'we want a good musical archaeologist of the rank of Jahn or Nottebohm or Ambros – and why should not you be he? (and a great deal better?)'.[61] If anybody won George Grove over to the potential benefits of a home-grown 'musicology', it was William Barclay Squire. For his part, Hubert Parry played a different but equally important role as Grove's technical adviser on purely musical issues. He studied printed and manuscript music at the Museum to convey his opinion and suggest exemplars, and wrote authoritatively on forms, genres and compositional devices – some 120 entries, including big ones such as 'Form', 'Sonata', 'Suite' and 'Symphony'.[62] But perhaps his most significant contribution was psychological. Every editor needs a confidant and a sounding board. Grove needed one who understood music in ways he did not but who could also appreciate his tastes and emotional responses. When the work began to build up and Parry was not so close at hand, Grove missed him. He wrote to his friend in April 1880:

> I want some one near me whose advice & assistance I can lean upon – & now you are away I feel all abroad. The big articles I am easy about, but the hundreds of little ones, which, though not important want a musician to deal with them – they frighten me.[63]

There is a clue here about Grove's fundamental insecurity: he was in charge of a book that he now realized was seriously behind and still had to cover a lot of routine specialist things, more than he had perhaps imagined. Fuller Maitland, a good pianist, could easily pick up a lot of these entries, including performance terms and smaller forms.[64] He also began to serve, with Squire, on a sort of sweep-up team for late corrections as well as for entries that had been missed or done inadequately earlier in the alphabet. At one stage Grove envisaged the two of them compiling the Appendix together, but that task eventually fell to Maitland alone, always careful and efficient in his work if not as warmly attached to the editor in a personal way.

From Maitland's single surviving letter to Grove in the Macmillan archives, an early one, we see the novice assistant reporting his progress, aiming to please, in July 1879:

> My dear Mr. Grove,
>
> I have taken all the articles except Marchand & Magyar to Bedford Street, together with Mendel [*Musikalisches Conversations-Lexikon*], for which

please accept my best thanks. As to Magyar, I had an introduction to Reményi, who knows all about it, but he being in Russia there is no time to write to him. However, I hope for information from Mr. Lichtenstein in Edinburgh which ought to come in a day or two. Meanwhile, I have got a lot from the Monthly Musical Record for 1877, two articles without signature, apparently by Barry [Charles Ainslie Barry], which contain all I want, only I don't know about "cribbing". I have not taken any of his ideas or things, but I suppose fact may be taken, he having got them out of German articles in papers, &c. Should one own one's obligation in any way, or write to him for permission to use his materials? Of course when Lichtenstein's information comes, I can use that in preference to the M.M.R. but suppose it doesn't?!! I am so sorry to trouble you, but what is to be done? Marchand is just ready.

Yrs ever,
J.A. Fuller Maitland[65]

This letter opens a window on research and writing methods used in the *Dictionary* – consultation of other dictionaries and recent music periodicals, direct enquiry of experts, concern over the acknowledgment of sources – reminding us that past techniques were not at all dissimilar to current ones. Examples recur many times in Grove's letters and in other material including Husk's notes.[66] We know, for instance, that the British Museum collections were a constant resource for questions on earlier music,[67] but that for newer music and books, Grove begged or borrowed from his publishing friends such as Chappell and Novello.[68] The editor also freely lent works from his own library where this would get someone going or solve a query. Besides Mendel's dictionary, and Dr Johnson's, he used that of Fétis, and books on individual composers or national traditions, including Spitta's Bach biography, Nottebohm's Beethoven studies, Karasowki's life of Chopin, Sowinski's book on Polish musicians and Proske's *Musica divina* collection.[69] Among his most frequently consulted periodicals were the *Neue Zeitschrift für Musik*, the *Revue et gazette musicale* and the *Musical World*.[70] Of course Grove had never been shy of asking or writing directly for advice and information – from his performer friends Joachim, Piatti and Pauer,[71] his contacts in officialdom such as W.G. Cusins, and from authorities abroad, whether a M. Bannelier (on French military music) or the eminent Alphonse Goovaerts. In a pinch, the editor even sent an office junior across London to interview a subject's mother.[72] His imagination was the only limit to his quest for information. On the issue of acknowledgment, Grove's advice to contributors had originally been straightforward: 'In citing authorities it is desirable to do so immediately after the statement to be supported, and not to put a long catalogue of names and works at the end of the article which can only be verified with difficulty.'[73] But this instruction soon proved too limited. Many authors gave direct sources in the prose as well as further suggestions and any personal acknowledgments at the end. Grove's attitude was generally accommodating, with footnotes offering a useful alternative. Composer work-lists and bibliographies were never *de rigueur*. Where they were offered, the editor accepted and printed them – features that, together with the author's initials on each article, put his book in the vanguard of reference publishing.

Our picture of internal office systems remains vague because much of the editorial work was done at Grove's home in Sydenham (after mid-1877), and the printing in small tranches at Oxford; all the edited copy and proofs, together with most of the contributor correspondence, seem to have disappeared.[74] But certain procedures are clear enough in Grove's letters to Parry and Squire. Once submitted, manuscripts were acknowledged and their receipt recorded.[75] Action then depended on the seniority of the contributor, the quality and interest of the piece, and, presumably, Grove's assessment of his future dependence on that writer. Where the article was good enough to 'blue', the editor marked it up fairly swiftly and sent it for typesetting; in little more than three weeks a galley proof could be returned to the contributor.[76] When a batch of galleys accumulated within a letter, Grove then passed this to a sub-editor for sense reading, which produced further suggestions for tightening, cross-checking and general improvement. The galleys were in some ways more like 'live' working copy than finished articles, and even page proofs could continue to throw up new ideas or names needing explication.[77] Meanwhile, where a submitted manuscript was unsatisfactory, Grove had either to work it over himself, give it to one of his assistants to fix (with guidance), or re-commission the article – contingent on topic, available time and finding a competent writer.[78] In rare cases, a hoped-for contributor simply backed out, leaving Grove in difficulty at a late stage: thus we might have had Jenny Lind-Goldschmidt or even Clara Novello as the author of 'Singing', for example, rather than Harry Deacon.[79] As to matters of style and consistency, Grove's printed rules were admirably brief: headings for people should give full names in their original form; those for terms should give equivalents in French, German and Italian; and cross-references should be indicated by the use of small capitals. All three rules have been retained to the present day, along with some presentational forms that apparently evolved quickly and naturally.[80] Much less consistent – and notoriously difficult to control in a multi-author book – are matters of orthography and language, name forms and work titles, dates and abbreviations. To his credit, Grove worried far less about whether one should say 'Leipsic' or 'Leipzig', 'Ninth Symphony' or '9th Symphony', than that each sentence should add something interesting and relevant to the reader's understanding.

The problem was that quite a few sentences turned out to be interesting and relevant – more than Grove or his publisher had counted on, and many more than he felt able to cut. The cumulative effect, together with all the new ideas as work progressed, was disastrous for the schedule and extent of the *Dictionary*. Part of the difficulty came from the editor's open-handed commissioning policy, notably with senior contributors.[81] It is also true that Grove's encounter with the fruits of music research, including his own, surprised no one more than himself and began to affect his views about what the *Dictionary* should contain. On the one hand, as an experienced editor he knew when an article was too long or diffuse; and he was aware that some authors were producing more than was necessary, or more than his personal taste might have allowed for the same subjects.[82] But on the other hand, gradually it dawned on him that music embraced more than the concert repertoire of his lifetime, and that musical history was intriguingly relational and suggestive. At the bottom of a letter to Squire in late 1879 he wrote:

> NB. Worries of an Editor – Rockstro sends me a Life of Monteverde – admirable & most readable & thoroughly new, but filling 8 pages! when 4 is the utmost I ought to allow. Mrs. Julian Marshall sent a life of Morlacchi filling 3 ditto when 1 is all I can give.
>
> [PS] Monteverde was quite the Wagner of his day.[83]

Five years later, we find Grove telling the same colleague, by the mid-1880s something of an authority on early English keyboard music, not that he should shorten his article on 'Virginal Music' but that he should remember to add something about a certain relevant manuscript in the British Museum 'which looks alarmingly interesting'.[84] The editor's keenness is unmistakable, even though the alarm here was more about time than length. Grove's next sentence reads: 'I don't want to hurry you but all of a sudden someday I shall be gasping for the article.' Regardless of length or time constraints, however, Grove now wanted every possible detail that might increase the novelty and authority of his book. By 1884 the *Dictionary*'s reputation went before it, and reader expectations had risen.[85]

The editor's growing reluctance to impose cuts may have been connected, too, with the knowledge that his own big articles, 'Beethoven', 'Mendelssohn' and 'Schubert', were 'awfully long'.[86] The research for these had engrossed and excited him, and the writing, carried on amid everything else, had barely been controlled or submitted to another editorial hand. But perhaps from the start, they were going to be special anyway. Falling fortuitously in the letters B–M–S, like an engineer's tripod, this group was surely designed to spread Grove's main pieces across the publishing schedule, at the same time forming the book's central structure and pointing its appeal to his imagined readers. It was a good idea in principle, and produced what were popularly considered the biographical glories of the book (these three entries were retained, with few changes, to the fourth edition in 1940).[87] Yet the familiar style and detail of these articles, and their extraordinary length when compared with anything else in the book (except 'Schumann'), are so out of step as to suggest Grove was on a different planet from his other contributors, or at least unable to put the claims of the whole *Dictionary* before those of his own research. The discrepancy was noted by critics, at least one of them a *Dictionary* contributor. Handel was given ten pages, Mendelssohn 58; J.S. Bach five pages and Schubert 63 – figures that cannot possibly be explained by contemporary taste and awareness.[88]

The inflationary trend across the whole book is seen at its simplest in successive title-page declarations, from 1879, 1880 and 1883, of yet one more volume in the total series.[89]. Whereas some degree of stretching was evident early on – a quarter of the way through the original planned two volumes, for example, published entries were still only in the B's and C's – a much greater expansion began to show from the beginning of Volume III, in the P's. The cause was not merely wordy contributors or Grove's enthusiasm for Schubert, but a conjunction of factors in how the work was managed from about 1880 – just the time when Grove's contract was drawing to a close, when Squire and Maitland with their more scholarly tendencies began to influence content, and when, at a practical level, earlier problems came home to roost. Topics that had been difficult to assign and thus pushed down in the alphabet, for instance, were now tackled and creatively renamed: rather than 'Military Band' or 'Military Music' we have the ingenious headword, and amazingly detailed entry, 'Sounds and Signals, Military'.[90] Even subjects Grove had earlier resisted, including acoustical ones, began to be slipped in when he could find a suitably intelligible author.[91] Similarly, musical people who had been inadvertently, or even deliberately, left out when their slot came up – Campra, Logroscino and Salmon, to name three – were reconsidered in light of the wider net cast by the editors from this period.[92] For alphabet letters already passed, the Appendix became an ever more handy receptacle. But Grove also inserted, where he saw the opportunity, substantial signed footnotes to related articles in a later letter by a different author. Florence Marshall's 'Logroscino' appears within Rockstro's 'Opera', for example, and Husk's 'Salmon' comes under Hipkins's 'Spinet'[93] – raising the obvious question of how a user was ever to find these entries (another problem yet to be solved). As if old loose ends were not enough, new ones kept popping up. There were fresh discoveries about early music, some of it much earlier than the limit of 1450 Grove had originally set but impossible to ignore; a steady growth in the output and importance of modern composers; and an eager influx of information from centres well beyond London – Philadelpia and Rome, for example.[94] Entries in all these categories seem to multiply through the last two volumes.

As scope grew wider and time stretched ahead, the coverage in material still in preparation naturally began to swell. A kind of 'mission creep' set in that Grove seemed powerless to control – made worse by the feeling, after about 1881, that he no longer needed to. Although he had tried to re-negotiate his contract as early as May 1879, foreseeing the workload and asking Macmillan and Craik for a special agreement about the *Dictionary*, the publishers had been unmoved. Indeed they were surprised he even asked since they had given him a chance to pull out of the project two years before and he had refused.[95] But in June of Grove's last contracted year, 1880, Alexander Macmillan contrived a way to keep the editor going for a final stint: he offered an additional one-off payment of £800 on completion of the *Dictionary*, and an increase of £200 on Grove's salary as editor of the *Magazine*. The editor gratefully accepted.[96] Moreover, that July Grove enjoyed a grand testimonial dinner with a purse of 1,000 guineas given by friends and colleagues. Though this event was ostensibly a general appreciation of his wide-ranging career, it was perfectly timed – and certainly supported by Macmillan – to bolster Grove in a personal way and keep the project afloat. The additional gift of a gold chronometer, an accurate timepiece, must have seemed more than apt.[97] With his employment as literary adviser officially over, however, any incentive to finish by a certain date was effectively removed. From 1882 a sense of drift carried the book still further into the future. Parry got busier with composition, and Grove became involved in RCM planning. Squire ploughed on, but the chief editor found it hard to concentrate on the *Dictionary* and Maitland came to the fore, ensuring the most up-to-date information was inserted in the Appendix – from Alkan's death date to a full Beethoven work-list and major new entries on Byrd, Dvořák, 'Negro Music' and 'Psalter'.[98] Things had moved on since 1874: the Appendix took up three fascicles.

If one vignette captures the challenge and changing mood of this later period, it must be the crisis over Squire's 'Waltz' in 1885. He had accepted the commission with other dance entries years before, but was unaware of the exact moment the article would be needed, meantime working on other ones in the U's and V's besides doing some translation. By mid-September Grove began asking about 'Waltz', hinting that it might be required soon, depending on the extent of page proofs for part 21 (Volume IV, part 3). On 30 September the editor knew the answer:

> Dear S.,
>
> I am afraid that I am in a horrid fix about Waltz. It is <u>just</u> wanted to fill up the last sheet of the new Part – I don't really know what to do. Could you not possibly suspend your translation and do the article[?] The Part has dragged on so that I dare not delay it farther.
>
> Yours most perturbed
>
> G. Grove[99]

In fact Squire could not do the article in a hurry and Grove used the stop-gap of a forward cross-reference – 'WALTZ and WALTZ À DEUX TEMPS.

(See p.385.)'. Then he carried on with succeeding entries. When 'Waltz' was eventually printed 18 months later, after 'Water Music', it was of course out of sequence – not the first time Grove appeared to have misfiled several pages.[100] To make matters worse from Squire's perspective, the editor in his zeal to enliven things had taken the liberty of inserting a vivid physical description, from Henry Crabb Robinson's *Diary*, of how the waltz was danced at Frankfurt about 1800 ('The man places the palms of his hands gently against the sides of his partner . . . '). The intervention was not appreciated; Squire felt it discrepant with the scholarly tone he had achieved elsewhere in the entry and said so. Grove apologized, but did not really understand the complaint.[101] For him, scholarship and 'interest' were never mutually exclusive. Yet the balance of priorities in his *Dictionary* had indeed subtly shifted. The book was no longer quite the one he had set out to publish.

'Fancy all Prague in a state of astonishment over us!' (November 1880)

Despite its difficulties and shortcomings, the *Dictionary of Music and Musicians* was a stunning achievement. The book placed an unprecedented range and complexity of music information on the page clearly and attractively, using music examples and fine illustrations and embodying both fact and assessment. From the first fascicle, the press began singing the *Dictionary*'s praises and pointing out faults – a sure sign of impact. Music journals were predictably picky. The *Musical Times* reviewer carped about inaccuracies and omissions but waxed lyrical about some longer entries, including 'Beethoven', 'Bellini', 'Bennett', 'Berlioz', 'Bishop' and later 'Harmony'; he was scathing about 'Hummel'.[102] Such comments, pro and con, were gifts to Grove. They got people talking, and supplied details that could be inserted as corrections later.[103] Reaction in the newspaper press was more generally positive, applauding the book's breadth, lucidity and reader appeal.[104] Important in a different way were reviews in literary journals. At least two of these pieces were broadly friendly, Henry Sutherland Edwards's essay in the *New Quarterly Magazine* (1878) and Louis Engel's in *Temple Bar* (1882).[105] But two more, in the *Edinburgh Review* (1881, 1883), though articulate, were at root deeply critical, especially of Parry's articles ('inclined to be wordy and diffuse') , Grove's lack of control as editor, and both 'Mendelssohn' and 'Schubert'. Not surprisingly, the anonymous writer, Henry Heathcote Statham, was a disaffected contributor whose classical tastes and alliances differed from Grove's more Romantic ones.[106] Grove decided Statham was 'a cankered soul' and tried to comfort Parry.[107] Meanwhile a counterbalance came in almost universal amazement at the idea of what Grove was attempting, and how well he was succeeding. In late 1880 he received a card from Frantisek Urbánek, the Czech music publisher, responding to the gift of a specimen fascicle. Grove passed Urbánek's reaction on to Squire: 'He says "Ihr Dictionary ist ein excellentes Werk, wir all bewündern es". Fancy all Prague in a state of astonishment over us!'[108] Friends in England, too, notably some not in music, were equally enthusiastic, confirming Grove in his support for the amateur.[109] Yet these forms of reception are modest compared with the implicit public acceptance of Grove's *Dictionary*, by the early 1890s, as the new international standard to be corrected. London concert programmes carried emendations to particular entries, as did ongoing 'letters to the editor' in music magazines. A raft of other music reference works came into being that either credited or criticized the *Dictionary*, such as James D. Brown's concise *Biographical Dictionary of Musicians* (1886), with its bibliographical slant, and David Baptie's books giving attention to Scottish composers (1894) and glee composers (1896) he felt Grove had ignored.[110] It was as if Grove's book had tapped a deep vein of British feeling about music, galvanizing research and at the same time opening a new market for differentiated works in the same field.

But what about tangible demand for the *Dictionary* itself between 1878 and 1901? Is it plausible that a book so widely acknowledged, though long in production, was not actually very profitable? In mid-1880, Macmillan & Co. had explained to Grove that the *Dictionary* was unlikely to be remunerative to them.[111] In considering this aspect of the book's reception, we need to look closely at its printing and publishing. Hard sales figures have not survived but print runs are available. Together with reprinting patterns and an estimate of costs and income over the length of the project, these shed considerable light on the question of profitability.

Table 8.1 shows the makeup of each volume in fascicles, the spread of alphabetic coverage, and the date each fascicle was first published.[112] Twelve had been projected, 25 were produced. A single fascicle was normally 128 pages long and sold for 3s 6d – with the two double numbers (15/16 and 17/18) and the triple appendix (numbers 23–5, slightly shorter than three full fascicles) priced accordingly. The parts were issued, like a periodical, with removable paper covers bearing advertisements inside and out.[113] (See Plate 10.) Respective title-pages, and half-titles, were issued with the last fascicle of each volume, and 'cloth cases for binding' were available separately at 1s. From October 1880, new collectors could purchase Volumes I and II already cloth-bound (21s each), though all the parts were also available separately and the *Dictionary* continued to be issued and sold that way; individual fascicles were still available, at the original price, as late as 1899.[114] As Table 8.1 shows, to the beginning of 1881 (part 13) Grove maintained a quarterly output; publication then slowed and became increasingly irregular. Keeping up with the fascicles may have been confusing or clumsy for some original buyers, while intending ones perhaps waited until publication was complete before making their purchase. Eventually the whole *Dictionary*, bound in cloth, cost £4 4s. The

Table 8.1 Original publication of *A Dictionary of Music and Musicians (A.D 1450–1889)*

Vol. I part	1: Aar–Ballad	January	1878*
	2: Ballad–Boieldieu	April	
A–Imp	3: Bolero–Concert-Pitch	July	
	4: Concert-spirituel–Ferrara	October	
	5: Ferrarese del Bene–Guitar	January	1879
	6: Gung'l–Impromptu	April	
Vol. II	7: Improperia–Libretto	July	1879
	8: License–Mendelssohn	October	
Imp–Pla	9: Mendelssohn–Mozart	January	1880
	10: Mozart–Opera	April	
	11: Opera–Palestrina	July	
	12: Palestrina–Plain Song	October	
Vol. III	13: Planché–Richter, Hans	January	1881
	14: Richter–Schoberlechner	July	
Pla–Sum	{15		
	{16: Schoberlechner–Sketches	August	1882
	{17		
	{18: Sketches–Sumer is icumen in	July	1883
Vol. IV	19: Sumer is icumen in–Tirarsi	July	1884
	20: 'Tis the Last Rose of Summer – Verschworenen, Die	March	1885
Sum–Zwi	21: Verse–Water-Music	September	
	22: Watson–Zwischenspiel	Spring	1887
	{23	began printing early	1888
Appendix	{24		
	{25:	finished May	1889
Index and Catalogue		printed June	1889
		published	1890

*The part 1 preface and list of contributors are dated 'Christmas, 1877' but the cover is dated January 1878. In fact the print order was entered at Oxford University Press on 28 December 1877 but not completed until 21 February 1878.

bibliographical and binding variety often found in original sets is one of the most obvious signs that the work was planned and executed in bits, over time. To pull together disparate strands, make the *Dictionary* easier to use, and draw attention to topics and contributors a reader might otherwise overlook, Macmillan employed Mrs Edmond R. Wodehouse to compile an index and catalogue of contributors; these appeared together in a single slim volume in 1890, and sold at an additional 7s 6d.[115]

Table 8.1 also reveals, in the headword ranges, a feature of serial publishing that could be exploited commercially. The double-column text was printed continuously within a volume. Obviously a long article might run across two fascicles in the volume, with a break occuring in the middle of a sentence (e.g. as in 'Mozart' in 9–10), or even in the middle of a word ('Ballad' in 1–2). To some degree this was inevitable since the length of a fascicle was predetermined and the text was not, giving rise to the convention of abrupt textual breaks. But publishers and clever periodical writers (not least Charles Dickens) could also deliberately plan or dramatize breaks to whet the reader's appetite and ensure subsequent purchase of each successive part. A glance at the article coverage in the fascicles of Grove's work shows that breaks happened to fall, or were employed, fairly consistently within the middle two volumes, culminating in what appears to be the anomaly of a break *between* the last two volumes, in the article 'Sumer is icumen in'. In this case, rather than break a word or sentence Grove edited the article – extended by a full transcription of the 'Sumer' canon – so as to conclude one section of it neatly and draw the reader's attention onwards to the next section, in the coming volume, with a tantalizing trailer.[116] Another result, of course, was that the headword 'Sumer is icumen in' would eventually be printed twice, perhaps in gold leaf, on the spines of two adjacent bound volumes. Given the singular importance of the 'Sumer' canon to early English music and the possible precedence over medieval European music it suggested – a matter in lively debate at the time – we can only guess that Grove, influenced by Rockstro (the contributor) and William Chappell (an early authority on the Harleian manuscript containing the piece), meant to highlight this entry as much as possible. The music had already been considered, and a 'photographic facsimile' reproduced, in the appropriate section of Rockstro's earlier 'Schools of Composition'. But Chappell's extraordinary dating of *c* 1226–36 for the canon, and its attribution to a monk of Reading Abbey, 'John of Fornsete', encouraged Grove to milk the patriotic potential of the piece in two ways – to attract attention (and buyers) for the *Dictionary* and, perhaps more questionably, to help raise money for the nascent Royal College of Music. His fund-raising work reached its height at precisely the time he was working on 'S' entries (from late 1881 to early 1883).[117]

All the printing work for the *Dictionary* was undertaken at Oxford University Press, in the first instance because Macmillan & Co. had been London selling agents for OUP books since the 1860s. Contact was cordial, discounts were likely and the printing house was just then expanding its work for outside clients. Oxford also had ready access to paper stocks at its Wolvercote mill, a clear advantage for a serial work in which the edition size might change from part to part. Although little relevant correspondence between the two companies survives, the Oxford printing house ledgers are full of references to 'Grove's D. of M.' from December 1877 to October 1901 and give a highly detailed picture of work done and charges made – far more than Macmillan's own records for the same period. It is chiefly from the Oxford ledgers that the information in Figure 8.1 derives.[118]

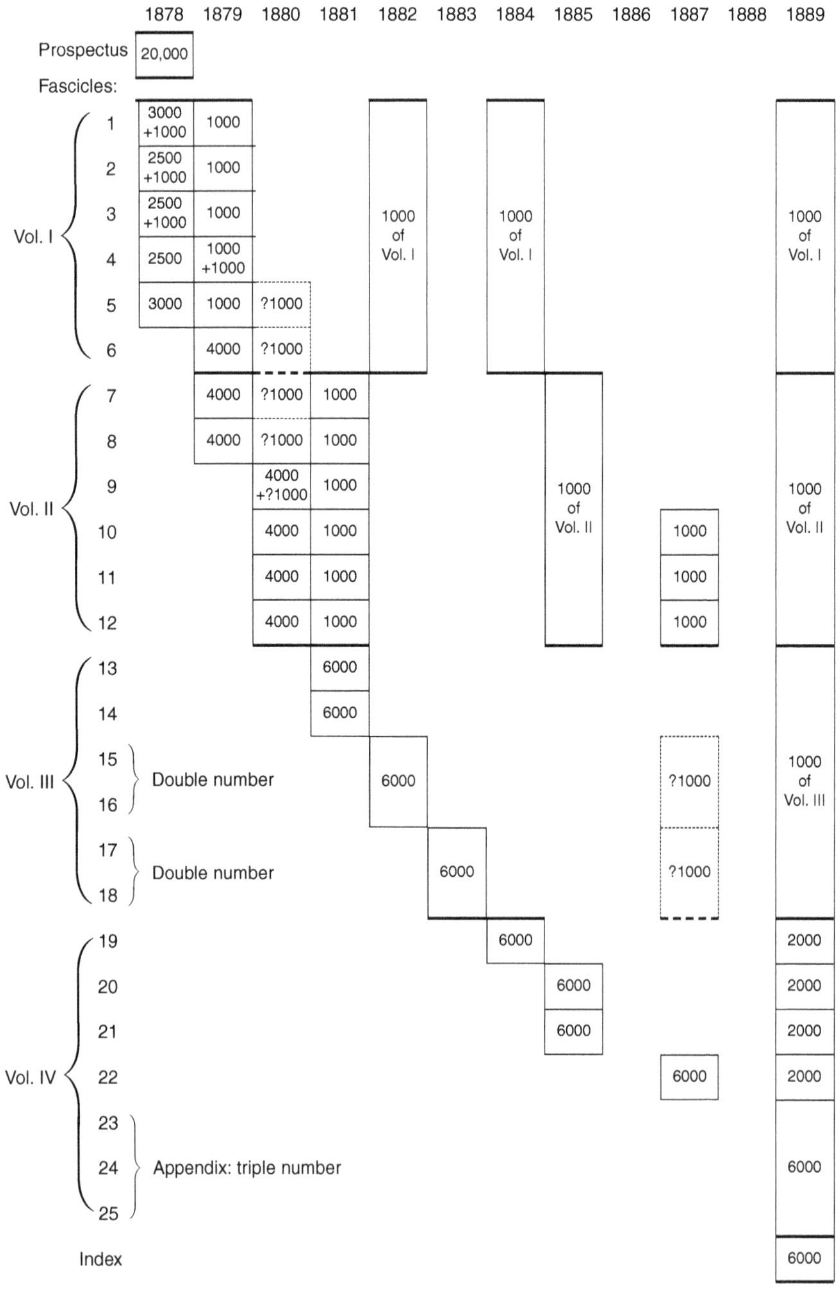

Figure 8.1 Print runs by fascicle, 1878–1901. *Sources*: Clarendon Press Ledgers Nos. 2–5 (OUP Archives, Oxford) and BL Add. MSS 55912 and 55913.

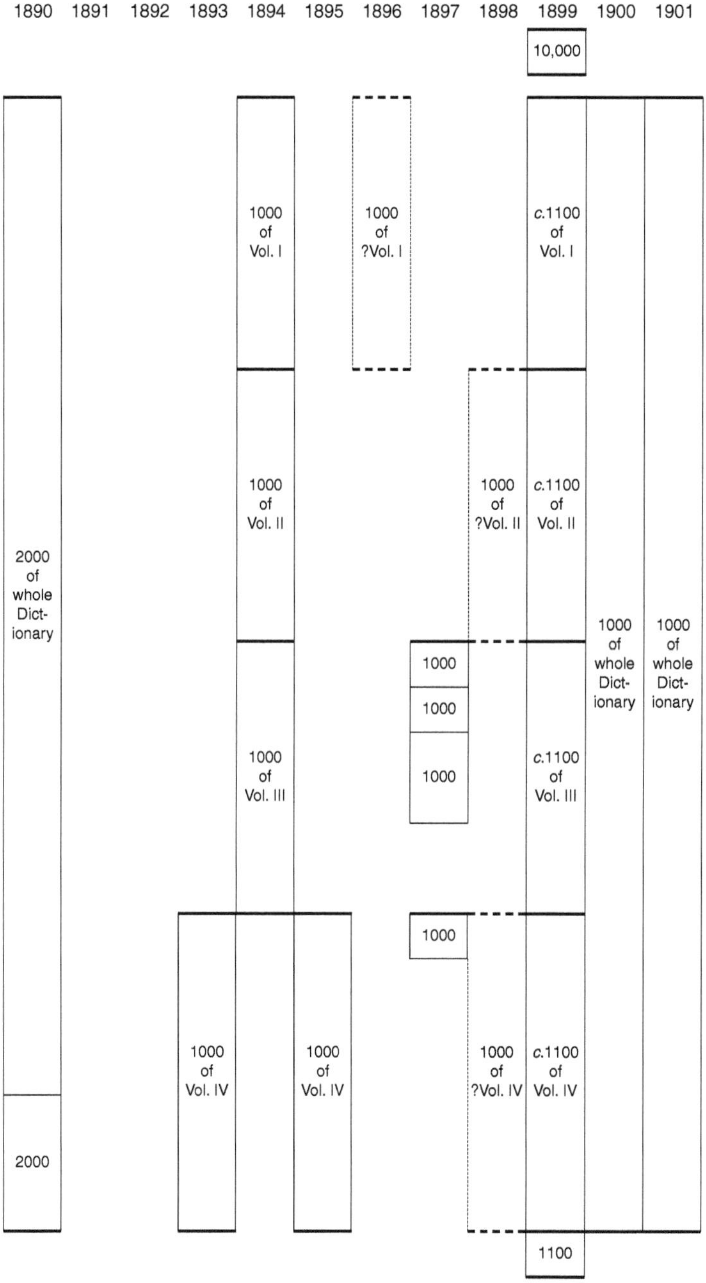

Dotted box and ? indicates a printing fee charged but parts unspecified.

The diagram essentially shows how many copies of each fascicle were printed across the period, from initial publication and any immediate additions, to reprints of complete volumes and ultimately of the whole *Dictionary*. Several patterns are clear from these figures. First, getting the original print order right – matching demand to avoid the risk of unsold copies – took some guesswork and adjustment: 3,000 was a bit high for the first fascicle, but by the sixth, 4,000 was not quite high enough; from part 9 (the middle of Volume II) experiments of up to 5,000 or 6,000 were feasible, and from part 13 (Volume III) onwards, 6,000 became the regular edition size.[119] Second, back numbers were reprinted to keep pace with each jump in the new size, and there was a gradual trend towards the printing and stitching of parts into volumes. Third, the pattern of comprehensive reprints was similarly conservative, with a pull-back in the middle, but it showed an overall trend upwards. The first one, of 2,000 copies, was executed in 1890, just after the whole publishing sequence was completed (note that the Index was not reprinted until 1899, and in any case never reached the number of copies of the *Dictionary* itself). Four years later a short-run reprint of 1,000 copies was undertaken. Then in 1899, a new advertising campaign launched yet another reprint operation, spread out steadily, of approximately 1,000 copies a year over each of the years 1899–1901.[120] This is commonly referred to as the 1900 reprint. It seems to have been the final effort to extend sales of the *Dictionary* before work began on a contemplated second edition.

Allowing for the vagueness of a few ledger entries (reprints of unspecified parts, indicated by dotted boxes with query marks in Figure 8.1, we can see that the total figure of *Dictionary* copies printed by late 1901 came to something between 14,000 and 16,000 – a range much higher than we might have expected from Alexander Macmillan's dour tone with Grove in 1880. And although this may still seem a lot lower than the numbers for J.R. Green's hugely popular *Short History of the English People* (1874) or for a bestseller like Lewis Carroll's *Alice's Adventures in Wonderland* (1865), both published by Macmillan,[121] the *Dictionary*'s performance was nevertheless remarkable for a large reference work on a single subject. Above all, Oxford's measured pattern of reprinting suggests that each upward boost was a response to genuine demand, not idle speculation. Of course 15,000 printed – to take the mean average – does not automatically translate into 15,000 sold: there were promotional giveaways, deposit and wasted copies, perhaps a certain number held in reserve for stock purposes. But even a conservative estimate of sales, rounded downward to, say, 14,000, would have yielded an income on the order of £61,950.[122] If we set known and hypothetical expenditure against that figure, the likely value of Macmillan's copyright on the *Dictionary* begins to come into focus (see Table 8.2).

Simply to subtract total costs from total receipts, however, is unrealistic as a gauge of profitability in such a lengthy project; for it was precisely the relationship between time and money that represented the great risk, and

Table 8.2 Expenditure on the *Dictionary of Music and Musicians*

Item	*Sum (£)*
George Grove's salary	7800
Other editorial costs	3716[123]
Contributors' fees	3125[124]
Paper and printing	6621[125]
Trade discount to booksellers	7434[126]
Advertising	975[127]
Macmillan overheads	2975[128]
Total estimated expenditure	£32,646

potential, of Macmillan's commitment. That is, since time *was* money and rather a lot of it was tied up before any net inflow could be detected, we need an account of cashflows, out and in on an annual basis, to reach a meaningful calculation of probable return on investment.[129] Luckily, such a timed reconstruction is possible for the *Dictionary* from 1874 to 1901, thanks to exact print orders in the OUP ledgers. The outcome is instructive. When both the costs and the income of the project are plotted year by year – using the best available evidence for timings of payments to suppliers and contributors, meanwhile estimating sales conservatively and reckoning publisher's discount at an average of 12 per cent[130] – it becomes clear that cumulative expenditure on the project would have reached a peak in 1880 (the year Macmillan told Grove there would probably be no profit); that from 1881 there would probably have been a net inflow of cash every year but two (1886, 1888); and that all the publisher's initial outlay would have been returned by 1889, followed by well over a decade of further strong inflows ('profit' in a naive sense). To put it in modern financial terms, estimated cashflows over the period 1874–1901 imply an internal rate of return of 11 per cent, which is to say they behaved like a deposit account accruing 11 per cent per annum throughout the period and returning capital in full. Was this actually a strong performance? By comparison, yields on Government bonds at the time were around 2.5–3 per cent.[131] At the very least, Grove's instinct had been right when he replied to Alexander Macmillan's warning note that he still hoped the *Dictionary* 'might turn out a very good property to you'.[132]

As early as March 1892 the editor was lobbying Frederick Macmillan about a second edition that would incorporate the Appendix with the main sequence. Grove strongly suggested publication in numbers again, for buyers who could not afford four volumes at once. The 'extremely intelligent' person he recommended to do the compilation was the critic Charles L. Graves[133]. Nothing much came of this idea, however, which would have entailed expensive re-setting, so Grove tried again five years later, writing to his old office-mate George Macmillan, now a director of the company:

> Have you ever thought of the necessity (or at least the advisability) of having a new edition of the Dictionary, or if not...a second appendix?
>
> A great many musical men have gone out of the world, and a great many come into it since 1890 or indeed since 1879 when we published the first volume; and so much change has taken place...that I think we ought at least to consider it. – To name only two, the development of Wagner and the rise of the Russian School. In England also a great deal has taken place which ought to be dealt with.[134]

But again, discussion dragged and in autumn 1898 Grove was still pushing for a decision. He had now reached agreement that Fuller Maitland would do the editing and J.S. Shedlock would help with 'Beethoven'.[135] As we have seen, the firm instead decided to reprint the first edition one more time. Grove had to accept this strategy, though he knew the *Dictionary*'s success had vindicated his earliest intuitions and the book would appear in an up-to-date revision one day. He died in May 1900. Macmillan & Co. authorized the start of the second edition nearly two years later, in March 1902.

Before work commenced on that version, the main points at issue were the following: extent (what to cut, what to add, and whether the whole thing could be squeezed into the same amount of space); how to deal with Grove's big articles (whether to condense them a bit, publish them separately and condense a lot, or completely re-commission); the possible use of composers' portraits (to increase popular appeal); whether Graves ought to co-edit the book with Maitland (to help maintain the pace of work); and whether to publish in parts again.[136] All these points show the firm's acknowledgment of difficulties with the first edition. Maitland conferred with both Parry and Graves before reporting back to George Macmillan. The clear feeling was that it was best to leave Grove's articles as they stood, but jettison Rockstro's 'Schools of Composition' as well as entries on people who were not themselves musicians; that an article on acoustics was needed among other big topics, and hence a fifth volume was desirable; and that composer portraits, suggested by the company, were not wanted (Parry thought they would lower the dignity of the book). Further, Maitland much preferred to 'let the whole work appear at once' so that earlier parts of the alphabet would not appear so out of date with the rest, and he was privately against the idea of collaborating with Graves.[137] Almost like clockwork, the five volumes of the second edition – what Maitland himself called 'the new Grove' – appeared at regular intervals from 1904 to 1910. In content the book was a careful amalgam rather than a new work, just as Grove had suggested, and it too had its critics and supporters.[138] Up to 1922, *Grove 2* reached a total print order of 7,000 copies.[139] Although this number was less than half that of the first edition, owing partly to the exigencies of the First World War and its aftermath, the *Dictionary* now took 'Grove' into its title for the first time, monumentalizing the man as well as his achievement. It was the beginning of a truly modern music-reference phenomenon, yet one ever further removed from the founder and his world.

*

At the end of a large and challenging project, one is tempted to look back and see how things might have been done differently, or how they should have been done in the first place. But George Grove was a journalist, not a historian: he looked ahead, not back. And posterity has surely been better served because his *Dictionary* was a quirky affair, bumpy and uneven, open to new ideas and personal foible as work unfolded, rather than perfectly controlled or rigidly consistent. For the great underlying value of the *Dictionary of Music and Musicians* has always been historiographical.[140] A continuous record of 16 years' effort, by a community of identifiable authors on topics seen to be important at the moment of writing, it was out of date as soon as each fascicle was published. If the flexibility Grove displayed was meant to counter obsolescence, that ultimately failed, as it was bound to; information and opinion developed constantly between 1874 and 1890 and of course have never stopped. On the contrary, Grove knew that the book's reflection of change, like a morning newspaper, added hugely to its interest for contemporary readers. It continues to attract modern ones. Looking into the *Dictionary* now, we can identify with those readers, making links and connections but also discovering endless contingencies that spark further explanation and refinement. The process itself is a sign of the ongoing usefulness of the book, and a salutary reminder not of how ignorant or amateurish our Victorian predecessors were, but of how much they got right and of how exciting the initial work must have been. Modern musicology, and modern publishing, would do well to recapture the co-operative spirit, purpose and precision Grove's project achieved.

Yet the first *Dictionary of Music and Musicians* might so easily have never happened. In one sense the idea was perfectly timed. When Grove first approached Macmillan music and historical research, professional infrastructures and the popular 'drawing power' of musicians had come together to make such a work possible for the first, and perhaps the last, time. Any earlier and there would have been insufficient materials and unequal contributors; any later, and there would have been too many specialists and too much information for a coherent book addressed to all. Even so, the project was nearly cancelled for lack of entrepreneurial confidence. It was Grove's determination alone that saved the book, and his peculiar combination of skills and interests that stamped it with humanity rather than genius. As a civil engineer, he knew about competing forces and shifting sands; as a site manager, he knew how to organize equipment and people. Both kinds of experience served him well when original plans had to be altered, and tensions arose. But above all, it was his intellectual curiosity as a listener – self-taught – and his journalistic skill as an editor that brought the *Dictionary* to life. These are the real roots of Grove's legacy, and reflect alike a strong performing tradition in nineteenth-century Britain and an unsurpassed literary one, each with its overlapping circles of keen concert-goers and voracious readers.

Larger meanings are harder to pin down. Perhaps the best clue lies in the force of print in a culture that was increasingly devoted to it. A book on any topic is a solid artefact with fixed words and sentences, reproduceable in any number of copies, holding the power of persuasion. A big reference book attempting to define and explain music through clear and authoritative voices, for the first time in English, rightly claimed international attention in the 1870s and 1880s. What the *Dictionary of Music and Musicians* particularly signified in Britain comes into view when we set it against other kinds of music endeavour taking place there at the same time, and against artefacts in other cultural spheres – painting, sculpture, books of fiction or poetry, buildings. That is, a monumental English book on music by its very nature inscribed and endorsed the musical intelligence of the nation, when neither evanescent musical performance nor native composers could do the job.[141] For Grove and others in the Victorian clerisy like him, what mattered indeed was not so much Britain's own musical eminence or the lack of it (Grove never believed British composers were a patch on the best German ones anyway) as the nation's unique capacity to understand, incorporate and champion good music, whatever its origin, style or date. Perception, breadth of judgment, susceptibility to musical art and study: these were the values Grove promoted in his *Dictionary*. And in its weighty but intricate form the book came to be regarded, like the Britannia Bridge or the Crystal Palace, as one more sign of a civilized, free and advanced society.

To what extent the same book may have paved the way for the Royal College of Music is another matter. Curiously – or perhaps logically under the circumstances – this was not the first time in nineteenth-century Britain that a music dictionary alluding to national accomplishment coincided with the founding of a London conservatoire. John Sainsbury's *Dictionary of Musicians from the Earliest Ages to the Present Time* (1824), also international in scope, was from its outset designed to encourage public subscriptions for the struggling Royal Academy of Music in the early 1820s.[142] By contrast, Grove never set out to use his *Dictionary* in this or any other way, and in both content and execution his book was in a different league from Sainsbury's. But given an enterprise culture in which music enjoyed little or no state support and literature could aid any cause, both Sainsbury and Grove saw the benefit of exciting patriotic feelings when purely musical ones were insufficient to build national training schools. Allowing himself to be swayed by the possibilities of English historicism and a kind of English musical precedence – and latterly by a hope of the RCM directorship – Grove clearly fell in with official attempts to get patriotic money out of the social and business elite in the early 1880s.[143] Eventually, this short-term goal had little effect on either the direction or validity of the *Dictionary*; in any case, Grove knew perfectly well that the historiography of early English music was still incomplete.[144]

More broadly interesting is the speed at which this stout printed book bestowed a whole new identity on the editor as a literate musical expert – a gentleman – above the fray of working musicians and cloistered academics. The *Dictionary* itself became a virtual centre of cultural authority – a national institution – independent of all schools, academies, universities, libraries, concert halls, choirs, orchestras, publishers and periodicals.[145] Was it merely a passing illusion, this lift-off for Grove and his book, or the breakthrough into respectability that music in England had always sought? The man has gone, but the book is still here, consciously remaking itself for new generations of committed listeners and readers. That is surely what George Grove would have hoped for, and all he ever really wanted.

Notes

This chapter is an expanded version of a paper read at the Royal College of Music in June 2000, and presented in another form at the 67th Annual Meeting of the American Musicological Society in Atlanta, Georgia, in November 2001. For financial assistance I am indebted to the *Music & Letters* Trust and to Goldsmiths College, University of London.

1. Grove to William Barclay Squire, 17 December [1881] referring specifically to the editing of W.S. Rockstro's long and effusive article on the modern British school (British Library [hereafter BL] Add. MS 39679, f.66). Elsewhere Grove declared publicly about the *Dictionary*: 'The work is full of drudgery and has to be done in a hurry' (*Musical World*, 58, 31 (31 July 1880), p.485).
2. The *New Grove*'s record alone would have dumbfounded Alexander Macmillan. From 1980 to the end of 1999 it sold 55,000 copies – 25,000 in hardback and 30,000 in paper. I am grateful to Ian Jacobs for these figures.
3. Grove had flashes of vanity, but was irritated by popular perceptions of him as some kind of musical hero. In 1897 he admitted to F.G. Edwards: 'But to tell the truth, I am perfectly sick of trying to tell the details of my life. People will insist on thinking of me as a musician, which I really am not in the very least degree. I took quite as much interest in my investigation into the natural features and the little towns of Palestine which I did for Smith's Dictionary of the Bible, or for Arthur Stanley's "Sinai and Palestine", as I did for Beethoven and Mendelssohn; indeed perhaps more…' (Grove to Edwards, 15 September 1897, BL Egerton MS 3091, ff.207v-8). Among modern attempts to cast Grove in the opposite role of villain, Robert Stradling and Meirion Hughes's *The English Musical Renaissance, 1860–1940: Construction and Deconstruction* (London and New York, 1993) is similarly wide of the mark in its depiction of the content and purpose of the *Dictionary* as essentially nationalistic (pp.19–21). Given notions of German musical hegemony in late nineteenth and early twentieth-century Britain, such a reading is predictable but superficial and ill-founded.

4. From a one-page announcement: 'Preparing for Publication: the Dictionary of Music (A.D. 1450–1874)', London: Macmillan & Co., March 1874; bound with 'General Directions for Contributors' and several headword lists (Royal College of Music, Library XXII.E.24 (4), copy of A.J. Hipkins). Note that the original dictionary title was simply 'of Music'; biography, the last of the intelligent inquirer's interests, was subsumed within the general subject. Grove was probably contacting potential contributors by January 1874, but there is no evidence of a printed prospectus before this one, of March.
5. His first and longest instruction in the 'General Directions for Contributors' spelt out what he wanted: 'Contributors will be kind enough to compress their articles as much as possible, consistently with giving all necessary facts of and about the subject. The aim should be to make the articles interesting to the amateur, without sacrificing exact treatment; avoiding technical statement and technical words as far as possible, and putting the subject in a non-professional point of view. In biographies, anecdotes, if characteristic and authentic, should by no means be excluded, as they often preserve important traits of character.'
6. For a cogent overview of the subject, see James B. Coover, 'Dictionaries and encyclopedias of music', *The New Grove Dictionary of Music and Musicians*, ed. Stanley Sadie (London and Basingstoke, 1980), v, pp.430–59; revised in *The New Grove Dictionary of Music and Musicians*, 2nd edn (London, 2001), vii, pp.306–20.
7. Preface to Vol. I of *A Dictionary of Music and Musicians (A.D. 1450–1879) by Eminent Writers, English and Foreign* (London, 1879), dated 1 April 1879, p. v.
8. Coover repeatedly points out that deeper national coverage of the music and musicians in the country of a dictionary's compilation – even in the best international ones such as Gerber and Fétis – has been both a firm tradition and, for users, a strength.
9. The earliest *Musical Times* review of the *Dictionary* registers this skepticism, suggesting that the earnest editor 'has scarcely yet fully realised' the difficulties of his scheme. *Musical Times*, 19, 420 (February 1878), p.84.
10. For this and many of the details in this section, I am indebted to Robert Collison, *Encyclopaedias: Their History Throughout the Ages* (New York and London, 1964, 2nd edn 1966), pp.xiii–xvi, 1–20, 174–228 (at 12). From the mid-nineteenth century, practical explications increasingly replaced the lengthy philosophical discussions prominent in older encyclopedias.
11. Grove worked for seven years as Smith's principal assistant on *A Dictionary of the Bible* (published 1860–63). In 1864 he undertook a further assignment, on Smith's *Atlas of Ancient Geography, Biblical and Classical* (1874). Smith had already made his reputation with the scholarly *Dictionary of Greek and Roman Antiquities* for Murray (1842), and followed it with dictionaries of *Greek and Roman Biography* (1849) and *Greek and Roman Geography* (1857), both later recalled by Grove as examples of Murray's enterprising spirit (see n.40 below).
12. See Giorgio Tonelli, *A Short-Title List of Subject Dictionaries of the Sixteenth, Seventeenth and Eighteenth Centuries as Aids to the History of Ideas* (London, 1971); see also the remarkable collection of early subject dictionaries in the Department of Special Collections, Glasgow University Library. Even Dr Johnson's *Dictionary* (1755) was designed as an aid to professional writers, printers and proof-readers.
13. Coover, in 'Dictionaries and encyclopedias' and in his *Music Lexicography* (Carlisle, PA, 1971), is my first point of reference for this vast subject. Here I give only the barest outline.

14. Walther's *Musicalisches Lexicon*, issued in Leipzig, was the first music encyclopedia and prototype for all subsequent ones; it was also one of the first ever to include living persons. Moreover, Walther was the first music lexicographer to collect information by sending inquiries to other authorities; he did not hesitate to offer opinion and speculation about music. Gerber's *Historisch-biographisches Lexicon der Tonkünstler*, also issued in Leipzig (1790–92), relied on Walther's work, but later appeared in a much-improved second edition (*Neues historisch-biographisches Lexicon der Tonkünstler*, 1812–14) complementing the first.
15. Dictionary instalments as running magazine features were especially popular in England. Although an abridged version of J.-J. Rousseau's music dictionary of 1768 had appeared in the *New Musical and Universal Magazine* in 1775–76, it was Samuel Arnold and Thomas Busby who in the 1780s executed the first, and most ambitious, original music dictionary in an English periodical – 'An Universal Dictionary of Music', appended to weekly musical parts of the *New Musical Magazine* (London, 1783–85). The text, nearly 500 pages, covered terms, topics and biographies, and continued to the letter 'M' before publication ceased; it was probably chiefly Arnold's work (drawing on Grassineau, Rousseau, Burney and Hawkins), and not the same thing as Busby's later *Complete Dictionary of Music* (London, 1801). Among later music magazines attempting a lexicon department were *Musical Miscellanies* (1784) and *The Harmonicon* (1823). See Leanne Langley, 'The English Musical Journal in the Early Nineteenth Century' (PhD diss., University of North Carolina, Chapel Hill, 1983), pp.446–53, 508–14.
16. Two prime examples are James Grassineau's *A Musical Dictionary of Terms* (London, 1740), heavily reliant on Brossard in translation; and John Sainsbury's *Dictionary of Musicians from the Earliest Ages to the Present Time* (London, 1824), based on William Bingley's *Musical Biography* (London, 1813) and on the Choron-Fayolle *Dictionnaire historique des musiciens* (Paris, 1810–11). Such transfers were common publishing practice in England – not only legal but desirable where the original was in a foreign language, out of print or difficult of access. Neither Grassineau nor Sainsbury is a negligible work, however. Sainsbury's book is important for its original material on living musicians as well as for the social and political context in which it was produced; see Leanne Langley, 'Sainsbury's *Dictionary*, the Royal Academy of Music, and the Rhetoric of Patriotism', in *Music and British Culture, 1785–1914: Essays in Honour of Cyril Ehrlich*, ed. Christina Bashford and Leanne Langley (Oxford, 2000), pp.65–97.
17. See Alvin Kernan, *Samuel Johnson & the Impact of Print* (Princeton, NJ, 1987), pp.181–203.
18. Ann Parry, 'The Grove Years 1868–1883: a "new look" for *Macmillan's Magazine*?', *Victorian Periodicals Review*, 19 (1986), pp.149–57, demonstrates this point. Indeed, partly to accommodate more articles on musical, historical and religious topics, Grove deliberately reduced the *Magazine*'s literary content, notably serialized novels – an extraordinary innovation at the time.
19. Novello, Ewer & Co.'s Music Primers began with Ernst Pauer's *The Pianoforte* in 1877 (Stainer's own *The Organ* was third in the series) and achieved more than forty titles under Stainer's editorship (latterly with Parry) to the 1890s; these included textbooks in harmony, analysis, fugue and tonic solfa, as well as dictionaries of terms, pianists and violin makers. Grove's series for Macmillan also began in 1877, with Franklin Taylor's *A Primer of Pianoforte Playing*, but failed to achieve momentum.

20. F.-J. Fétis's *Biographie universelle des musiciens* (Brussels, 1835–44; revised and enlarged, 1860–65) and Gustav Schilling's *Encyclopädie der gesammten musikalischen Wissenschaften, oder Universal Lexikon der Tonkunst* (Stuttgart, 1835–8; supplement, 1841–2) were landmark works, setting new standards. Despite its inaccuracies and bias, Fétis's book was readable, clear and full of personality. Schilling's was massive, containing much reliable information not available elsewhere. Both were used by Grove (his copy of the second edition of Fétis is now in the RCM Library).
21. Mendel's work (12 vols, Berlin, 1870–80; 2nd edn, 1883), like Schilling's, was encyclopedic but expressly addressed to 'Gebildete aller Stände'. It was produced by a team of musical experts under Mendel's direction until his death in 1876, and thereafter completed by August Reissmann (from 1877 Francis Hueffer was on the committee). One of the most highy valued music-reference works of the period, it may have been a direct inspiration to Grove for its familiar approach, ease of use and collaborative working method; he certainly consulted it and recommended it to his own contributors.
22. Part-issue was not only congenial to Grove from his *Magazine* work, but probably crucial in selling the dictionary idea to Macmillan. By spreading costs and generating income before publication was complete, the company would be able to offer each part at an affordable price, encouraging gradual purchase of what many readers could not have afforded all at once. The title as we know it must have been fixed by late 1877, with 'Musicians' added for reader appeal.
23. 'Sir George Grove, C.B.', *Musical Times*, 38 (1897), pp.657–64 (at 662).
24. See Percy M. Young, *George Grove, 1820–1900. A Biography* (London, 1980), pp.105–13.
25. By 1873 Grove had been editing the *Magazine* for five years, carefully introducing new critical ideas and a distinctive character without offending existing readers; he often consulted Alexander Macmillan. For a comparison of the magazine with its main competitors, *Blackwood's Edinburgh Magazine* and *Cornhill Magazine*, see the introduction to *Macmillan's* in *The Wellesley Index to Victorian Periodicals, 1824–1900*, ed. Walter Houghton, then Jean H. Slingerland (5 vols, Toronto, 1966–89), I, pp.554–6. Contributing writers during Grove's 15-year tenure included Matthew Arnold, Walter Pater, James Bryce, Max Müller, E.B. Taylor, J.R. Seeley, A.P. Stanley and Henry James, and on musical subjects Edward Dannreuther, Henry Sutherland Edwards, Edmund Gurney, Francis Hueffer, John Hullah, Henry Leslie, Julian Marshall, John Oxenford and William Pole. Ann Parry concludes that this was the heyday of the magazine ('The Grove Years', p.156).
26. BL Add. MS 54793, f.77.
27. See G.L. Craik to Grove, 2 August 1877, BL Add. MS 54793, f.91; and pencil draft of [Frederick] Macmillan to Grove, n.d. [early May 1879], ff.137–8. The sub-text of early negotiations must have centred on the company's fear that a specialist dictionary would be an expensive undertaking with no guarantee of profit. They built in their own exit route, at the same time hoping Grove's other output would help finance the project.
28. See Michael Musgrave, *The Musical Life of the Crystal Palace* (Cambridge, 1995), pp.161–72.
29. From the 1860s the ineffectiveness of the Royal Academy of Music was a matter of general agreement, leading to a quasi-official investigation into the state of music education at home and abroad (by the Society for the Encouragement of Arts, Manufactures, and Commerce, 1866). For the result, and discussion of the proliferation of music colleges after 1870, see Cyril Ehrlich, *The Music Profession in Britain since the Eighteenth Century* (Oxford, 1985), pp.88–120.

30. See Hugh Cobbe's account of the founding and early years of the Society, based on its minute books, in 'The Royal Musical Association, 1874–1901', *Proceedings of the Royal Musical Association*, 110 (1983–4), pp.111–17. Some dozen of the original 22 'gentlemen' invited to the first organizational meeting, including Stainer and Pole, became contributors to Grove's *Dictionary*: seven had just been listed in his March 1874 prospectus.
31. Preface, p.iii.
32. 'Larynx' (not to mention 'Ear', 'Laryngoscope' and the explanation of the formation of the hand in 'Fingering') was the work of F. Champneys, Medical Registrar of St Bartholomew's Hospital. Coover, 'Dictionaries and encyclopedias of music', calls attention to Stainer and Barrett for this very article.
33. For a brief description of the ninth edition (25 vols, Edinburgh, 1875–89), see Herman Kogan, *The Great EB: the Story of the Encyclopaedia Britannica* (Chicago, 1958), pp.51–5. Its success was hugely extended by a reissue in 1898, with American-style advertising, a bargain purchase plan and the sponsorship of *The Times* (pp.81–3). From 1902 the 10th edition (a 10-volume supplement) was under the editorial aegis of *The Times* (cf. n.137 below).
34. In 1871 Grove rejected Freeman's review of the last volume of J.A. Froude's *History of England* because it indulged in personal insult; see Young, *George Grove*, pp.120–1, and Parry, 'The Grove Years', p.155.
35. In 1876 Macmillan considered taking on the new English dictionary being prepared by the Philological Society (a project begun in 1858), but could not reach agreements about leadership and finance. The project was eventually accepted by Oxford in 1879 under the editorship of Dr James Murray and completed in 1928, despite rising costs, tardiness and gigantism, as the *Oxford English Dictionary*. By contrast, Smith miraculously kept his promise of publishing one volume of the *DNB*, edited by Leslie Stephen and later Sidney Lee, each quarter from 1885, completing the 63rd volume in 1900 and the three-volume supplement in 1901. Smith's family later presented the copyright and stereotype plates – and responsibility for carrying on the work – to Oxford University Press. Both projects are discussed in Peter Sutcliffe, *The Oxford University Press: an Informal History* (Oxford, 1978). For an illuminating discussion of gaps in original *DNB* coverage, see *The Dictionary of National Biography: Missing Persons*, ed. C.S. Nicholls (Oxford and New York, 1993), pp.v–vii.
36. On Stainer: '...he is so perfunctory, and gets so much more out of that brown head, & browner imagination, than from books' (Grove to Squire, 12 September [1885], BL Add. MS 39679, f.112). On Prout: 'I have a high regard for his abilities but (between ourselves) he is such a snob that I can never like him' (Grove to F.G. Edwards, [23 January 1889], BL Egerton MS 3091, f.8). On Oakeley: '...a mere thin aristocratic prig with no inside to get into. His great talent is a painful sensitivity to pitch ' (Grove to C. Hubert H. Parry, 12 October [1874], Shulbrede Priory, Lynchmere, Sussex; this and all subsequent letters of Parry's are quoted by kind permission of Miss Laura Ponsonby).
37. Grove to Squire, 27 May [1879], BL Add. MS 39679, ff.7–8.
38. Recounted in Sutcliffe, *The Oxford University Press*, p.32.
39. From 1863 to 1880 Alexander Macmillan held the appointment of Publisher to the Press. He was not a partner in the usual sense but an agent with London commercial experience – able to attract new business, advise on book promotion and improve profits. The relationship was largely harmonious despite some differences of approach; see Sutcliffe, *The Oxford University Press*, pp.16–32.

40. The first clear indication of a threat to the dictionary, and hence to Grove's personal finances, appeared in his letter of 5 March 1877 to Hubert Parry: Macmillan & Co. were waiting for profits from Grove's recently published geography primer, meanwhile pressing him for another book, a geography classbook, before taking a final decision on the music project. Four months later he wrote of his frustration at the continuing threat: 'The Americans won't take up "Grove's Dictionary" and M. & Co. are again beginning to talk of giving it up. Fools – if they only had the enterprise of Murray whose Dictionaries of Gk & Roman Geography & Biography did not pay him for years! But they have not' (Grove to Parry, 25 July [1877], Shulbrede Priory). It was in 1877 that ongoing peripheral costs such as translation, artwork and the setting of music examples began to mount.
41. Statement dated 31 July 1877, with alterations in Grove's hand, BL Add. MS 54793, f.90.
42. Grove to Craik, 31 July 1877, BL Add. MS 54793, f.88.
43. Grove to Craik, 29 July 1877, BL Add. MS 54793, f.86 (note that the book's extent was now already up from the original estimate by 300 pages). In giving the company his undertaking, Grove was careful to point out why the dictionary required so much time: 'To drive a team of contributors half of whom are amateurs, and half can get 3 times the pay we can give them elsewhere, takes a frightful amount of goading & coaxing & correspondence: and the editing and correcting & checking and completing – as I feel bound to do it – is a matter of great labour and incessant thought & occupation.'
44. C.L. Graves, *The Life & Letters of Sir George Grove, C.B.* (London, 1903), p.229. They worked together closely for two or three years.
45. See n.4 above. The published lists, with more than 3,000 headwords, were meant to elicit comment from contributors and give a sense of the intended scope and organization of the material; Hipkins annotated his copy. I am grateful to Peter Horton of the RCM Library for making this source available to me.
46. Grove was probably helped by W.H. Husk on the first of these (Husk was librarian to the Sacred Harmonic Society and an antiquarian with interests in English vocal music), and by Franz Gehring on the second.
47. Rev. T.P. Hudson (later Canon Pemberton), a Yorkshire clergyman and author of a book on trigonometry, was wrongly called Rev. J.P. Hudson on the prospectus, and confusingly given the initials T.P.P. on one early list and T.H.P. in the *Dictionary*'s Index volume. An accomplished cellist, he typified a kind of amateur writer Grove used at the outset (Hudson suggested entries on some 250 names in his area, but contributed only 20).
48. Mrs Walter Carr, a parson's wife in Coventry, had worked for Grove as a German translator on the *Magazine* ('excellent for style & spirit': Grove to G.A. Macmillan, 14 September [1877], BL Add. MS 54793, f.102), and was liked for her speed and dependability. She crafted more than 150 articles on eighteenth- and nineteenth-century Continental composers (up to the letter 'H'). Chouquet, a music journalist, historian and keeper of the instrument museum at the Paris Conservatoire, contributed steadily on French topics until his death in early 1886. Stone was a medical doctor, acoustician and expert on wind instruments, and a founding member of the Musical Association. He and Franklin Taylor, a pianist long friendly with Grove, both wrote music books for Macmillan in the 1870s.

49. 'Old Husk', clerk to a firm of solicitors, was a workhorse for Grove, answering queries, checking sources, compiling hundreds of small entries on relatively minor composers and institutions. Through the library of the Sacred Harmonic Society, with its printed music, periodicals, histories and dictionaries (notably Sainsbury's), he had ready access to material; he was also adept at making direct personal enquiries. Vol. II of his 'Remains' shows some of his working methods (see n.66 below).
50. See A.H. King, 'William Barclay Squire, 1855–1927: Music librarian', *Musical Pursuits: Selected Essays* (London, 1987), pp.187–99, at 189; and J.A. Fuller-Maitland, *A Door-keeper of Music* (London, 1929; 2nd edn, 1932), pp.86–7, 214–19.
51. See Jeremy Dibble, *C. Hubert H. Parry: His Life and Music* (Oxford, 1992), pp.127–8, 134, 151.
52. All contributors, including Grove, were probably paid £1 per 1,000 words (i.e. per page of printed text: double column, 500 words a column). See draft letter from Frederick Macmillan to Grove, n.d. [early May 1879], BL Add. MS 54793, f.138, alluding to payment for Grove's copy on top of his salary. See further, Grove to Squire, 5 January [?1887], BL Add. MS 39679, f.141v, offering Squire, if he would edit the Appendix, 'a proper sum for the Editing and 20/ a page for writing'.
53. Grove to Parry, 14 July [1875], Shulbrede Priory.
54. Grove to Squire, 7 May 1879, BL Add. MS 39679, ff.5v–6. In general, Grove's advice to assistants about keeping things short, or cutting down as much as possible, was strongest in the first few years of work, to 1880.
55. Grove to Squire, n.d. [July 1879], BL Add. MS 39679, f.16.
56. Grove to Squire, 26 June [1879], BL Add. MS 39679, f.9 (suggesting Schauer and Koch as sources); 15 July [1879], ff. 20–1 (enclosing information on Luther's letters, recently published in the *Revue et gazette musicale*); 10 August 1879, ff.22–3 (referring to a facsimile of Luther's musical autograph in the *Neue Zeitschrift für Musik*).
57. Grove to Squire, n.d. [July 1879], BL Add. MS 39679, f.15.
58. Grove to Squire, 23 September [1879], BL Add. MS 39679, f.34. Several articles on individual libraries, commissioned separately, were already in type. Grove had been impressed by Nottebohm's Beethoven sketch studies, linking MSS in several libraries to form a coherent picture of compositional activity. But it was Squire who fleshed out the 'Libraries' idea by continuing to gather information from still more collections. See Grove's letters to him of 29 October [1879], ff.35–6; 26 February [1880], f.38; and 21 November [1884], f.107.
59. Letters of August and September 1879 (BL Add. MS 39679, ff. 28–34) show Grove's reliance on Squire for translations of German poetry; a letter of the following year (19 August [1880], f.41) shows that Squire could handle Chouquet's French. Later, the editor asked his assistant to read and help revise 'Mendelssohn' after its initial publication, owing to 'a great opinion which I have formed of your sense & judgment' (Grove to Squire, 20 November [1882], BL Add. MS 39679, f.85).
60. Grove to Squire, 20 December [1882], BL Add. MS 39679, f.87. On Squire's work for the *DNB*, see further, BL Add. MS 39680.
61. Grove to Squire, 30 December [1884], BL Add. MS 39679, f.108. During this period Squire had held a clerkship in a solicitors' firm; he contemplated a possible move into the BM, and the change of career, very carefully before taking action.

62. None of the big ones came easily or quickly after Parry decreased his involvement as sub-editor. He began work on 'Sonata' in October 1880, agreed a year later to do 'Symphony' (which Grove had thought of asking Frederick Corder to do), but in the event accepted and finished 'Suite' first, by early 1883 ('Suite' had once been assigned to Prout). Parry's 'Symphony' was extremely late, adding to the delay in the publication of part 19 (July 1884).
63. Grove to Parry, n.d. [April 1880], Shulbrede Priory. Grove seems to have elevated Parry to a special level not only out of genuine friendship and intellectual regard, but because he was a practising creative musician (unlike Squire or Maitland).
64. Maitland picked up where Prout had left off on some of these – in the middle of the alphabet – while Grove turned to Frederick Corder for others (having once considered the young composer Henry Gadsby).
65. Maitland to Grove, 25 July 1879, BL Add. MS 55236, ff.1–2.
66. BL Add. MS 39864, vol. II of Husk's 'Remains', contains among other things replies to Husk's queries, such as one from Prout enclosing his autobiography (dated Dalston, 3 January 1878, f.137); and one from W. & A. Gilley, the owners of the Pantheon, Oxford Street, offering to open their files (also dated 3 January 1878, f.172). There are also notes such as this one: 'Dear Husk, Does "Spring Gardens" call for any notice in the Dictionary? I do not want it unless it is really requisite. Please let me hear from you. G. Grove' (postcard, 13 September [1882], f.173).
67. Grove went frequently and had his own regular attendant, one Hawkins, who fetched things for him (1886); he also sent assistants there to double-check details in MSS or early printed music (e.g. of John Shepherd). Oxford collections, including Christ Church Library, were occasionally consulted through catalogues; the editor regretted he had no funds to send Squire to Oxford in person.
68. Grove to Parry, 25 July [1877], Shulbrede Priory: 'I have told Novellos to send you a copy of Day [Alfred Day's *Treatise on Harmony*, 1845] – take care of it as I don't want to have to buy it.' This *ad hoc* borrowing system relied on goodwill from friends and publishers at home and abroad. Macmillan & Co. offered no budget for reference tools.
69. Grove used Fétis in part as a double-check on minor figures, writing to Husk after his sentence about the composer Norcome, 'Nothing is known of his biography', appeared in the *Dictionary* : 'It's all in Fétis' (5 September [1880], BL Add. MS 39864, f.128); a correction was generated for the Appendix. The editor lent Spitta's book, with its new information on Bach's use of Vivaldi, to Parry for his 'Arrangement' article. Karasowski's book, in a recent English translation (1879), was pushed at Squire for quotes about the mazurka and polonaise. Sowinski's *Les musiciens polonais et slaves anciens et modernes* provided a useful source on less familiar music (Grove's copy is now in the RCM Library). The editor sent Proske's collection to Parry in 1876 as a help in his work on historical styles.
70. Grove had inherited Otto Jahn's personal copies of both the *Neue Zeitschrift* and the *Allgemeine musikalische Zeitung* (which he later passed to the RCM).
71. It was Joachim who encouraged Grove to approach 'Spitta of Berlin' about any points on which he was having difficulty in early German music (Grove to Squire, 30 June 1879, BL Add. MS 39679, f.11). Piatti was the editor's first thought when a dance-movement form needed verification or example (Grove to Squire, 15 July [1879], f.20). Pauer was a useful tipster for information and opinion on keyboard literature (Grove to Parry, 26 October [1880], Shulbrede Priory).

72. The subject was J.H. Mapleson and the despatched interviewer, 'Jones'. Grove told him to go to Oakeley Square, find Mrs Mapleson and, after explaining about the *Dictionary*, to extract all he could on her son's career (Grove to Jones, 29 July [1879], BL Add. MS 54793, ff.139–40).
73. 'General Directions for Contributors', RCM Library (see note 4 above).
74. Grove often wrote on stationery headed 'Macmillan's Magazine. Dictionary of Music and Musicians. Lower Sydenham, S.E.' In 1886 he complained to Edith Oldham about household servants tidying his papers so that he could no longer find things (letter of 6 November, quoted in Young, *George Grove*, p.188). And in 1897 F.G. Edwards described Grove's 'den' and the books in his study at Sydenham ('Sir George Grove, C.B.', p.657). The loss of edited copy and proofs is far less surprising than that of personal letters, some from eminent contributors and friends, which were surely written to him (cf. the large selection quoted in Graves, *Life & Letters*). Lady Grove must have destroyed a considerable number.
75. Grove kept a record of manuscripts received but not of edited copy sent to the printer. Hence occasional queries or losses, in the period before proofs were returned, could cause panic – as when 'Philadelphia' went astray (Grove to Squire, Wednesday, n.d. [1880], BL Add. MS 39679, f.37).
76. One of Squire's dance entries, 'Matelotte', was sent to the printer on 15 July 1879 and returned by 10 August. Going quickly to galleys not only gave a form of security and multiplicity in the days before typewriter carbons and photocopiers: it was easier on the eyes, and more accurate and efficient for the publishing schedule.
77. Grove asked for Parry's 'sharpest attention' to a batch of 'B's' in April 1876 (letter of 29 April, Shulbrede Priory), and to part 5 in proof in November 1878 (letter of 21 November). A read-through of 'Handel' in part 6 revealed omission of an entry on Buononcini; so Grove concocted a long footnote, for insertion on page at the reference in the Handel article.
78. Parry's memory of his editing days, recounted to RCM students in 1895, is illuminating: 'If you could have seen the state in which some of the articles were sent in you would wonder how they were ever got into shape. I remember we not only had to recast the details of the language of many of them, but to turn the articles inside out and upside down, to put the end at the beginning and the middle at the end, and to cut out whole paragraphs of rigmarole, till we were driven nearly distracted' (quoted in Young, *George Grove*, p.293). Among entries that had to be completely re-done are 'Tattoo', originally given to Pontigny (who was 'quite stumped' about it: Grove to Squire, 23 July [1883], BL Add. MS 39679, f. 97), and 'University Musical Society, Cambridge', first given to 'Cobbs' (Grove to Squire, 12 September [1885], f.112).
79. Grove to Squire, 17 December [1881], BL Add. MS 39679, f.66v: 'I had hoped that Mad. Goldschmidt would have taken it but she has thrown me over & now I am in doubt whether to ask Clara Novello or her sister Sabilla – or to go to a man like Deacon who knows the subject thoroughly & will do it justice though he has no wide spread fame.'
80. Exact birth and death dates were given where known, for example (though in prose rather than standardized headings); small Roman type was used for list material at the ends of articles; families were organized under the oldest member, with younger ones in separate paragraphs underneath; large subject entries, such as 'Music-printing' and 'Schools of Composition', were subdivided into numbered sections.

81. Several factors may account for this. Grove did not know in advance exactly what he wanted in every entry, nor how proportions ought to fall out across the book; his enthusiasm for the project, and eagerness to get good writers, came first. Once the experts were there, he tended to rely on them; apart from tight editing (in some cases), he was reluctant to rein in compelling work. Ultimately his sensitivity to individual writers added to the variety, readability and authority of the text.
82. Rockstro, for one, habitually wrote too much – 'so utterly unnecessary and absurd' (Grove to Squire, 12 September [1885], BL Add. MS 39679, f.112). But Grove needed him on early music.
83. Grove to Squire, 29 October [1879], BL Add. MS 39679, f.35v. The published articles on Monteverdi and Morlacchi are probably not far from what was sent in, being nearly five and three columns, respectively.
84. Grove to Squire, 30 December [1884], BL Add. MS 39679, f.108. The music manuscript in question was Lady Elizabeth Rogers's virginal book. In the event Squire did not mention it.
85. Press reviews had been appearing since 1879, pointing out mistakes and gaps but generally noting improvement in successive parts. In 1884 a *Guardian* piece reviewing the *Dictionary*'s second and third volumes more favourably than the first caught Grove's eye in particular (Grove to Squire, 21 November [1884], BL Add. MS 39679, f.107v). Meanwhile, in 1882, Riemann's vast *Musik-Lexikon* had appeared in Leipzig. Grove recognized the scholarly direction in which things were moving, and knew he had to keep up.
86. From Grove to Squire, 20 November [1882], BL Add. MS 39679, f.85, about 'Mendelssohn'. For *Dictionary* reprinting purposes Grove allowed small changes to this article (following reaction from the Mendelssohn family), but he still felt that though long, it was consistent and not susceptible of major cuts.
87. For a mid-twentieth-century view of the editorial problem presented by the three articles, and for its solution, see Eric Blom's Introduction to *Beethoven, Schubert, Mendelssohn by Sir George Grove* (London, 1951), pp.vii-ix.
88. The most pointed criticism came from Henry Heathcote Statham in the *Edinburgh Review* (see n. 106 below). Beyond Grove's enthusiasm and specialist knowledge, there are practical explanations for the length of these essays. Not only were they partly conceived in the manner of magazine articles (e.g. 'Beethoven' was directly influenced by Dannreuther's *Macmillan's* piece on the composer, of July 1876: see Grove to Parry, [21 October 1876], Shulbrede Priory), but at an early stage Grove had thought of publishing them collectively as a book, and even hoped to write a fourth one, on Schumann (see Grove to Marian Bradley, 16 August 1880, quoted in Graves, *Life & Letters*, pp.257–8; and Grove to F.G. Edwards, 4 May 1881, BL Egerton MS 3091, ff.3–4). Wide public praise for 'Beethoven' encouraged Grove to pursue the same approach for the others; eventually, pressed for time and weary when doing 'Schubert' ('I am pretty sick of it': Grove to Parry, 1 October [1881], Shulbrede Priory), his loss of focus expressed itself in inordinate length.
89. The title-page to the first volume reads 'in two volumes', that to the second volume 'in three volumes', and that to the third 'in four volumes'.
90. Although not the full story on military music, this article, by Squire, was a *tour de force* under the circumstances; it survived in part down to the sixth edition (as 'Military calls'). In helping Squire find sources for it, Grove remembered 'a man

named Kappey, Bandmaster to H.R. Engrs at Chatham, an old & very intelligent German, who does editing for Boosey, & has some literary knowledge' (Grove to Squire, 20 September [1881, *sic*: 1882], BL Add. MS 39679, ff. 60–1). It was J.A. Kappey who eventually wrote 'Wind-band' and corrected 'Saxophone'. Placing Squire's entry at 'S' was not really satisfactory; Maitland re-named it 'Military Sounds and Signals' in the second edition.

91. James Lecky wrote on acoustical topics starting with 'Node'. Grove described him to Parry as 'a nice bright little Irishman who appears to know his subject thoroughly and to be possessed with the necessity of making it intelligible' (1 December [1879], Shulbrede Priory).
92. Campra had been considered by Grove but rejected, presumably for space constraints and lack of an author. Squire raised the omission in 1879 and had this reply from the editor: 'I remember debating over him and should like much to talk to you about that and the great question of who to leave out...' (7 May 1879, BL Add. MS 39679, f.5). Squire's friend Mrs Wodehouse did an entry for the Appendix.
93. Grove got Husk to help with Salmon: 'You have mentioned him under Lock, but there should be a notice of the nature of his proposed notation. Hipkins mentions him incidentally under Spinet and this affords an opportunity for a note upon him. Could you kindly let me have something?' (Grove to Husk, 6 September [1882], BL Add. MS 39864, f.140).
94. Places, namely towns and cities, were not thought of as a discrete subject area and treated systematically, but were included when a given contributor could describe a local music tradition of importance. Grove's own 'Leipzig' and 'Manchester' are the clearest early examples, in addition to Miss Phillimore's 'Bologna', 'Florence' and 'Naples'. London never received this treatment (nor did Berlin, New York, Paris, Vienna), although some institutions of such places were entered individually (e.g. 'Gesellschaft der Musikfreunde', 'London Sacred Harmonic Society', 'Norwich Festival', 'Philharmonic Society of New York, The'). The full marketing potential of place entries was not fully realized by Macmillan until the 1980s.
95. See the company's draft letter setting out their view in Frederick Macmillan to Grove, n.d. [early May 1879], BL Add. MS 54793, ff.137–8.
96. Grove to Alexander Macmillan, 17 June 1880, BL Add. MS 54793, f.141.
97. The origins and purpose of the testimonial, on 19 July 1880, were discreetly mysterious. Grove's friend Ernest von Glehn, who hired St James's Hall for the event, was supposed to have been the moving spirit behind it (Graves, *Life & Letters*, p.251); the immediate 'occasion' was Grove's retirement from the Board of the Crystal Palace Company (see an announcement in *The Times*, reprinted in the *Musical World*, 58, 11, 13 March 1880, p.173). Dean Stanley and Arthur Sullivan gave the speeches, and the Archbishop of Canterbury made the presentation – signed by some 300 of their eminent contemporaries in science, art and literature (including Macmillan). For Grove's reply, including his acknowledgment of *Dictionary* colleagues and of Alexander Macmillan's 'liberality and generosity...throughout this long and difficult undertaking', see 'Mr George Grove's Testimonial Speech', *Musical World* 58, 31 (31 July 1880), pp.484–5. Given Grove's previous send-off from the Crystal Palace secretaryship, and his ongoing worries about money, his job and the *Dictionary*, one is tempted to infer some particular Macmillan involvement in the testimonial (the company now desperately needed him in good spirits). But there is equally no reason to doubt the sincere feeling and wide public esteem shown by this episode.

98. The Appendix gives a fascinating snapshot of international music scholarship, 1879–89. To mention only a few examples, Gustav Nottebohm and Alexander Thayer are acknowledged for 'Beethoven'; Squire corrected and updated both Rockstro's 'Byrd' and his own 'Musical Libraries'; Giannandrea Mazzucato contributed a substantial new entry on Boito, as Maitland did on Dvořák, and H.E. Wooldridge on 'Psalter'. Augustus Hughes-Hughes wrote on 'Histories of Music', F.H. Jenks on 'Negro Music', and J.R. Milne on 'Schütz' – all nicely balanced by a survey of 'Recording Music Played Extemporaneously' by T.L. Southgate.
99. Grove to Squire, 30 September [1885], BL Add. MS 39679, f.117.
100. Five articles from 'Silvana' to 'Sivori, Ernesto Camillo' (including 'Sinico') were inadvertently left out of part 15/16. To his embarrassment, Grove realized the mistake too late ('Fancy! I have omitted Sinico and Sivori!!!!!': Grove to Squire, 20 September [1882], BL Add. MS 39679, f.60). He then had to place the missing articles after 'Sketches' in part 17/18. Maitland's explanation (*A Door-keeper of Music*, p.216) that Grove had been eager to get on to 'Sketches', a subject that specially interested him, is embroidery.
101. See Grove to Squire, 28 July [1887], BL Add. MS 39679, ff.134–5: 'I am very sorry for my mal à propos addition to Waltz. Tho' I confess I cannot see the discrepancy, nor I think will any one else do so. But still I am heartily sorry and beg your pardon...'.
102. See *Musical Times*, 19, 420 (February 1878), pp.84, 93; 19, 424 (June 1978), pp. 336–7; and 20, 435 (May 1879), pp.270–1. It was Dannreuther's tone in the Hummel article, and his assessment of the composer as a 'dull classic', that the reviewer most disliked.
103. The *Musical Times* writer made this point, offering his corrections in the spirit of getting facts right since the new work was clearly 'more than a gossiping book' (*Musical Times*, 19, 420 (February 1878), p.93). Corrections were indeed inserted more than once in reprints of early parts of the *Dictionary* (see n.119 below).
104. Some examples from 1878–9: 'What is modestly called a "Dictionary" might have fairly been entitled an "Encyclopaedia," for the editor has included in his scheme everything that belongs to music, or is allied, or is even distantly related to it. It would be a great mistake to regard this work as useful only for purposes of reference. It is a collection of interesting and valuable articles...which amateurs...will read from beginning to end' (*Daily News*). 'This promises to be for music what the best encyclopaedias are to general literature and science' (*Guardian*). 'We have no hesitation in advising all students of music, nay more, all amateurs, to order this work. ...No one can make even a superficial examination of the parts already published without perceiving that this Dictionary will meet a real want' (*Manchester Examiner*).
105. See *New Quarterly Magazine*, 10 (1878), pp.591–613, in which Edwards stresses the range and interest of the first four parts, as well as the quality of 'Beethoven'; and *Temple Bar*, 64 (1882), pp.541–56, in which Engel gives an anecdotal survey of fact and opinion in the *Dictionary*. Both writers were minor contributors. Edwards's piece is the more rambling and partial; Engel noted the disproportionate space given to Mendelssohn ('a glaring imbalance').
106. See *Edinburgh Review*, 153 (1881), pp.212–40; and 158 (1883), pp.475–509. Both articles are attributed to Statham by the *Wellesley Index*. The first one (January 1881) covers the *Dictionary*'s first two volumes. Statham thought 'Mendelssohn' not only long but outdated; some of the space should have been given to Bach. He liked 'Beethoven'. Parry is depicted as a clumsy writer with ultra-modern

tastes, and Hueffer as too partial on Liszt, while Rockstro gets high praise. The second article (October 1883) considers Grove's 'Schubert' along with three monographs on Chopin and Liszt: raising doubt about Schubert's importance becomes a means to attack Grove and 'the Sydenham creed'. Whatever else may be the background to this critical struggle, Parry and Grove had disliked Statham's rather overweening article on William Sterndale Bennett for the *Dictionary*, with its 'arrogance & conceit' (see Grove to Parry, 4 August [1876], Shulbrede Priory). After 'Bennett', Grove asked him to write only 'Carillon' and 'Registration'.

107. Grove to Parry [14 August 1883], Shulbrede Priory. This letter was actually Grove's response to yet another strong criticism of Parry, published anonymously in the *Guardian* in summer 1883: 'There is a nasty animus all through, but his strictures on you are so obviously inspired by personal feeling as to take away all the force or weight they might have had... The idea of abusing you for gushing[,] and praising Rockstro for conciseness[,] is too rich. ...I feel pretty sure that the author of the article is Statham. He follows the same line, & with some of the same expressions, in his article in the Edinburgh. He is... a cankered soul and very much to be pitied.'

108. Grove to Squire, 19 November [1880], BL Add. MS 39679, f.45v. The gift fascicle had presumably been a gesture of thanks for assistance as well as a means of promoting the *Dictionary*. Some years later, another foreign reaction impressed the editors. Adolphe Jullien, an Appendix contributor, reviewed the *Dictionary* 'in several French papers in glowing terms, and really excellently' (Maitland to G.A. Macmillan, 22 May [?1891], BL Add. MS 55236, f.3).

109. Grove's awareness of this part of his readership is revealed in his reminder to Parry to spell out musical details (e.g. of a sequence) so that untrained listeners could appreciate them: 'I am sure it is our attention to such things, that makes our Dictionary so popular with people like Spencer Lyttleton [*sic*], F. Harrison & all that tribe...' (Grove to Parry, 29 August [1881], Shulbrede Priory).

110. Other dictionaries created in the wake of Grove's include W.H. Cummings's slight *Biographical Dictionary of Musicians* (London, 1892), F.J. Crowest's undervalued *Dictionary of British Musicians* (London, 1895), and James D. Brown & Stephen S. Stratton's *British Musical Biography* (Birmingham, 1897), besides more specialized works such as Ernst Pauer's *Dictionary of Pianists and Composers for the Pianoforte* (London, 1895). Meanwhile, before Grove's book was complete, its scope and title were reflected in an American publication, J.D. Champlin and W.F. Apthorp's *Cyclopedia of Music and Musicians* (New York, 1888–90).

111. See Grove's reply to Alexander Macmillan, 17 June 1880, BL Add. MS 54793, f.141, reiterating his personal commitment: 'I was distressed to find, from the light thrown upon the subject on Tuesday, that the work is not likely to be remunerative to you. I had always hoped that it might turn out a very good property to you, and the prospect of the reverse is to me a bitter disappointment. However if care and pains on my part can alter this, you will not have to complain of me.' With hindsight, we might well wonder how far Macmillan really believed his own dire financial predictions at this time, and how far he was just trying to inhibit Grove and curb growth of the book. This was also the moment when the publisher offered one additional payment, but only on completion.

112. Publication dates are taken from original fascicles held by the Department of Portraits and Performance History, Royal College of Music, and from a complete set

in the possession of Dr Stanley Sadie. I am grateful to Oliver Davies and Paul Collen at the RCM, and to Stanley Sadie, for allowing me to examine this material.

113. Macmillan & Co. promoted their own books here, but other prominent advertisers included Debain, Pleyel, Augener, Chappell, Novello, Joseph Goddard, and Dr Moffat, whose Ammoniaphone 'for voice cultivation by chemical means' appears to have been warmly endorsed by the Rev. H.R. Haweis and Adelina Patti.
114. Information from Macmillan trade catalogues (1896, 1899, 1903) and the *Bibliographical Catalogue of Macmillan and Co.'s Publications from 1843 to 1889* (London, 1891) in the company archive at Basingstoke. I wish to thank Robert Machesney and Alysoun Sanders for their assistance with these sources.
115. Mrs Wodehouse, a friend of Squire's, seems to have suggested the Index herself, to improve the *Dictionary*'s usefulness. Grove encouraged the idea, and strongly advised that she ask the firm to pay her for it (Grove to Squire, 24 August [?1883], BL Add. MS 39679, f. 105). The ancillary 'Catalogue of Articles Contributed by Each Writer in the Dictionary' was compiled at the same time.
116. 'And now, having compared the views entertained by the best historians of the past century with those set forth by the latest and most competent critics of the present day, it remains only that we should place before our readers the results of our own careful and long-continued study of the original MS' (iii, p.768).
117. Grove was never one to miss a strategic opportunity. Although he knew the evidence for precedence was only suggestive (as 'Sumer' clarifies) – and he never believed in anything like a modern British supremacy in music – he still wanted to pique public curiosity, stir discussion and excite interest, to the advantage of both projects. Timing was everything (see also n.143 below).
118. For access to the OUP Archives and assistance in locating Clarendon Press Ledgers Nos 2–5, I must thank Dr Martin Maw, Archivist, Oxford University Press. For permission to reproduce information from them, I thank the Secretary to the Delegates of the Press. The relevant sections are as follows: No. 2 (pp.242, 455), No. 3 (pp.241–2, 256–8, 261), No. 4 (pp.70–2, 74, 495), No.5 (pp.10–14). Some reprint orders of 1899–1901 also appear in two Editions Books in the Macmillan Archive at the British Library (BL Add. MSS 55912 and 55913); these broadly agree with the more detailed Oxford records. Macmillan's Editions Book for the 1870s and 1880s, however – still held by the firm at Basingstoke – is blank for the *Dictionary* entry (p.402), probably because its purpose was to keep track of monograph paper stocks. I am grateful to Dr John Handford, former Archivist at Macmillan, for his help and advice in this matter.
119. Specific ledger entries show that when an adjustment upwards was necessary to meet demand for the first five parts – up to October 1879 – corrections were inserted and charged for each time. There were thus as many as three 'editions' of parts 1–4, and two of part 5. At about this time the idea of the appendix took root; corrections then appear to have been generally held back to reduce costs and minimize confusion.
120. Exact figures for each part varied according to stock in hand, eg. from 800 to 1,300 or more, suggesting not only an uneven sale but a practical drive to make up complete volumes; see BL Add. MS 55912, ff.101v–104r. At least some of these copies were destined for export to the USA, bound in brown cloth and issued with a title-page dated 1902.
121. Green's book sold 35,000 copies in its first 18 months; *Alice* sold 180,000 between 1865 and 1898. Figures cited in Rosemary T. VanArsdel, 'Macmillan and Company', *British Literary Publishing Houses, 1820–1880*, ed. Patricia J. Anderson and Jonathan Rose (Detroit, 1991), p.185; and Richard D. Altick,

The English Common Reader: a Social History of the Mass Reading Public, 1800–1900 (Chicago, 1957), p.389.

122. Calculation based on an average price per set of £4 8s 6d, to reflect the mix of formats available between 1878 and 1901 (individual fascicles, Appendix and Index, whole volumes, complete bound sets with or without the Index, etc). In effect, collecting all the parts separately from the beginning (at £4 13s 6d) would have been slightly more expensive than buying the basic bound set at the end (£4 4s).
123. This is an estimate comprising modest retainers for Parry, Squire and Maitland; translation; the origination cost of woodcut illustrations; the preparation of music examples; the editing of the Appendix (see n.52 above); and Mrs Wodehouse's fee for the Index.
124. Estimated at £1 per page of text (500 words a column, 2 columns a page); see n.52 above.
125. This is the total of all relevant paper and printing charges in the Oxford ledgers, December 1877 to October 1901 (not including any trade discount OUP may have deducted on account with Macmillan). Besides the fascicles themselves, Oxford printed the prospectuses of 1877 and 1899, the fascicle wrappers and the volume title-pages, also charging for 'electro mounted' woodcuts, wrappering, stitching and boxing-up, and corrections made to plates.
126. Reckoned as 12 per cent of retail sales income on 14,000 sets (at £4 8s 6d each; see n.122 above). A standard trade discount to retailers in this period was 24 per cent (cf. the account between Kegan Paul, Trench, Trübner & Co. and J.& E. Bumpus Ltd of Oxford Street, 1889, in the Bumpus papers at the City of Westminster Archives, Acc M:418). It is not however clear that most, or even many, *Dictionary of Music* customers bought their sets through bookshops rather than from the publisher. Thus I have assumed a mix of sales through retailers and direct to the public.
127. This is a guess, based on Macmillan's customary use of advertising; see Sutcliffe, *The Oxford University Press*, p.31.
128. Reckoned notionally as 10 per cent of all the above expenditure, and embracing costs such as editorial postage, secretarial assistance, storage and free carriage of stock to booksellers.
129. For this point, and technical assistance on the calculations that follow, I am indebted to Stanley Sadie and Paul Scruton.
130. I spread overheads, for example, equally over the first 17 years (1874–90); allocate stipends for sub-editors to the respective years of each one's known involvement; and cost contributors' fees to the four years when each volume was completed (£768 in 1879, £769 in 1880, £768 in 1881 and £820 in 1889), as in Macmillan's practice with *Grove 2* (see Maitland to G.A. Macmillan, 13 July 1905, BL Add. MS 55236, ff.20–1). For publishers' discount, see n.126 above.
131. As per the financial columns of the *Daily Telegraph* for May 1894. See also almanacs of the Birkbeck Bank, Chancery Lane, which in 1888 paid 2 per cent interest on current accounts and 3 per cent on deposit accounts (BL pressmark PP.2492.d.).
132. Grove to Alexander Macmillan, 17 June 1880, BL Add. MS 54793, f.141.
133. See Grove to Frederick Macmillan, 27 March [1892], BL Add. MS 54793, ff.160–61; Grove to G.A. Macmillan, 2 April 1892, f.162; and Graves to Grove, 1 April 1892, f.163. C.L. Graves was a music reporter for the *Daily Graphic* and had had critical engagements on the *Spectator* and *Athenaeum*. He approached Grove in the first instance about work as a reader at Macmillan's. Grove's recommendation secured him an entrée and probably some editorial work; later

the firm published his biographies of Grove (1903), Alexander Macmillan (1910) and Parry (1926).

134. Grove to G.A. Macmillan, 2 September 1897, BL Add. MS 54793, f.167.
135. See Grove to G.A. Macmillan, 30 October 1898, BL Add. MS 54793, ff.172–3; 8 November 1898, f.174; 13 November 1898, ff. 175–6; and 29 December 1898, ff.177–8.
136. See Maitland to G.A. Macmillan, 4 March [1902], BL Add. MS 55236, ff.5–6.
137. Maitland to G.A. Macmillan, n.d.[March 1902], BL Add. MS 55236, ff. 7–8. On working with Graves, Maitland had explained in his earlier letter (4 March, see n.136 above) that he was 'dead against collaborating with anybody; there must be one responsible person in such a work as this, and to collaborate means not a saving of time or trouble, but an increase of both.' Further, he doubted that Graves could help with the real work – at least not as much as subordinate colleagues he had already used in the musical part of the *Encyclopaedia Britannica* (10th edition).
138. An outspoken critic was Henry Davey, who claimed that the first edition – 'not very happy in its inception and subsequent carrying-out'– had now not been revised sufficiently (*Musical Herald*, December 1904, pp.372–3). Though he approved some of the new contributors, he attacked Maitland as incompetent and listed 46 factual errors spotted in a week's reading. Concerned to defend himself, Maitland wrote to G.A. Macmillan answering every point and explaining the background (i.e. that Davey was angry he had not been asked to contribute). See Maitland to Macmillan, 1 December [1904], BL Add. MS 55236, ff.11–16.
139. Macmillan Editions Book, p.888. The original print run was 2,000 copies.
140. Maitland confirmed this in his explanation to George Macmillan of why he had let some articles stand without updating them (and often placed new material within square brackets): '...in many of these cases...I thought it best not to bring the old articles up to date, but to let the different conditions of fashion, etc. speak for themselves. ...In such articles as some of the old-fashioned ones, like Hullah's etc (more particularly when the writers are dead) I allowed sentences to remain which, as such things acquire a certain historic interest as the work of their authors, are not quite accurately descriptive of present-day conditions' (BL Add. MS 55236, f.12). This approach to the text, born of expediency and commercial considerations as much as reverence for original authors (Grove above all), marked a major step in the 'canonization' of the *Dictionary*.
141. In the nineteenth century there were only two monumental 'complete editions' for English composers, Purcell and Handel; neither was very complete nor very successful.
142. The origins of Sainsbury's book in the RAM fiasco of 1823 are explored in Langley, 'Sainsbury's *Dictionary*, the Royal Academy of Music, and the Rhetoric of Patriotism' (see n.16 above).
143. Since late 1879 Grove had been a member of Prince Christian's executive committee to establish a national conservatoire, and he was approached with increasing frequency for his help in the sensitive negotiations that followed (cf. David Wright's chapter in the present volume). Among fund-raising speeches he is known to have written, that for the Duke of Albany at Manchester on 12 December 1881 (quoted in Young, *George Grove*, pp.159–60) is especially confident in its assertion of the primacy of English music, notably through 'Sumer is icumen in'. The speech was promotional, provocative and

shrewdly judged for the audience. By late February 1882, when the RCM directorship was probably dangled in front of Grove, we might fairly detect a conflict of interest between his 'scholarly' editorial work and personal concern for his own future – though he also knew the difference between a reference book aspiring to accuracy and a one-off speech whose sole purpose was to stir emotion and raise cash.

144. Grove had a genuine curiosity about English music history, and its rhetorical possibilities in making the RCM's case, but he deferred to others for verification of his hunches. Even when, in the run-up to the opening of the College, he tried to get Squire to publish separately 'all the evidence of music being more advanced in England than it was on the Continent before the 18th century', he had to back down when the young scholar refused, indicating he did not have full information. See Grove to Squire, 26 March [1883], BL Add. MS 39679, f.92; and 28 June 1883, f.96. Later, after the RCM was safely established, Grove persisted in his quest but from a different, less self-interested angle: 'I am very much exercised with the fact that when you encounter the English school about 1530 it is in full maturity, and that all traces of its progress between the Round of 1230 and 1530 seem to have almost vanished; & yet there must have been such a period of infancy and youth before the manhood of Tallis & Byrd. ... The subject ought to be gone into by somebody or other' (Grove to Squire, 23 February 1887, BL Add. MS 39679, f.143).

145. Then as now, readers imagined that an authoritative research service existed somewhere in the *Dictionary*'s collective mind. Even Giuseppe Verdi wrote, in 1896, asking about an Italian cantata of Vincenzo Galilei's mentioned by Rockstro in the Appendix. Rockstro was dead, Grove was stumped, and Squire fielded the query. See Grove to Squire, 17 June 1896, BL Add. MS 39679, f.161.

Part 4

The Royal College of Music

9
Grove's Role in the Founding of the RCM

David Wright

Regard for Grove as Founding Director

On 5 November 1894, a specially convened meeting of the Royal College of Music Executive Committee was held to receive news of the resignation, through ill health, of the RCM's founding Director, Sir George Grove.[1] Lord Thring paid tribute to Grove (pp.38–9):

> He [Thring] could not but recollect the many meetings held 12 years ago [as a member of Prince Christian's Executive Committee to establish the Royal College]...it had often been his duty to appear to oppose Sir George Grove [and] that he feared his opposition had sometimes had an unpleasant aspect...[but] that he never knew any man who bore the reproaches, or he would rather say the ill temper, of his Colleagues so kindly or so generously as Sir George Grove, nor did he ever know any man who worked with such singleness of purpose.

The meeting ended with a formal resolution, proposed by Prince Christian, recording the Council's gratitude (pp.41–2):

> It has been through his [Grove's] untiring zeal and energy, and his constant watchfulness over its interests, that the Royal College of Music has in so short a time attained its present high position; and, whatever its future destinies may be, it will never be forgotten how largely the influence which the College has been the means of exercising on the musical education of the country, was due to its first Director, Sir George Grove.

This extraordinary meeting (called on the signature of five members) gives valuable insight to the standing that Grove enjoyed: from the social and professional eminence of those attending (chaired by Prince Christian, it was attended by the Duke of Westminster, two Lords and five knights, including Sullivan and Stainer); and by the very warmth of the tributes that were paid. We get a sense that there were strong tensions between those concerned in the process of establishing the RCM, and that Grove was perceived to have dealt with these in a manner that brought him personal as well as professional credit. There was common admiration for, as Thring put it, Grove's 'singleness of purpose'. But while Prince Christian's resolution again emphasized Grove's energy, it also acknowledged Grove's breadth of vision for the College, and his ability to harness together a variety of philosophical and musical strands into a coherent purpose. All of these aspects were clearly recognized by contemporaries as ingredients of Grove's multi-faceted and extraordinarily talented persona. Examining Grove's role in the founding of the RCM, the sheer potency of the man and the extent of his achievement continues to resonate over a hundred years later.

We also have a practical measure of the debt that the RCM Council felt was due to Grove, in the shape of the award of a substantial annual pension of £700 'in recognition of the signal services rendered to the College as first Director',[2] decided upon at its next meeting two days later. This was not a casual gesture, for the College, having just moved into its new, much larger building and with associated start-up and increased running costs, was about to face a predicted deficit of £1,079 for the current financial year, and double that for the next. So what did these founding members of the RCM Council feel was so unique about Grove's contribution that they should have acknowledged it by the outpouring of such regard and such a generous pension?[3] Perhaps not far from several minds was the consideration that quite apart from the RCM being seen in its own terms as an institution of national musical significance, its establishment had been expressly undertaken as a royal initiative, with the Prince of Wales personally identified with its successful foundation. So failure to launch the College and to secure its early future would have caused considerable embarrassment to its royal and noble patrons, further compounded by the earlier royal involvement with the RCM's now compromised predecessor, the National Training School for Music (NTSM). But as the *Musical Times* report of the RCM's opening ceremony makes clear,[4] it was to be a very close call indeed, with a disappointing level of public subscription that amounted to some £110,000 (sufficient for only 50 scholarships) as opposed to the target figure of £250,000–£300,000.[5] Without Grove, it is clear that the enterprise, which represented a grand but not altogether coherent vision – and one that was very closely identified with the initiative of its aristocratic patrons – is likely to have foundered. Given this additional dimension, Grove's 'singleness of purpose' in bringing the RCM into being and giving it credence and viability, also represented a notable saving of collective face, for which many, including the heir to the throne, had cause to be grateful. But for British musical life, the RCM represented a significant artistic and educational endeavour, and the arguments made in favour of its foundation show that those involved saw the project as a worthy, even a high minded undertaking. As will be seen, it was because of the strength of Grove's own advocacy, and by his marshalling of the ideas of others, that the case for establishing the RCM was given such a robust and energizing philosophical basis. It was a very different start from that of the NTSM.

The unpropitious context

Grove had to contend directly with an accumulated range of unfavourable perceptions and negative attitudes that produced antipathy, even hostility to the proposition of a Royal College of Music. These suggest something of the inherent nature of the difficulties facing Grove when he assumed responsibility for the RCM, first as a member of Prince Christian's Executive Committee (which he had joined by November 1879) with responsibility for fundraising, and then, appointed by the Prince of Wales, as Director elect. It is possible to argue that, if anything, the significance of Grove's personal role in founding the RCM has been understated, given the musical, philosophical and educational cross-currents he had to keep in play during the fundraising process. From today's historical perspective, with the strength of the conservatoire role within the UK's higher music education system firmly established, and with the casual assumption of Victorian society's automatic deference to royalty, it is easy to think of the successful establishment of the RCM as a foregone conclusion, requiring no great feat of enterprise. For with the Prince of Wales's active patronage leading the fundraising and the fact that the College was following in the footsteps of a predecessor institution, the National Training School which had had Arthur Sullivan as its first Principal, it might be thought that Grove indeed had found himself fortunately placed. Not surprisingly, perhaps, this was a view which Sullivan himself, with an eye to his historical reputation, later sought to foster:

> The Royal College of Music was founded on the basis of the Training School which I had conducted. It was to all intents and purposes the same institution. They took over our building, our library and our teaching staff. Sir George Grove was appointed Director and carried on the institution on the lines which I had already laid down...So you see that the National Training School was really the forerunner and parent of the Royal College of Music.[6]

But this misrepresents the situation very considerably, for the NTSM under Sullivan's direction was the opposite of a model institution, and more of an impediment to the establishment of the RCM than otherwise. Nor does Sullivan's version take account of the intervening year between the NTSM's closure and the opening of the RCM. The stark reality is that the NTSM proved inadequate to its task and unable to live up to what had been promised to its original subscribers. It was a failure occasioned on one hand by Sullivan's deficient and uncommitted leadership, and insufficient funding on the other. Yet it was Grove himself who helped to establish the myth of the NTSM as a successful experiment, in the entry he wrote for his *Dictionary*, which described the School's training as 'systematic and thorough', and emphasized its achievement in the education of its four most brilliant students. But when Grove penned this entry there still lingered the very faint hope that government might be induced to take a greater financial role in the RCM, and so it was not the time to allude to the deficiencies of its predecessor, even had Grove been prepared to comment less than favourably on the work of Sullivan, who was a close friend.

Study of the Minutes of the NTSM's Committee of Management and contemporary press coverage shows that the School's brief life represented wasted opportunity and unfulfilled expectations, of academic scandal and dilettantish attitudes. Lacking sufficient capital, and forced by circumstances to run for an additional, sixth, year under its own financial steam, the NTSM accordingly was obliged to request a second tranche of subscriptions from its donors, not all of whom agreed to provide. Whether consciously or not, this reluctance reflected the unsatisfactory reality of the NTSM's situation, which was that, starved of income and unable to attract a critical mass of students of above average ability or to cover the range of orchestral instruments, the NTSM was reduced to a parody of those continental conservatoires it was formed to emulate. Therefore it can be seen that the determination of the Prince of Wales to make a further attempt to establish a national conservatoire in the shape of a successor institution to be called the Royal College of Music, flew in the face of this first, NTSM, experience. But it was also in defiance of the British government's steadfast refusal to assume the full financial and educational responsibility for a national school of music, unlike the French government who undertook such responsibility for the Paris Conservatoire, an institution on which the RCM was modelled. Given this background, it is no surprise that subscriptions to establish the RCM did not come easily, and Grove was therefore called upon, as the morally and socially acceptable face of the new College, to win the hearts and minds of potential subscribers by making the philosophical and social case for the RCM and to demonstrate the economic viability of music as a profession for its scholars. Simultaneously, he had to fulfil the academic leadership expected of a Director in recruiting staff and establishing the curriculum.

Origins of the founding of a national training school for music

The move to establish a national institution for advanced musical training based on the European conservatoire model, had its origins in the spirit of national endeavour in the arts and sciences that followed the 1851 Great Exhibition. The (later Royal) Society of Arts, promoters of the Exhibition, enabled by its financial success and prompted by their Patron, Prince Albert, assumed the role of advocating wider and cheaper educational opportunities in music. This was followed through with some energy by the extremely effective Henry (later Sir Henry) Cole, the prime mover behind the success of the Great Exhibition and the person ultimately responsible for driving through the scheme for the South Kensington museums. The Society of Arts established a Committee to investigate and report on 'the State of Musical Education, at Home and Abroad', specifically:

> To ascertain the principles and the nature of the administration by which the general musical education of the people of this country may be systematically conducted on a scale and with results at least equal to those of the Academies which flourish on the Continent of Europe.[7]

The report of the Committee, which was written by Cole, took evidence of accounts of the work and organization of ten European conservatoires together with a series of British institutions, primarily the Royal Academy (founded in 1822), the Military School of Music at Kneller Hall and a range of Cathedral foundations. Comparison between the Royal Academy of Music and the Paris Conservatoire emphasized the dismal state of current British provision. The advantages of the Paris Conservatoire lay not only in its physical resources, its national student catchment and the rigour of its examination system; but in the fact that it was supported entirely by the state, so able to offer free education to all. By making the nature of European provision more generally known, the Society of Arts report sought to elicit the support needed to rectify the situation in London, firstly through the reform of the RAM, and then, when that failed, by establishing a National Training School with free education and national access based on competitive entry.

Sir Henry Cole was undoubtedly the prime mover behind the founding the National Training School for Music, and it was due to his energy and determination that it opened at Easter 1876 in purpose built premises opposite the west side of the Royal Albert Hall. It was a major undertaking that involved the raising of public subscriptions 'to endow the scholarships to provide for the free education and maintenance of the students', the assignment of land by HM Commissioners for the 1851 Exhibition and the donation of the building itself. Cole secured royal support for the School, particularly that of Prince Alfred, Duke of Edinburgh, Queen Victoria's second son and an enthusiastic amateur violinist. From the outset, the intention of the Society of Arts was that the School should be founded 'with the full intention and under the confident hope that it will eventually be transferred to the responsible management of the State'.[8] In other words, the NTSM was originally envisaged as an experiment, designed to kick-start the government into implementing the Paris Conservatoire model perceived to be so beneficial for French national musical life by the Society of Arts in their 1866 report. The plan was that the NTSM should be supported by public subscription for a limited period, after which, on the basis of its demonstrable success, it would be handed over to a grateful government who would then assume full financial responsibility. This accounts for the fact that originally the NTSM scholarship subscriptions were intended to run for only five years. But the government was to remain impervious to all attempts to induce it to fund a national conservatoire, happy instead to give the NTSM and the RAM each a token annual amount of £500 per annum at a time that the Paris Conservatoire was reported to be receiving £12,000 in state funding.[9] It is not altogether surprising that the government preferred to take an unsentimental view, happy to see the coexistence of two independent colleges rather than moving to create a single one that would enjoy national status, but which would also expect full state support.

The NTSM's financial plight

Very shortly after its opening in 1876, it became clear that the NTSM simply did not have enough income to run on, and in July 1877, the Committee of Management made an appeal to HM Commissioners for the 1851 Exhibition for financial help, which was rejected. In acknowledgement of this letter of appeal, Earl Spencer, the Chief Commissioner, expressed privately his own view of the predicament that the NTSM project was now in:

> I am jealous of the doctrine put forward by the Society of Arts that if the School succeeds during five years of independent life the Government ought, and are expected to take it completely under its own management. I think that is a broken reed to lean upon and that the Treasury are not likely to undertake the charge of providing for Musical Education if they find two Institutions existing who do this work with small Government assistance....the amalgamation of the two institutions would nearly, if not altogether, reduce the deficit which exists in the finances of the School....The greater strength which the union would give to the Musical School of the Kingdom, coupled with some plan for affiliating the School to a University for the purpose of giving degrees in music would, in my opinion, justify the Commission in coming forward with a considerable grant[10].

When Earl Spencer's response was reported back to the Committee of Management, its members realized the expediency of seeking to merge the NTSM with the rival RAM in order to secure the goal of a single national college and also to rescue the financial situation. Originally, the NTSM operation had been projected on the basis of an income that offered 300 scholarships, but it opened in 1876 with only 68 scholars (by 1880 it had limped to only 92 scholars plus 16 fee-paying students). So anxious had been the Committee of Management (which as constituted did not have a musician on it) to get things underway, that its individual members gave personal guarantees for a start-up loan offered by Coutts Bank,[11] and when Sir Henry Cole 'demonstrated that the school could be worked on an income of £4,800 per annum',[12] they began recruiting staff. A very rough indication of the extent to which the NTSM operation was both under-funded and essentially uneconomic in scale, can be seen by contrasting the £4,800 income which Cole felt was viable to run it in 1875, against the fact that in 1879, the RAM achieved an operating surplus of £87 on an income of £13,924 from some 400 students.[13] Significantly, the targets set to run the RCM at its opening were given as 100 scholars and an income of £10,000–£12,000.[14]

The fact that in 1880 the RAM now felt itself strong enough to reject the proposed merger with the NTSM and to continue as an independent institution, even given the undoubted attraction of a new South Kensington site, reflected a considerable change in its fortunes. It was this refusal which triggered the scheme for a new, independent Royal College of Music.[15] For after years of uninterrupted decline, the RAM had become markedly more healthy as an institution, with an unprecedented increase in its student numbers from about 60 or 70 in the 1860s, to 363 in 1877 and reaching over 400 in 1880. It was, as we have seen, now making a small financial return, and with a history and Royal name of its own it was in a position to take advantage from the upsurge in the numbers seeking musical tuition. But the issue of the RAM's independence against what was, in effect, an NTSM takeover prompted the expression of strong institutional jealousies and stands on respective loyalties, further fuelled by what was perceived as the grand manners and high handed actions of South Kensington. Inevitably such perceptions began to play a significant part in shaping and dividing public attitude.[16] Clearly this refusal to merge increased Grove's difficulties in selling the RCM's case to a country which had already experienced two calls in quick succession on its money for scholarship subscriptions in the cause of music education.

The failure of the NTSM's educational provision

The argument for establishing a national school of music in London was based on a widening perception of British under-achievement in music and the recognition that if the position was to be improved, Britain was in very strong need of an institution corresponding in function, purpose and standards to those of the main European conservatoires. Unlike today's tendency towards an international orchestral sound, the nineteenth century prized distinctive national styles of playing, something which had obvious implications for the cohesion and quality of any ensemble whose players had been trained in different traditions. So the desire for a national style of music had as much an implication for the performance situation as it did for composition. This is underlined in the concerns expressed by the redoubtable John Ella, whose Musical Union chamber concerts, running from 1845 to 1881, gave London the first regular opportunity to hear the canonical chamber music repertoire played by some of the greatest continental players. Ella was a regular visitor to Europe and knew about the performance situations in a variety of centres, and his perspective on the role of the National Training School is therefore particularly valuable. Commenting in the *Orchestra*, Ella remarks that:

> Within a few weeks, lately, in Paris, I have heard splendid orchestral concerts, of eighty and 100 musicians, besides those of the Grand Opera and the Opera Comique, composed entirely of native talent, well-educated musicians. For unity of style, taste and feeling, the result of national schools, we have nothing in London to compare with the first class orchestra of Paris, and, for the same reason, those of Vienna. Our cosmopolitan London orchestras are composed of the surplus talent of the continent, some educated, others uneducated, and no two of the same style of playing. With the immediate prospect of a national school for the gratuitous education of the musically gifted youths of this country, let us hope that, eventually, we may have our orchestras complete of well educated native musicians.[17]

This makes Ella's agenda for the NTSM very clear, and it was one in which he was to be disappointed, for by the autumn of 1876 the School's 74 scholars (17 males, 57 females) were made up of 42 pianists, 22 singers, nine violinists and one organist. In December 1877, Sullivan reported the concern of the Board of Professors to the Committee of Management:

> The orchestral practices, of so much importance as distinguishing a National School of Music from a private venture have been hitherto wanting, and can no longer be delayed without obvious injury to the career of the students and without the danger of compromising the reputation of the school.[18]

At this meeting, Sullivan requested £230 to cover the cost of 'orchestral assistance', or one professional string player per part and the hire of music for a year. Eventually, some two years later, in June 1880 Sullivan was able to report to the Committee that the orchestral class had been established and consisted of nine each of first and second violins, two violas, six cellos, one flute, one clarinet, and 'the other wind instrument parts are taken by the pianists'.[19] Some of even this body of instrumentalists were pianists playing their second study, for the School's Fourth General report, indicating that the figures are substantially the same as for the Report for the previous year, gives the principal study numbers as 57 piano, 32 singing, 14 violin, five organ, one flute.[20] This all represented a lamentable situation when compared to continental conservatoires, and so cosmopolitan a figure as Ella could not have been but bitterly aware of the shortcomings of a supposedly national institution that could not muster even the most usual brass and woodwind orchestral instruments. This situation gives an insight into a series of conflicting tensions about the NTSM's work that would undermine Grove's case for the RCM. Firstly, the scholarship scheme, the principle on which the NTSM was founded, was not attracting national talent, or, from another viewpoint, preference was being given to the genteel pursuits of piano and singing in an institution which saw itself as not having responsibility for serious orchestral training. It is this sort of inability to deliver a perceived need which generated a sense that the NTSM had failed, and the consequent resentment against the proposed RCM scheme by many professional musicians. It also helps to explain the polarization of opinion to the effect that that the RCM was a plaything of the nobility for the training of amateurs, while the RAM was under the control of musicians for the training of professional performers[21]. Neither of these perceptions was an accurate representation, as we shall see, but it is indicative of the negative attitudes which Grove had to surmount.

For all its splash of royal support and high-minded intentions, the NTSM was never much more than a hand-to-mouth operation whose education was effectively no different to that offered by some of the other private, fee-charging schools,[22] such as the RAM (which in 1877 had 363 students), the Crystal Palace School and the London Academy of Music (founded in 1861, which had upwards of 400 students in 1877). It was the NTSM's immense good fortune that its scholarship places did bring to it a few exceptionally talented students, such as Eugène d'Albert from Newcastle, Frederic Cliffe and Walter Alcock, whose presence at the institution (or in Alcock's case his subsequent reputation), masked what seems to have been the uninspiring mediocrity of many of their fellows. But the worst blow to the aspirations so boldly set out for the NTSM was to come in the Examiners' report for the summer period 1880; worst, in the sense that by striking at the very heart of the effectiveness of its work and general standards, it fatally damaged the NTSM's name and effectively ensured that the NTSM mission could only be pursued under another identity.

The examiners, Charles Hallé (Chair), Sir Michael Costa, Sir George Elvey, Otto Goldschmidt and Henry Leslie, submitted a damning report on the summer exams which was received by the School's Committee of Management at its meeting on 14 July, 1880.[23] The examiners called into question the very process of assessment which they had heard; the suitability of what they had heard for the purpose of examination; the quality of the students' progress in general (with named exceptions such as Eugène d'Albert); and the quality of instruction they were receiving. They concluded with emphatic criticism of Sullivan's effectiveness as Principal, remarking that they had 'failed to observe an executive cohesion in general' in respect of the School's work. Sir Julius Benedict, although one of the examiners, declined to sign this report, and so let the School off the hook, allowing Sullivan and the staff to call it an 'incomplete' report. The Committee of Management resolved that their confidence in the Principal and the staff is 'in no wise diminished in consequence of this report', sending a copy of that resolution to the examiners. Sullivan submitted his resignation, and no reaction to this is recorded in the minutes.[24] The Fourth General Report of the NTSM is masterly in its deadpan expression of the situation:

> Owing to some unfortunate want of understanding between the Authorities of the School and the Examiners, the Examination, though going on for two days, was not formally conducted; and in a Report which the Examiners made to H.R.H. The Prince of Wales, it was admitted that the Examination which had been held was not an Examination in the strict sense of the word, and neither fair nor advantageous to Master or Pupil. Under these circumstances, it was arranged that another Examination of a more strict, formal, and searching character should be held at the earliest convenience of the Examiners.[25]

Needless to say, there is no record of this subsequent examination ever being held. However, news of this scandal circulated within professional circles and appeared in the press. Under the heading 'Royal Musical Schemes', the *Musical World* reproducing a report on the incident from the Citizen, remarks:

> ...we are inclined to think that after reading the [Examiners'] report, [the Prince of Wales] formed a strong opinion as to the expediency of promoting musical instruction through some more efficiently-conducted and influential medium than the South Kensington Training School.[26]

The article concludes with the thought that not the least benefit of some government subsidy for the proposed RCM would be to make it subject to government supervision.

Sullivan described this report by the Examiners as a 'backstairs' intrigue' led by Hallé, who was revenging himself for Sullivan's own appointment as conductor of the Leeds Festival,[27] but a more likely explanation is that it was a direct response to a perceived waste of the NTSM opportunity. There has to be some doubt as to Sullivan's own commitment to the NTSM ideal, not least in terms of his attitude: 'My hand was always in my pocket to help some poor student to get daily food. Oh, the curse of this free education bringing up a class of educated, helpless paupers!'[28] Financially, Sullivan was very well placed to help, with an income in 1880 of £9,998 12s 6d (the Prime Ministerial salary was £7,500),[29] and shortly after his resignation he was able to lose £450 (£50 more than his NTSM salary) in one night at the gaming table, returning two days later to win £350.[30] However, Sullivan's attitude to scholarships was in fact indicative of a wider public resistance to the idea of scholarship provision against which Grove needed to argue in order to secure the endowments upon which the RCM would depend.[31] All in all, the unhappy experience of Sullivan as Principal of the NTSM was a caution for the future and a warning that eminence as a composer or performer, even on the part of a royal favourite, was itself no guarantee of vision as a Principal. An important observer of the highly unsatisfactory situation at the NTSM had been Sir Francis Knollys, Private Secretary to the Prince of Wales. Knollys, with others in the Prince's royal household, is likely to have been concerned to ensure that, if his master insisted on backing the establishment of a new conservatoire, then this time it would have to be with a more suitable person in control. This perhaps helps to explain the strength of Knollys's practical support for Grove in the process of setting up the RCM, as will be illustrated below.

Grove's appointment as Director

As may be imagined, George Grove's appointment as the RCM's first Director flew in the face of the expectation that the principal of a conservatoire should be a professional musician of some distinction. After all the Royal Academy had had Sterndale Bennett and Macfarren as Principals, and Arthur Sullivan and John Stainer had been the successive Principals of the National Training School. In conferring Grove's knighthood, the Prince of Wales said: 'Mr Grove, although not an active musician, has done more for the development of musical taste in England than many composers and executants.[32] But a letter from Henry (later Sir Henry) Leslie, the choral conductor, to Lord Folkestone dated 9 January 1883 (four days before the publication of the RCM's Prospectus) marked 'private and confidential' suggests something of the private reservations which are likely to have been felt by several:

> I fear very much a mess will be made with the start of the R. College of Music. How can an amateur, who knows absolutely nothing of even elementary music education properly control a professional body in the highest artistic culture? The Prince of Wales has asked me (perhaps also others) to advise Mr Grove on any practical points he may require, and of course I shall do so to the best of my ability. But the lookout is to my mind, a sad one.[33]

Despite the likelihood of *amour-propre* being behind this particular attack (Leslie had been Principal of the short-lived private National College of Music, had given evidence to Cole's Society of Arts Music Education committee, and doubtless felt himself more suited and certainly more qualified than Grove to direct the RCM), evidence of this sort of response to Grove's appointment makes necessary some attempt to answer the question as to why such an unusual choice of Director should have been made, and which of Grove's acknowledged qualities gave it viability. The first consideration, and one which contemporaries clearly raised, was why was it that George Grove was chosen to establish and then to lead the RCM in preference to a music professional of established repute, such as (for the sake of argument) John Ella? This particular assessment, although hypothetical, is useful because it affords a clearer understanding of Grove's very individual locus, both personal and professional. As has been seen, Ella's forcefully argued article in the *Orchestra* was strong evidence of his concern for the training of professional performers, and his interest in the NTSM was clearly demonstrated. While there is no evidence that Ella (1802–88) had presented himself as a candidate, and although ruled out by age and health from the hurly-burly of the fundraising process itself, on the face of it he might be said to have had sufficient credibility to be a first, figurehead Director in the RCM's initial years. Through his Musical Union, Ella had established for himself a cachet in society and a huge reputation as a shaper of musical taste. As the programmes of the Musical Union show, Ella was up to date with the work of European composers and able to secure the services of top continental talent such as Clara Schumann, Joachim, Vieuxtemps and Piatti.[34] He was a practical musician, and although not formally educated to Grove's own level, the Musical Union concerts had featured programme notes from their inception in 1845, well before Grove's own notes for the Crystal Palace. But this speculation – why Grove and not Ella – is useful precisely because it provides a clear measure of the contemporary recognition (despite the reservations of such as Henry Leslie) that was afforded Grove as a man of credibility and significance in the musical world, with, in addition, a sense that his star was still further on the ascendant. For in March 1880, Ella had written to Grove, enclosing a draft testimonial on his own behalf which he asked Grove to endorse, an action which is eloquent indication of Ella's perception of Grove's standing in the scheme of things. Interestingly, Grove chose to decline,[35] and couched his refusal in modest, even self-deprecatory terms, referring to Ella's achievements in a way that could cause Ella no offence, while being resolute in withholding the requested testimonial.[36]

Perhaps another reason for Grove's appointment lay in the very diversity of views (including those of the educationalist, John Hullah) as to what role, or indeed, the range of roles it was envisaged that the College should endeavour to fulfil within its published mission. These different views continued to coexist, largely unresolved, and resulted in a broadly-based philosophy of training that viewed RCM students as teachers and general music practitioners as well as professional performers. A quintessential British compromise, it was something that Grove, with his liberal vision of the role of music in society was much better equipped to bring about. Indeed, the speech he wrote for the Duke of Albany describes music as a 'civilising, humanising element in life',[37] and draws specific attention to the disservice to British music in general that was caused by its London focus, the 'over concentration, the want of diffusion of music in England'.[38] However, in terms of the importance of the RCM as a conservatoire for the training of British performers, Grove, with his practical involvement in the Crystal Palace concerts, reinforced by August Manns' concern for high standards of orchestral performance, would have been only too aware of the problems of working with a restricted pool of London orchestral players and the damage done to performance standards by the infamous deputy system that had been exacerbated by rehearsal clashes between the Crystal Palace and Philharmonic Society orchestras.[39] Consequently, Grove would have been very conscious that the RCM had a responsibility to respond to this situation through the training of professional instrumentalists.

Grove's relationship with the Prince of Wales's household

Although the process of establishing the College demanded a very disparate range of skills, including fundraiser and development officer (to use our modern equivalents) as well as philosopher, musical-scholar and educationalist, there was to be no separation of personnel. In other words, Grove saw the task as an entirety. It is probable that this was very much at his own wish, for although he was to profess an element of surprise at the fact that he was to be Director as well as Founder, his economic circumstances did not give him much latitude. In 1880, Grove was facing the end of his seven-year contract at *Macmillan's* (which had started in 1874 at £1,300), and although he was to receive another year's salary in order to expedite progress on the *Dictionary*, he was at this stage worried about his future.[40] The RCM was offering the much smaller initial salary of £750, and even that was effectively conditional upon the College's successful establishment. Grove was only too well aware of the magnitude of the task he had to accomplish and the uncertainty of its outcome. Yet this must have seemed to him to have been a chance worth taking. The range of skills that the role demanded played very much to his strengths, while the opportunity to instigate, and then to head what was being heralded as an important national institution, also carried with it the promise of a significant measure of public honour. Indeed, it is more than likely that the anxious future which Grove was facing had the effect of sharpening his determination to succeed with the RCM, as well as determining his strategy to assume what was virtually a solo role in the process. For, seen in the context of his personality and achievements to date, Grove is likely to have felt that he was more able to rely upon himself than upon anyone else to deliver under these difficult circumstances, and chose to work this way in order to minimize his vulnerability.

The suggestions in the press that a considerable part of the impetus behind the wish to see the RCM rise, phoenix-like, out of the NTSM's ashes was in order to save royal face, almost certainly meant that the search must have been on amongst the Prince of Wales's advisers to identify someone who could successfully pull off this new scheme without further embarrassment to the Prince. It would have been recognized as a daunting assignment, and correspondence that has survived from Sir Francis Knollys to Grove, suggests that theirs was a pivotal relationship in setting up the College, with Knollys sometimes steadying Grove. This passage from a letter of 1882 is indicative, significantly changing from the third person to the first, then reverting back again:

> He [the Prince] is certain to see Mr Gladstone during the winter after Parliament has adjourned, when he will not lose the opportunity to speak to him about it [Government funding for the RCM].
>
> I [Knollys] hope that you will always write to me as openly as possible whenever anything occurs to you which you think may benefit the College.
>
> HRH entirely approves of your suggestion...[41]

Several other letters indicate the extent of the support that the Knollys either himself gave or arranged to be given. The following passage from Knollys to the Duke of Albany's private secretary about the fundraising meeting to be held at Salisbury, relates to the need to ensure an impressive aristocratic turn out for the event:

> It is very desirable that as many of the important and influential Residents in the County as is possible should be present, and the Prince of Wales thinks that Lord Bath and Lord Folkestone should be asked to attend, among others, if they have not already signified their intention to do so.[42]

There is almost a sense of easy complicity about an exchange relating to a meeting at Swansea when a telegram was sent in support of the project, drawing the tenuous connection that the Prince, 'can not forget the magnificent reception the Princes received at Swansea the year before last'. Knollys writes to Grove:

> HRH was very glad to hear of your successful meeting at Swansea and that his telegram had a good effect. You were quite right to telegraph to me [Knollys], and as you know the Prince is always anxious to help you and to render the work which you are carrying on in so highly a satisfactory manner easier for you when he can do so.[43]

It is evident, and not surprising, from the loneliness of the responsibility that Grove was bearing, that the pressure took an especial toll at times, as Knollys was able to perceive. In a letter marked 'Private' written during the run up to the RCM's official opening ceremony, Knollys wrote: 'Let me take this opportunity of saying that the Prince will be ready at all times to support you and to strengthen your hand in every possible way.'[44] Paradoxically, the burden of this constant royal presence, with its particular weight of responsibility, must have added considerably to Grove's worries in a task which, as was becoming ever more apparent, would fall far short of the subscription target necessary to ensure scholarships for all the planned student places. For what Grove was contending with was a very complex situation which at times was hard to define. That he achieved a level of success that was sufficient for the College to run on, is a real vindication of the decision to cast him in this lead role. We have also to admire the perception of understanding (or the NTSM lesson learned) that, once opened, the RCM needed a Grove to set it firmly on track, rather than a Sullivan or a Stainer.

Grove's impact on musical life

Grove, despite his lack of formal musical training, combined work in the practical domain of organizing and delivering London's most adventurous and prestigious orchestral concert series at Crystal Palace, with the more reflective, but no less active, roles of critic and scholar. This breadth of experience, taken together with his work outside music, made Grove particularly sensitive to an exceptionally wide range of those stimuli that were currently shaping events and attitudes in British public life. The well-developed antennae that made him such a brilliantly informed editor of *Macmillan's Magazine* – a notably broad-based and liberal-minded publication that brought together the worlds of the arts and the sciences – meant that he was able and well placed to function as both point of intersection and as a conduit to refocus and channel energies from a variety of sources. In this sense, Grove was the engine that powered the RCM into being through his combination of administrative vigour, astute use of contacts, ability to work usefully with those for whom he felt little rapport, and an inner strength and sense of self-worth, which, although sometimes threatened by depression, gave him the strength to submerge his own personality in the interests of his main objective. We can, perhaps, get a broad sense of the impact that Grove had in modernizing London's musical culture and taste in the nineteenth century, by viewing his achievement in relation to that of Sir William Glock as Controller of Music at the BBC.[45] The role of an individual in bringing about a process of profound change of attitude can soon be hidden as the products of these changes themselves become culturally assimilated. As has increasingly become the case with Glock, so it is with

Grove. For it was Grove's own advocacy of Beethoven and Schubert as well as more contemporary composers through his programming of their works at the immensely popular Crystal Palace concerts, together with presenting performers such as Clara Schumann and Joachim, which meant that Grove, more than any other single individual of his time brought about the wider realignment of London's musical life. Grove and Glock each utilized to maximum effect the very different means that were available to them in a way that now seems to us to be visionary. Grove's mission to educate, as we now would tend to express it, was as evident in his editing of *Macmillan's Magazine* as in his Crystal Palace programme notes, and this profile made him a powerful beacon in the establishment of a national college for the training of musicians.

Presenting the case for the RCM

But was the primary role of a Royal College of Music to train performers, or was it to train teachers, so building upon the scope given to music by the 1870 Education Act? There is some evidence to suggest that Grove found it expedient to keep the possibility of both these roles simultaneously in play, and so to avoid any implication that they could be construed as mutually exclusive. Thus on one hand the RCM's stated objective, as established in every version of the RCM Prospectus circulating in 1882 and 1883, could align it with the performance mission of the conservatoires of Paris and Vienna, institutions with whose purpose Grove was very familiar, while not contradicting another influential dynamic, that of the quality of school music provision. This latter was a cause which Grove helped to propagate in *Macmillan's Magazine*. The philosophical case for the RCM as it was perceived by Prince Christian's executive committee was presented by Charles Sumner Maine in his article, 'A Conservatoire of Music for England'.[46] It argued that the lack of permanent concert provision in all but a relatively few English towns – so unlike the situation in Germany – constituted a powerful case for the establishment of a national college, thereby identifying such an institution with the need to train the many performers necessary to reverse this situation. But then, if not actually prompted by Grove, then certainly with his approval, Maine carefully broadens the remit of such an institution. He says that it should certainly correspond to European conservatoires, but '*adapted to English wants and requirements*' [my emphasis]. It should be also:

> ...a centre for all matters connected with music and for the settling of such questions as the long-disputed one of musical pitch. It should hold examinations and grant certificates; and last, but not least, it should fix the standard for what is to be taught in Elementary schools and should control them by efficient inspection.[47]

This explicit association of an educational remit for a national conservatoire served several purposes. While there was the genuine desire to spread the effectiveness of music education in schools, the accomplishment of this aim was also a means of exerting moral and practical pressure for government funding of the Royal College. The intention, formulated with John Hullah, was that a limited number of selected trainee teachers should spend a period at the RCM before being transferred to a centre from which they would assist in teaching music at elementary schools:

> ...candidates for the office of musical examiner in elementary schools be required to attend a course of special instruction at the Royal College at the close of which their general musical knowledge, and especially their skill and tact as examiners, should be tested and certified by the professors of that institution.[48]

But identification of this educational role for the RCM also offered a means of camouflaging the provision of public money to an institution that offered opera training, for Maine ends by stating that although scruples might prevent public money going to a National Theatre, no one could object to government funding to a conservatoire undertaking such a public role as he had described; 'Our project appeals to all', he concluded, hopefully. Another statement of the case for a national conservatoire is made in relation to opera, again in *Macmillan's Magazine*, by the writer, music critic and librettist Dr Francis Hueffer, who also contributed to *Grove 1*. It laments the lack of operas written by English composers and sung by English opera singers, but, on the basis of the success of Carl Rosa's season at Her Majesty's Theatre, an experience which proved that native British singing voices were able to do justice to even the most difficult works in the international repertoire, Hueffer argues the case for the establishment of a permanent English opera company in London.[49] Possibly, however, Grove feared that Hueffer's uninhibited advocacy of English opera with its taint of the theatre might have offended some readers, hence the manner in which Maine concluded his later article. Whether this was the case or not, these two articles show Grove as an expert in shaping and marshalling the arguments of a cause amongst the cultured professional readership of *Macmillan's Magazine* on whom he would be relying to help influence opinion in the fundraising effort. It is just this sort of sensitivity in creating potential allies for a cause that reminds us that Grove had already proved his ability as a fundraiser in his work for the Palestine Exploration Fund, involving the judicious use of letters to *The Times*, and establishing a network of influential contacts. Thus well before the RCM project, Grove had a well-established public profile as someone who was able to get things done, highly rated by those he dealt with as possessing the personal qualities of stability, intellectual energy and breadth of mind, and trusted as an enabler and facilitator. Certainly Grove emerges as a more sympathetic figure by far than did his great contemporary and champion of the NTSM, Henry Cole, whom Lord Derby called 'the most generally unpopular man I know'.[50] Cole was certainly indefatigable, a superb administrator, but, by all accounts, without a human touch in handling people. Interestingly, although Cole achieved so much in his lifetime, he failed to bring about the success of the project for a national school of music that meant so much to him. Grove, who was certainly Cole's match in indefatigability, and certainly had a greater quality of warmth, despite his occasional touchiness and asperity of manner, did achieve the RCM by selling its case, rather than just by asserting it, and doing so in terms of a quality of vision that gave the institution a strong philosophical basis. It is an interesting contrast of styles in the pursuit of a worthy, but elusive objective.

The significance of the RCM's charter

A second important objective was declared for the RCM specifically broadening the College's base beyond its training mission, and so giving it an additional public role and regulatory function that greatly enhanced the College's status and significance in national life. This objective was set out as paragraph 12 of the form of the prospectus printed for circulation at fund-raising events in late 1882, although at some, possibly later, stage this sensitive paragraph was quietly dropped.

> In addition to its educational duties, the College will undertake the more extended functions of a university; and will conduct examinations and give musical degrees or certificates of competency in music throughout the British Empire. With this in mind a scheme will be prepared for affiliating musical schools and Colleges which may desire to be associated with the Royal College, and for forming a musical Senate composed of representative musicians from all parts of the Empire, and charged with the duty of fixing standards of examination for degrees, and of advancing by general regulations the art and science of Music.[51]

This duty provided an important additional lever to the case for establishing the College. It harnessed the RCM with the wider drive to establish chartered professional bodies, such as those for solicitors, accountants, druggists or pharmacists, and veterinary surgeons, charged with the regulation of their respective profession – a movement towards identifying and establishing professional standards which had reached something of a formative stage at around 1881.[52] The intended prestige of the RCM's regulatory status was signalled in a speech given by the Duke of Connaught at a meeting, hosted by the Lord Mayor, of merchant bankers and other City professionals at the Mansion House on 20 March 1882. In it, the Duke said that the RCM would have a role comparable in musical terms to that of the Medical Council in medicine, namely, as the seat of a 'musical Senate' constituted of affiliated colleges (including the RAM) that would arbitrate and offer guidance on musical issues and establish common standards for certificates and diplomas in music. In *Chartered Surveyors*, his history of that profession, F.M.L Thompson sets out the significance of chartered status:

> Incorporation by charter was a privilege highly prized by institutions, as a mark of their maturity and of their public recognition. This was not so for legal reasons...It was so for social and moral reasons. In part it was because a charter conferred on an institution [gave it] moral authority over all the members of its profession, moral responsibility for supervising their conduct and a moral, though not a legal monopoly of regulating entry into the profession...the grant of a charter was proof that a society had passed a careful scrutiny of its credentials, its worthiness, its capacity to fulfil its aims, and its generally representative character.[53]

In this context, the granting of a Royal Charter to the RCM had a symbolic as well as a practical significance, and one that was likely to cause considerable jealousy, from those who would feel that the RCM had yet to prove its worth for such a role, as well as from backers of the RAM who would baulk at this signal mark of favour. It also caused serious concern among the universities, who protested strongly at the right of the RCM to award degrees. But for the purposes of fundraising, it offered the RCM privileged status that set it clearly apart and distanced it from its NTSM predecessor, and also from the RAM, neither of which enjoyed these rights. But, as Thompson's assessment suggests, propriety had been stretched in awarding such a charter on a new and as yet untried institution. Grove's record as a scholar of substance would have lent much-needed credibility to the RCM as a chartered institution invested with such powers as these. As an engineer, who had been admitted 'a graduate' of the Institution of Civil Engineers in February 1839, Grove was very conscious of the seriousness of professional training and of the significance of professional qualifications. And as a noted lexicographer, Grove's instincts would have responded strongly to the concern for a proper ordering of knowledge, and provision for its coherent dissemination.

Selling the concept of the RCM: Grove's fundraising themes

The fundraising speech that Grove made at Leeds,[54] in the centre of the industrial heartlands, illustrates exactly how Grove used his breadth of experience to formulate his case for the RCM. The purpose of the speech was to make the audience 'better acquainted with the objects and scope of the institution' and Grove does so in a speech of considerable astuteness.

It ranges widely in subject matter, blending historical reference, national patriotism and local pride, in a manner that in moving between sophistication and tub-thumping rhetoric also gives a strong flavour of the public attitudes of his time. But perhaps its most interesting theme is a vision of the arts that is based on their potential to encompass both aesthetic significance and practical need. This shows Grove the engineer's ability to relate to the functional importance of industrial design for his audience of manufacturers, but he emphasizes that the graphic nature of the skill made it a branch of the visual arts. Thus, by analogy with the 'usefulness' of music, Grove brings industrial manufacturers into closer contact with his vision for the RCM. He also reminds his audience of the significance of technology in infrastructural advances, such as the building of railways, bridges and canals, with the message that there are new technical skills involved in achieving 'progress' in any sphere, whether artistic or scientific: who is going to teach such skills, and who is going to ensure that they are being taught properly? That, translated onto the musical domain, was to be the role of the RCM, hence the necessity of its being properly established.

In arguing his case, Grove also makes shrewd play upon the role and personal commitment of members of the royal family, emphasizing the prestige and importance that the RCM would have as a national institution, a status that would in turn reflect well upon those subscribing to it. He illustrated this by saying that the RCM would enjoy the prestige in music that the Royal Academy of Art had in painting as an institution of musical stature which Britain presently lacked: 'The college would thus possess the character of a University, and be the head English musical centre. All the most distinguished people connected with English music would be directed…to its council and managing board.'

He said that it was because of the present lack of a national institution, that '[a] large number of English students were driven…at an impressionable period of their lives, to the continent for the purpose of study, and who by that means naturally became not English but German musicians.' Grove owned a history of the Leipzig conservatoire in which he had marked the names of many of its British students.[55] It was one of the claims that Macfarren, on behalf of the RAM, was most anxious to counter, but, typically, Grove's claim was based on knowledge of the numbers involved. He argues that:

> In his [Grove's] opinion it was their [his audience's] duty to [contribute towards scholarships to] keep our English boys at home, to educate them here, and to make our English music as national, as characteristic as our literature, and our painting, and our manufactures, and other things of which we were so proud as Englishmen.

But the audience should not for a moment consider that music meant frivolity:

> The College would be a place of work, and not of recreation and amusement – strict examinations being kept up throughout. Students would have to go there with the intention of learning music in the best possible way, and treating it as a serious matter of life.

Grove would himself have been known to several of the audience as a fine exemplar of the virtue of diligence.

Grove's speech has a strong historical dimension, arguing that as a fact of history, music was a British birthright and not a foreign import. To prove his case, Grove calls particular attention to the round, 'Sumer is icumen in', doing so in terms that evoke industrial process (with composition as something that had been 'invented', resulting in 'productions'), an acknowledgement of the significance of British manufacturing industry that will have appealed to the Leeds audience:

> It [Sumer is icumen in] was written 150 years before any other piece of music which could be found on the continent, and showed that at that time we were 150 years in advance of those great learned Flemings and Italians whom we had always been in the habit of considering the inventors of music. More than this, the music in question was not written in the learned, crabbed style which marked the first productions of the Flemish and Italian contemporary schools...

Grove had used the example of 'Sumer is icumen in' in the speech he had ghost-written for the Duke of Albany's address in Manchester in 1881, where the corresponding passage has no such industrial allusion.[56]

Grove concludes with a direct appeal to contemporary local pride, prefaced by the admonition that even though many people in Leeds had been familiar with the provision offered by the NTSM, Grove had noticed that Leeds had not provided a single one of its scholarships. By contrast, he pointed out that the NTSM's building had been donated by a single individual. This example of generosity also meant that the money now being raised for RCM scholarships would be able to be used entirely for that purpose, and not for bricks and mortar. This new appeal was Leeds' opportunity to redeem its reputation:

> The college was certain to be founded, whether Leeds assisted or not, because the Prince of Wales had made himself personally responsible. How would it look if a great town like Leeds, or a great district like the West Riding, had no part in the matter? Besides, it would not be fair. Leeds would probably be the first to knock at the college doors, for they would be certain to send up some of their clever Yorkshire boys, with their fine musical voices, for training in the college. What was £3,000, £5,000, or £10,000 for a great town like Leeds? It meant in many cases,

> a mere scratch of the pen and a little diminution at the banker's, which would never be regretted, but which, on the other hand, would always be a source of thankfulness to the donor.

There is something curious about the way that this speech is presented by the *Musical World*, which emphasizes the degree of ambivalence with which the RCM case was being received by the professional musical community. On the face of things, Grove should have found it helpful to have the text of his appeal more widely circulated through this journal, but it in fact appears (printed side-by side in parallel columns) with a speech that G.A. Macfarren had given in Manchester on behalf of the Royal Academy of Music. Direct comparison was therefore not only intended, but unavoidable, and by this stage in the campaign, the themes of Grove's fundraising were obviously well known to Macfarren, who uses this Manchester opportunity to counter, or to spoil, some of Grove's aspirations for the RCM, by presenting the RAM's achievements to date as those of an established European-style conservatoire which already enjoyed national standing. So the reader was therefore seeing the claims of the respective institutional positions being counterpointed against each other, and not always to Grove's advantage. For example, Macfarren argues that there was in fact no necessity for English students to go abroad to complete their study, and cites the case of an Academy student who won the Mendelssohn Scholarship but who was asked to leave the Leipzig Conservatoire because his Academy training meant that he had already covered the ground of the Leipzig syllabus. Indeed, Macfarren pointed out, foreign students came to study at the RAM. He said that although the RAM offered some orchestral training, the economic conditions for orchestral players were so poor that this activity did not offer a respectable, living wage, which explained the preponderance of foreign players in British orchestral life. Accordingly, there was no imperative to develop this area further. It is indicative that such an argument, with its implied dismissal of either the importance or significance of high orchestral standards, was far removed from Grove's own musical philosophy.

Conclusion

We have seen how, in making the case for the RCM, Grove sought to present the College as a vital element within the wider context of national life. He considered that the argument for the RCM should not be considered only on a narrow musical basis, but as a broader issue of education. He highlighted the development of art education over the past thirty years, and says that given the chance, music education would mean that in fifty years' time the musical tastes of the people would have developed in ways they presently could not foresee, and that this change would bring social as well as artistic benefit. This reference to art education is an allusion to the work of Sir Henry Cole. In 1852, Cole was made General Superintendent of the Schools of Design. There were 20 schools in all, with provincial branches and a London centre (the forerunner of the Royal College of Art). Nearly half their funds came from the government (£7,500 grant-in-aid in 1851) and the rest by public subscription; this was a situation that was in notable contrast to the £500 annual government grant given to the NTSM and the RAM. Cole brought his model for these schools to bear on his thinking for the NTSM, and it continued to be an influence in the early discussions about the RCM, both in the system of scholarships and for John Hullah's proposed scheme for training specialist music teachers at the College.[57] Cole built up the model of provincial schools feeding their most talented students into the London centre, in an education that was based on a rigidly systemized process of exercises and examinations.[58] It was a system that brought Cole a bad contemporary press, with Dickens characterizing him as a soulless, bureaucratic school inspector in *Hard Times* (1854): 'A mighty man at cutting and drying...always with a system to force down the general throat like a bolus'.[59]

The benefits of the broader social dimension of the RCM, something that was implicit in its merit-based scheme of scholarship education, was reinforced by the Prince of Wales in his speech at the RCM's opening ceremony:

> ...the time has come when class can no longer stand aloof from class.... I claim for music the merit that it has a voice which speaks in different tones, perhaps, but with equal force to the cultivated and the ignorant, to the peer and the peasant.[60]

This report of the opening also makes specific mention that the students of the new institution include 'a mill-girl, the daughter of a bricklayer, the son of a blacksmith, and the son of a farm labourer'. So what had Grove achieved as the RCM opened on 7 May 1883 after 44 fundraising meetings across the UK and the other associated activities pressing the RCM's case? On one level it was a disappointing 50 scholarships and no government funding. The *Musical Times*, in its report of the College's inauguration, described the £110,000 raised by public subscription as 'by no means munificent or encouraging', as 'equal to a twelve-thousandth part of the national income, or about one-third of a farthing per head of the population'. It sought to account for this, saying that 'We are all honourable men and lovers of music; but to the ordinary educated Englishman, music is an abstraction until united with some essential'.[61] It is an assessment which also reflects Grove's shrewdness in handling his Leeds audience. But despite disappointment at the total amount raised, it was sufficient to start the RCM on a sound footing, and in achieving this, Grove established the conditions for the renaissance of British music in the twentieth century. He created a successful institutional situation that could harness the work of composers such as

Parry and Stanford, together with influential instrumental and singing teachers. The result was the training of such numbers of talented students of the next generation as to generate a critical mass of British composers and performers. In turn, their work began to transform public attitudes to music. It is an achievement which substantiates the aspiration that Grove originally had for the RCM, and which he articulated so clearly during his speech at Leeds, in a passage which was emphasized by the *Musical World*:

> *He [Grove] believed that there was such a period of development coming upon music in the next fifty years as had never been seen in England, and that it would be one of the most characteristic things of that period of our history.*[62]

Notes

1 Minutes are in RCMA 007/2, pp.32–42.
2 RCM Council (7 November 1894), RCMA 007/2, p.44. The motion was proposed by Sir Arthur Sullivan.
3 The same meeting fixed the salary of Grove's successor at £800.
4 *Musical Times*, 24, 484 (June 1883), pp.309–10.
5 *Monthly Musical Record*, 12, 136 (1 April 1882), p.80.
6 Arthur Lawrence, *Sir Arthur Sullivan – Life Story, Letters and Reminiscences* (London, 1899), p.111.
7 Society for the Encouragement of Arts, Manufacturers and Commerce, *First Report of the Committee…on the State of Musical Education, at Home and Abroad*, 27 June 1866 (London, 1867).
8 NTSM Committee of Management Meeting (29 May 1873) RCMA 001/1, p.18a.
9 Reported by John Ella in 'Professor Ella's lecture on Spohr's "Jessonda"', *Orchestra*, New Series, 19 (February 1876), p.202.
10 Text given in NTSM/CMM (26 July 1877), p.176.
11 NTSM/CMM (26 June 1875) RCMA 001/1, p.55.
12 NTSM/CMM (19 November 1875) RCMA 001/1, p.64.
13 Figures given in G.W.E. Brightwell, 'The National Training School for Music 1873–1882: Catalyst or Cul-de-Sac?', University of Durham MA thesis, 1998, p.73.
14 *Monthly Musical Record*, 12, 136 (1 April 1882), p.81.
15 NTSM/CMM (16 February 1880) RCMA 001/1, p.224.
16 Indicative is the article 'Royal College of Music' commenting on the fundraising meeting Grove held in Bath, reprinted from the *Bath Evening Chronicle* in the *Musical World* (29 July 1882), p.469.
17 John Ella, 'Professor Ella's lecture on Spohr's '"Jessonda"', *Orchestra*, New Series, 19 (February, 1876), p.202.
18 Sullivan's report to the NTSM Committee of Management, meeting on 10 December 1877 (RCMA 001/1), p.186
19 RCMA 001/1, pp.238–9.
20 NTSM Fourth General Report (Easter 1881), p.98.
21 This perception is reinforced by the *Monthly Musical Record*, 12, 136 (1 April 1882), p.82, which reported that the names of the RCM Executive Committee had not yet been released, 'but we are assured that "they will command the confidence alike of the public and of the musical world." Of this committee the professional element ought to form a principal ingredient'.

22 In addition to the commentary on the orchestral situation, Sullivan's December 1877 report to the Committee of Management also observed, 'The organization of the school is...in every way satisfactory, *so far as its means allow it to go* [my italics]....But at present the teaching (with the exception of the Choral Class) is purely individual, and differs in principle but slightly from that one might expect to find in any good private school'. NTSM/CMM (10 December 1877), RCMA 001/1, p.185.

23 NTSM/CMM (10 December 1877), RCMA 001/1, pp.244–8.

24 Sullivan in fact resigned at the meeting of 13 May 1881 (RCMA 001/2, pp.23–5), an announcement received with suitable expressions of regret and gratitude (Stainer was appointed to succeed him at a salary of £400). But as the minutes of that meeting show, Sullivan's leadership had not emerged unscathed from the exams held in March 1881, the Examiners' report for which was presented also on 13 May.

25 NTSM, Fourth General Report (Easter 1881), p.9.

26 *Musical World*, 59, 4 (22 January 1881), p.54.

27 Arthur Jacobs, *Arthur Sullivan* (Oxford, 1984; 2nd edn, 1986), p.150.

28 *Ibid.*

29 *Ibid.*, p.155.

30 *Ibid.*, p.151.

31 This is illustrated in the reservation expressed by EH Turpin in a passage headed 'Royal College of Music' reprinted from the *Musical Standard*, in the *Musical World*, 60, 29 (22 July 1882), p.443. Even C.V. Stanford, appointed by Grove to the RCM, continued to inveigh against scholarship provision in his *Pages from an Unwritten Diary* (London, 1914), p.213.

32 *The Times*, 8 May 1883.

33 Letter held in the ownership of the Earl of Radnor, who has kindly given permission for this passage to be quoted. I am grateful to Celia Clarke for drawing it to my attention.

34 For an illuminating discussion of Ella's work and significance, see C. Bashford, 'John Ella and the Making of the Musical Union', *Music and British Culture, 1785–1914: Essays in Honour of Cyril Ehrlich*, ed C. Bashford and L. Langley (Oxford, 2000), pp.193–214.

35 This must have been a somewhat problematic request in the light of Grove's membership of Prince Christian's Executive Committee, given Ella's accumulation of influential enemies in the press and in the music profession.

36 I am grateful to Christina Bashford for information regarding this request by Ella and for valuable discussion of this issue.

37 *Music in England and the Proposed Royal College of Music: Three Addresses delivered by the Duke of Edinburgh, Duke of Albany and Prince Christian at Manchester 12 December 1881* (London, 1882), p.9.

38 *Ibid.*, p.8.

39 See Michael Musgrave, *The Musical Life of the Crystal Palace* (Cambridge, 1995), p.76.

40 I am grateful to Leanne Langley for alerting me to this point.

41 RCMA 0096/1, dated 8 October 1882.

42 *Ibid.*, letter dated 28 November 1882.

43 *Ibid.*, letter dated 17 March 1883.

44 *Ibid.*, letter dated 16 April 1883.

45 Interestingly, at the time of his BBC appointment in 1959, Glock had been approached to become the Principal of the Guildhall School of Music and Drama.

46 Charles Sumner Maine, 'A Conservatoire of Music for England: Report of Prince Christian's Executive Committee since its foundation by the Prince of Wales', *Macmillan's Magazine*, XLI, 242 (November, 1879), pp.145–53.
47 *Ibid.*, p.149.
48 John Hullah, Report to the Lords of the Committee of Council on Education on 'The Examination in Music of the Students of Training Colleges in Great Britain', *Musical World*, 59, 45 (5 November 1881), p.708.
49 Francis Hueffer, 'The Chances of English Opera', *Macmillan's Magazine*, XL, 235 (May, 1879), pp.57–65.
50 Quoted in Elizabeth Bonython, *King Cole: a Picture Portrait* (London, n.d), p.2.
51 The Royal College of Music Prospectus, copies dated 1 October and 15 November 1882, held in the RCM's Department of Portraits & Performance History, file marked '1882 Matters'. The version of the Prospectus which omits paragraph 12 is undated.
52 F.M.L. Thompson, *Chartered Surveyors: the Growth of a Profession* (London, 1968), p.177.
53 *Ibid.*, pp.173–4.
54 Reported in the *Musical World*, 60, 28 (15 July 1882), pp.427–9.
55 Dr Emil Kneschke, *Das Conservatorium der Musik in Leipzig. Seine Geschichte, seine Lehrer und Zöglinge. Festgabe zum 25jährigen Jubiläum zum 2.April 1868* (Leipzig [1872]). RCMA XXII.A.5(1). I am grateful to Peter Horton for drawing this to my attention.
56 'Music in England and the Proposed Royal College of Music: Three addresses… at Manchester 12 December 1881', p.11. The text is included in a bound volume from Grove's library containing miscellaneous papers, indexed on the inside front cover in Grove's hand. Against the entry for this Duke of Albany's speech is the remark 'written by G. Grove'. RCM Library, press mark XXII B.20.
57 *Vide* John Hullah's 1880 report to the Lords of the Committee of Council on Education, on 'The Examination in Music of the Students of Training Colleges in Great Britain', in *Musical World*, especially the passages given in vols 59, 44 (29 October 1881), p.692, and 59, 45 (5 November 1881), p.708.
58 A systematic scheme of local music examinations was established by the Associated Board of the RCM and the RAM in 1899.
59 Quoted in Bonython, p.9.
60 'Royal College of Music', *Musical Times*, 24, 484 (June 1883), pp.309–10.
61 *Ibid.*
62 *Musical World*, 60, 28 (15 July 1882), p.428.

10
Grove as First Director of the RCM

Janet Ritterman

On 10 October 1894, scarcely more than a fortnight into the new academic term, Sir George Grove took a decision that had been weighing on his mind for several months. With a heavy heart he wrote to the Prince of Wales, President of the Royal College of Music, to offer his resignation. He was then 74; the post of Director he had held since 1882.

The decision was hard and, as he said in his letter, caused him 'very real distress': for the past 12 years the Royal College of Music had been Grove's 'world'. He had become, in his own words, 'heart and soul devoted' to its work. But the inevitability of the decision he recognized: as his letter explained:

> my health has of late suffered considerably, I have lost much of my energy, nerve, and spirits, my faculties are not what they were, and I have been at length most unwillingly forced to the conviction that it will be for the interests of the College that I should resign my trust in favor [sic] of a younger and more active man.[1]

To those closest to him, the announcement will have come as no surprise. At the beginning of May that year the state opening of the new college buildings had taken place, and the College had now moved into its new home in Prince Consort Road.[2] By any standards, this was a remarkable achievement, and one whose significance was acknowledged later that same month when, at the request of the Queen, Grove was honoured with the Order of the Companion of the Bath (CB) in recognition of the 'eminent services' which he had 'rendered to the public in connection with the Royal College of Music'.[3]

In private correspondence Grove had spoken frankly of his intention to 'cut the knot somehow' once the College had moved into its 'new house'. Advancing years and the relentless pressure of the task had taken their toll. Anxieties, both real and imaginary, were weighing in on him: Grove recognized that he was censuring himself for not being as vigorous as previously, and expressed fears that 'through me some misfortune is impending on the College I love so dearly.'[4] Those closest to him professionally had watched with mounting concern. Some, such as his long-standing friend, Sir Arthur Sullivan, a member of the College's Governing Body, the Council, had attempted to suggest ways of alleviating the pressures of the role, but Grove recognized that, for him, this was unrealistic. In May his close colleague, George Watson, Registrar of the College, whom he regarded as his 'right hand man', had fallen ill.[5] Grove, his own health failing, recognized that the time had come to submit his resignation: in a letter to the Bishop of Lichfield written a few days later, he described himself as having been beaten 'by age and overwork'.[6]

The Council, doubtless anticipating this outcome, seems not to have encouraged Grove to reconsider his decision. Accepting his resignation with regret, the President's letter reflected the sense of what the College was losing: in his reply to Grove, couched in the warmest of terms, the Prince wrote:

> To one who has worked so hard as you have, and with such great success in promoting the interests of the College, one would gladly see you take that rest and repose which you have so thoroughly deserved; but for the sake of the College, I and all connected with it deeply regret your decision.[7]

At a special meeting of Council held in early November, this tone of regret was echoed as members expressed their gratitude to Grove for 'his unselfish and increasing devotion to the College since its foundation'. It was, they acknowledged, 'through his untiring zeal and energy, and his constant watchfulness over its interests, that the Royal College of Music in so short a time attained its present high position' and, they asserted, 'whatever its future destinies may be, it will never be forgotten how largely the influence which the College has been the means of exercising on the musical education of the country, was due to its first Director Sir George Grove.'[8] The Chairman, Lord Charles Bruce, writing to Grove, urged him not to be anxious for the future:

> You have laid a sound foundation and build thereon a noble edifice with which your name will be ever identified. We, the Governing Body, can never forget all you have done for us, for without you the College could not have become what it is, one of our most important National Institutions.[9]

In December 1894 Grove retired as Director. Just before Christmas he wrote to Walford Davies,[10] a composition scholar who was to join the College staff in the following year. It was, he confessed, 'a terrible wrench to me leaving my dear College. I did not know how much I should feel it till the moment actually came and even now I am not at all happy as to the result.'[11]

Grove's unhappiness sprang from the loss of his 'world', not from the choice of his successor. This was an outcome which delighted him. Parry, whom he had known for twenty years, and had been appointed to the College as Professor of Musical History in 1883,[12] had, Grove believed, 'all my virtues and others that I could never aspire to'.[13] He was confident that he and Parry shared similar principles and sense of purpose: as he said in the same letter to Walford Davies, 'I believe that he [Parry] will look on the work a good deal from my point of view and think that the breeding up of good young men and women is as much the duty of the Director as making them good musicians.' It was an aspect of the role of Director about which he looked back with what he described as 'great satisfaction' on his efforts.[14] Parry, for his part, who had worked closely with Grove even before the College had opened, was conscious of what retirement must have meant to Grove himself. In an affectionate Boxing Day letter, he identified with the mixed emotions that he imagined Grove must be feeling, explaining that he realized 'too vividly and painfully what it must be to you, with all your energies and sympathies fully alive, to be giving up a thing so engrossing and valuable as the College work.'[15] In his address on taking up office, observing that Grove's influence was likely to 'last long beyond the limited vista of the lives of even the youngest' of the students then at the College – a prediction amply realized – Parry urged his listeners not only to develop their talents to the full, but also to serve others, and work at becoming 'honourable and refined men and women.'[16]

The 1895 Spring Term began under Parry's leadership. Heartened by the choice of new Director, cheered by the good wishes of the Council, who had awarded him a pension of £700 a year[17] (his successor's salary was £800)[18] and honoured by the invitation to become a member of the Council,[19] Grove's spirits had been raised during the final weeks of his directorship by the many expressions of affection and admiration which he received from students, members of teaching staff, former students, parents, friends and colleagues. A bust was commissioned,[20] professorial staff combined to commission a portrait,[21] and in March 1895 a concert organized by Parry, was given by students of the College in Grove's honour.[22] Devoted to the music of Schubert – a choice sure to have delighted Grove – it included performances of four songs, framed by the D minor Quartet and the B flat Trio (op. 99), and the *Moments musicaux* for piano (op. 94).[23] In July Grove returned to the College to receive one further tribute from the College – this time an address, signed by present and former students. His reply on this occasion, again reflected some of the key values that had guided him as Director. 'One thing I have tried to show you', he said,

> that ability and hard work are of no avail unless backed by character; that, great work as the study of music is, there is one thing still greater – to be good, to be unselfish, to be thoughtful of others; and hereafter when the bust which you intend to present me with shall be placed in this noble building, I trust that it may be recognized as the likeness of one to whom that was the great object of his life.[24]

In this, Grove's hopes were largely fulfilled. It was precisely in these terms that many of those within the College remembered Grove as Director. The recollections of students and staff allude to countless instances of his kindness, his enthusiasm and his generosity of spirit. Stanford, appointed by Grove as professor of composition and orchestral playing in 1883, described him as someone who 'was always...working for others, rather than himself'[25] and regarded as 'one of Grove's greatest gifts' the fact that he 'never stinted his praise, when it was deserved, or closed his mouth to gratitude or appreciation.'[26] The obituary published in *The Times*, while describing Grove as 'a man of wide culture', similarly referred to him as someone 'of particularly kindly and generous nature to the younger generation of native musicians, whom he was already ready to help with sound advice.' 'Probably no young musician of serious aim', the writer concluded, 'ever appealed for help and advice in vain to Sir George Grove.'[27]

To the writer of this obituary, the fact that Grove was, in musical terms, an amateur, had in his particular case proved to be anything but a disadvantage. 'Perhaps for the very reason that he was an amateur and that, as a consequence, his enthusiasms were evidently disinterested,' he observed, 'he [Grove] acquired an influence in the world of music which was at least as great and as widespread as that of any professional musician.' For if an amateur, it was as an amateur infused with a passionate love of music as an art and capable of communicating this powerfully to others. Walford Davies, when reflecting on the significance of this in relation to Grove's achievements as Director, wondered whether it was these qualities of the amateur which

> together with his human kindness, formed his best qualification for a great professional post. I think this must have been so. And I believe most of us who had the good fortune to come under his influence would gratefully acknowledge that our own musical fires were kindled and fed by the Director's unique, unfailing enthusiasms for our great Art.[28]

Stanford also referred to Grove's uniqueness in terms of his capacity to influence others: Grove was, he reflected, 'like nobody else in the world...'

> From his opening speech at the College to the day he resigned, he kept the highest ideals steadily before the eyes of every man and woman within its walls, and by his insistence, by example as well as precept,

upon general culture, raised the niveau of musical education in England to a height which it had never before attained. This fact alone is a monument to his memory, and to an influence which succeeding generations may find difficult to emulate but impossible to destroy.[29]

Appointment

Grove's freely acknowledged amateur status gives rise to interesting questions about his appointment as Director. Had events turned out as originally planned, had the Royal College of Music already been well-established, Grove would almost certainly not have been appointed to this role or indeed have been attracted to it. But at the point when Grove appears to have become centrally involved in the movement that led to the establishment of the Royal College of Music, plans for a new national conservatoire in London were at a critical juncture. Although the tide of public opinion was by then slowly beginning to turn in favour of the establishment of a new institution on these lines, the hurdles to be surmounted were considerable and the means of achieving the goal far from certain.

In turning vision into reality, Grove's role became pivotal. Already connected with the work of Prince Christian's committee (the committee established in 1878 which attempted unsuccessfully to bring together the Royal Academy of Music and the proposed College), Grove appears to have been invited to join the committee established by the Prince of Wales to take forward the plans for the new institution in July 1881.[30] By May 1883 the Royal College of Music had come into being, Grove was installed in South Kensington as Director, the first students were admitted, and the first Council meeting had taken place.[31] At the opening ceremony on 7 May the Prince of Wales, commending the 'skill and success' with which Grove had worked 'in the difficult task of organising the Royal College', announced that he had been offered a knighthood, in acknowledgement of the services which he had rendered 'to the promotion of the Art of Music in this country'.[32] Sullivan and Macfarren (the latter then Principal of the Royal Academy of Music)[33] were honoured at the same time. Although Grove in a private letter written a fortnight later professed that he had always hoped to go to his grave 'with no change from the "Mr Grove" [that he] had been so long known by',[34] and Macfarren (aged 71 and blind) was apparently even more reluctant to accept the honour extended to him, all three went together to Windsor Castle before the end of May, to receive their knighthoods together from Queen Victoria.[35] Whether ruffled feathers were smoothed by these simultaneous awards, history does not record.

Whether it was because of his literary and advocacy skills, or his organizational experience that Grove was recruited to the Prince of Wales's committee, both were soon put to good use. In the period leading up to the opening of the Royal College of Music, Grove's formidable capacity for hard work was tested to the full. In December 1881, three members of the Royal Family – two of the Prince of Wales's brothers, the Duke of Albany and the Duke of Edinburgh, and his brother-in-law, Prince Christian – addressed a large public meeting in Manchester to assess the measure of support for the plan. The impact of the speeches, reported verbatim in *The Times* on the following day,[36] owed much to Grove's musical knowledge and experience, to his command of the arguments, and to his literary skills. Eloquent appeals were made to English patriotism by comparing native musical achievements with those from the Continent; specific examples of Government support in Europe for national conservatoires were presented.[37] In the closing speech, arguments for the role of music as a social leveller were strongly in evidence, support for the new College being enlisted on the grounds that 'music is an art which both the rich and the poor are intended to enjoy'. To cheers from the gathering, reported as three thousand in number, Prince Christian asked for

> sympathy and co-operation in advancing throughout the United Kingdom the cultivation of this noble art by encouraging and aiding an institution by means of which those who have been endowed by Providence with genius or talent, though not with wealth, may acquire an independence for themselves and exercise an beneficial influence on their country.[38]

The water having been tested in Manchester, two months later, at the end of February 1882, the Prince of Wales called a meeting at St James's Palace. To this were invited 'representatives of the counties and towns of England, the dignitaries of the Church and other religions and educational bodies, distinguished Colonists and the representatives of foreign Powers'.[39] With this meeting, the campaign moved into its final phase. A cartoon in the magazine *Punch* carried the wish that the protagonists should soon be heard outside the confines of the Palace, especially since, as it wryly observed, 'the notes seem to be coming in from all quarters'.[40] The hope was realized almost immediately, with Grove as its instrument. Support in principle having been secured from civic leaders in many parts of the country, the national campaign was launched. The capital sum of between £250,000 and £300,000 – approximately £4.5 million at 2002 values – was established as the fundraising target. Grove, despite his other commitments, agreed to co-ordinate the fundraising for the next six months. From March 1882 until the opening of the College in May the following year, he addressed public meetings throughout the country – 44 in all[41] – wrote speeches, produced documents, doing all that was necessary for the launch of the College from temporary accommodation in the Duchy of Cornwall Office in Buckingham Gate.

Within a week of the meeting at St James's Palace, it seems that the Prince of Wales had named Grove as Director of the enterprise. At the time there appears to have been no formal notice of the appointment in the press.

Instead an inconspicuous item in the *The Times*, buried at the foot of one of the back pages, advised the readership in confidential tones that 'We have reason to believe that Mr George Grove will be invited to take a leading part in the management of the new Royal College of Music, with the title of "Director" of the institution.'[42] When compared with the extensive reportage of so many other details, large and small, of the establishment of the College, this way of breaking the news of Groves' appointment seems curiously at variance with the general approach. It seems likely therefore that the style of announcement reflected not only the fact that the project was still 'on the drawing board' and was entirely dependent on fundraising if it were to be realized, but also the fact that the less controversy such an announcement provoked, the easier the task would be. Grove himself initially adopted a similarly 'low key' approach: writing to the publisher John Murray to seek financial support for the new College, shortly after the announcement had appeared in *The Times*, Grove represented his role in provisional terms, commenting that 'it seems I am to be Director in the event of its being established.'[43]

The task which Grove had shouldered was anything but a sinecure: the fundraising target was high; the risks attached to failure of the scheme were great; opposition from those who viewed the scheme as unwelcome was fanned by the press. Success seems likely to have been dependent on minimizing the attention attracted by dissenting voices. This may help in part to explain the choice of 'Director' as the title which Grove was to hold. Then, as now, the customary title in other British music schools, and the title that Sullivan and Stainer had held at the National Training School for Music, was that of 'Principal' (i.e. 'Principal Professor'). In view of Grove's lack of professional training in music, his appointment as 'Principal' may well have given scope for further criticism of South Kensington amateurism – a feature of much of the opposition voiced by those who saw the establishment of a Royal College of Music as a threat to the Royal Academy of Music. But to those who were aware of European precedents, it cannot have escaped their notice that in Paris and Brussels the title of 'Directeur' was the norm, and these were among the institutions on which the new College was to be modelled. And at that stage there was, of course, no RCM professoriate of which Grove could be described as 'Principal'.

As the news of Grove's appointment trickled out, public response seems to be been generally positive. The April issue of the *Musical Times*, noting that it had already been announced that the new institution would have a governing body consisting of 'a Council, intrusted with the function of making by-laws for the regulation of the College, and of an Executive Committee charged with the details of the administration', expressed pleasure that Grove's name had emerged as its leader: 'what is most needed for the new College', wrote the anonymous contributor,

> is a Principal endowed with the rare combination of gifts, both practical and artistic, which would give him sufficient authority to smooth down and, if necessary, to overrule such differences of opinion and disputes of privilege as are apt to spring up between and within governing bodies and executive committees. The success of the two most prominent music schools on the Continent shows the enormous importance of individual initiative. The Conservatoire of Paris was virtually the creation of Cherubini; the Conservatorium of Leipzig literally that of Mendelssohn. We have not among us a Cherubini or a Mendelssohn. But a man combining business tact and social influence with a genuine love and a thorough knowledge of music would probably serve the purpose as well.[44]

Comment in other publications makes clear that speculation about the choice of leader for the new College had been rife. The *Monthly Musical Record*, observing that 'the appointment of Dr. George Grove as "Director" will give general satisfaction', since 'it would indeed be difficult to name any one of higher literary musical ability or of wider experience', admitted to a sense of relief that the rumour which had been circulating that 'this important post would be occupied by some distinguished foreigner' had proved unfounded.[45] Which foreign names may have been bandied about offers tantalizing scope for speculation.

It is unlikely that any foreigner, distinguished or not, would have been able to achieve in the time available what needed to be done. At this stage Grove's job was to translate the broad vision of the role of the new institution into working reality. This he did almost unaided, on an extremely tight time-scale. The plan was to open in spring 1883, provided that sufficient funds were raised. Although Grove inherited a building (that of the National Training School) and had a clear sense of the problems to which the Royal College of Music was intended to provide solutions, in April 1882 there was still an enormous distance to be travelled before the new institution could open its doors to students. Grove was still occupied with the *Dictionary of Music and Musicians*, yet within 14 months, between March 1882 and May 1883, first working alone and then later with the assistance of George Watson, who was subsequently appointed as the first Registrar of the College, Grove raised funds for the institution by his programme of visits around the country, appointed staff, developed and publicized the scholarship scheme to which prospective pupils could apply, and established a framework for the management and administration of the College. The role of founding Director in any organization demands more than vision. Grove had not only the vision but also the capacity to take forward various issues simultaneously, maintaining a clear overview while shifting constantly between major concerns and operational minutiae. His eye for detail was fastidious; his vision of the whole and his total commitment to it were a source of inspiration.

It is interesting to conjecture what at this stage Grove may have known of the organization of other conservatoires – how much he devised without drawing on precedent, how much reflected the knowledge that he had acquired of practices elsewhere.[46] The speeches that Grove crafted for the public meeting in Manchester in December 1881 show that at this stage he had made it his business to discover how leading conservatoires in mainland Europe were funded.[47] He could already count leading figures in European conservatoires, such as Joachim and Clara Schumann, among his circle of friends and professional contacts. It is evident from Grove's copy of the monograph by Emil Kneschke, produced in 1872 to celebrate the 25th anniversary of the founding of the Leipzig Conservatorium,[48] held in the RCM Library, that this was one of the sources which he had studied in detail. Pages showing the number of students from Great Britain who had studied in Leipzig are neatly annotated in his hand.[49] The provision of a musical education of a quality sufficient to ensure that British students no longer regarded study in Germany as indispensable was one of the challenges which Grove identified as a key task for the Royal College of Music.[50]

The plan that the College would admit students by competitive examination, awarding scholarships to cover the tuition costs of a significant proportion of them, was a scheme which distinguished it from existing British music schools of the time,[51] and as expected attracted widespread attention.[52] Grove's announcement during some of the public meetings that scholarships would be available to 'all comers and all nations' gave rise to opposition in certain places,[53] and helped to fan a certain anti-German feeling. In view of this reaction it was perhaps not surprising that at the opening of the College, the Prince of Wales chose to describe the 'object' that he had in view as being 'Imperial as well as national', and that Grove's account of the four private scholarships that had been established, in addition to the 50 Foundation scholarships, included reference to two from Australia – the Elder and the Clarke Scholarships from South Australia and Victoria respectively.[54] By the end of the first year, there were 53 scholars and 100 paying students on the books, the latter having more than doubled in the year from the 42 who enrolled in May. There were then in total only nine students from abroad – four from Australia, and one each from Switzerland, Germany, Belgium, Canada and California. The feared German invasion did not materialize.

Choosing colleagues

While the task of fundraising – critical to the success of the new institution – consumed a considerable amount of Grove's time in the period leading up to the opening of the new College, perhaps the most significant of the tasks that Grove undertook during these months was the selection and appointment of those who were to teach. With the College's purposes clear – 'an institution to provide musical instruction of the highest class' – Grove went directly to those whom he regarded as leaders in their field. For this, his Crystal Palace and Macmillan networks proved invaluable. Some of those whom he approached were performers and composers whose qualities and reputations he knew at first hand from Crystal Palace concerts: the pianists Franklin Taylor and Arabella Goddard were among those who fell into this category. Some, like Parry and Stanford, Grove also knew from the work that they had undertaken for him on the *Dictionary*; others, like Pauer and John Francis Barnett, had in addition taught at the National Training School.

In selecting those who were to teach at the new College, Grove aimed high and looked widely. Not all of those whom he approached felt able to accept, mainly because of existing professional commitments. Charles Hallé, in a letter to one of his daughters written in August 1882, refers to a letter from Grove informing him that he was being offered 'the professorship of the first pianoforte class in the Royal College'. This offer, Hallé explained in a subsequent interview with Grove, he could not accept because of his crowded engagement books.[55] An undated manuscript note by Grove preserved in the correspondence between Grove and the Prince of Wales in the RCM Archives, which lists names of those whom he may have intended to invite to teach, suggests that at some stage others such as the violinists, Joachim and Wilma Norman Neruda[56] – both regular performers at the Crystal Palace concerts – were also considered. If approached, neither accepted, probably for similar reasons.[57] In the circumstances, this outcome may have encouraged more favourable attitudes to the establishment of the new institution: one published report of the opening ceremony commented on the favourable reception given to Grove's announcement of the names of professors. Since, the writer reasoned, an enterprise like this 'must be in all essential respects of a national character if it is to contain within itself the elements of vitality', 'the name of Englishman after Englishman [fell] pleasantly on the ear'.[58]

Grove's inclusion of Joachim's name on his list of possible professorial appointments was perhaps more a signal of the level sought and the educational and musical philosophy which was to characterize the RCM than an indication that he intended to attempt to obtain his services on a regular basis. Joachim was at that time the head of the Hochschule für Ausübende Tonkunst in Berlin, a role that he had held since 1868 and where he was to remain for almost forty years. Joachim did, however, pay regular visits to the Royal College of Music during Grove's directorship. On some visits he performed with the students,[59] on other occasions, he acted as an examiner.

From the founding of the College, standards were closely monitored by a board of visiting examiners. Initially six in number, its members were appointed each year to conduct the annual practical examinations and comment on the progress of the pupils[60] by producing a substantial written report, addressed to the Prince of Wales which was then published for presentation to the Council and the Corporation.[61] In 1884, 1885 and 1892, Joachim served as a member of this board. Several of the others whom Grove did not persuade to make a regular teaching commitment, he was also able to interest in the work of the College on this basis: Hallé, Sullivan and Stainer all served in this capacity during Grove's time as Director.[62]

Despite some refusals which must have disappointed him, Grove succeeded in making strong appointments to the teaching staff of the College, several of whom were to create 'schools' of performance or composition, whose influence continued well beyond Grove's directorship. For the opening of the College, Grove made 42 appointments. As the list in Table 10.1 shows, most were appointed as 'teachers'. Eleven were appointed with the title of 'professor' and formed the Board of Professors which, under Grove's chairmanship, was responsible from the outset for the oversight of the work of the College. Among the most prominent of the established 'names' whom Grove appointed were leading performers such as the singer Jenny Lind (Madame Goldschmidt) and the pianists Ernst Pauer and Franklin Taylor.

In making his selection, Grove clearly sought more than age and experience: those appointed as professors ranged in age from Jenny Lind, then 63, who came out of retirement to teach at the new institution, to young men in their thirties, like Stanford, Parry and Bridge. These three, whom Grove appointed to teach composition, harmony, counterpoint and the history of music, had already demonstrated qualities of musical leadership while at university. All three were beginning to make their way professionally as composers. Frederick Bridge, at 39 the eldest of the three, had recently been promoted to organist of Westminster Abbey. Stanford, only 31, was among those who had studied in Leipzig. The Leipzig influence was clearly in evidence among the first generation of professors whom Grove sought to attract to the College.

The orchestral instrumentalists whom Grove appointed – 'honoured names', as he called them[63] – tended to come from different backgrounds. Most were well-established in their respective fields and familiar figures in London musical life. Among them was stalwarts such as Charles Godfrey, responsible for military music, then bandmaster of the Coldstream Guards; Henry Lazarus, a highly respected clarinettist, with fifty years of playing experience, who had taught at Kneller Hall, and was the author of a significant clarinet method book; the trumpeter, Thomas Harper, also known for his method books, and the Welsh harpist and composer, John Thomas, who had a distinguished reputation as virtuoso and teacher.

The Times, commenting on the appointments at the time of the opening, noted that with the exception of Jenny Lind and Arabella Goddard, there was perhaps a shortage of names 'of European reputation'. This, it concluded, was probably all to the good, since the 'star' system, 'bad enough on

Table 10.1 Professors and teachers at the RCM, 1884

PROFESSORS AND TEACHERS.

Those marked with an asterisk are members of the Board of Professors.

SINGING.

* Madame Lind-Goldschmidt (Scholars only).
* Mr. H.C. Deacon.
* Mr. Albert Visetti.
Mr. Gustave Garcia.
Miss Gertrude Mayfield.
Mr. Richard Latter.

CHORAL AND SIGHT SINGING.

Mr. Eaton Faning.

PIANOFORTE.

* Mr. Ernst Pauer.
* Mr. Franklin Taylor.
Madame Arabella Goddard.
Mr. John Francis Barnett.
Mr. R. Hensler.
Mr. Eaton Faning.
Mr. Frederic Cliffe.
Mr. Stephen Kemp.
Mr. A.J. Caldicott, Mus. Bac.
Miss Edith Jerningham.
Miss Helen Synyer.
Mr. Herbert Sharpe.
Mr. Algernon Ashton.

ORGAN.

* Mr. Walter Parratt, Mus. Bac.
Dr. George C. Martin, Mus. Doc.
Dr. F.E. Gladstone, Mus. Doc.

VIOLIN.

* Mr. Henry Holmes.
Mr. Richard Gompertz.

VIOLA.

Mr. Richard Gompertz.

VIOLONCELLO.

Mr. Edward Howell.

DOUBLE BASS.

Mr. A.C. White.

CLARINET.

Mr. Henry Lazarus.

OBOE.

Mr. George Horton.

FLUTE.

Mr. W. Lewis Barrett.

BASSOON.

Mr. William B. Wotton.

HORN.

Mr. Thomas E. Mann.

TRUMPET.

Mr. Thomas Harper.

TROMBONE.

Mr. Samuel Millar.

HARP.

Mr. John Thomas.

MILITARY MUSIC.

Mr. Charles Godfrey.

COMPOSITION.

* Dr. C. Hubert H. Parry, Mus. Doc.
* Dr. C.V. Stanford, Mus. Doc.

COUNTERPOINT.

* Dr. J.F. Bridge, Mus. Doc.

HARMONY.

* Dr. J.F. Bridge, Mus. Doc.
Mr. Eaton Faning.
Dr. A.J. Caldicott, Mus. Bac.
Dr. F.E. Gladstone, Mus. Doc.
Mr. James Higgs, Mus. Bac.

HISTORY OF MUSIC.

* Dr. C. Hubert H. Parry, Mus. Doc.

DECLAMATION.

Mrs. Kendal.
Mrs. Arthur Stirling.

ITALIAN.

Signor Perini.

ENSEMBLE CLASS (CHAMBER MUSIC).

* Mr. Henry Holmes.

ORCHESTRAL PRACTICE.

* Mr. Henry Holmes.
* Dr. C.V. Stanford, Mus. Doc.

Source: Royal College of Music General Regulations, 1884, pp. 6–7

the operatic stage', would be 'simply fatal in an institution devoted to serious study'. In the version of the Prospectus which he produced in early 1882, Grove had committed the College to providing teaching by 'the most eminent musicians attainable'.[64] In the opinion of *The Times'* commentator, this was precisely what he had done: as the writer confirmed, in the British context names such as Pauer, Franklin Taylor, Barnett, Lind-Goldschmidt, Visetti, Bridge, Stanford, Parry, Holmes, Harper, Lazarus and Thomas inspired real confidence.

Building a reputation

Grove's single-minded determination to appoint the best and to provide strong musical and pedagogical direction through the Board of Professors helped to position the College nationally, and was a key factor in ensuring that the standards that the students achieved and the systematic nature of the training were soon to attract favourable comment. A review of the first public concert given by College students outside the College in June 1885, towards the end of the College's second year, concluded that 'The Royal College during its brief existence, has made rapid advances, and there is every reason to think that it will steadily continue to do so.' The choice of programme, seen as bearing 'testimony to the comprehensive knowledge and catholicity of taste for which the principal of the College, Sir George Grove, is known as a musical critic and historian', was seen as giving further grounds for confidence in the quality of the training provided, as was the playing of the orchestra, described by the reviewer as 'perhaps the most remarkable creation of the Royal College'. This was because it was the pupils who were performing: as the reviewer commented with surprise and pleasure, the orchestra consisted 'with few exceptions, of scholars, exhibitioners, and paying students, male and female'.[65] All this gave grounds for confidence. While the Royal College of Music had 'not as yet produced a Beethoven or Joachim, or even a D'Albert', the reviewer conceded, 'if a genius of the first order should arise, we may feel satisfied that Sir George Grove and his staff of professors will know how to lead him in the right direction.'[66]

Opera studies formed an essential ingredient of Grove's vision for the College. Annual opera productions became a feature of the work of the College from Summer 1885, the second year of the RCM's existence. The absence of appropriate training for opera was a constant theme among late nineteenth century commentators, and a problem which Grove was committed to addressing. It was a subject to which he alluded in his report to the Council in April 1886, where he wrote that 'there is a direct want of players and singers versed in the practical work of opera, and a livelihood may thus be expected to present itself to those who leave the College with this training'. This, he pointed out, was a view which had already been expressed in notices which had appeared in the press after the first College opera production.[67] Always closely in touch with the daily life of the College, Grove was quick to recognize that in a music school the presence of opera training, with its own particular rhythms and demands, did not necessarily make for an easy life. In the same report, while conceding that 'the practical training is indisputably of a most beneficial kind', he noted the impact that opera training tended to have on the daily College routine – '[w]hat we have to do is to keep our operatic studies in due proportion, and prevent their interfering with the more regular and quiet work in College.'

Grove's role in the nurturing of opera training was singled out for commendation in the press after the second College production – a performance of Cherubini's *Les deux journées*, given at the Savoy Theatre – when the *Times* reviewer, comparing the work of the College with that of Continental counterparts, observed that:

> Under Sir George Grove's intelligent and enthusiastic superintendence the college has in a few years established a position of which the most famous and most ancient teaching bodies of the Continent need not be ashamed. Here the art is taught in its noblest aspects and in all its branches, including the dramatic, too much neglected by older institutions. A few years ago it seemed a [sic] utopian hope that we should ever have in this country a music school which would be able to supply Mr. Carl Rosa with dramatic singers, even as the Paris Conservatoire supplies the Grand Opera and the Opéra Comique. Yesterday's performance brought such contingency within measurable distance.
>
> Equally excellent was the musical training shown throughout, and in this fact the real importance of the occasion must be discovered. A school cannot create genius, but it can rear what talent is placed at its disposal by careful and intelligent fostering.[68]

Similar commendations can be found in the detailed written reports prepared by the Annual Examiners. The Annual Examiners' Report for 1891, a year when the Board included the violinist Ysaÿe, who then taught at the Brussels Conservatoire, commented that the examination of the string teaching had 'shown that the teaching staff of the College is one of the first in Europe, and that the instruction given is at an equally high level', adding that the chief violin class and the orchestral class 'are trained in a specially artistic manner'.[69] Further evidence of the distinctiveness of what was established at the Royal College of Music can be found in a report written by Frank Damrosch, the founder of what was to become The Juilliard School, after his visit to Europe in 1904. In most European institutions that Damrosch visited (these included Paris, Leipzig, Berlin, Vienna and Brussels) he was disappointed to find that 'there is no unity of pedagogical effort. Each teacher teaches according to his own lights without regard to a broad general plan or to the instruction which the student receives from others'. This he contrasted with what he found at the Royal College of Music:

> A notable exception to this rule is the Royal College of Music in London, where Sir Hubert Parry is in constant touch with all teachers and these again with others; and where there is a well-defined plan of work which is carried out intelligently by each teacher as a part of a whole.
>
> On the continent I found that, while the course of study as outlined in the various prospectuses would be fairly comprehensive, the student did not really get the full benefit of such opportunities as the institution offered, because the various subjects of study were not properly correlated....[70]

While these comments date from ten years after Grove's retirement as Director, it was Grove who had created the framework, established the working principles, and appointed the colleagues who were to produce these results. The pattern of studies, shown in Table 10.2, was distinctive for its time, and led Grove's Annual Examiners more than once to comment favourably on 'the complete musical education which is made indispensable for all Pupils at the Royal College'.[71] As Charles Hallé had pointed out before the College opened, the concept of there being a full course of instruction which students were expected to complete, rather than students doing what they pleased for as long as they pleased, distinguished the Royal College of Music from many existing institutions.[72] By the time that Damrosch visited the Royal College of Music, some of the most talented of the students during Grove's directorship were now members of the teaching staff, continuing the traditions that he had established – among them the pianist, Marmaduke Barton, the composer Charles Wood, and the composer and organist Walford Davies.

Building for the future

The Annual Examiners' Reports, which commented on progress year on year, while generally encouraging, did not refrain from making explicit comment on areas seen as meriting attention. The 1889/90 Report included the recommendation that an increase in the number of scholarships offered to the wind instrument pupils 'would be of advantage, as players of wind and brass instruments who have received a thorough musical education are still greatly needed in many first-class orchestras.'[73] After earlier reports referring gently to the limitations of space within the building, in their 1886/87 report the examiners observed emphatically that '[w]ant of sufficient accommodation, especially for pianoforte and organ practice, is a hindrance to progress', stressing that it was 'highly desirable that better provision is made'.[74]

Grove had accepted the post of Director in the knowledge that the building adjacent to the Royal Albert Hall, which had been the home of the National Training School, was intended to be a temporary home for the new College (Plate 4). The Prospectus which he produced in 1882 included the confident statement that 'Grounds for the erection of Collegiate Buildings will be provided by the Royal Commissioners of 1851 on their estate'.[75] However this was contingent on the College raising funds for the erection of a suitable building, as the first Annual Report of the Council made clear.[76] In the College's first few years the Council was reluctant to take on further major expenditure. Money was tight, since the hope that the College would receive a government grant had not yet been realized.[77]

From the outset, Grove's vision for the Royal College of Music far outstripped its immediate surroundings in Kensington Gore. In his 1886 report to the Council, he raised the issue of accommodation, clearly not for the first time.

> 'I desire again to urge the fact that the College suffers materially from [the confined size and bad arrangement of the College House]...It can never fulfil the purposes for which it was designed by our Founder, with due discipline and efficiency, without a Collegiate Building, where teaching and residence should be comprised under one roof.[78]

In pursuing this goal, the observations of the Annual Examiners were doubtless of some assistance. Echoing their remarks, in 1887 Grove again described the work of the College as 'extremely inconvenienced and prejudiced by want of space'.[79]

Grove's private correspondence suggests that this – and the financial stability which the College managed to achieve in the first few years – helped to strengthen resolve,[80] though he himself was briefly distracted by the death of the Principal of the Royal Academy of Music, Sir George Macfarren, and concerned that there might be a further attempt at an amalgamation of the two institutions.[81] By Christmas 1887 a solution to the building question was at hand. Grove's delight is evident in his letter to Edith Oldham, a former student, in mid January 1888. 'And now I must tell you a bit of real news', he wrote:

> I have just secured the money for building the new College! – This week I took a rich Yorkshireman to the Prince, and he promised H.R.H. £30,000 and if 30 wasn't enough 40, and if 40 not enough, £50,000!...I am determined to have a building with the character of a college – that all the pupils shall remember with love and affection.[82]

Samson Fox, a Leeds businessman,[83] had contacted Grove to offer to HRH the Prince of Wales £30,000 for the erection of a new Collegiate building. For this purpose the 1851 Commissioners granted a one-acre site on the

Table 10.2 Course of instruction at the RCM, 1884

COURSE OF INSTRUCTION.

The full course of instruction in the College occupies three years, and may, in the case of Scholars, be further extended with the sanction of the Council. On the other hand, a Scholarship may be terminated at any time by the Council should the progress or conduct of the Scholar be unsatisfactory.

Students are not admitted for a shorter period than one year.

The following are the subjects of study:-

Composition.
Harmony and Counterpoint.
Organ.
Pianoforte.
Harp.
Violin.
Viola.
Violoncello.
Double bass.
Wind instruments.
Solo singing.
Declamation.
Italian.
Choral singing.
Sight singing, dictation, &c.
Concerted music (instrumental).
Orchestral practice, including playing from score.
The History of Music, and other subjects relating to Music.

From the above subjects a Student may adopt the following course, or a part of it, with the consent of the Director:-

Weekly Schedule

1. Principal Study. – Two lessons of one hour each (in conjunction with two other students) in either singing, violin, viola, violoncello, double bass, piano, organ, harp, wind instrument, or Composition (the last if sufficiently advanced in Harmony).
2. *Second Study*. – One lesson in one of the various branches named in the preceding section.
3. *Harmony*. – One lesson of one hour in class. This is obligatory unless under very special circumstances.
4. *Counterpoint or Composition*. – One lesson of one hour in class, after the pupil has passed the requisite grade in Harmony.
5. *Italian*. – One lesson of one hour in class; provided that singing is taken as principal study.

Table 10.2 *continued*

6. *Declamation.* – One lesson of one hour in class; provided that singing is taken as principal study.
7. *Sight singing, dictation, &c.* – One lesson of forty-five minutes.
8. *Choral Singing.* – One lesson of one hour.
9. *Ensemble Playing.* – Two hours' practice in class if sufficiently advanced.
10. *Orchestral Practice.* – Two hours, if sufficiently advanced.
11. *History of Music.* – Lectures as announced from time to time.

The Pupil's Concerts are at present held fortnightly.

Source: Royal College of Music, General Regulations (1884), VII, pp. 20–1.

corner of Prince's Gate and Exhibition Road.[84] This was later to be replaced by the offer of the site in what is now Prince Consort Road, provided that a building appropriate to what was seen as a 'more desirable' location was erected.[85] These demands persuaded Samson Fox to raise his offer to £45,000 – over £2 million in today's values.[86]

For Grove the next six years, the second half of his 12-year term as Director, were to be dominated by the creation of the new building. Designed to accommodate 400 students, rather than the 247 then enrolled,[87] this was to supplement the building in Kensington Gore, which the College planned to retain. With his declared aim 'to build for all time and provide for all possible extension'[88], the building of a new home for the College was, as Grove said, to give him 'no end of trouble and anxiety'.[89] But he was, in every respect, the ideal person to oversee the project. His qualifications and experience as a civil engineer meant that he was well equipped to deal with the many technical issues which the new building raised. Arrangements for the installation of up-to-date equipment such as telephones and electric lighting[90] were among the multitudinous issues that demanded his attention. As Peter Horton wrote in the handlist prepared to accompany the exhibition, 'Grove's World', Grove had 'knowledge of new technology, experience as an organizer and project manager and a concern for thoroughness and accuracy that were to serve him well in all his subsequent activities'.[91] The successful completion of the College's new building was one of the great achievements of Grove's period of office as Director. The state opening of the new building in May 1894 – a brilliant affair, in marked contrast to the low-key opening of the College just over a decade earlier,[92] which had been marked by 'an absence of fuss and parade' – was to be the culmination of Grove's period as Director.

Establishing standards

It would have been easy for Grove to allow his time as Director to be dominated by fundraising and by the creation of the new building. Despite the time and effort that both of these activities demanded of him on a continuing basis, he made major contributions to the work of the College and to British music education as a whole through the attention he gave to the processes of teaching and examining and to the establishment of national standards. The Royal Charter made clear the role that College was intended to hold as a 'central teaching and examining body'. One of the first tasks to which Grove turned his attention was the establishment of a high-level award. By the end of the first year of the College's existence, Grove was able to outline the plan to award 'Certificates of Proficiency, bearing with them the title of "Associate" ...to such pupils of the College and other persons who may present themselves for examination'.[93] By 1886, examination requirements were in place for the Associate of the Royal College of Music (ARCM). Of the 36 candidates who entered that year, ten were successful, seven of whom were either present or former students of the College or the National Training School.[94] By the summer of the year in which Grove retired as Director, there were 231 holders of the award, spread throughout the country, some holding the 'teaching' award which had been introduced in the second year, 1887, rather than the 'performing' award. Over half (57 per cent, or 131) had not studied at the Royal College of Music (or the National Training School for Music).[95]

The agreement reached in 1889 for a joint arrangement between the Royal Academy of Music and the Royal College of Music for conducting local music examinations – the arrangement that led to the establishment of the Associated Board of the Royal Schools of Music[96] – was a development similarly of national importance.[97] It led in the first year to entries from 1,141 candidates for examinations which were held at 46 local centres throughout the country. In the activities of the Board Grove played a key part, as did others associated with the College. The Chairman of the RCM Council was the Chairman of the Board; the Prince of Wales became its President. In this, as in many other things, Grove's political sense and his alertness to the implications of national developments was key to the development of the College's national standing. The College's response to the proposed 'Teachers Registration and Organization Bill' of 1891, written by Grove,[98] provided strong and informed resistance to the proposals which, as Grove had been quick to see, would have been damaging to the interests of the College, the Associated Board and to music and musicians in general.

Care for individual students

Grove's response to the Select Committee spoke as much of his care for young musicians as it did of his concern for established professionals. Despite his many other achievements while Director it is perhaps his care for those who formed part of his RCM 'family' that most distinguished Grove from other institutional leaders of his time. Although the number of students increased significantly during his directorship, he maintained a close personal interest in the achievements and welfare of his pupils, as his correspondence, reports and the recollections of former students and colleagues testify. He was liberal in his approach and, as Stanford later recalled, 'less hide-bound and more cosmopolitan' in his views of the possibilities of music in this country than 'most of the leading professional musicians of the day.'[99] In his commitment to music as a means of creating greater social harmony and in providing opportunities for talent, irrespective of birth or social background, Grove wholeheartedly identified with the vision articulated by the Prince of Wales. Grove's guiding hand can clearly be detected in the Prince's announcement at the opening of the College that of the 50 scholarships which had been awarded, half were held by boys and half by girls; that the 50 came from all parts of the British Isles, and that among them, 'a mill-girl, the daughter of a brickmaker, and the son of a blacksmith' had won scholarships for singing, while the son of a labourer had won a scholarship for violin.

As Director, Grove often spoke of feeling 'like the father of a big family'. This paternalistic view of his role certainly coloured much that he did and said. Accounts of the care and attention that he gave to individual students and to student matters are legion. Admittedly, in his Royal College of Music 'family', Grove may well have found outlets for his giving nature that were harder to create in his own domestic circle. But while there were some particularly close relationships, it was not simply one or two individual students who were the beneficiaries of his attention: his generosity of spirit seems to have embraced virtually all those who crossed his path – and this despite the fact that during his directorship, the number of pupils increased more than threefold, from 92 when the College opened, to 311 (a sixth of them scholars) in the year in which he retired. The style which Grove adopted will have been influenced by the average age of the pupils. This was lower than today: at the opening of the College the majority of the Scholars were between 14 and 17 years old (one as young as nine).[100]

Students' health and strength were matters of particular personal concern to Grove: within the first year of its existence, the College had appointed an honorary physician.[101] Among the first of the pastoral matters to which Grove turned his attention was the provision of food and lodging houses for students,[102] and to the establishment of a 'Committee of Ladies' to oversee the latter. These were among the features which particularly caught the attention of the American, Frank Damrosch.[103] In 1904, such provision – and the atmosphere that it helped to create – was far from commonplace.

Grove diligently attended student performances, whether on or off site, whether by present or former students. His biographer, Graves, noted that Grove's 'engagements in one fortnight in December included four concerts either given by old pupils or at which they took a prominent part.'[104]

Walford Davies recalled the occasion when Grove kept 'a casual promise to come out to Hampstead to a concert at which many of his students were to play, though in his own words "Hampstead seemed as far off as the Sahara." '[105] Grove took students to concerts, to Crystal Palace and the Monday Pops in particular. He contacted parents and guardians, advised on students' progress, commented on reports, attended examinations. It is heartwarming to sense the sensitivity and concern which he must have shown towards the 15-year-old Samuel Coleridge-Taylor, who will have been the College's first black student when he enrolled in 1892. Without care of this kind it is doubtful that the young composer's student years would have been so successful.[106] But Grove seems to have given this quality of attention to all who needed it. After all, it was, he believed, by learning from the students and gaining their confidence that one became an effective Director. When Parry was appointed, he wrote to one of them : 'It depends upon the pupils to make him [Parry] an excellent Director. If they put the same confidence in him that they have put in me, he will rise to the occasion; so please remember that, and act upon it…'.[107] True though it may seem a century later, it cannot have been a common Victorian view.

Those leaving he urged to keep in touch: addressing the College in 1887, when pupils who had joined the College at its opening were beginning to depart, Grove expressed the hope that 'all his children would write to him at least once a year when they left College, to let him know of their welfare'.[108] These letters, and their occasional visits, delighted him and quickly led him to devise a plan by which leavers could keep their names 'on the books' of the College.[109] He reported enthusiastically on pupils' success in getting teaching posts and other musical appointments in his reports to Council, in his addresses to the College and in his correspondence. He seems to have devised a system whereby details of former pupils' activities were displayed in College. He immediately established a scheme to provide those who left the College after not less than 12 months with a Testamur of residence and of good conduct, and copies of all reports written on their progress.

The benefits on overall morale can be detected in various recollections of those who were part of the College during these years. One of Grove's obituarists, a regular recipient of his letters and cards, quoted Grove's conviction that '[t]o have helped anyone on in the world is surely one of the greatest pleasures there is.'[110] This characterized Grove's relationships with his pupils. Students – both boys and girls – were in no doubt that the Director had their interests at heart. This included singers as much as instrumentalists, even though, as Stanford maintained, Grove found singers and singing less interesting than instrumentalists and instrumental music.[111] As one student later recalled: 'There were certainly various drawbacks, but in spite of these there was a beautiful feeling in the place, due, I believe, chiefly to Sir George…'[112]

Conclusion

It was a case of a round peg in a round hole. As Director, Grove found an ideal outlet for his talents and fulfilment of his most deeply held convictions. The role of Director gave him the opportunity to draw together the diverse skills, experience and understanding that he had acquired during his busy life. Alexander Mackenzie, Principal of the Royal Academy of Music from 1888, and Grove's close neighbour in Lower Sydenham, commented that he was 'always brimful of schemes for the success of his beloved school'.[113] It provided a focus for his boundless intellectual energy. Few conservatoires then or since have found in the one person, a talented writer and public speaker, an industrious researcher, a meticulous administrator, a diligent correspondent, an experienced civil engineer and a successful fundraiser as well as a knowledgeable and dedicated musician and individual of wide culture. Without ever losing sight of the fundamental purposes for which the College had been founded, Grove put all these qualities to the service of the new institution, in a blend and with a human touch that was uniquely his own.

In personal as well as in professional terms he demonstrated abundantly those qualities generally associated with effective leadership, while never neglecting the concerns of the individual student or colleague. In an age where finely graded distinctions by age and class were the norm, Grove's approach must have been unusual in its openness and lack of pretension. There are so many accounts which speak to his warmth, kindness and deep humanity; and he was a prodigious correspondent, writing 'letters and postcards galore', sometimes two a day to the same person, as one regular recipient recalled. Grove had a gift for friendship: many of his students and colleagues experienced the care and concern that made them want to remain friends for life.

Of criticism there was some, particularly of the scholarship scheme ('a sort of epidemic in the country, to the imperilling of individual effort')[114] and of the extent of Grove's real support from British music. Stanford, writing in 1914, with perhaps more than a modicum of self-interest, expressed the view that Grove 'never in his heart believed in the creative work of his own country' and that '[a] half-century of barren mediocrity [i.e. 1830–80] had accustomed him to look abroad for anything and everything'. It is a charge hard to sustain in the face of the encouragement for British composition which Grove gave through his activities inside and outside the College, and of his urging of the need in music to make efforts to 'have our own English things'.[115] The roll call of composers who studied at the College during Grove's directorship would be sufficient to question the fairness of the judgement. It was a view that Stanford was to modify: in subsequent writings he acknowledged that Grove in his later years, had 'laid a sure foundation for English music in his directorship of the Royal College of Music.'[116]

This he did, and more. He was uniquely fitted for the task which confronted him. He fulfilled the role of Director in a way that cast a long shadow. Within a decade of its foundation, and in a climate of some political uncertainty, Grove had ensured that the new institution had a committed staff, a clearly delineated curriculum, a national system of examinations, effective arrangements for the artistic and educational oversight of the institution as well as for its governance, a scholarship fund, a fitting home, a well-equipped building, a pattern of endowments, a government grant, a national and a growing international reputation. The key tasks which the Prince of Wales envisaged the new institution as undertaking were already begun. The appointments which Grove made, as well as the establishment of national systems of examination, had set the College fair to become a 'national centre'.

Good scholarship requires that one recognizes one's own position in the story that one is weaving, and the value systems that one brings to any investigation. As the current Director of the Royal College of Music, I have found it a moving experience, and a thought-provoking and humbling one, to spend time following the traces of Grove as Director. There is a line in Antonia Byatt's novel, *The Biographer's Tale*, where she ponders whether 'all writing has a tendency to flow like a river towards the writer's body and the writer's own experience'.[117] When a current holder of a role reflects on the achievements of his or her predecessors, there is an almost irresistible inclination to 'read' the evidence in ways that help to make sense of today's story. Clearly in the case of Grove there is more than one story to be told, and Grove's achievements seen in the light of the challenges of today's conservatoires may well be among these. But it is not in this spirit or with this purpose that this chapter has been conceived. Rather the aim has been to focus on the way in which Grove as Director related to – and challenged – the society in which he found himself, and worked to change it. Close examination of Grove's contribution as Director draws attention to the fact that many of the positive aspects of the atmosphere which people associate with the Royal College of Music – features difficult to describe, but strongly felt – are qualities which Grove himself valued highly and sought to engender in the College that he founded.

Frank Howes, in his book *The English Musical Renaissance*, describes Grove as having 'served music as administrator, scholar, educationalist and evangelist' and as practising and preaching a gospel that 'was broadly based on wide reading and a wide experience of life'.[118] It was these qualities and this style that marked out Grove as Director. He was, as Howes describes, 'a characteristic product of the Victorian age at its best: high ideals, unwearied effort, broad culture, ingratiating personality and public spirit'. Little wonder then the Royal College of Music still bears the signs of his guardianship: there can be few stronger foundations on which to build.

Notes

1 Royal College of Music (RCM) Council, Minute Book, II, pp.33–4 (RCM Archives 0007/2).
2 At that period, the College academic year began after Easter, the Summer Term being the first term of the year. This tradition continued throughout Groves' directorship.
3 Grove was informed of the award on 25 May 1894. See extract from the letter to his brother quoted in C.L Graves, *The Life and Letters of Sir George Grove, C.B.* (London, 1903), p.408.
4 Letter of 10 August 1894 to Miss L. Heath, quoted in Graves, *Life & Letters,* p.409.
5 This was an extended absence. In a letter to the Council in July that year, Watson thanked the Council for the 'prolonged leave of absence' that he had been granted. Appointed in 1882 as 'organizing secretary' for the College (a title originally applied to Grove's role), George Watson became Registrar in 1884 and Secretary in 1894, and also acted as secretary to the Associated Board from its inception in 1889. He died in February 1896. His obituary in *The Times* (18 February 1896) was written by Grove.
6 Graves, *Life & Letters*, p.412.
7 RCM Council, Minute Book, II, pp.35–7 (RCM Archives 0007/2).
8 Ibid, pp.41–2.
9 Graves, *Life & Letters*, p.414.
10 Henry Walford Davies (1869–1941) had entered the RCM in 1890 as a scholar for composition, and studied with Parry and Stanford. On the death of William Rockstro in July 1895, Parry appointed him as a teacher of counterpoint.
11 Letter of [23] December 1894 (RCM Library MS, Walford Davies Letters XLII/H); also quoted in part in Graves, *Life & Letters,* p.416.
12 Parry received the letter of appointment as Professor of Musical History at the College on 1 January 1883 (see Charles L. Graves, *Hubert Parry, His Life and Works* (London, 1926), 2 vols, I, p.239). His work at the College, which included the teaching of composition, began before the formal opening of the College in May 1883 (*ibid.*, pp.242–3).
13 Graves, *Parry*, vol. I, p.357; also quoted in Graves, *Life & Letters*, p.416.
14 Letter of [23] December 1894 (RCM Library MS, Walford Davies Letters XLII/H); also quoted in part in Graves, *Life & Letters*, p.416.
15 Graves, *Life & Letters*, pp.416–17; Graves, *Parry*, vol. I, p.357.
16 Sir C. Hubert H. Parry, *'Sir George Grove, 1894', College Addresses delivered to pupils of the Royal College of Music*, ed. H.C. Colles (London, 1920), pp. 42–3.
17 RCM Council, Minute Book, ii, pp.44–5 (RCM Archives 007/2).
18 *Ibid.*, p.47.
19 *Ibid.*, pp.44–5; see Graves, *Life & Letters*, p.414, for the offer of an immediate place on Council.
20 Through the subscriptions of former students.
21 Reproduced in Graves, *Life & Letters*, plate between pp. 420 and 421.
22 Graves, *Parry*, vol. I, p.358.
23 RCM Concert Programmes, Concert no. 201, 6 March 1895.
24 RCM Library MS 7296, *George Grove, Farewell Address*, 12 July 1895. The address is quoted in part in Graves, *Life & Letters*, pp.422–3.
25 Charles Villiers Stanford, *Interludes, Records and Reflections* (London, 1922), p.137.
26 Charles Villiers Stanford, *Pages from an Unwritten Diary* (London, 1914), p.218.

27 *The Times*, 29 May 1900.
28 Graves, *Life & Letters*, p.349.
29 Stanford, *Pages from an Unwritten Diary*, p.227.
30 H.C. Colles and J. Cruft, *The Royal College of Music: a Centenary Record, 1883–1983* (Prince Consort Foundation, 1982), p.5.
31 On 3 May 1883 at Marlborough House. The minutes of the meeting record that a report in *The Times* that day had stated that students were 'unable to comply with the College Regulation, to pay the yearly fee of £40 [approximately £2,000 at 2002 values] in one sum'. The Council swiftly arranged for payments to be made in three instalments of £15, £15 and £10.
32 See Colles, *Royal College of Music*, pp.10–11; Graves, *Life & Letters*, pp.288–9. Details of the opening ceremony were widely reported in the press: see, for example, *Musical World*, 61, 19 (12 May 1883), pp.283–5 (which include the texts of the speeches of Grove and HRH The Prince of Wales) and *The Times*, 8 May 1883.
33 Macfarren had succeeded Sterndale Bennett as Principal of the Royal Academy of Music in 1875, a post which he held until his death in 1887, aged 74.
34 RCM Library MS 7326, letter to Mrs Macmillan, Sunday 20 May [1883].
35 See Herbert Sullivan and Newman Flower, *Sir Arthur Sullivan* (London, 1927), p.133.
36 *The Times*, 13 December 1881, p.6.
37 'How is it then, that, while such an abundance of music is brought to us and made for us and consumed by us, we often hear it said from the other side of the Channel, that England is not a musical nation?...If we are a musical nation, why do we draw our supply of music so largely from abroad?'; There is a national Conservatoire in Paris, aided by an annual State subvention of £10,000. At Vienna there is also a Conservatoire with a large State subvention. At Berlin the Royal High School for Music receives £7,500 a year, the Royal Conservatoires at Brussels and Liege [sic] have £8,100, while in Florence, Milan, Naples, St. Petersburg, Moscow, and even in Prague, Wurzburg, Toulouse, and other less considerable towns of the Continent, schools of music will be found recognized or aided by Government. (Cheers)...In the case of England, I am aware that the State and the public ought to go hand in hand in any undertaking of this description, and what I submit to you is...hat the institution so formed should be assisted by the public, and be recognized and subsidized by the State [Cheers].'
38 *The Times*, 13 December 1881, p.6.
39 'Addresses of Their Royal Highnesses The Prince of Wales and The Duke of Edinburgh, at a Meeting at St. James's Palace, Tuesday, February 28th, 1882', Royal College of Music (20 June 1882), p.14.
40 *Punch*, 11 March 1882.
41 See Grove's speech at the opening of the College, quoted in full in the *Musical World*, 61, 19 (12 May 1883), pp.283–5, for examples of towns and cities visited.
42 *The Times*, 8 March, 1882, p.11.
43 Letter of Grove to John Murray of 16 March 1882 (the John Murray Archive).
44 *Musical Times*, 23, 470 (1 April 1882), pp.195–6. The item was reprinted (with certain changes) in *The Times*, 12 April 1882, p.4.
45 *Monthly Musical Record*, 12, 136 (1 April 1882) p.81.
46 After the College was established, Grove made visits to other institutions, such as Frankfurt, Paris and Vienna, to see at first hand how they operated (see Graves, *Life & Letters*, pp.343, 345, 367).
47 See note 37 above.

48 Dr Emil Kneschke, *Das Conservatorium der Musik in Leipzig. Seine Geschichte, seine Lehrer und Zöglinge. Festgabe zum 25jährigen Jubiläum zum 2. April 1868* (Leipzig [1872]. I am indebted to Peter Horton for drawing my attention to this volume.

49 The list of pupils by country (pp.69–70) show that in the first 25 years, 109 British students had studied in Leipzig (73 men and 36 women), by comparison with those from Saxony (253) and Prussia (284). The British students were the third largest contingent, followed by Russians (90) and those from North America (85).

50 Prominent London-based musicians who had studied in Leipzig included Alexander Mackenzie (who became Principal of the Royal Academy of Music in 1888), Sullivan, Carl Rosa, Ethel Smyth, Franklin Taylor and Stanford.

51 In a letter to the *Musical World*, 60, 4 (28 January 1882), p.57, John Francis Barnett, later to become a teacher at the College, wrote: 'In the history of musical education in this country, the fact of nearly 100 students, selected by competition, studying together during the space of five years, is without parallel.'

52 This proved to be the case. For the first open scholarships there were 1,588 applications. See *Musical World*, 61, 18 (5 May 1883), p.270.

53 *Musical World*, 60, 13 (22 April 1882), p.244.

54 *Musical World*, 61, 19 (12 May 1883), pp.283–4.

55 *Life & Letters of Sir Charles Hallé, Being an Autobiography (1819–1860) with Correspondence and Diaries*, ed. C.E and M. Hallé (London, 1896), p.308.

56 Neruda, Bohemian-born, married Charles Hallé in 1888. For a biographical account of Neruda, see 'Lady Hallé's first appearance in England', *Musical Times*, 41, 692 (1 October 1900), pp.652–4.

57 'List of proposed members of the professorial staff' (RCM Archives, 0096/1). The third of the violinists on Grove's list, John Carrodus, who was then leader of the Covent Garden orchestra, was also among those whom Grove did not manage to appoint.

58 *Musical World*, 61, 19 (12 May 1883), p.284.

59 'Report of the Council to the Fifth Annual General Meeting of the Corporation', 24 July 1888, p.13. (RCM Archives 0008/1). Details are amplified in Grove's letter to Edith Oldham, dated 2 March [1888] (RCM Library MS 6864/88), which refer to Joachim performing the Beethoven Triple Concerto (with Hausmann and Fanny Davies) and then the Violin Concerto with the student orchestra in an 'orchestral practice' session.

60 'Pupil' was the generic term used. The pupils were divided into 'scholars' (or 'exhibitioners'), whose tuition was provided without charge, and 'students', who paid for their tuition.

61 The other members of the Board of Examiners appointed at the opening of the College were: Joseph Barnby, Manuel Garcia, Otto Goldschmidt, Sir Frederick Gore Ouseley and John Stainer. Extracts from the examiners' reports were normally included in the Annual Reports of the Council to the Annual General Meetings of the Corporation (RCM Archives 0008/1).

62 For an account of Hallé as examiner see Grove's letter to Edith Oldham, dated 27 March 1888 (RCM Library MS 6864/93).

63 In his speech to open the College. See *Musical World*, 61, 19 (12 May 1883), p. 283.

64 The Royal College of Music, *Prospectus* (early 1882), pp. 1, 2. See also Chapter 9 of this book, p.219 and n.52.

65 The reviewer observed that 'The strings are of a good quality, and their attack is firm and crisp. There is an excellent clarionet [sic] and a satisfactory flute.'

66 *The Times*, 25 June 1885, p.6.
67 'Report of the Director to the Council', p.28, in 'Report of the Council to the Third Annual General Meeting of the Corporation', 3 July 1886 (RCM Archives 0008/1). Acts 1 and 2 of *The Marriage of Figaro* had been given on 22 July 1885.
68 *The Times*, 25 June 1886, p.12. Grove comments on the performance in his 1886 Report to Council (see note 68).
69 'Report of the Eighth Annual Examination, 1891', p.2, in 'Reports of Annual Examinations – 1884 to 1896' (RCM Archives, 0012/1). The printed report includes the full text of Ysaÿe's comments (in French) which, 'at the request of M. Ysaÿe' was appended in full (p.3).
70 Frank Damrosch, *Institute of Musical Art 1905–1926* (New York, 1936), p.8. I am indebted to Andrea Olmstead for drawing my attention to this. Olmstead, who quotes from this source in her book, *Juilliard. A History* (Urbana and Chicago, 1999), also mentions Damrosch's recognition that the endowed dormitory and dining room – both established during Grove's directorship – were among the distinctive and beneficial aspects of student life at the Royal College of Music (see Olmstead, *Juilliard*, p.18).
71 'Report of the Council to the Seventh Annual General Meeting of the Corporation', 9 July 1890, p.8 (RCM Archives 0008/1).
72 'No Teachin [sic] Power in England', *Musical World*, 60, 10 (11 March 1882), p.155.
73 'Report of the Council to the Seventh Annual General Meeting of the Corporation', 9 July 1890, p.8 (RCM Archives 0008/1).
74 'Report of the Council to the Fourth Annual General Meeting of the Corporation', 15 July 1887, p.9 (RCM Archives 0008/1).
75 Prospectus (1882), p.4, para. 6.
76 'His Majesty's Commissioners for the Exhibition of 1851 have intimated, through their Chairman, that they will view with favour any scheme for the enlargement of the College as soon as sufficient contributions have been provided.' 'Report of the Council to the First Annual [General] Meeting of the Corporation', 28 May 1884, p.8 (RCM Archives 0008/1).
77 In July 1888 the Honorary Treasurer reported that the College had 'during the last five years succeeded in showing a surplus over revenue over expenditure of something like 500l. a year.' By the end of that year the reserves amounted to £2,800 ('Report of the Council to the Fifth Annual General Meeting of the Corporation', 24 July 1888, p.18). The assumption, frequently expressed in the press and in other College papers, had been that the government should be approached for a grant 'after everything has been done by way of public enterprise' (cf. the *Monthly Musical Record*, 12, 136 (1 April 1882, p.80). Despite repeated efforts by the Council, the College received no government grant until after it moved into its new building. The grant was then £500 p.a., matching that already received by the Royal Academy of Music.
78 'Report of the Director to the Council' in Report of the Council to the Third Annual General Meeting of the Corporation', 3 July 1886, p.29 (RCM Archives 0008/1).
79 'Report from the Director to the Council' in 'Report of the Council to the Fourth Annual General Meeting of the Corporation' 15 July 1887, p.19 (RCM Archives 0008/1).
80 Letter to Edith Oldham, 2 November [1887] (RCM Library MS 6864/81), mentions that 'We are thinking seriously of our new Building but only thinking as yet.'

81 Letters to Edith Oldham, dated 2 and 20 November [1887] (RCM Library MS 864), ff.81and 82.
82 Letter to Edith Oldham, 18 January 1888 (RCM Library MS 6864), f.84.
83 Fox's private address was Grove House in Harrogate.
84 'Report of the Council to the Fifth Annual General Meeting of the Corporation', 24 July1888, p.14 (RCM Archives 0008/1). The minutes of the eleventh meeting of the Council, held on 10 May 1888, include a 'draft Memorial' prepared by Grove as from the President and Council of the College, to be sent to the 1851 Commissioners to request the grant of a suitable site for the new College building (see RCM Council, Minute Book I, pp.66–70). This requests that 'the new Buildings should be erected in a commanding position, on a site of sufficient area for the construction of an edifice which in size, proportions, and Collegiate character should be appropriate and adequate to the objects and requirements of the College; such site to be capable of extension as the operations of the College increase in the directions named in the Charter.'
85 Royal College of Music, Council, Minute Book, I, pp.88–90 (RCM Archives 0007/1).
86 In a letter to Grove dated 25 February 1889, later reproduced in the Council minutes of the 14th meeting of the Council, held on 1 March 1889 (see Minute Book I, pp.88–90) the 1851 Commissioners said that their plans for 'a broad road across the Gardens' led them to offer the College a different site for the new building, provided that the proposed building was 'of a character which would justify the allotment of such a site'. This, the letter indicated, would require the College in raising additional funds. The next Council meeting (31 May 1889), reported that Samson Fox had given the sum of £45,000. In recognition of his contribution, Samson Fox was invited to join the Council of the College.
87 'Director's Report to the Council', in 'Report of the Council…[to the] Sixth Annual General Meeting of the Corporation', 18 July 1889, p.23 (RCM Archives 0008/1).
88 Letter to Edith Oldham, [19 February 1888], (RCM Library MS 6864/87).
89 Ibid.
90 Royal College of Music, Executive and Finance Committees, I, 9 June 1892, 1 July 1892, 3 December 1892.
91 'Grove's World. An Exhibition to Mark the Centenary of the Death of Sir George Grove (1820–1900)'. Handlist prepared by Peter Horton (Royal College of Music, 2000), p.4.
92 For comment on this, and the reasons for the style adopted in this occasion, see *Musical World*, 61, 19 (12 May 1883), p.283.
93 'Report of the Council to the First Annual [General] Meeting of the Corporation', 28 May 1884, p.10 (RCM Archives 0008/1).
94 'Report of the Council to the Third Annual General Meeting of the Corporation', 3 July 1886, pp.8–9, 40.
95 'Report of the Council…[to the] Twelfth Annual General Meeting of the Corporation', 8 July 1895, pp.32–6. Seven holders of the award were from overseas, four of these from Australia.
96 'Report of the Council to the Sixth Annual General Meeting of the Corporation', 18 July 1889, p.11; 'Report of the Council to the Seventh Annual General Meeting of the Corporation', 9 July, 1890, pp.10–11. For Mackenzie's account of the process and the opposition experienced by Grove and Mackenzie within their respective institutions, see Alexander Mackenzie, *A Musician's Narrative* (London, 1927), pp.167–8.

97 The Royal Academy of Music had previously conducted local examinations but these had run into difficulties (see Mackenzie, *Narrative*, p.166).
98 Royal College of Music Council Minute Book, I, inserted in minutes for 26th meeting (15 May 1891, opposite p.171), RCM Archives 0007/1.
99 Stanford, *Pages from an Unwritten Diary*, p.212.
100 *Musical World*, 5 May 1883, p.270.
101 'Report of Director to Council', in 'Report of the Council to the First Annual [General] Meeting of the Corporation', 28 May 1884, p.11 (RCM Archives 0008/1).
102 There were seven lodging-houses in the first year, 12 a year later. The committee was formed only in the second year.
103 See Damrosch's comments on the distinctive and beneficial aspects of student life at the RCM quoted at note 70.
104 Graves, *Life & Letters*, p.348.
105 Graves, *Life & Letters*, p.349.
106 'Samuel Coleridge-Taylor', *Musical Times*, 50, 793 (March 1909), pp.153–8. I am indebted to the dissertation work of Marianne Lee, RCM Masters student, for drawing my attention to other sources relating to Samuel Coleridge-Taylor.
107 Graves, *Life & Letters*, p.416.
108 Graves, *Life & Letters*, p.322.
109 *Ibid.*
110 *Musical Times*, 41, 689 (1 July 1900), p.460.
111 Stanford, *Pages*, p.224.
112 *Ibid.*
113 Mackenzie, *Narrative*, p.137.
114 Stanford, *Pages from an Unwritten Diary*, p.213.
115 Graves, *Life & Letters*, p.299.
116 Stanford, *Interludes*, p.137.
117 Antonia Byatt, *The Biographer's Tale* (London, 2000), p.214.
118 Frank Howes, *The English Musical Renaissance* (London, 1966), p.49.

11
The Documentary Legacy: Grove's Library and Papers at the RCM

Peter Horton

> 'I have been sending up a quantity of music to College from this house lately, a vast lot, 2 carts full – Periodicals and miscellaneous music of all kinds – and yet without treading on my own special library – i.e. the scores of Mendelssohn Beethoven, Schubert &c. books about them & a collection of many volumes of Pamphlets – It is quite wonderful what a quantity I have accumulated, it will make quite a department in the Library and will serve to keep my name green after I am passed away.[1]

The image of two carts laden with books and music slowly wending their way through the suburbs to the urban bustle of South Kensington in February 1891 is an attractive one. But what relevance, one might ask, does it have to the Royal College of Music at the beginning of the twenty-first century? That journey, however, saw the removal of one part of the library of Sir George Grove from his home in Lower Sydenham to the College he had headed for its first 11 years and where his legacy is as much in evidence today as it was a century ago. Indeed, Sir Christopher Wren's epitaph in St Paul's Cathedral, 'Si monumentam requiris circumspice' ('If you want to see my memorial look around you') is just as applicable to Grove at the RCM, and nowhere more so than in the Library. Through his books, pamphlets, programmes, periodicals, scores, manuscripts and letters he is almost as present today as he was during his lifetime. Even something as seemingly insignificant as his initials or a brief comment on a student's entry in the Registers of Scholars or Students reminds us of the extent to which he was involved in the daily life of the College and of the interest he took in those he dubbed his 'children'. When speaking of his 'documentary legacy', however, it is principally those printed and handwritten works listed above which come to mind and which paint such a fascinating picture of the man, his interests, friends and travels.

How long after death does someone become a historical figure rather than a recently departed one? I ask this because there is always a period during which yesterday's figures are in limbo and it is at such times that their legacy is in the greatest danger of being lost, destroyed or dispersed. This was certainly true of Grove. As his first biographer, C.L. Graves, described, he left a quantity of diaries and pocket books which Lady Grove placed at Graves' disposal.[2] Neither they, nor many of the letters from which he quoted, have been seen since and one can only presume that Graves, considering that his quotations told enough of the story, saw no need to retain the originals.[3] Further casualties befell the collection of books and scores which came to the RCM. Some, like the 34 volumes of *The Athenaeum* which formed part of that first instalment in February 1891, have disappeared without trace as have, one suspects, others which duplicated works already held. That said, plenty remains and during the century since his death further material has been added, including a collection of letters to Edith Oldham, a collection of annotated programmes and the manuscript of his moving address to the students in July 1895.[4]

In addition to references in Grove's letters, the arrival of material from Sydenham is recorded in both the RCM Gift Book and the College Annual Reports. Although rarely explicit, they usually contain sufficient information to allow one to identify with reasonable certainty what each gift contained. Thus the large donation reported in July 1891 (including *The Athenaeum*, 34 volumes of the *Musical World*, 20 volumes of Proske's *Musica Divina*, together with 'many volumes of various other musical periodicals; a large quantity of music (say) 400 pieces, including Vocal Scores of Oratorios, Full Scores of Concertos and Symphonies, Pianoforte Music, Vocal Music, etc., etc., by various composers')[5] is clearly what was sent in February 1891 – although curiously it was not noted in the Gift Book until April – and many volumes bear a bookplate with the words 'The Gift of Sir George Grove. 1891'. An equally large collection arrived seven years later and here, within what was described as 'About 650 Volumes of Musical Literature, about 350 Volumes of Music, Autographs of Beethoven, Mendelssohn, and Schubert (including that of the Unfinished Symphony [i.e. No 7 in E major]), and a Quantity of Sheet Music',[6] lay the heart of his collection – 'my own special library', as mentioned at the start of this chapter – which he had been unable to part with earlier. Now, with its departure from Sydenham, there was surely tacit acknowledgement that his days of musical scholarship had drawn to a close.

Grove was an inveterate scribbler and much of the interest in his books and scores lies in the annotations so many of them contain. Sometimes these consist of no more than dates of performances with the name of conductor (and soloist) and it is interesting to see that most of these date from no earlier than the late 1850s or early 1860s (i.e. from the time he started to write programme notes in earnest). A number of scores, however, contain more informative marginalia: at bar 184 of the finale of Beethoven's Fifth Symphony, for example, he corrected the clarinet parts which were printed a third too low for 23 bars), while he frequently marked passages which particularly interested him and several of these were later used as musical examples in his two books, *Beethoven's Nine Symphonies* (which he was persuaded to compile by George Henschel, conductor of the Boston Symphony Orchestra) and the rather more expansive *Beethoven and his Nine Symphonies*. Their aim was set out in the preface to the former:

> I had been well grounded in vocal music, particularly in Händel and the old Italian and old English schools; but modern orchestral music was a new world to me, and one that puzzled me at the same time that it delighted me. I felt impelled to put down the discoveries which I made in these unknown regions, as I made them. And thus the papers reprinted in the following pages arose . . .
>
> Their aim is to enable my readers to appreciate what I have learned more quickly than I was able to learn it, because I had no guide, but was forced to find it out for myself.[7]

First-hand evidence of Grove's determination to 'find it out for myself' can be seen in the first movement of the Seventh Symphony where, at bar 309, he added figures to the bass line to help him understand the harmony better; the phrase subsequently reappeared as example no.15 in *Beethoven and his Nine Symphonies*. A further link between score and book is found in the 'Eroica' where the words from Tennyson's *Ode on the Death of the Duke of Wellington* that he was later to quote in print are found written above the Funeral March:[8]

> In the vast cathedral leave him, [bars 139–43]
> God accept him, Christ receive him. [bars 145–50]

Tucked into the back of the score there is also a slip of paper with another comment on the section which immediately follows (bar 160): 'triplets – look at Leonora No 3. They occur in much the same kind of connexion – as if the feeling were too great to bear any longer and he bursts out into a kind of joke'.[9] Such little details add a human touch. Sometimes an old score needed replacing and he characteristically annotated his 'new' copy of Beethoven's Ninth Symphony 'G. Grove. Oct. 1894. Bought at Schott's – (London) – a copy which Mr Volkert said had been there for 40 years'; three years later he returned to its predecessor (which had first accompanied him to the Crystal Palace in April 1865) 'My own old copy G. Grove April 7. 1898'.[10] In total he possessed no fewer than four scores of the work, including a much prized copy of the first edition. Occasionally one find works from earlier collections, among them Otto Jahn's which was sold after his death in 1869: Grove's annotated copy of the catalogue is to be found among his bound volumes of pamphlets, with Beethoven's first and second symphonies (lots

1063–4) and Mendelssohn's third and fourth symphonies (lots 1944–5) marked. He successfully obtained all four – with some typical scribbled notes on a programme for the Crystal Palace Wednesday orchestral concert on 17 May 1871 inserted into the last – but a number of the lots he was interested in either escaped him or are no longer at the RCM.[11]

No less fascinating are the 48 bound volumes of pamphlets, mostly (but not exclusively) on a wide range of musical topics. At the front of the first volume are a Crystal Palace Programme for 16 March 1865 and Guinea season ticket admitting until 30 April 1865, suggesting that it was bound up in that year, with subsequent volumes probably being put together every two or three years. The third, for example, contains Köchel's *Die kaiserliche Hof-Musikkapelle in Wien, von 1543 bis 1867*, published in 1869 and 'Mr. Grove's Copy' of the catalogue of works performed at the Monday Popular Concerts between 1859 and 1868. They also reveal some surprising facts. Although Grove was no great lover of Wagner's music he possessed many of his literary works, both in German and in English translation, among them an English libretto to *Die Walküre*, privately printed in London 1873 (for the Wagner Society founded a year earlier by Edward Dannreuther). Likewise, while many relate to those composers we particularly associate with Grove, others suggest a continuing interest in music of earlier periods: alongside publications on Handel and Bach there is Edmund Schebek's *Zwei Briefe über Johann Jacob Froberger* (1874). And to corroborate an interest in earlier German and Austrian music, one of the marked lots in the catalogue of Jahn's sale was a volume containing toccatas and fugues by Froberger and works by Muffat, Kerll, Murschhauser and Eberlin.[12]

Another intriguing aspect of the book and pamphlet collections is the light they shed on Grove's travels and his many friends and acquaintances. His copy of Miel's *Notice sur la vie et les ouvrages de Cherubini*,[13] for example, was inscribed 'given me by Madame Cherubini at her house' (May 1861) and others were presented by the German musicologists Max Friedländer and F. Gustav Jansen. Preserved in one volume are the admission ticket and accommodation receipt for his stay in Bonn during the 1870 'Beethoven-Fest'. Other visits were to Vienna in search of further compositions by Schubert, where a great friend was the music historian and librarian of the Gesellschaft der Musikfreunde, Carl Ferdinand Pohl.[14] Grove's account of his historic discoveries in 1867 was printed in his appendix to Arthur Coleridge's translation of Kreissle von Hellborn's *Franz Schubert*, but pasted into the back of his copy of the German edition is a page of Pohl's notes on Schubert, including some fascinating information on the problems which beset the copying of Schubert's *Incidental Music to Rosamunde* for use at the Crystal Palace on 28 March:

> Sunday 23d febr: [1868] As the copyist did not come also this morning, and [I] became anxious and went to Hernals where he lives. He gave me the Nr. 1 (Entr'act) which was finished. (If I had known that there are

> only a few leaves I would have copied it myself). The overture also will be ready till 4 or 5 o'clock and I send it also directly by the lettrepost [sic]. All the rest I told the man to bring to Spina that the whole shall be send [sic] to you – the Becker-Quartett is much liked here – very disagreeable for Hellmesberger. God bless you! Yours Pohl.[15]

Another acquaintance was the German conductor and scholar Hermann Kretzschmar whom he entertained in 1895:

> Tomorrow is an exciting day [he wrote to his confidante Edith Oldham on 12 April.] I shall have plenty to do – I go up early in the mg. To say Good bye to Joachim at Victoria at 11, then Ethel [Sharpe] is to play at the C.P. at 3 and then I have to bring a German musician (with the crack jaw name of Kretzschmar) and his wife home to dinner. [Sidney] Waddington and his wife are also coming…'.[16]

Two months later Kretzschmar sent two of his publications as a 'thank-you' offering and thanked Grove for his 'great kindness to me when in England': clearly touched, Grove had the letter bound up with the articles.[17] Uncut pages prove that a number of unsolicited pamphlets remained unread!

Although the majority of books and pamphlets at the RCM are on musical topics, a number reflect other aspects of Grove's career. *A Report of the Assyrian Excavation Fund* (1855), for example, serves as a reminder of his own role in the establishment of the Palestine Exploration Fund, while a further link with the Middle East was provided by a Crystal Palace colleague, James Fergusson. General Manager from 1856–58 and initiator of the so-called Assyrian Court, Fergusson was also an architectural historian and authority on the topography and architecture of the Holy Land. Another of his multifarious interests was military fortification and his (un-read) publications on proposals for improving the defence of Portsmouth are among the more unusual items in the collection![18] At first sight two pamphlets on the rebuilding of Trinity Church, Hamilton, Bermuda, after its destruction by fire in 1884, appear equally unpromising. Within, however, are hidden details of a hitherto unknown episode in Grove's early career when, in 1846, he had superintended the preparation of the site:

> The cap of the hill had to be taken down and the foundation carried to considerable depth, owing to the irregularity of the rock, and fissures in the strata. The Committee were fortunate in securing the services of Mr. George Grove, C.E., who had been engaged in erecting the Lighthouse on Gibbs' Hill.[19]

Among the items reprinted was the address from the mechanics and labourers to Grove on his departure from the island:

> ...we...are unwilling to allow it [Grove's departure] to pass without making an acknowledgement of the manner in which you have exercised your superintendence over us, and of the light which has been reflected upon our trade, by your kind and opportune teaching. We sincerely regret the speedy termination of your charge over us, for whether we consider your urbane manner as a director, – your scientific knowledge as a superintendant...your general deportment as a gentleman, and a Christian, which has been so conspicuous throughout, we are equally bound, by a sense of gratitude and respect, not only to offer this tribute of regard, but to cherish a thankful recollection of your unbounded kindness and liberality.[20]

Grove's reply was no less characteristic: after expressing his thanks, he concluded with words from the Catechism which were surely as applicable to himself as those he addressed: 'My duty is, to learn and labour truly to get my living and to do my duty in that station of life to which it has pleased God to call me'.[21]

Grove's transformation from civil engineer to administrator to writer on music has been covered in earlier chapters and led to the long series of annotated programmes for the Crystal Palace concerts, to which he contributed for over forty years. Although in the 1880s he intimated to William Barclay Squire his intention of leaving his own set to the RCM, they never reached the College and disappeared from sight for the next century.[22] It was thus a happy coincidence when a large part of this collection was offered for sale almost exactly one hundred years after his death and the College was able to buy it. Its interest, as ever, lies in the many annotations and alterations it contained and they provide yet more evidence of his compulsive need to revise or improve. Rarely was the same note reprinted exactly as it had appeared before, but the most substantial additions were invariably reserved for those works particularly dear to him – the orchestral music of Beethoven, Schubert and Mendelssohn. Those on the Beethoven symphonies subsequently formed the basis for his two books on the subject.

It is with some effort that one remembers that, in so far as music is concerned, Grove was largely self-taught. Although, as shown in an earlier chapter, his mother had introduced him to the *Messiah* and the family attended the Sacred Harmonic Society Concerts at Exeter Hall, and he also heard a variety of works played as organ voluntaries at Clapham Parish Church, only after he had started his engineering apprenticeship with Alexander Gordon did he set about acquiring a better knowledge of music, spending many hours in Novello's music shop, attending evensong at Westminster Abbey and copying music in the British Museum. The legacy of these hours in Bloomsbury is the collection of music manuscript books he left, which chronicle both his own musical education and his later musicological work. The first series include numerous transcriptions from the British Museum

Library where, in the early 1840s, he spent many happy hours among the printed and manuscript music. Many examples are from the English church composers of the sixteenth, seventeenth and eighteenth centuries, others from sixteenth-century Italian composers or Handel – in other words just those fields he later described as having provided his introduction to music: 'vocal music, particularly...Händel and the old Italian and old English schools'.[23] Another early project was a projected thematic catalogue of the instrumental music of Bach. Three manuscript books survive, arranged by genre and probably copied in the late 1840s and early 1850s.[24] (One of the collections named as a source for his material was Friedrich Griepenkerl and Ferdinand Roitzsch's *Johann Sebastian Bach's Compositionen für die Orgel,* published between 1844 and 1850.)

A further stage of Grove's musical exploration began on 22 February 1865, the date entered into the front of the first of a series of four small oblong music manuscript books, his so-called 'commonplace books', into which he copied down brief snippets of music which had caught his ear or eye.[25] Many were examples of a similar phrase being used by different composers – or the same composer in different works – and a large number reappear in his later series of articles 'The History of a Musical Phrase Attempted'.[26] But we also find notes in the first volume of the Schubert discoveries he made on his historic visit to Vienna with Arthur Sullivan in October 1867 and a sketch of the opening bars of the Scherzo of the 'Unfinished' Symphony, reprinted in the Crystal Programme notes every time the work was performed. Beethoven comes to the fore in the second volume, with an extensive one- or two-stave reduction of the first movement of the 'Eroica' Symphony, begun during his summer holiday at Chamonix on 10 August 1874; another entry contains excerpts from Schumann's music to Goethe's *Faust* which he had heard at the Schumann Festival at Bonn in 1873. Volume III is dominated by fragments for inclusion in 'The History of a Musical Phrase Attempted', among them a chant sung by the sailors in San Juan harbour in Puerto Rico as they heaved the lead in 1840 and the cry 'Heave over jolly copper' sung by children in the 'streets in Bermondsey below the Railway viaduct where the train stopt [sic] to take tickets on the C.P. line in 1853, 54'.[27]

In Grove's fascination with the way the same musical building blocks could be used in such a variety of different ways by so many composers one can surely see the mind of the engineer being brought to bear upon music, and an examination of one such pattern of notes – the opening theme of the finale of Mozart's 'Jupiter' symphony – forms the basis of 'The History of a Musical Phrase Attempted'. Like the Crystal Palace programmes, Grove's working copy (with the pages of the articles pasted into a guard-book) was not among the materials which he donated to the RCM Library, but passed into the possession of Novello & Co. Here it remained until the sale of the remnants of the firm's library in 1996 when, as part of a miscellaneous job lot, it was fortuitously purchased by the RCM. Once again we are confronted by his almost obsessive urge for completeness, with numerous manuscript additions to both the printed examples and his commentary. Not the least interesting item is a torn-up letter from Hanslick used as a bookmark! Grove had apparently invited him to the RCM:

> I regret not to... accept your invitation, because I am invited Thursday by Mr Pauer to dinner. After the dinner we will come over together to the Concert of your 'College of Music', where I hope [to have] the pleasure to see you'.[28]

Hanslick's account of his stay in London unfortunately contains no mention of a visit to the College, so we can only speculate whether he was present for a programme of music by Bach, Beethoven, Handel, MacCunn, Rheinberger and Spohr in the West Theatre at the Royal Albert Hall.[29]

Undoubtedly the largest and in many ways most interesting part of Grove's legacy at the RCM is to be found in the hundreds of letters preserved in the Library. By far the largest number are to the former student Edith Oldham who entered the College when it opened in 1883 and later became one of Grove's closest confidantes.[30] By the summer of 1884 he had begun a regular correspondence with her which continued after Edith left the college for her native Dublin in 1887. The letters contain many glimpses of everyday life at South Kensington, but also reveal the vulnerable nature behind the façade of cheerfulness and confidence. In March 1889, for example,

> I ought to tell you, dear, that I have been really very bad this winter. It is not only that I am overworked and have had a bad cold – but I seem to feel that I have taken a step downward, and to be less able for my duties and 'responsibilities' than I was. I do stupid things, forget events, & in consequence take steps I ought not to, and neglect the most obvious things, and get bewildered; and then worry myself so sadly, not only at the faults which I have made, but at the fact that I am so deteriorated as to make them: and then I think at once that I shall be disgraced and shewn to be a mean humbug, and altogether get into a dreadfully bad way – I suppose it is the inevitable consequence of being so near the limit of three score & ten![31]

Occasionally, too, there are hints as to why he needed to unburden himself to others, for whatever her virtues his wife did not share his interests in music and literature:

> Lady G.... is one of those uncommunicative people who do themselves so much wrong... It's a sad loss to me because one must talk & let out to

> some one, else one dries up; and there is nothing on which I can talk to her. The College she has no interest in – Music ditto – my friends d[itt]o.[32]

Among his surviving letters to other students are ones to Walford Davies and Charles Wood, both of whom he lived to see appointed to the staff of the College. Writing to the latter in May 1888 he revealed an unexpected sympathy for the music of Grieg.

> I went to Grieg's concert tonight & heard his sonata in A minor (Pf & Violin) played by him & Neruda & 3 songs sung by mad. Grieg – They touched me extremely, by the beauty of the thoughts and a wild mountain simplicity more than by any art in the treatment – but I found some of the ideas strangely fetching'.[33]

His interest, however, extended to all those 'children' who had passed through 'his' college, to whom he was indeed a father figure and whose careers he followed with keen interest and great pride in their subsequent achievements. Although rather fewer in number, there are also many letters to professional colleagues, in particular the music critic J.W. Davison whom he knew well from his Crystal Palace days.

Finally one comes to the small collection of papers relating to the planning or the running of the College, among them the list of names of those Grove would have liked to have seen appointed professors[34] (see chapter 10). Several were on the staff of the Crystal Palace School of Art (among them Franklin Taylor and J.F. Barnett), but they also included such eminent performers as Joachim, Sims Reeves, Charles Hallé, Mme. Norman-Neruda and Jenny Lind-Goldschmidt, many known to him personally. For most of Grove's term as Director the RCM occupied the former National Training School for Music building (later home of the Royal College of Organists), but from 1888 plans for much larger new premises in Prince Consort Road were being drawn up. The design was by the distinguished architect Sir Arthur Blomfield and among the miscellaneous papers is a single sheet dated December 1889 on which Grove jotted down what he thought the number and dimensions of the various rooms should be. Here, surely, we can see a link with his comment in a letter to Edith Oldham that he 'must go and look through the Conservatoires of Leipzig, Frankfurt, Berlin, Vienna &c with a view to our new College.'[35]

It is impossible in the space of a few thousand words to convey the true scope of Grove's documentary legacy to the Royal College of Music. Even its full extent is not clear, though this will gradually become more apparent as the re-cataloguing of the collection of scores continues. The remarks on his pamphlet collection likewise only touch the surface and much surely remains to be discovered about them and the web of connections they reveal. Yet even a glimpse of this material sheds light on the personality and character of this fascinating man who stood like a colossus over the fledgling college. There can be no more fitting way to end this brief account than by quoting the words he used in July 1895 on being presented with an address signed by 488 past and present students to mark his retirement:

> My dear friends – pupils of College, past and present, I thank you heartily for your kind and appreciative address, and especially for the signatures appended many of which are those of dear friends whose recollection I hope always to cherish.
>
> I am sure that I need not tell you what a touching occasion this is to me, because I know that you are feeling very much the same as I do myself. I am now, as I said, addressing the whole body of pupils past and present, whom I have done my very best to serve during the twelve happy and earnest years in which I was Director of the College. During that time I worked as hard for you as ever I could…
>
> Yes, one thing I have tried to do. I have tried to shew you that authority is strengthened by affection; that enthusiasm and esprit de corps are strong motive powers; that ability and hard work are of no avail unless backed by character; that, great work as the study of music is, there is one thing still greater – to be good, to be unselfish, to be thoughtful of others.[36]

Notes

1 Letter from George Grove to Edith Oldham [1 February 1891] (RCM MS 6864/173).
2 Charles L. Graves, *The Life and Letters of Sir George Grove, C.B.* (London, 1903), v.
3 Among other losses are the letters from C.F. Pohl whose correspondence with Grove, Graves considered 'would fill a volume' (Graves, *Life and Letters*, p.207).
4 The letters to Edith Oldham (MS 6864) came from the estate of her husband, Dr Richard Best, in 1960; the Crystal Palace programmes (MS 7328) were purchased at Sotheby's in May 2000 and the Address (MS 7297) privately in 1999, with the assistance of the Friends of the National Libraries.
5 'Report of the Council to the Eighth Annual General Meeting of the Corporation', 30 April 1891 (RCM Archives 1138), p.32.
6 'Report of the Council to the Fifteenth Annual General Meeting of the Corporation', 30 April 1898 (RCM Archives 1128), p.12.
7 George Grove, *Beethoven's Nine Symphonies* (Boston, 1884), pp.viii-ix.
8 George Grove, *Beethoven and His Nine Symphonies* (London, 1896), p.73.
9 See RCM Library, LVIII, A.6, pp.105–6.
10 RCM Library, LVIII.B.29, inside of front cover.
11 Among other works acquired by Grove at this sale were scores of Mendelssohn's third and fourth symphoniesa, a manuscript of J.H. Knecht's *Le portrait musical de la nature our grande symphonie* (a programmatic precursor of Beethoven's 'Pastoral' Symphony, MS 926) and various literary works (see RCM Library XXII.A.4[5]).
12 Lot 2377. There is no evidence from the Library catalogue that Grove succeeded in acquiring the lot.
13 An offprint from the *Moniteur Universal*, 24, 25 and 29 August 1842.

14 Carl Ferdinand Pohl (1819–87) had lived in London between 1863 and 1866, where he worked in the British Museum on Haydn and Mozart sources, but it is not known whether his friendship with Grove dates from this time.
15 See RCM 41865.f.1. The numbers in question were presumably the *Balletmusik* No. 1 and the *Balletmusik* No. 2, both first heard at the Crystal Palace (and in England) on 16 March 1867.
16 RCM MS 6864/15.
17 See RCM XXII.B.17(8–9). The articles in question were 'Die Venetianische Oper und die Werke Cavalli's und Cesti's' and 'Monteverdi's "Incoronazione di Poppea"', offprints from the 1892 and 1894 volumes of *Vierteljahrsschrift für Musikwissenschaft* respectively.
18 James Fergusson, *The Peril of Portsmouth; or, French Fleets and English Forts*, 3rd edn (London, 1853), *Portsmouth Protected: a Sequel to The Peril of Portsmouth* (London, 1856) (RCM XXII.D.24 [11, 10]).
19 Thomas S. Reid, *Trinity Church Bermuda: a Sketch of its History drawn from Various Sources* (Bermuda, 1886), p.8 (RCM XXII.D.24 [15]).
20 *Ibid.*, Appendix D.
21 *Ibid.*
22 See BL Add. MS 39679, ff.136–7. I am grateful to Leanne Langley and Christina Bashford for bringing this to my attention.
23 'George Grove, *Beethoven's Nine Symphonies* (Boston, 1884), p.viii.
24 RCM MS 1174.
25 RCM MSS 2134–37.
26 'The History of a Musical Phrase Attempted', *Musical World*, published serially from (2 October 1886 (vol. 64, no.40, pp.627–8), to 14 May 1887 (vol. 65, no. 20 p.371–2)). Grove's final instalment is dated 11 May 1887.
27 RCM MS 2136, f.36v.
28 Letter dated 'London 25 May [1886]. See RCM MS 6859a.
29 See Eduard Hanslick, translated Henry Pleasants, *Music Criticisms 1846–99* (Harmondsworth, 1963), pp.246–74.
30 Grove's letters to Edith Oldham were extensively drawn on by Percy Young for the preparation of *George Grove: a Biography* (London, 1984).
31 RCM MS 6864/114.
32 RCM MS 6864/88.
33 Letter dated 16 May 1888 (RCM MS 7056/11).
34 RCM Archives 009611. Although the document appears to be in Grove's hand, doubts remain over its authenticity.
35 Letter to Edith Oldham, 10 June [1888] (RCM MS 6864/104).
36 RCM MS 7297, ff.1, 8. The following RCM manuscripts are known to have come from the collection of Sir George Grove. MS 378 Mendelssohn: Overture *Die Hebridean:* copyist's full score of the December 1830 version; [586] Schubert: Symphony No. 7 in E major: autograph full score in sketch form; [2174] Beethoven: single leaf of autograph sketches (Bagatelle WoO 60 & two canons WoO 168 – MS of neither work listed Kinsky-Halm, *Das Werk Beethovens* (Munich 1955); [2175] Beethoven: 2 fragments of autograph sketches; [2176] Beethoven: 2 quarto pages containing an extract of a translation of a Buddhist religious work, beginning 'Gott ist immateriell', said to have been kept framed on his writing table (see further 'Beethoven Autograph' in *Beethoven's Letters*, with explanatory notes by Dr A.C. Kalischer, trans. with preface by J.S. Shedlock, London, 1909; 2nd edn 1972), pp.393–4; [4813] Schumann: Partsong for female voices 'Die Capelle' op. 69/6 (presented by Clara Schumann).

Chronology

1820 13 August	George Grove born at Thurlow Terrace, Clapham
1828	Attends School on Clapham Common (Greaves's, later Elwell's School)
1832	Attends Stockwell School (under Charles Pritchard)
1834 August–Dec 1835	Attends Clapham Grammar School (under Charles Pritchard)
1836 January	Articled to Alexander Gordon, engineer, Westminster
1836	Publication of the *Musical World*
1837 30 November–1838 17 January	Visit to Belgian railway system with Gordon
1838 9 January	Opening of North Wing Reading Room of the British Museum.
1839	Seconded to Robert Napier, engineer, Glasgow
1839 26 February	Admitted as graduate, Institute of Civil Engineers
1840 end	Returns to London from Glasgow
1841	Publication of the *Singing Class Circular*, later the *Musical Times*
1841 October	Sent to Jamaica to supervise construction of the lighthouse at Morant Point as Resident Engineer
1843–1846	Sent to Bermuda for 3 years to supervise lighthouse construction at Gibbs Hill, Hamilton, Bermuda; in 1846 superintends preparation of the site for the rebuilding of Trinity Church, Hamilton
1846 6 August	Returns from Bermuda
1846 autumn	Employed on Robert Stephenson's extension of the railway system from Birmingham under his assistant C.H.Wild
1847–8	Appointed resident Engineer at construction of Chester General Railway Station under C.H.Wild
1848 1 August	Chester General Station opens
1848 autumn	Holiday in Paris with his brother Edmund
1848–50	Assistant Site Engineer on the Britannia Tubular Bridge project, Bangor, N. Wales
1849 20 June	Floating of the first tube of the Britannia Bridge, Bangor, North Wales
1850	Foundation of the Leipzig *Bach Gesellschaft*. (Publications 1851–99)
1850 6 February	Appointed Joint Secretary of the Society of Arts (with J. Scott Russell)

1850 March	Appointed full Secretary of the Society of Arts
1850 3 December	Admitted as Associate of the Institute of Civil Engineers
1851 May–Sept	The Great Exhibition, Hyde Park
1851 23 December	Marries Harriet Bradley
1852	Foundation of New Philharmonic Society
1852 May	Appointed Secretary of the Crystal Palace Company, Sydenham
1852 2 April	Death of Grove's father
1852 May	Moves to house at Church Meadow, Sydenham (later No. 1)
1853 25 April	Birth of Lucy Penrose Grove
1854	Meets Alfred Tennyson and A.P. Stanley
1854 10 June	Opening of the Sydenham Crystal Palace
1855 October	August Manns's first season as Director of Music, Crystal Palace
1856 26 January	Grove's first programme notes (for the Mozart Centenary concert, Crystal Palace)
1856 March	Death of Grove's mother
1857 27 January	Birth of Walter Maurice Grove
1857–1863	Work on Dr William Smith's *Dictionary of the Bible*
1857 June	Preliminary Handel Festival at Crystal Palace
1858–94	Publication of the Collected Edition of Handel (*G.F. Händels Werke*) by Breitkopf und Härtel, Leipzig (under Friedrich Chrysander)
1858 July	Grand Handel Demonstration at Crystal Palace
1858 late August–7 October	First visit to the Holy Land
1859	Opening of St James's Hall, London: Arthur Chappell's Popular Concerts begin
1859 8 April	Birth of Julius Charles Grove
1859 July	Handel Commemoration Festival at Crystal Palace
1859	Appointed Assistant Editor of *Macmillan's Magazine* under David Masson First issue 1 November 1859
1860 summer	Moves to new house in Sydenham High Road, Lower Sydenham
1860 28 August	Holiday in Brussels, Rhineland, Austria, Switzerland, Paris, Oberamergau
1861 September–10 October	Second visit to Holy Land: Haifa, Nazareth, Damascus, Beirut, Jerusalem
12–13 October	Attends Yom Kippur Ceremony at Nabloos [Nâblus]
1861 December	Death of the Prince Consort
1861 Christmas eve	Death of Mary Bithia Grove
1862–3	Work on Dr Smith's *Dictionary of the Bible*
1862–5; 1888	Publication of Beethoven Collected Edition (*L. van Beethovens Werke*) by Breitkopf und Härtel, Leipzig
1862 16 January	Birth of Millicent Stanley Grove

1862 Spring	First appearance of Joachim at the Crystal Palace concerts Sullivan's music for *The Tempest*
1862 1 May	Second Great International Exhibition, South Kensington
1862 September	Spends ten days in Oxford
1863	Completion of Smith's *Dictionary of the Bible*
1863 15 June	Death of Lucy Penrose Grove from scarlet fever
1863 June	First appearance of Clara Schumann at the Crystal Palace Concerts
1864	Birth of Arthur Grove
1864 early August	Three weeks holiday in Switzerland: Basel, Lucerne, Andermatt, Brieg, Chamonix, Geneva, Lausanne, Berne, Interlaken; Strasbourg, Paris
1865	Invited to produce a new edition of the Bible
1865	Meets Alexander Macmillan
1865 Easter	Short visit to Paris with Emmanuel Deutsch
1865 22 June	Launching of the Palestine Exploration Fund
1866	Offered position of Keeper at South Kensington Museum by Henry Cole
1866 10 March	First performance of Arthur Sullivan's Symphony in E at the Crystal Palace concerts
1866 October	Visit to Tennyson
1867 end July	Visits Paris for the International Exposition
1867 May	Applies for position of Librarian of House of Commons
1867 24 September–27 October	Visit to Vienna; also Baden, Munich, Prague, Dresden, Leipzig, Berlin
1868 6 March–23 March	6-week tour of Italy: Florence, Vesuvius, Naples, Rome (meets the Pope and Franz Liszt), Turin
1868 May	Takes over editorship of *Macmillan's Magazine* from Masson
1868	Unsuccessful application for post of Secretary at Lloyds
1868 August	Visits Frederick Gore-Ouseley at the College of St Michael and All Angels, Tenbury
1869	Foundation of the Metaphysical Society. Grove a founder member, but not recorded as attending after 19 December 1871
1869 early September	Attends Three Choirs Festival at Worcester. Sullivan: *The Prodigal Son*
1869 11 September–8 October	Visit to Italy, via Paris [attends International Exposition], Bologna, Turin, Naples
1869 8 November	Speaks at Newark for the Palestine Exploration Fund
1869 late	Undertakes a Biblical atlas for Dr Smith's *Atlas of Ancient Geography* (Murray)
1870 August	Visits Paris (after the end of the Franco-Prussian War)
1871 27 February	Election to the Athenaeum (proposed by Dean Stanley; seconded by Dr William Smith)

1871 29 March	Opening of the Albert Hall, Kensington Gore
1871 early June	Visit to Paris with Sullivan and Wilhelm von Glehn
1871 17 August	Travel to Bonn (Beethoven Centenary: 20–23 August); Switzerland: Basel, Lucerne, Brünig Pass; Mürren in Bernese Oberland
1872 2–21 August	Holiday in Scotland: Glasgow, Oban, Bonavie, Inverness, Loch Carron, Skye
1873 2 April	First UK public performance of Brahms's *A German Requiem* by Philharmonic Society, at St. James's Hall
1873 17 July–end August	Bonn (Schumann Festival). Thuringia: Wildbad, Freudenstadt, Rippoldsau, Freiburg
1873 September	Announces resignation from the Crystal Palace
1873 18 December	Foundation of the National Training School for Music
1874	Publication of Mendelssohn Collected Edition (*F. Mendelssohn-Bartholdy Werke*) by Breitkopf und Härtel, Leipzig
1874 January	Assumes full responsibility for editing at Macmillan Prospectus issued for the *Dictionary of Music and Musicians* in 2 volumes 1874. Appointed to the Board of Directors of the Crystal Palace
1874 31 July	A month's holiday in Switzerland: Chamonix, Bel Alp, Andermatt, Lucerne, Basle
1874	Interest in Chinese porcelain; sketches for 'Handbook of the Bible' (unpublished work)
1875	Publication of the music magazine *Concordia* by Novello
1875 1 February	Death of Sterndale Bennett
1875 16–18 May	Visits Düsseldorf for Lower Rhine Music Festival
1875 May and June	Visits to Thomas Grove at Penn
1875 16–18 May	Lower Rhine Music Festival
1875 29 June	Awarded degree of Doctor of Civil Laws by Durham University
1876	Grove plans a Primer on the commercial development of Great Britain
1876 5 February	Cardinal Manning visits Grove at the Crystal Palace
1876 14 February	Elected a member of the Royal Geographical Society
1876 26 April	First performance by the Bach Choir: Bach, *Mass in B minor*, conducted by Otto Goldschmidt (St James's Hall)
1876 Easter	Opening of the National Training School for Music, Kensington Gore
1876 summer	Socializing in Sydenham includes meeting Anthony Trollope
1877 January	Publication of Grove's *A Primer of Geography*
1877 30 April	Wagner visits England: Grove meets him

1877 8 May	Attends the UK premiere of Brahms's First Symphony at Cambridge under Joachim
1877 30 April	Wagner arrives in England. Grove meets him during his visit
1877 May	Meets Anton Rubinstein in London
1877 September	Visits brother Edmund at Saltburn
1877 13 July	Prince of Wales convenes meeting on the envisaged National Conservatoire of Music
1878 6 March	Death of Louise Scott Russell
1878 5 September–14 November	Visit to North America with Dean Stanley and Harper: Boston, Baltimore, Virginia, Niagara, Toronto, Montreal, Quebec, Lake George, Massachusetts, New York
1879	Mendelssohn research
1879 early	Two visits to Cambridge for CUMS concerts
1879 24 July	Visits Eleanor Grove at Sevenoaks, including Knole Park
1879 April	First volume of the *Dictionary of Music and Musicians* published
1879 May	Richter Concerts commence at St James's Hall
1879 29 September–16 October	German research trip for Mendelssohn: Cologne, Hanover, Leipzig, Magdeburg
1880 February	Mendelssohn fascicle of the *Dictionary* published
1880 April	Meets Ernest Renan in London. Visits Westminster Abbey with him and Matthew Arnold
1880 end April	Germany trip with Millicent Grove; Cologne; Bonn (Schumann Festival 2–3 May); Wiesbaden. Frankfurt
1880 19 July	Presentation to Grove at St James's Hall banqueting room. He gives autobiographical speech
1880 20 September–early October	Schubert trip: Frankfurt, Nuremberg, Wiesbaden, Vienna
1880 October–February 1881	First complete cycle of the Schubert symphonies at Crystal Palace
1880 November/December	Correspondence with Frl. Carola Geisler Schubert
1881 9–27 April	Holiday in Italy via Paris: Turin, Milan, Verona, Venice, returning through Botzen and Munich
1881 17 May	Cambridge: attends CUMS performance of Parry: *Prometheus Unbound*
1881 July	Invited to join the Prince of Wales's committee
1881 18 July	Death of Dean A.P. Stanley
1881 September	C.V. Stanford in Vienna. Researches Schubert for *Dictionary*
1882	Foundation of the *Dictionary of National Biography*
1882 28 February	Prince of Wales meeting at St James's Palace for RCM

1882 March	Grove undertakes organizing subscriptions for the RCM for 6 months
1882	Schubert article published in the *Dictionary of Music and Musicians*
1882 7 March	Cambridge. CUMS Concert: Joachim plays Brahms's Violin Concerto.
1882 May	Correspondence with Clara Schumann on Spitta's *Dictionary* article on Schumann
1882 20 October	First reference to Grove as Director of the RCM appears in *The Times*
1883 7 May	RCM opens. Grove receives knighthood
1883	Summer holiday: Yorkshire; Northumberland, Norfolk
1883 August	2 weeks' holiday with Edmund Grove at Saltburn
1883 late August	Visits friends in Northumberland and Norfolk
1883 September	Attends Worcester Festival: Hears Dvořák's *Stabat Mater*
1883 December	Relinquishes editorship of *Macmillan's Magazine*
1884 March	Visits 6 Sussex churches in 3 days
1884 early June	A week in Paris with Millicent Grove
1884 August	2 weeks' holiday in the Engadine
1884 22 October	Speaks in Portsmouth for the RCM
1885–97	Publication of Schubert Collected Edition (*F. Schuberts Werke*) by Breitkopf und Härtel, Leipzig
1885 Spring	Visit to churches near Salisbury
1885 12–31 August	Visits Switzerland with Millicent Grove: Lucerne, Interlaken. Meets Julius Stockhausen and Georg and Lillian Henschel
1885 December	Discussion of an available plot for the new RCM building
1886	Deaths of many close friends in this year
1886 8 April	Reception for Liszt at Grosvenor Galleries, later at Crystal Palace
1886 10 May	First London performance of Brahms's Symphony No. 4 under Richter at St James's Hall
1886 30 April	Receives degree of LLD, Glasgow University
1886 23 June	Cherubini. *Les deux Journées* by RCM students under Stanford
1886 August	Visits Edmund Grove at Saltburn
1886 late September	Visits Thomas Grove at Penn
1886 October	Attends Leeds Festival: Sullivan's *The Golden Legend*
1886 10 November	Run down by cab in Knightsbridge. 3 days in bed
1886 early December	Travels to Alassio with Harriet for dying Millicent Grove, who dies 16 December

1887 14 March	Queen Alexandra House opened as women's hall of residence for the RCM in Kensington Gore
1887 28 April	Death of C.F. Pohl in Vienna. Grove writes *The Times* obituary
1888	Joins Board of the Carl Rosa Opera Company
1888	Discussions concerning new RCM building
1888 10 September	Report of Grove's address to the College of Organists in the *Musical World*
1889 March	Attends dinner for Joachim at Cambridge
1889 4 April	Run down by cab in Piccadilly. In bed 10 days
1889 August–10 September	Vienna Beethoven trip with Manns: Cologne (visits Conservatoire); Frankfurt, Nuremberg, Bayreuth (*Tristan und Isolde, Parsifal*), Regensburg, Vienna (meets Artaria), Interlaken, Lucerne, Ringgenburg (meets Lili Wach)
1889 October	Attends Leeds Festival; interest in Beethoven's Symphony No. 9 as conducted by Sullivan
1890 8 July	Foundation stone of RCM new building laid.
1890 1 August	Visits Tennyson
1890 14–16 August	Visits his brother Thomas at Penn
1890 19 August	Visit to Norway: visit with son Julius Charles
1890 10 September	Attends marriage of youngest son, Arthur
1891 early months	Illness
1891 February	Cab accident in London
1891 Easter	Visits Paris Conservatoire: Works in Library there
1891 August	Holiday, mainly in Switzerland: Paris, Lausanne, Riffal Alp, Berlin
1891 June	RCM orchestra performs Brahms's Symphony No. 4
1891 October	Attends Birmingham Festival. Parry *Blest Pair of Sirens*; Brahms's Symphony No. 3
1892 early	Unwell: Attacks of lumbago, winter hearing problems
1892 15 April	Travels with Arthur Sullivan to Biarritz, Bayonne, St Jean de Luz
1892 2 August–3 September	Travels to Bonn, Vienna (Music Exhibition), Salzburg, Interlaken, Ringgenburg, Thun (with Walter Parratt)
1892 September	Attends Gloucester Festival. Parry: *Job*
1892 6 October	Death of Tennyson. Grove attends funeral on 12 October
1893 January	Visit to the Riviera with Sullivan for health
1893 mid-August–28 September	Visit to Ragatz for cure; Interlaken
1893 December	Queen's Hall opens in Langham Place
1894 2 May	RCM new building opened.
1894 25 May	CB conferred on Grove by the Queen
1894 June	Attends Handel Festival at the Crystal Palace

1894 22 June	Hears Tchaikovsky's Symphony No. 6 at the Philharmonic under Alexander Mackenzie
1894 August	Brief Scottish holiday
1894 17 October	Grove's resignation from the RCM accepted by Prince of Wales
1894 November	C.H.H. Parry appointed Grove's successor
1894 21 Dec	Grove's last day at RCM
1895	Sells the geographical and biblical sections of his library
1895	Working on *Beethoven and His Nine Symphonies*
1895 12 February	Gives Beethoven paper to the Musical Association
1895 4 April	Distributes prizes at Sydenham High School
1895 30 April	Attends 70th Birthday celebration for Manns at Grafton Galleries
1895 May	Grove sits for the RCM portrait by Charles Furse and bust by Alfred Gilbert
1895 20 Nov	Performance of Purcell, *Dido and Aeneas* by RCM students at Lyceum Theatre under Stanford
1895 23 Oct	Elgar's *Bavarian Dances* performed at Crystal Palace by Manns
1895 28 October	Run down by cab in Victoria St. Unhurt
1895 end	Grove takes the young singer Clara Butt to Paris for lessons with Marie Trélat
1895 December	Presentation to Grove at RCM by Parry of the Furse portrait
1896 March	Publication of *Beethoven and His Nine Symphonies*
1896 4 July	Attends *Tristan und Isolde* at Covent Garden
1896 27 July	Scottish holiday: St Andrews, Edinburgh, Portobello, Melrose
1896 September	Attends Hovingham Musical Festival
1896 October	Attends Bristol Festival
1896 end	Handwriting weakens. Employs an amanuensis
1897	Queen Victoria's Diamond Jubilee Year. Relinquishes programme-note writing for the Crystal Palace
1897 3 April	Elgar: *King Olaf* performed at Crystal Palace by Manns
1897 6, 10 April	Attends Bach's *St Matthew Passsion* by Bach Choir under Stanford (in German)
1897 June	Attends his last Handel Festival at Crystal Palace
1897 August	Hears of death of A.W. Thayer
1897 Summer	Grove begins to feel deafness, arthritis and memory loss
1897 October	Article on Grove appears in the *Musical Times*
1897 30 October	Distributes prizes at St Michael and All Angels Boy's School, Lower Sydenham
1897 28 November	Death of Marie Benecke, eldest daughter of Mendelssohn

1897 9 November	Death of Thomas Grove, Grove's eldest brother. Grove involved with problems with his estate
1897 August	Visits Lincolnshire: Churches at Boston, Lincoln, Heckington
1898	Declining health
1899 Winter	Grove increasingly oblivious to surroundings
1900 28 May	Grove dies. Funeral at St Bartholomew's Church, Sydenham, conducted by Dean of Westminster, Dean Bradley. Buried in Ladywell Cemetery, Lewisham, South London
1914 31 March	Harriet Grove dies and is buried with her husband.

Appendix 1: Grove's Published Writings[1]

Books

Geography, No. 4 of History Primers, ed. J.R. Green (London, 1877).

Beethoven's Nine Symphonies: Analytical Essays, with a Preface by Georg Henschel (Boston, 1884).

Beethoven and His Nine Symphonies (London, 1896; 2nd edn, 1896; 3rd edn, 1898; rept London/New York, 1962).

Beethoven und seine neun Symphonien, trans. Max Hehemann (London/ New York, 1906).

The Story of David, with a Preface by W. Addis, privately printed after 1900[2].

Contributions to books by other authors

A.P. Stanley, *Sinai and Palestine in Connection with Their History* (London, 1856), Appendix.

Clark, Samuel, *The Bible Atlas of Maps and Plans to Illustrate the geography and Topography of the Old and New Testaments and the Apocrypha with Explanatory Notes… and a complete Index of the Geographical Names of the English Bible* (London, 1868; 2nd edn, 1875): index of geographical names.

Kreissle von Hellborn, Heinrich, *The Life of Schubert*, trans. A.D. Coleridge (London, 1869): Appendix, pp.297–332.

Hiller, Ferdinand, *Mendelssohn, Letters and Recollections*, trans. M.E. von Glehn (London, 1874): Editor's Preface pp.xxxiii–iv.

Mendelssohn's Psalms [in English with piano accompaniment] (London, *c.* 1876), Preface.

Fay, Amy, *Music Study in Germany* (Chicago, 1880): Introduction, pp.v–vi.

Hensel, Sebastian, *The Mendelssohn Family 1729–1847 from Letters and Journals*, trans. C. Klingemann and an American collaborator, 2 vols (London, 1881): 'Advertisement', pp.v–vi.

Jahn, Otto, *The Life of Mozart*, trans. P.D. Townsend, 3 vols (London, 1882): Preface.

Rockstro, W.S., *The Life of George Frederick Handel* (London, 1883): Preface.

A Short History of Cheap Music (London, 1887): Preface.

Early Letters of R. Schumann, originally published by his Wife (Jugendbriefe), trans. May Herbert (London, 1888): Preface.

Chambers Encyclopedia (London, 1890): Entries of Orlando Gibbons, Beethoven and Handel. [Copies in BL 78998.0.12] Only the last is acknowledged by the addition of 'G'.

Edwards, F.G., *The History of Mendelssohn's Oratorio 'Elijah'* (London, 1896): Introduction, p.iii.

Translations and editions

Guizot, F., *The Fine Arts, their Nature and Relations* (London, 1853), from *Etudes surles beaux arts en general* (Paris, 1852): translator.

A.P. Stanley, *Sinai and Palestine in Connection with Their History* (London, 1856): editor.

An Atlas of Ancient Geography, Biblical and Classical (London, 1874): editor.

Mendelssohn's Psalms [in English with piano accompaniment] (London, *c.* 1876): translator and editor.

Taylor, Franklin, *Primer of Pianoforte Playing* (London, 1877): editor.

A Dictionary of Music and Musicians (London and New York, 1879–89): editor.

Analytical notes and addresses

Analytical notes, Crystal Palace Concerts 1856–96.

Analytical notes, Richter concerts at St James's Hall, May 1879–96.

Preface to the programme of J.S. Bach, *St Matthew Passion* (Bach Society, 'second public performance').

'Beethoven Symphonies': Introduction to the performance of the nine symphonies at the Richter concerts commencing 10 May 1880.

'A Few Words of the Successive Editions of Beethoven's Ninth Symphony' *Proceedings of the Musical Association*, 1894–95. Paper read on 12 February 1895.

'Explanatory Notes by Sir George Grove CB' for a performance of Handel's Israel in Egypt, Windsor, 26 March 1896.

'Sir George Grove's Address, 30 October 1897', *Report of the Third Annual Old Boy's Social Evening, St Michael and All Angels Boy's School, Lower Sydenham*, 21 November 1897.

Address at Sydenham High School for Girls, 4 April 1895, *Sydenham, Forest Hill and Penge Gazette*, 4 April 1895.

Articles and reports in the press

On the Floating of the First Tube of the Britannia Bridge, by 'a correspondent' under 'The Provinces', *Spectator*, 23 June 1849.

'On a Song in The Princess', *Shilling Magazine*, 3, February 1866.

'Tears, Idle Tears', *Macmillan's Magazine*, November 1866.

'The New Testament under New Aspect', *Macmillan's Magazine*, September 1869.

'Mr Deutsch and the Edinburgh Review', *Macmillan's Magazine*, August 1873.

On opening the Sacred Harmonic Society season, *Daily News*, 27 September 1881.

Concerning a map by the Palestine Exploration Fund, *Pall Mall Gazette*, 25 October 1881.

[Unsigned] Obituary Notice of John Scott Russell, *The Times*, 10 June 1882.

On the derivation of the name of Phoenix Park, Dublin, *St James's Gazette*, 6 October 1883.

In response to a criticism of Sullivan's departure from 'serious music', *Pall Mall Gazette*, 16 October 1883.

Concerning a complete and trustworthy edition of Schubert, *Pall Mall Gazette*, 30 November 1883.

Concerning an error in the Authorized Version of Proverbs 1.17, *Pall Mall Gazette*, 4 December 1883.

'The secret of sir Michael Costa's Success' by a correspondent, *Pall Mall Gazette*, 1 May 1884.

On Brahms' Fourth Symphony, *St James's Gazette*, 10 May 1886.

On Brahms's Fourth Symphony, *St James's Gazette*, 12 May 1886.

On suburban commuter transport, *St James's Gazette*, 10 June 1886.

Poor attendance at Hallé – Neruda concert, *St James's Gazette*, 14 June 1886.

Comment on *The Times* account [14 June] of the opening of a new organ, *St James's Gazette*, 15 June 1886.

'A blunder in The Spectator', *St James's Gazette*, 5 August 1886.

'A Country Church', *St James's Gazette*, 27 September 1886.

'The History of a Musical Phrase Attempted', *Musical World*, serially from 2 October 1886 to 14 May 1887.

On Sullivan's *The Golden Legend, St James's Gazette*, 8 October 1886.

On [Beethoven's] 'C minor Symphony', *Musical World*, 3 November 1888.

On a performance of Schubert's 'Waldesnacht', *St James's Gazette*, 8 February 1887.

On a performance of Schubert's *Ganymede*, *St James's Gazette*, 23 February 1887.

On German press responses to the music of Sullivan, *St James's Gazette*, 23 April 1887.

Obituary of C.F. Pohl, *The Times*, 11 May 1887.

'Beethoven' [unsigned review of Nottebohm: *Zweite Beethovenian*], *Musical Times*, June 1887.

Address to the College of Organists, *Musical World*, 10 September 1887.

'On Beethoven C minor Symphony', *Musical World*, 3 November 1888.

'Canon by Mendelssohn', *Musical World*, 1 December 1888.

'Beethoven's Marches', *Musical World*, 29 December 1888.

'A Letter of Beethoven's', *Musical World*, 19 October 1889.

'Royal College of Music Scholarships', *Musical Herald*, April 1891.

'Madame Sophie Lowe's Concert', *Pall Mall Gazette*, 6 May 1891.

'The Birds in the Pastoral Symphony', *Musical Times*, special Beethoven issue, 15 December 1892.

'English Music', *Strand Musical Magazine*, February 1895.

Obituary of George Watson, unsigned, *The Times*, 18 January 1896.

'Madame Schumann' by a special contributor', *Scottish Musical Record*, June 1896.

[Appreciation of] 'Joseph Joachim', *Musical Times*, April 1898.

'Mendelssohn's *Overture* to 'A Midsummer Night's Dream,' *Musical Times*, 1903, pp.728–38.

'Mendelssohn's *Hebrides* Overture', *Musical Times*, 1905, pp.531–3.
'Mendelssohn's Violin Concerto', *Musical Times*, 1906, pp.611–15.
'Mendelssohn's Oratorio 'St Paul', *Musical Times*, 1909, pp.92–4.

Letters to the Editor

The *Spectator*

1853	11 June 'Sebastian Bach's Music ('Constant Reader')
1890	4 October 'The Cat's Toilette'
1891	21 October 'Lord Rodney'
1892	5 November 'Crossing the Bar'
1893	27 May 'Beethoven'
1894	3 February 'Links with the Past'
1894	30 June Declaration on the Inspiration of the Scriptures
1895	19 January 'A French Whittaker'
1897	16 October 'Rossini and Beethoven'

The Times

1860	5 September 'The Holy Plays in Bavaria'
1864	7 March 'Jerusalem Explored'
1864	21 March [Pierotti's 'Jerusalem']
1865	3 January [Palestine Exploration]
1865	21 February [Mendelssohn's 'Trumpet Overture']
1866	17 January, 12 February, 21 February, 20 March, 3, 9, 23 April, 21 May [Palestine Exploration Fund]
1867	5 August, 26 September, 14 November, 4 December [Palestine Exploration Fund]
1867	3 September 'Titian's "Peter Martyr"'
1869	7 January 'A Discovery in Jerusalem'
1870	10 February/24 March 'On the Moabitish Antiquities'
1871	10 November 'The Survey of Palestine'
1873	15 August 'The Palestine Exploration Fund'
1874	14, 19 October; 2, 17 December. 'Palestine Exploration'
1875	5 August 'The Palestine Exploration'
1877	28 March 'Palestine Exploration'
1878	8 January 'Welsh Nomenclature'
1878	4 February 'La Marseillaise' and 'God Save the Queen'
1881	27 June 'St. Mark's, Venice'
1881	28 September 'Another Unknown Symphony by Schubert' (also published in *Daily News*)
1881	19 October 'Schubert's Missing Symphony'
1882	21 November 'A Musical Explorer'
1882	25 November 'The Sacred Harmonic Society Library'
1883	21 May 'An Incident for the Psychic Society'
1883	14 August 'Imagery in the Psalms'
1883	6 November 'The Song of Schubert'
1885	10 September 'September Primroses'
1885	10 December 'A Concerto by Beethoven'

1886 16 June 'The Dream of St Jerome'
1886 6 December 'New Musical Publications'
1886 7 December 'The Performance of Oratorios'
1887 9 February 'The Crystal Palace'
1887 4 October 'A Symphony by Richard Wagner'
1888 30 January 'The Royal College of Music'
1889 29 June 'Warning about a Person calling himself Dr Heinrich Pauer'
1889 18 September 'Grattan Cooke and Mendelssohn'
1889 2 October 'The Schubert Monument in Vienna'
1889 28 October 'Leeds Festival'
1890 4, 15 March 'Madame Arabella Goddard'
1890 27 March 'The Arabella Goddard Concert'
1891 26 February 'An Interesting Event in English Musical History'
1891 15 September 'The Autographs of Beethoven's Manuscripts'
1891 22 December 'Facsimiles of Beethoven's Works'
1892 12 September 'The Gloucester Festival Band'
1892 14, 22 October 'Timbuctoo' and 'Jehoshaphat' [sic]
1893 17 January 'St Mary's Oxford'
1894 11 September 'Mendelssohn and Schumann'
1897 2 August 'Shakespeare and the Thrush's Song'

Pall Mall Gazette

1870 18 April 'A Conscientious Parish Clerk'

Musical World

1876 19 February 'Mr Manns and Flamingo'

Daily News

1881 28 September 'Another Unknown Symphony by Schubert' (also published in *The Times*)

The Athenaeum

1881 19 November 'Schubert's Gastein Symphony'

St James' Gazette

1886 2 November 'Brahms and Beethoven'
1887 21 February 'Persian Hyperbole'
1890 29 January 'The Encore Nuisance'

Daily Graphic

1890 31 July 'Education in Music in Ireland'

Strathearn Herald

1895 27 April 'Letter to J. Maxtone Graham'

Sunday Times

1896 26 April 'The Lamoureux Concerts'

Leeds Mercury

1896 12 October 'The Normal Diapason Pitch'

Sydenham, Forest Hill and Penge Gazette

1897 25 September/ 4 October 'Some Sydenham Disappearances'

Notes

1 Based on the list in Percy M. Young, *George Grove. A Biography* (London, 1980), pp.299–313, with additions.

2 Young, *George Grove*, p.299.

Appendix 2: Crystal Palace Programme-Note Writers

compiled by Christina Bashford

The following list derives from information contained in programmes at the Royal College of Music, London (the Library and Department of Portraits and Performance History), the British Library, London, Manchester Central Library (the Henry Watson Library), and Bromley Central Library, and contains data on notes supplied for Crystal Palace concerts between 1856 and 1900. Because none of these libraries contains a full set of Crystal Palace programmes for the whole period, some gaps in coverage remain.

The list is divided into five sections, as follows: (1) notes by Grove; (2) notes by Manns; (3) notes by Barry; (4) notes by other identifiable note-writers; (5) notes by unidentified note-writers. The range of years over which notes for a particular composition appeared are indicated as, for example, 1876–90: this does not mean, however, that they necessarily appeared in each year of this range. More detailed information including precise dates of concerts, lists arranged alternatively by work and by concert, and data on the many works that received unsigned notes, is to be found in a database located electronically at http://www.brookes.ac.uk/music/cplists.

1. George Grove ('G.')

Composer	Work	Dates
Auber	Overture, *Masaniello*	1874–90
Bach	Brandenburg Concerto No.3	1883–7
	Brandenburg Concerto No.4	1885
	Brandenburg Concerto No.5: 1st movement	1896
	Christmas Oratorio: Pastoral Symphony and Cradle Song	1874
	My Spirit was in Heaviness (cantata)	1875
	Organ Prelude and Fugue in E minor	1870
	Organ Prelude and Fugue 'St Anne'	1870
	Orchestral Suite No.1 in C	1875
	Orchestral Suite No.2 in B minor	1876–94
	Orchestral Suite No.3 in D	1872
Granville Bantock	Overture, *The Fire Worshippers*	1893
Barclay Jones	Symphony No.1 in C minor	1896
J.F. Barnett	Offertoire for organ	1888
Herbert Bedford	Prelude, *Kit Marlowe*	1898
Beethoven	'Adelaide' (air)	1874
	Allegro con brio for violin and orchestra in C WoO5	1879

	Choral Fantasia, op.80	1887–99
	'Die Ehre Gottes in der Natur' (song)	1877
	Egmont: incidental music	1869–87
	'Es blüht ein Blümlein' (romance for soprano and harp)	1888
	King Stephen: Chorus of Maidens	1874
	'Liederkreis', op.98 (*An die ferne Geliebte*)	1870
	Mass in C	1875
	'Mit Mädeln sich vertragen' (aria)	1888
	Overture, *Coriolan*	1870–1900
	Overture, *Die Weihe des Hauses*	1870–73
	Overture, *Egmont*	1869–98
	Overture, *Fidelio*	1870–98
	Overture, *King Stephen*	1871–4
	Overture, *Leonora* No.1	1870–91
	Overture, *Leonora* No.2	1868–97
	Overture, *Leonora* No.3	1868–98
	Overture, *Namensfeier*	1873
	Overture, *Prometheus*	1886–99
	Piano Concerto No.1 in C	1870–91
	Piano Concerto No.2 in B flat	1870–91
	Piano Concerto No.3 in C minor	1870–96
	Piano Concerto No.4 in G	1869–98
	Piano Concerto No.5 in E flat	1870–98
	Prometheus: ballet music	1869
	'Remorseless Friend' (recit/aria from *Fidelio*)	1880
	Rondo for piano and orchestra in B flat WoO6	1872
	Septet, op.20	1871–4
	String Quartet, op.18/5: Andante cantabile + variations	1878
	Symphony No.1 in C	1869–98
	Symphony No.2 in D	1869–99
	Symphony No.3 in E flat 'Eroica'	1868–98
	Symphony No.4 in B flat	1868–98
	Symphony No.5 in C minor	1869–99
	Symphony No.6 in F 'Pastoral'	1868–98
	Symphony No.7 in A	1869–1900
	Symphony No.8 in F	1870–98
	Symphony No.9 in D minor 'Choral'	1869–99
	The Mount of Olives (oratorio)	1868–90
	The Praise of Music (cantata), op.136	1873
	The Ruins of Athens: Overture and incidental music	1870
	Triple Concerto, op.56	1874
	32 Variations for piano in C minor	1882–3
	Violin Concerto (including arr. for piano and orchestra)	1869–99
	Violin Sonata in A, op.47 'Kreutzer'	1872–8
W.H. Bell	Symphonic Prologue, *The Canterbury Tales*	1898
Julius Benedict	Moderato and Allegro in C; Scherzo in A	1875
	Piano Concerto No.2 in E flat	1877
	Symphony in G minor	1873

George Bennett	Serenade in Symphonic Form in A	1887
W.S. Bennett	Overture, *Parisina*	1875–93
	Overture, *The Naiads*	1871–99
	Prelude and Funeral March to Sophocles's *Ajax*	1880
	Symphony in G minor, op.43	1875–95
Berlioz	*Hamlet: Marche funèbre*, op.18/3	1889–91
	Harold in Italy	1878–93
	La damnation de Faust: excerpts	1880–99
	L'enfance du Christ	1886
	Overture, *Benvenuto Cellini*	1871–97
	Romeo et Juliette: 'Queen Mab scherzo'	1880
W.T. Best	Festival Overture in C	1876
Bizet	*Roma* (suite No.3 for orchestra)	1880
Boieldieu	Overture, *Les deux nuits*	1874
J.H. Bonawitz	Piano Concerto in A minor, op.36	1880
Brahms	Hungarian Dances for orchestra	1874
	Piano Concerto No.1 in D minor	1872–99
	Serenade No.1 in D	1873
	Serenade No.2 in A	1875
	Song of Destiny, op. 54	1874–97
	Symphony No.1 in C minor	1877–91
	Symphony No.2 in D	1878–98
	Variations on a theme by Haydn, op.56a	1874–83
	Violin Concerto	1879–1900
J.F. Bridge	Overture, *La morte d'Arthur*	1889
Dora Bright	Piano Concerto No.1 in A minor	1891
Ignatz Brüll	Piano Concerto No.1	1881
	Piano Concerto No.2 in C, op.24	1878
Herbert Bunning	*Village Suite*, op.45	1896
Miss E.A. Chamberlayne	Scherzo, 'Ariel', for strings, harp and flute	1895
Cécile Chaminade	Concertstück for piano and orchestra	1896
	Suite, *Callirhoë*	1896
Cherubini	Concert Overture in G	1892–3
	Overture, *Ali Baba*	1872
	Overture, *Anacréon*	1870–95
	Overture, *Faniska*	1873–86
	Overture, *Les abencérages*	1872
	Overture, *Les deux journées*	1870–83
	Overture, *Lodoiska*	1873–85
	Overture, *Médée*	1869–77
Chopin	Grand Fantasia on Polish airs for piano and orchestra	1880
	Piano Concerto No.1 in E minor	1879–96
	Piano Concerto No.2 in F minor	1881–98
Frederic Cliffe	Symphony No.1	1889–99
C.H. Couldery	Overture, *To the Memory of a Hero*	1890
W.G. Cusins	Overture, *Love's Labours Lost*	1875
Eugen D'Albert	Prelude, *Der Rubin*	1896
Francis Davenport	Prelude and Fugue for orchestra	1879
Delibes	Suite, *Sylvia*	1879–88

Dvořák	Slavonic Dances, op.46	1883
	Symphony in D, op.60	1882
Rosalind Ellicott	Dramatic Overture	1891
Gade	Overture, *Nachklänge von Ossian*	1895
	Violin Concerto in D, op.56	1886
Henry Gadsby	Overture, *The Witches' Frolic*	1874
	Symphony in D 'Festal'	1888
Edward German	Dances from *Henry VIII*	1892–3
	Marche solennelle	1893
	Overture, *Richard III*	1890
Friedrich Gernsheim	Violin Concerto in D, op.42	1880
F.A. Gevaert	Overture, *Le billet de Marguerite*	1876
Paul Gilson	*La mer*	1897
Benjamin Godard	*Concerto romantique* in A minor, op.35	1888
Goetz	Symphony in F, op.9	1879–99
	Violin Concerto in G	1880
Goldmark	Overture, *Sakuntala*	1889–96
	Symphony 'The Country Wedding'	1878–88
Georg Goltermann	Cello Concerto in B minor	1883
Gounod	*Le tribut de Zamora*: ballet airs	1881
	Overture, *La nonne sanglante*	1875
	Roméo et Juliette: ballet music	1891
	Symphony No.2 in E flat	1871
Grieg	Overture, *In Autumn,* op. 11	1888–96
	Suite for orchestra, op.46	1889
Johan Halvorsen	*The Triumphal Entry of the Boyards*	1896
Handel	'Arioso' (from *Alcina*), arr Helmesberger	1880
	'Chandos' Te Deum	1876
	Concerto for harp or organ, op.4/6	1885–7
	Concerto for keyboard op.4/4 in F	1875–95
	Concerto for oboe, op.3/2 in B flat	1878
	L'allegro, il penseroso ed il moderato	1874
	'Nasce al bosco' (aria from *Ezio*)	1874
	Ode on St Cecilia's Day	1869
	'Ombra mai fui' [largo] (aria from *Serse*: for voice, also arr for instruments)	1878–88
	Overture, *Ariadne*	1885
	Overture, *Esther*	1874
	Overture, *Giustino*	1891
	Overture, *Semele*	1892
	'Where'er you walk' (aria from *Semele)*	1889–96
Hasse	'Mea tormenta' (aria from *Maddalena*)	1875
Haydn	Cello Concerto in C	1894
	Cello Concerto in D	1894
	Symphony No.44 in E minor	1874
	Symphony No.73 in D 'La chasse'	1879
	Symphony No.84 in E flat	1875–97
	Symphony No.85 in B flat 'La reine'	1894
	Symphony No.88 in G	1872–8
	Symphony No.92 in G 'Oxford'	1869–92

	Symphony No.93 in D	1876–86
	Symphony No.94 in G 'Surprise'	1881
	Symphony No.96 in D	1873
	Symphony No.97 in C	1874
	Symphony No.98 in B flat	1871–80
	Symphony No.99 in E flat	1869–90
	Symphony No.101 in D 'The Clock'	1885
	Symphony No.102 in B flat	1871–98
	Symphony No.104 in D	1872–92
	The Creation	1882
George Henschel	Serenade for strings, op.23	1878
Adolf Henselt	Piano Concerto, op.16	1891–5
Arthur Hervey	Overture in G	1892
Henry Hiles	Overture, *Youth*	1893
Ferdinand Hiller	Piano Concerto in F sharp minor, op.69	1876–9
Heinrich Hofmann	*An Italian Love Story*	1881
	Frithjof Symphony, op.22	1879
Hummel	Piano Concerto in B minor, op.89	1877
Humperdinck	*Hänsel und Gretel*: Traum-Pantomime	1895
Joachim	Theme and Variations for violin and orchestra	1880–84
	Violin Concerto in D minor, op.11 'In the Hungarian Style'	1872–89
	Violin Concerto in G	1875
Joncières	*Sérénade hongroise*	1884
August Klughardt	Cello Concerto in D, op.59	1896
Lachner	Suite No.6, op.150	1875
Henry Leslie	Symphony in D 'Chivalry'	1881
Litolff	*Concerto-symphonique* No.3 in E flat	1874–83
Hamish MacCunn	*Lord Ullin's Daughter*	1888–93
	Overture, *The Dowie Dens o' Yarrow*	1888–92
	Overture, *The Land of the Mountain and the Flood*	1887–98
	Suite, *Highland Memories*, op.30	1897
G.A. Macfarren	Overture, *Joseph*	1877
	Overture, *King David*	1884
	Violin Concerto	1875
W.C. Macfarren	Overture, *Othello*	1896
A.C. Mackenzie	*Benedictus* for orchestra	1888–90
	From the North (3 Pieces for orchestra)	1895
	Highland Ballad for violin and orchestra, op.47/1	1894
	Jason: Recit, Air and Intermezzo	1882
	Scherzo for orchestra	1879
	Scottish Rhapsody No.2	1881
	The Little Minster: 3 entr'actes	1898
Charles Macpherson	Overture, *Cridhe an Ghaidhil*	1895
Massenet	*Esclarmonde*: Interlude	1889
	Le Cid: ballet music	1886
	Manon: Minuet	1884
Mendelssohn	*A Midsummer Night's Dream*: incidental music	1874–81
	Duet for clarinet and bassett horn	1868

	Elijah	1871
	Fugue for strings, op.81/4	1876
	Hymn of Praise, op.52	1870–98
	'Infelice/Ah ritorno' (concert aria, op.94)	1870–72
	Loreley (opera): excerpts	1868–91
	Octet, op.20	1869–95
	Organ Sonata No.1 in F minor	1870
	Organ Sonata, op.65/6 in D major/minor	1871
	Overture, *A Midsummer Night's Dream*	1870–99
	Overture, *Athalie*	1870–96
	Overture, *Calm Sea and Prosperous Voyage*	1869–93
	Overture, *Die schöne Melusine*	1875–95
	Overture, *The Hebrides*	1868–99
	Overture, *Ruy Blas*	1871–97
	Overture, *St Paul*	1872–81
	Overture, *Son and Stranger*	1870–82
	Overture in C, op.24	1874–85
	Piano Capriccio in F sharp minor, op.5	1871–83
	Piano Concerto No.1 in G minor	1870–96
	Piano Concerto No.2 in D minor	1879–85
	Psalm 42	1872
	Psalm 95	1874–6
	St Paul	1872–89
	Serenade and Allegro Giojoso, op.43	1877–80
	String Symphony No.11 in F: Adagio in E flat	1877–82
	Surrexit Pastor, op.39/3	1874
	Symphony No.1 in C minor	1871–7
	Symphony No.3 in A minor 'Scotch'	1868–99
	Symphony No.4 in A 'Italian'	1871–1900
	Symphony No.5 in D minor 'Reformation'	1875–90
	The Evening Bell for piano and harp	1876
	The First Walpurgis Night	1870–91
	'Trumpet Overture', op.101 (in C)	1868–92
	Violin Concerto in E minor	1869–1900
Moscheles	Piano Concerto No.3 in G minor, op.60	1875
Mozart	Adagio in E for violin and orchestra K261	1885
	Clarinet Concerto: Adagio	1885
	'Ma che vi fece/Sperai vicino' (recit/aria)	1878–82
	'Non temer' (recit/aria)	1895
	Overture, *Die Zauberflöte*	1873–98
	Overture, *Don Giovanni*	1875–96
	Overture, *Idomeneo*	1890
	Overture, *Il Seraglio/ Die Entführung*	1875
	Overture, *La vilanella rapita*	1873
	Overture, *Le nozze di Figaro*	1869–71
	Piano Concerto No.18 in B flat K456	1871
	Piano Concerto No.20 in D minor K466	1869–97
	Piano Concerto No.23 in A K488	1872
	Piano Concerto No.25 in C K503	1876
	Piano Concerto No.26 in D 'Coronation' K537	1872–85
	Piano Concerto No.27 in B flat K595	1872

	Sinfonia Concertante for oboe, clarinet, horn and bassoon in E flat	1887
	Sinfonia Concertante for violin and viola in E flat	1883
	Symphony No.26 in E flat	1872
	Symphony No.31 in D 'Paris'	1868–92
	Symphony No.35 in D 'Haffner'	1877–94
	Symphony No.36 in C 'Linz'	1879–90
	Symphony No.38 in D 'Prague'	1869–84
	Symphony No.39 in E flat	1871–99
	Symphony No.40 in G minor	1872–95
	Symphony No.41 in C 'Jupiter'	1871–97
	Thamos, King of Egypt: music (selection)	1883
	Violin Concerto in D K218	1874
Paganini	Violin Concerto 'Le streghe'	1886
Parry	Overture, *Guillem de Cabestanh*	1879
	Piano Concerto in F sharp major	1880–95
	Symphony in G	1883
Piatti	Cello Concerto in D minor, op.26: Andante and Finale	1882
H.H. Pierson	Overture, *As you like it*	1874
Godfrey Pringle	*Durand* (ballad for orchestra)	1893
Ebenezer Prout	Magnificat	1876
	Overture to Scott's *Rokeby*	1889
	Symphony in C	1874
	Symphony No.2 in G minor	1877
	Symphony No.3 in F	1885
Raff	Cello Concerto in D, op.193	1876–89
	Overture, 'Ein feste Burg ist unser Gott'	1876
	Piano Concerto in C minor, op.185	1885
	Symphony No.3 in F 'Im Walde', op.153	1878–93
	Symphony No.5 in E 'Lenore', op.177	1881–98
	Symphony No.8 in A 'Frühlingsklänge'	1879
	Symphony No.9 in E minor 'In Summer-time'	1880
	Violin Concerto in B minor, op.161	1877
Reinecke	*In memoriam*: Introduction, Fugue and Chorale	1878
	Overture, *Friedensfeier*	1872
Rheinberger	Piano Concerto in A flat op.94	1878
Ries	Piano Concerto in C sharp minor	1882
Julius Rietz	Clarinet Concerto, op.29	1887
Hermann Ritter	Concerté-fantasie for viola-alta No.2	1897
Rossini	Messe solennelle	1869
	Mosè in Egitto: ballet music	1877
Rubinstein	*The Demon*: ballet music	1878
	Feramors: ballet music	1876–81
Saint-Saëns	Cello Concerto No.1 in A	1880–98
	Fête populaire (from *Henry VIII*)	1884
	La jota aragonese	1890
	Piano Concerto No.2 in G minor	1889
	Piano Concerto No.3 in E flat	1879
	Variations on a theme of Beethoven for 2 pianos	1879

Schubert	*Der Hirt auf dem Felsen*	1894
	Deutsche Tänze	1888
	'L'adieu' (song)	1880
	Octet	1874–80
	Overture, *Des Teufels Lustschloss*	1880
	Overture, *Fierrabras*	1872–92
	Overture, 'In the Italian Style' in C	1874
	Overture, *Rosamunde*	1890–93
	Psalm 23	1888–94
	Quartet in D minor 'Death and the Maiden': Slow movement	1871
	Quartettsatz: Allegro	1876
	Rosamunde: incidental music	1868–92
	Symphony in C (originally, op.140)	1876
	Symphony No.1 in D	1880–81
	Symphony No.2 in B flat	1877–81
	Symphony No.3 in D	1881
	Symphony No.4 in C minor 'Tragic'	1870–81
	Symphony No.5 in B flat	1873–81
	Symphony No.6 in C	1868–81
	Symphony No.7 in E minor/E major (including completion by J.F Barnett)	1883–4
	Symphony No.8 in B minor 'Unfinished'	1868–1900
	Symphony No.9 in C [later listed as No.10 in C]	1867–1900
Schumann	Cello Concerto, op.129	1880
	Concertstück in G, op.92	1892
	Festival Overture	1876
	Manfred: music (selection)	1874
	Overture, *Genoveva*	1870–97
	Overture, *Hermann and Dorothea*	1869
	Overture, *Manfred*	1871–93
	Overture, Scherzo and Finale, op.52	1871–1900
	Overture, *The Bride of Messina*	1872–80
	Piano Concerto in A minor	1869–99
	Symphony No.1 in B flat	1869–99
	Symphony No.2 in C	1872–97
	Symphony No.3 in E flat	1876–98
	Symphony No.4 in D minor	1878–98
	Violin Fantasia, op.131	1881
Eduard Schutt	Piano Concerto in G, op.7	1882
Shakespeare	Concert Overture in D	1873
Edouard Silas	Elegy for piano and orchestra, op.34	1873
	Piano Concerto No.4 in B minor, op.116	1892
Spohr	Overture, *The Fall of Babylon*	1876
	Overture, *Jessonda*	1877–90
	Symphony No.1 in E flat	1874
	Symphony No.2 in D minor	1872
	Symphony No.4 'Die Weihe der Töne'	1871–90
	Symphony No.6 'Historical'	1870
	Violin Concerto No.6: movements	1875–81
	Violin Concerto No.7 in E minor, op.38	1874–96
Spontini	Overture, *Olympie*	1876–82

Stanford	Festival Overture in B flat	1877
	Symphony in B flat	1879
	The Veiled Prophet: Overture and ballet music	1882
Sullivan	Overture, *Di Ballo*	1870–98
	Overture, *In Memoriam*	1875–94
	Overture to Scott's *Marmion*	1874
	Symphony No.1 in E 'Irish'	1876–99
	The Light of the World: Introductions to parts 1 and 2, and selections	1873–96
	The Tempest: selection	1881
Svendsen	*The Carnival at Paris*, op.9	1880–92
Tchaikovsky	Piano Concerto No.2 in G [no analysis]	1890
Vieuxtemps	Violin Concerto No.4 in D minor, op.31	1881–7
Charles Vincent	Overture, *The Storm*	1897
Robert Volkmann	Overture, *Richard III*	1875
Wagner	'Faust' Overture in D minor	1874–94
Weber	Clarinet Concerto No.2, op.74	1874–86
	Overture, *Der Freischütz*	1870–98
	Overture, *Euryanthe*	1870–94
	Overture, *Jubilee*	1874–83
	Overture, *Oberon*	1870–99
	Symphony No.2 in C	1875–86
Widor	Symphony No.2 in A	1887
Wieniawski	Violin Concerto No.2 in D, op.22	1883–91
Thomas Wingham	Concert Overture	1875
	Symphony in B flat	1872

2. August Manns ('A.M.')

Composer	Work	Dates
Uberto Bandini	*Eleonora* (symphonic poem)	1881
Woldemar Bargiel	Overture, *Prometheus*	1867
Beethoven	*Fidelio*	1859
	Prometheus: ballet music (selection)	1863
	Overture, *Namensfeier*	1869
	Symphony No.3 in E flat 'Eroica'	1861–2
	Symphony No.7 in A	1865–6
	Symphony No.9 in D minor 'Choral'	1865–8
W.S. Bennett	Overture, *The May-Queen*	1871–8
	Overture, *The Woodnymph*	1874
Berlioz	Overture, *Béatrice et Bénédict*	1877
	Overture, *Les francs-juges*	1870–95
	Symphonie funèbre et triomphale [with W.G.]	1882
Bizet	Suite, *Carmen*	1891
Brahms	Academic Festival Overture	1881–94
	Serenade No.1 in D: selection	1863
	Tragic Overture	1881–97
Louis Brassin	Piano Concerto in F	1878
Bruch	Prelude, *Loreley*, op. 16	1877
	Violin Concerto No.1 in G minor	1870–99
	Violin Concerto No.2 in D minor	1877

Chabrier	*España*	1888
F.H. Cowen	Suite, *In the Olden Times*	1883
Ferdinand David	Violin Concerto No.5 in D minor	1865
Delibes	Scène du bal (*Le roi s'amuse*)	1886
Dvořák	Overture, *My Home*	1883
Gade	Overture, *Hamlet*	1873
	Overture, *Michael Angelo*	1870
	Symphony No.5	1860
Gluck	Overture, *Iphigénie en Aulide*	1878–98
Gounod	'Méditation' for violin and orchestra	1873
Handel	*Acis and Galatea*	1865–84
	Theodora	1874
Haydn	Symphony No.78 in C minor	1878
Ferdinand Hiller	Overture, *Demetrius*	1870
	Symphonie phantasie	1872
	Symphony in E minor, op.67 'Spring is Coming'	1870–71
Heinrich Hofmann	Hungarian Suite in F	1877
Alfred Holmes	Overture, *Le Cid*	1874
C.E. Horsley	Overture, *Euterpe*	1876
Lalo	*Symphonie espagnole*	1878–95
Liszt	*Hunnenschlacht*	1877
	Mazeppa	1876–86
A.C. Mackenzie	*La belle dame* (ballad for orchestra)	1884
Mendelssohn	*Loreley* (opera): Finale	1867–98
	Overture, *Calm Sea and Prosperous Voyage*	1866
	Symphony for strings in F minor	1878
	The Wedding of Camacho: ballet music	1881
	The Wedding of Camacho: selection	1871
Meyerbeer	Overture, *Struensee*	1876–85
Moszkowski	Six Character Pieces for orchestra	1886
Mozart	*L'impresario* (opera)	1861–5
	Symphony No.39 in E flat	1865
Popper	Cello Concerto in E minor, op.24	1891
Ferdinand Praeger	Prelude, *Manfred*	1880
Purcell	Yorkshire Feast Song	1877
Raff	Suite in C, op.101: Adagietto and Scherzo	1870
Julius Rietz	Festival Overture	1873
	Overture, *Lustspiel*	1873
Rossini	Overture, *Semiramide*	1867
Rubinstein	Adagio and Scherzo for orchestra [supplementary movements to Symphony in C, op.42]	1869
	Bal costumé, op.103	1885
	Don Quixote	1872–7
	Nero (ballet-divertissement)	1881
	Overture, *Dimitri Donskoi*	1875–94
	Symphony in C, op.42 'The Ocean'	1882
	Symphony No.5 in G minor, op.107 'Russian'	1881–95
	The Grape (ballet)	1884
Philippe Rufer	Violin Concerto, op.33	1881

Saint-Saëns	*Etienne Marcel*: ballet airs	1885–8
	La jeunesse d'Hercule	1877
	Le rouet d'Omphale	1879–98
Schubert	*Rosamunde*: incidental music & ballet airs	1866–7
Schumann	Overture, *Genoveva*	1866–9
	Overture, *Manfred*	1866
	Overture, *The Bride of Messina*	1865
	Symphony No.1 in B flat	1860
	Symphony No.2 in C	1866–8
	Symphony No.3 in E flat	1870–73
	Symphony No.4 in D minor	1869–75
Sgambati	Symphony in D	1882
Smetana	*Overture to a Comedy*	1884–8
	Vltava	1881–98
	Vysehrad	1882
Spohr	Violin Concerto No.9 in D	1877–93
Spontini	Overture, *Nurmahal*	1873
Sullivan	Symphony No.1 in E 'Irish'	1866
	The Merry Wives of Windsor: music	1884–6
Svendsen	*Rhapsodie norvégienne* No.3	1879
Ambroise Thomas	*Le roman d'Elvire*	1878
Vieuxtemps	Violin Concerto No.6 in G, op.47	1882
Wagner	*Parsifal*: Klingsor's Magic Garden and The Flower Maidens	1887
	Siegfried Idyll	1879–98
Thomas Wingham	Concert Overture No.4 in F	1878–93
	Symphony No.4	1883

3. Charles Ainslie Barry ('C.A.B.')

Composer	**Work**	**Dates**
Bach	Violin Concerto in A minor	1900
	Violin Concerto in E	1898
Antonio Bazzini	*Concertstück* for cello and orchestra, op.81	1892
	Overture, *King Lear*, op.68	1880
W.H. Bell	Symphony in C minor 'Walt Whitman'	1900
	The Pardoner's Tale	1899
Berlioz	*Faust*	1888–96
	Grande messe des morts	1883
	*La mort d'Ophélie, op.*18/2	1891
	Overture, *King Lear*	1883–99
	Overture, *Le corsaire*	1884–96
	Overture, *Rob Roy*	1900
	Overture, *Waverley*	1884–90
	Roméo et Juliette	1884–94
	Te Deum	1885
Bizet	Egyptian Dance (from *Djamileh*)	1893
Brahms	Piano Concerto No.2 in B flat	1882–91
	Symphony No.3 in F	1884–96
	Symphony No.4 in E minor	1889–99

Bruch	Violin Concerto No.3 in D minor	1892–5
Richard Burmeister	Piano Concerto in D minor	1891
	The Chase after Fortune	1894
Coleridge-Taylor	Ballad for orchestra in A minor, op.33	1898
Cornelius	Overture, *Barber of Bagdad*	1892
C.H. Couldery	Fantasia for trumpet and organ	1898
F.H. Cowen	Concert Overture in D	1886
D'Albert	Piano Concerto in A: Allegro moderato	1882
	Piano Concerto No.2 in E	1895–6
D'Indy	*The Enchanted Forest*, op.8	1896
Thomas Dunhill	Valse Fantasia for flute and orchestra	1899
Auguste Dupont	Piano Concerto in F minor, op.49	1883
Dvořák	Cello Concerto in B minor, op.104	1896–7
	Heroic Song, op. 111	1899
	Mass in D, op.86	1893
	Notturno for strings, op.40	1885–93[1]
	Overture, *Carneval*, op.92	1894–8
	Overture, *In der Natur*	1896
	Piano Concerto in G minor, op.33	1883
	Scherzo capriccioso, op.66	1884–91
	Symphony in F, op.76	1888
	Symphony in G, op.88	1893
	Violin Concerto, op.53	1888
Elgar	*Caractacus*: procession music	1898
	Sevillaña, op.7	1899
Field	Piano Concerto in A flat	1878
Gade	Violin Capriccio	1893
Edward German	*Fantasia on March Themes*	1898
	Hamlet	1897
Benjamin Godard	Violin Concerto No.2 in G minor, op.131	1899
Goldmark	Overture, *Im Frühling*	1890–96
	Overture, *Sappho*	1894
	Symphony No.2, op.35	1888
Georg Goltermann	Cello Concerto No.1 in A minor, op.14	1891
Grieg	Norwegian Dances, op.35	1892
	Peer Gynt: Suite No.1	1897
	Peer Gynt: Suite No.2	1893
	2 String Melodies, op.53	1892
Ernest Guiraud	Caprice for violin and orchestra	1900
Joseph Holbrooke	*The Raven* (symphonic poem)	1900
Jeno Hubay	'Hejre Kati' (from *Scènes de la Csárda*, op.32)	1892
Joachim	Notturno in A	1899
Julius Klengel	Cello Concerto, op.20	1893
	Concert Overture, op.35	1900
Lalo	Cello Concerto in D	1899
Frederic Lamond	Symphony in A	1890
Liszt	*Angelus* for strings (*'Prière aux anges'*)	1892
	Festklänge	1889–95

[1] Notes for 1884 and 1890 signed 'A.B' are almost certainly also by Barry

	Hungarian Rhapsody No.1	1892–6
	Hungarian Rhapsody No.4	1883–6
	Interlude, *Salve Polonia*	1884
	Les préludes	1884–94
	'Rakoczky' March	1886
	St Elizabeth [with J.B.]	1886
	Tasso	1892
	Totentanz for piano and orchestra	1890
MacDowell	Piano Concerto No.2	1900
A.C. Mackenzie	Overture, *Britannia*	1894
	Overture, *Twelfth Night*	1888–99
	Prelude, *Colomba*, op.28	1892
	Scotch Rhapsody No.1 in G, op.21	1883–95
	The Rose of Sharon: selection	1884
Charles Maclean	Pageant March	1898
Otto Manns Jr	Scherzo capriccioso	1899
G.W.L. Marshall Hall	Concert Overture	1893
	An Idyl [sic] for orchestra	1898
Mascagni	*Cavalleria rusticana*: Intermezzo	1892
Massenet	Cello Fantasia	1898
Maud Matras	Polish Sketches, op.9	1898
Méhul	Overture, *La chasse de jeune Henri*	1891–4
Moszkowski	*Boabdil*, op.49: selection	1892–3
	Violin Concerto in C, op.30	1894
Mozart	Violin Concerto No.5 in A K219	1884–93
J.L. Nicodé	*Faschingsbilder* suite, op.24: selection	1893
Paderewski	Piano Concerto, op.17	1890
Popper	Cello Concerto No.3 in G, op.59	1892–5
Raff	Symphony No.2 in C, op.140	1881
	Symphony No.10 in F minor, op.213 'Zur Herbstzeit'	1883
	Symphony No.11, op.214 'Winter'	1885
Jean Renard	Cello Concertino	1899
Rimsky-Korsakov	*Capriccio espagnol*	1900
	Mlada: dances	1896
Bernhard Romberg	Cello Concerto No.9: 1st movement	1899
Jacob Rosenhain	Piano Concerto in D, op.73	1890
Saint-Saëns	*Introduction and Rondo Capriccioso*, op.28	1892–8
	Piano Concerto No.4 in C minor	1890–98
	Violin Concerto No.3 in B minor, op.61	1891–7
Scharwenka	Piano Concerto No.3 in C sharp minor	1899
Bernhard Scholz	Symphony in B flat, op.60	1889
Schumann	*Song of Night*, op.108	1898
	Symphony No.4 in D minor [1st version, 1841] [with G.]	1841 1892
Sinding	Symphony in D minor, op.21	1896
Hans Sitt	Cello Concerto in A minor, op.34	1890
	Overture, *Don Juan d'Austria*, op.20	1891
Stanford	Serenade in G, op.18	1883
	Symphony No.4 in F, op.31	1889

Reginald Steggall	Suite for orchestra No.2	1899
Richard Strauss	*Also sprach Zarathustra*	1897
	Symphony in F minor, op.12	1896
	Till Eulenspiegel	1896–8
Sullivan	Overture, *The Sapphire Necklace*	1899
	The Merchant of Venice (masque)	1900
Tchaikovsky	*Capriccio italien*, op.45	1885–90
	Suite, *The Sleeping Beauty*	1900
	Symphony No.3 in D	1899
	Symphony No.5 in E minor	1895
Robert Volkmann	Cello Concerto in A minor, op.33	1886–1900
Wagner	*Das Rheingold:* Entry to Valhalla	1894–6
	Die Meistersinger: Introduction to Act 3	1890–97
	Die Meistersinger: Introduction to Act 3; Dance of the Apprentices; Closing Scene	1895
	Die Walküre: Ride of the Valkyries	1878–95
	Die Walküre: Wotan's Abschied & Feuerzauber	1885
	'Faust' Overture in D minor	1900
	Götterdämmerung: Siegfried's Journey to the Rhine (orchestrated Humperdinck)	1899
	Huldingungsmarsch	1900
	Kaisermarsch	1883–96
	Lohengrin: Introduction to Act 3	1892
	Lohengrin: Prelude	1890–98
	Parsifal: 'Charfreitagszauber'	1883–99
	Parsifal: 'Verwandlungsmusik' and Closing Scene	1885
	Parsifal: Prelude	1882–98
	Rienzi: Overture	1900
	Siegfried: 'Waldweben'	1882–99
	Tannhäuser: Act 3	1891–3
	Tannhäuser: Introduction to Act 2 and Elisabeth's Greeting	1890
	Tannhäuser: Introduction to Act 3	1886–92
	Tannhäuser: Overture	1897–1900
	Tannhäuser: Elisabeth's Prayer	1892
	The Flying Dutchman: Overture	1875–97
	The Flying Dutchman: Overture; Acts 2 and 3	1895
	Tristan: 'Isolde's Liebestod'	1883–95
	Tristan: 'Isolde's Verklärung'	1885
	Tristan: 'Nachtgesang' (from Act 2)	1893
	Tristan: Prelude	1883–96
William Wallace	*Anvil or Hammer* (symphonic prelude)	1896
	Overture, *In Praise of Scottish Poesie*	1894
	Prelude, *The Eumenides of Aeschylus*	1893
	Sister Helen (symphonic poem)	1899
	The Passing of Beatrice (symphonic poem)	1892
André Wormser	*Les lupercales*, op.5 ('Fêtes de Pan')	1892

4. Other Identified Note-Writers

Composer	Work	Dates
W.A. Barrett ('W.A.B.')		
Berlioz	*Symphonie fantastique*	1881–91
Antonio Bazzini		
Bazzini	Overture, *Saul*	1877
Joseph Bennett ('J.B.') – notes mostly reprinted from other programme books		
Bruch	*Kol nidrei* for cello and orchestra	1891
	Scottish Fantasy for violin and orchestra	1897
Frederic Cliffe	*Cloud and Sunshine*	1890
	Violin Concerto in D minor	1896
F.H. Cowen	Symphony No.3 in C minor 'Scandinavian'	1881–91
Dvořák	Symphony in D minor, op.70	1885
	Symphony in E minor, op.95 'From the New World'	1894–8
Henry Gadsby	*The Forest of Arden*	1887
Edward German	Suite in D minor	1895
	Symphony No.2 in A minor	1893
F.K. Hattersley	Concert Overture in E minor	1887
George Henschel	*Hamlet* suite, op.50	1893
Liszt	*St Elizabeth* [with C.A.B.]	1886
G.A. Macfarren	*St John the Baptist* (oratorio)	1875
	The Lady of the Lake (cantata)	1878
A.C. Mackenzie	Pibroch for violin and orchestra, op.42	1892
Parry	*L'allegro ed il pensieroso* (cantata)	1890
Sullivan	Overture, *Macbeth*	1891–8
Tchaikovsky	Symphony No.6 in B minor 'Pathétique'	1898–1900
Oscar Beringer ('O.B.')		
Chopin	Allegro de concert in A, op.46 for piano and orchestra	1880
Rubinstein	Piano Concerto No.3 in G, op.45	1876–80
George Case		
Schütz	*Lamentatio Davidis*	1890
Frederick Corder ('F.C.')		
Berlioz	*Lélio*	1881–7
Edward Dannreuther ('E.D.')		
Grieg	Piano Concerto	1874–1900
Liszt	Piano Concerto No.1 in E flat	1872–99
	Piano Concerto No.2 in A	1874–99
Rubinstein	Piano Concerto No.4 in D minor	1872–1900
Scharwenka	Piano Concerto No.1 in B flat minor, op.32	1877–98
Tchaikovsky	Piano Concerto No.1 in B flat minor, op.23	1876–97
Wagner	Overture, *Rienzi*	1872–97
	Prelude, *Die Meistersinger*	1884–1900

J.W. Davison ('J.W.D.')

W.S. Bennett	Piano Concerto No.1 in E flat	1872
	Piano Concerto No.3 in C minor	1878–82
	Piano Sonata 'Maid of Orleans'	1873

J. Dibdin

Hamish MacCunn	*The Cameronian's Dream*	1890–92

J.A. Fuller Maitland ('J.A.F.M.')

Lalo	Overture, *Le roi d'Ys*	1889
Saint-Saëns	*Phaéton*	1889

Francis Hueffer ('F.H.') - Notes reprinted from Philharmonic Society programmes

F.H. Cowen	Symphony No.4 in B flat minor 'Welsh'	1884[2]
A.C. Mackenzie	*La belle dame* (ballad for orchestra)	1885–96

W.Y. Hurlestone

Léon Boëllmann	Symphonic Variations for cello and orchestra, op.23	1898

George A. Macfarren ('G.A.M.')

J.F. Barnett	Overture, *A Winter's Tale*	1873–8
W.S. Bennett	Overture, *The Merry Wives of Windsor*	1876
	Piano Concerto No.4 in F minor	1874–9
W.G. Cusins	Overture, *Les travailleurs de la mer*	1875
Henry Gadsby	Intermezzo and Scherzo	1876
Alfred Holmes	Overture, *Ines de Castro*, op.42	1877
Joachim	Elegiac Overture	1878–94
Walter Macfarren	Overture, *Hero and Leander*	1881
Cipriani Potter	Overture, *Cymbeline*	1871
Rubinstein	Piano Concerto No.5 in E flat, op.94	1878

John Henry Mee ('J.H.M.')

Ebenezer Prout	Symphony No.4 in D	1887

Friedrich Niecks

Liszt	*The Ideals*	1881–6

Hubert Parry ('C.H.H.P.')

Goetz	Piano Concerto in B flat, op.18	1880
Rubinstein	Symphony No.4 in D minor, op.95 'Dramatique'	1880

Ebenezer Prout ('E.P.')

Hans von Bronsart	Piano Concerto in F sharp minor	1876
Haydn	Symphony No.100 in G 'Military'	1876

[2] This note was wrongly attributed to 'F.H.C' (i.e. Frederic Cowen) in the Crystal Palace Programme; see Frederic H. Cowen, *My Art and my Friends* (London, 1913), pp.127–8.

Raff	Suite in E flat for piano and orchestra, op.200	1877
Rubinstein	Symphony in C, op.42 'Ocean'	1877–9
Saint-Saëns	*Marche héroïque*, op.34	1876
Tchaikovsky	Overture, *Romeo and Juliet*	1876
Verdi	String Quartet in E minor	1877
Wagner	Festival March	1876
	Götterdämmerung: Siegfried's Death	1876–98
Weber	Overture, *Peter Schmoll*	1875
	Piano Concerto No.2 in E flat, op.32	1875
J.S. Shedlock ('J.S.S.')		
Raff	Symphony No.4 in G Minor, op.167	1875
	Symphony No.6 in D minor, op.189	1882
Ethel Smyth ('E.M.S.')		
Ethel Smyth	Serenade in D	1890
C.E. Stephens ('C.E.S.')		
Thomas Wingham	Serenade in E flat: Andante espressivo	1891
John Stainer ('J.S.')		
Henry Gadsby	Organ Concerto in F	1874
Ebenezer Prout	Organ Concerto in E minor	1872
Sidney P. Waddington ('S.P.W.')		
Ferdinand Dunkley	*The Wreck of the Hesperus*	1894
Dvořák	Overture, *In der Natur*	1894
	Overture, *Otello*	1894
H.K. Hofmann	Concertstück for flute and orchestra, op.98	1894
Joseph Hollman	Cello Concerto in A minor, op.12	1890
Saint-Saëns	Piano Fantasia 'Africa'	1894

5. Unidentified Note-Writers

Composer	Work	Dates
'M.B.'		
Dvořák	*The Wild Dove*	1900
Vieuxtemps	Violin Concerto No.5 in A minor, op.37	1900
'P.R.'		
Goldmark	*Merlin*: *Geisterreige*	1890
Raff	Violin Concerto No.2 op.206	1890
Saint-Saëns	*Ascanio* (ballet)	1890
Wagner	Finale to *Meistersinger*	1890
'W.G.'		
Berlioz	*Symphonie funèbre et triomphale* [with note by A.M.]	1882
Goldmark	Airs from *Königin von Saba*	1882

Ebenezer Prout	*Alfred* (cantata)	1883
	Alftruda's scena 'Hereward'	1880

'W.-S.'

Ferdinand Praeger	Fantasia in F for orchestra	1886
	Life and Love, Battle and Victory	1885

Appendix 3:

Grove's Programme Note on Beethoven's Symphony No. 5 in C minor for the Nineteenth Saturday Concert of the Crystal Palace Season 1879–80 (Editor)

SYMPHONY IN C MINOR No. 5 (Op. 67) . *Beethoven.*

1. Allegro con brio. C minor, 2-4.
2. Andante con moto. A flat, 3-8.
3. Allegro (Scherzo). C minor, 3-4 : Allegro (Finale), C major, 4-4.

We have now arrived at the fifth of Beethoven's Symphonies. It forms, in a certain sense, the climax of them—not that it is so great or so profound as the Ninth, or even perhaps as the Eroica ; but there is about it an energy, an audacity, an unexpectedness, which seem, perhaps, more directly typical of the man than anything else that he has left, and would probably cause most persons, when the name of Beethoven is mentioned, to think immediately of the C minor Symphony. A striking proof of the truth of this is found in the fact that Mendelssohn, of whose judgment on such a point there can be no question, did choose the C minor Symphony to introduce Beethoven to Goethe, who, though he had known the composer personally, knew nothing of his music till Mendelssohn's visit to Weimar in 1830. This distinct personality (if we may so style it) no doubt arises in great measure from the extraordinary nature of the opening subject. Learned doctors tell us that the well-known four notes which open the Symphony are only part of a longer and more extended subject. But whether this be true or not, certain it is that to the mass of hearers

is the real subject—the germ, the animating soul of the whole movement. It is this which strikes the ear like no other phrase in music, and at once rivets the attention beyond the power of the will. And this audacity once aroused can never be quenched till the last bar of the movement. The magical group of notes forces itself in at every moment. And we shall see that even the second subject—a suave and peaceful theme—is compelled to submit to its inroads. And herein does this movement furnish a true picture of its author, who, on the testimony of his most delicate pupils, though ugly, rough, and often hateful, could also be noble, cultivated, and sympathetic, and make every-one doat on him.

The C minor Symphony, though now known and fixed as No. 5, was not always so. In the programme of the first concert at which it was performed—22nd December, 1800, in the Vienna Theatre—it is not only preceded by the Pastoral Symphony, but is given as No. 6 ; while the Pastoral—now No. 6—is designated as No. 5. And the same thing was done in Vienna as late as 1813. The two were composed or completed, together, during the summer of 1808—as the two later twins, Nos. 7 and 8, were in that of 1813, and as the third pair would have been in 1817 had they ever come to the birth —had Beethoven's offer to Ries for the Philharmonic Society been carried out. But there is no doubt that the C minor has the priority of the two. True, the autograph manuscript, once in the possession of Felix Mendelssohn, and still in the hands of his family, bears neither date nor number, and has simply the words

"Sinfonie da L. v. Beethoven"

scrawled on it in red chalk. But that of the Pastoral Symphony is numbered 6th both in Italian and German, in Beethoven's own hand. And the score and parts of each, published in April, 1809, are numbered as we are accustomed to.

The two were brought out together, and each is jointly dedicated to the Prince Lobkowitz and Count Rasumowsky, noblemen who held a high place among Beethoven's patrons. The Prince's name appears on the title page of the Eroica Symphony, of the first six String Quartets, and of the Quartet in E flat (Op. 74); while the Count enjoys a safe eternity in the three immortal works which will be known as the "Rasumoffsky Quartets" as long as there are four artists in the world capable of playing them.

There is no doubt that the C minor Symphony had occupied the mind of its composer longer than the Pastoral. The actual composition of the first two movements appears to date from 1805, the time when Beethoven was also at work on the Pianoforte Concerto in G major;* and we have the authority of Mr. Thayer† for the fact that the themes of both the *Allegro con brio* and the *Andante* were noted down as early as 1800 or 1801. As the first Symphony, so different in its gentle grace to the vigorous abruptness of the No. 5, was written in 1800, this is very remarkable.

In speaking of the opening notes of the work (quoted above) some years after its composition, Beethoven is reported to have said, *So pocht das Schicksal an die Pforte*—"That is how fate knocks at the door;" and the phrase is a fitting text for a movement so full of the struggle of life—of conflicts, and victories, and laments, and triumphs, and every emotion that can affect the spirit of man, except happiness. One has neither the obligation nor the temptation, as in the case of some of the other Symphonies, to attach any definite meaning to the music,

* Nottebohm, in the new Thematic Catalogue, p. 61. This accurate investigator has elsewhere pointed out (Beethoveniana, p. 10) that the same rhythm exists in the first movements of both these works.

† *Chronologisches Verzeichniss*, p. 75.

or to construct any picture out of it. It is enough that it touches one's deepest and most sombre feelings, and carries one along unresistingly on its tremendous current. That the actual notes above quoted were those of a bird which Beethoven heard in the Prater is quite possible; but, as in the case of the four notes which form the groundwork of the *Allegro* of the Violin Concerto, and were suggested by the repeated knocks of a man shut out of his house in the dead of the night, the fact only shows how vast is the transmuting power of the imagination. This theme has been finely compared to the magic ball of the fairy story, which opens at the word of command, and produces whole kingdoms and nations, with cities, villages, mountains, rivers, armies, and myriads of people.

Allegro con brio.—The two subjects which provide the materials for this movement are as follows—first the opening one:—

No. 1.

—and next the counter-theme, a simple phrase of eight notes beginning at (*a*)—introduced by the Horn, and accompanied by the Basses in the rhythm of the former one:—

No. 2.

It is given out by the Violins, and is repeated first by the Clarinet and then by the Oboe.

These two subjects furnish all the material for the *Allegro*. In the first movement of the Eroica we noticed the occurrence of an "episode"—a distinct melody, not included or implied in either of the two main subjects; and in that of the No. 4 Symphony there was the same—a beautiful melody of four bars, having no relation to the principal themes, but introduced *de novo*, and repeated five times consecutively. But in the present case there is nothing of the sort, all the phrases are either repetitions of the whole or parts of the main theme, or are constructed out of them; and the workmanship is as close and solid as possible throughout. That so concise a treatment is consistent with the expression of the most tremendous emotion no one need be told who knows the Symphony.

As an instance of the crude and common-place form in which ideas that were ultimately to become his boldest first entered Beethoven's head, we quote the first of the above two subjects (No. 1) as it appears in the sketch book in its earliest form :—

No. 3. *Sinfonie, Allegro presto.*

The *Andante con moto* is in the key of A flat (as that of Mozart's G minor is in the key of E flat). The subject is given out by the Tenors and Cellos in unison, with a simple accompaniment, *pizzicato*, in the Double Basses :—

No. 4.

This is followed by a phrase for the Flutes, Oboes, Clarinets, and Bassoons, with its echo in the Violins :

No. 5.

There is then a second melody, which at first appears to be meant as a second strain to the first theme :--

No. 6.

—though it negatives that idea by ending in C major. The whole of the movement consists of repetitions of these three themes, with varieties in their forms and accompaniments. On the last repetition of that quoted as No. 5, Beethoven, by a slight alteration of the notes, a trifling extension of the phrase, and a management of *nuance* all his own, has produced one of the most pathetic and beautiful effects possible :

No. 7.

—immediately after this touching farewell, as if ashamed of being seen with the tears on his cheek, he urges the Basses into crescendo arpeggios, and ends the movement with a loud crash and an ordinary cadence.

The drollery of the *Andante* is almost as striking as its grace ; and nowhere is this more conspicuous than in a place where Beethoven has indulged his humour and his caprice by stopping the flow of the melody for eight bars to introduce a passage of mere pleasantry; which to those who first heard it must have seemed mere vanity and vexation of spirit, though we should now be very sorry to spare it.

No. 8.

Other passages of the same kind occur in the *Andante*—all examples of that determination to do what he liked, of which we noted an early instance in the first movement of the second Symphony. But none are so flagrant as that we have quoted.

"The *Scherzo*," says M. Berlioz, "is an extraordinary composition ; the very opening :—

No. 9.

—though containing nothing terrible in itself, produces the same inexplicable emotion that is caused by the gaze of a magnetiser. A sombre mysterious light pervades it ; the play of the instruments has something sinister about it, and seems to spring from the same state of mind which conceived the scene on the Blocksberg in Faust. A few bars only are *forte—piano* and *pianissimo* predominate throughout. In the second theme the triple rhythm of the opening movement reappears :—

No. 10.

The middle of the movement (the 'trio') is founded on a rapid passage for the Double Basses, *fortissimo*, which shakes the Orchestra to its foundation, and irresistibly recalls the gambols of an elephant :—

No. 11.  &c.

but the gamesome beast retires by degrees, and the noise of his antics is gradually lost. The theme of the *Scherzo* reappears, *pizzicato*, the sound diminishing at the same time till nothing is heard but the crisp chords of the Violins, and the droll effect of the upper A flat in the Bassoons rubbing against the G, the fundamental note of the dominant minor ninth. At length the Violins subside on to the chord of A flat, which they hold *pianissimo*. The Drums alone have the rhythm of the subject, which they reiterate with all possible lightness, while the rest of the Orchestra maintains its stagnation :—

No. 12.

The Drums sound C, since C minor being the key of the movement: but the chord of A flat, so long held by the Strings, forces another tonality on the ear, and we are thus kept in doubt between the two. But the Drums increase in force, still obstinately keeping up both note and rhythm; the Fiddles have by degrees also fallen into the rhythm, and at length arrive at the chord of the seventh on the dominant (G), the Drums still adhering to their C. At this point the whole Orchestra — including the three Trombones, hitherto silent—bursts like a thunderclap into C major, and into the triumphal march which forms the commencement of the Finale. The effect of this transition is obvious enough to the ear, though it may be difficult to explain it to the reader. With reference to it, it is sometimes said that Beethoven has, after all, only made use of the common expedient of following a soft passage in the minor by a burst in the major; that the theme of the Finale is not original; and that the interest of the movement diminishes instead of increasing as it goes on. To which I answer that it is no reflection on the genius of a composer that the means he employs are those already in use. Plenty of other composers have used the same expedients, but nothing that they have done can be compared for a moment to this stupendous pæan of victory, in which the soul of Beethoven, for the moment freed from its mortal drawbacks and sufferings, seems to mount to heaven in a chariot of fire. The four first bars of the subject may not be strikingly original, but the forms of the triumphant *fanfare* are but limited, and it is probably not possible to find new ones without forfeiting the simple, grandiose, pompous character which is native to that kind of phrase. But Beethoven evidently did not intend to continue the *fanfare* style after the first few bars, and in the rest of the movement—even as early as the conclusion of the first subject (see No. 15) —he quickly resumes the lofty and original style which never forsakes him. As to the interest not increasing as it goes on, the transition from the *Scherzo* to the Finale is probably the greatest effort of which music is at present capable, so that it would be simply impossible to have continued to increase it. And those who thus carp at one of the greatest works of human genius forget what a peculiar charm is given to the movement by the sudden reintroduction of the trio into the midst of it, an expedient most original, and producing an effect which has probably never been surpassed.

It was indeed a prodigious effort even to sustain so lofty a flight; but Beethoven has done it, notwithstanding the extent to which he has developed his subjects. And the mere fact that the beginning and end are equal in effect—which all allow—is, of itself, enough to make the hearer think the reverse, because the tremendous shock of the opening is enough to dwarf what comes after it, just as in a long row of columns the distant ones appear smaller than those in the foreground.

At the worst, the criticism we are noticing refers only to what may be called the *mise en scène* of the Finale, and leaves untouched the fact that the movement is so rich and magnificent that very few pieces would have a chance of being heard after it."

The subject of which we have given the commencement in the last quotation is very long, a burst of melody twenty-four bars in length; it ends in a more definite figure :—

No. 13.

—which again conducts to the second subject proper, in the key of G :—

No. 14.

After this we arrive at the end of the first section. That section is repeated; then comes the working out, in the course of which a most important and effective episode occurs in the re-introduction of the passage quoted in Nos. 12 and 13, with its characteristic rhythm. It is practically the same as that passage, though, except for a few bars at the close, the Drum is omitted; and it forms a most effective preparation for the return of the principal theme (No. 14) and the repetition of the first portion of the movement.

Before concluding, we may say that there is no truth whatever in the story sometimes promulgated that the Finale was originally intended by its author for the Eroica. Such an idea is neither true in fact, nor just in sentiment. The sketch books lend it no countenance, and the Eroica has its own Finale, which to those who hear it aright is a fitter Apotheosis for its hero than that which we are now hearing would be.

The C minor Symphony was last performed at the Saturday Concerts on November 16th, 1878. [G.]

Bibliography

Allcott, K., ed. *The Poems of Matthew Arnold* (New York: Barnes and Noble, 1965).

Allan, D.G.C. *The Houses of the Royal Society of Arts. A History and Guide* (London: Royal Society of Arts, 1866; 2nd edn, 1974).

Arnold, Matthew. *Essays in Criticism*, First Series, ed., with introduction and notes by Sister T.M. Hoctor (Chicago and London, 1964).

Arnold, Matthew. *Culture and Anarchy*, ed. with introduction by J. Dover Wilson (London: 1935; 2nd edn, 1960).

Ashton, Rosemary. *George Eliot. A Life* (London: Hamish Hamilton, 1996).

Bashford, Christina. 'Learning to Listen: Audiences for Chamber Music in Early-Victorian London', *Journal of Victorian Culture*, 4 (1999), pp.25–51.

Bashford, Christina. 'The Late Beethoven Quartets and the London Press, 1836–ca.1850', *Musical Quarterly*, 84 (2000), pp.84–122.

Bashford, Christina. 'John Ella and the Making of the Musical Union', in *Music and British Culture, 1785–1914: Essays in Honour of Cyril Ehrlich*, ed. C. Bashford and L. Langley (Oxford: Oxford University Press, 2000), pp.193–214.

Badura Skoda, E. and Branscombe, P. *Schubert Studies. Problems of Style and Chronology* (Cambridge, Cambridge University Press,1982).

Beaver, Patrick *The Crystal Palace 1851–1936: a Portrait of Victorian Enterprise* (London, 1970; 2nd edn, Chichester: Philimore, 1986).

Bennett, Joseph *Forty Years of Music 1865–1905* (London, 1908).

Bent, Ian, ed. *Music Analysis in the Nineteenth Century*, I: Fugue, Form and Style (Cambridge: Cambridge University Press, 1994).

Black, Alistair, *A New History of the English Public Library: Social and Intellectual Contexts, 1850–1914* (London and New York: Leicester University Press, 1996).

Bonython, Elizabeth. *King Cole: a Picture Portrait* (London: Victoria and Albert Museum, n.d).

Botstein, Leon. *Music and its Public: Habits of Listening and the Crisis of Musical Modernism in Vienna, 1870–1914*, (PhD diss., Harvard University, 1985).

Bradley, G.G. *Recollections of Arthur Penrhyn Stanley* (London, 1883).

Breuning, G. von. *Aus dem Schwarzpanierhaus. Erinnerungen von Ludwig van Beethoven aus meiner Jugendzeit* (Vienna, 1874).

Briggs, Asa. *Iron Bridge to Crystal Palace. Impact and Image of the Industrial Revolution* (London: Thames and Hudson, 1979).

Briggs, Asa. *A Social History of England from the Ice Age to the Channel Tunnel* (new edn., London: Weidenfeld and Nicolson, 1994).

Brightwell, G.W.E. *The National Training School for Music 1873–1882: Catalyst or Cul-de-Sac?* (University of Durham MA thesis, 1998).

Brown, Maurice J. *Schubert. A Critical Biography* (London, 1958).

Brown, Maurice J. *Essays on Schubert* (London, 1966).

Browning, Robert. *The Poetical Works of Robert Browning* [The Oxford Edition], 8 vols (Oxford: Clarendon, 1983–2001).

Byatt, Antonia. *The Biographer's Tale* (London: Chatto & Windus, 2000).

Buckler, William E. *Prose of the Victorian Period* (Boston, 1958).

Clark, Edwin. *The Britannia and Conway Bridges* (2 vols, London, 1850).

Cole, Henry. *Fifty Years of Public Works of Sir Henry Cole KCB* (2 vols, London, 1884).

Colles, H.C. and Cruft, J. *The Royal College of Music: a Centenary Record, 1883–1983* (London [Prince Consort Foundation] 1982).

Colloms, Brenda. *Victorian Visionaries* (London: Constable, 1982).

Creighton, Louise. *Life and Letters of Mandell Creighton*, (2 vols, London, 1904).

Creighton, Louise. *Memoir of a Victorian Woman*, ed. James Thayne Covert (Bloomington: Indiana University Press, 1994).

Curran, Eileen M. 'Verse in Bentley's Miscellany, vols 1–36', *Victorian Periodicals Review*, 32, 2 (Summer 1999), pp.103–59.

Dale, Catherine. 'Towards a Tradition of Music Analysis in Britain in the Nineteenth Century', *Nineteenth-Century British Music Studies*, vol.1, ed. Bennett Zon (Aldershot: Ashgate, 1999), pp.269–302.

Frank Damrosch. *Institute of Musical Art 1905–1926* (New York: Juilliard School of Music, 1936).

Davison, Henry. *From Mendelssohn to Wagner: Memoirs of J.W. Davison* (London, 1912).

Deutsch, Otto Erich, in collaboration with Donald E. Wakeling. *Schubert. Thematic Catalogue of all his Works* (London,1951).

Deutsch, Otto Erich. *Schubert, A Documentary Biography* (London,1946; rept 1977).

Doctor, Jennifer. *The BBC and Ultra-Modern Music, 1922–1936: Shaping a Nation's Tastes* (Cambridge: Cambridge University Press, 1999), pp.66–79. .

Edwards, F.G. *The History of Mendelssohn's Oratorio 'Elijah'* (London, 1896).

Edwards, F.G. 'Sir George Grove C.B.', *Musical Times*, 38, 654 (October 1897), pp.657–64.

Edwards, F.G. 'Schubert's Music in England', *Musical Times*, 38, 646 (February, 1897), pp.81–4.

Ehrlich, Cyril. *The Piano: a History* (Oxford: Clarendon Press, 2nd edn, 1990).

Ehrlich, Cyril. *First Philharmonic: a History of the Royal Philharmonic Society* (Oxford: Clarendon Press, 1995).

Ella, John. *Musical Sketches, Abroad, and at Home* (London, 1869).

Elkin, Robert. *Royal Philharmonic: the Annals of the Royal Philharmonic Society* (London [1946]).

Ernle, R.E. Prothero. *The Life and Correspondence of Arthur Penryhn Stanley, D.D.*, (London, 1893).

Fay, Amy. *Music Study in Germany* (Chicago, 1880).

Fergusson, James. *The Peril of Portsmouth; or, French Fleets and English Forts* (London, 3rd edn, 1853).

Fergusson, James. *Portsmouth Protected: a Sequel to The Peril of Portsmouth* (London, 1856).

Fétis, F.-J. *La musique mise à la portée de tout le monde* (Paris, 1830; 2nd edn, 1834); trans. from 2nd edn as *His Music Explained to the World: or, How to Understand Music and Enjoy its Performance* (Boston, MA: 1842).

Fifield, Christopher. *True Artist and True Friend: a Biography of Hans Richter* (Oxford: Clarendon Press, 1993).

Flood, W.H.G. 'Sir G Grove, C.B., a Centenary Appreciation', *Musical Times*, 61, 931 (September 1920), p.603.

Foster, Myles B. *History of the Philharmonic Society of London 1813–1912* (London, 1912).

Ganz, A.W. *Berlioz in London* (London: Quality Press, 1951).

Gardiner, Juliet, ed. *What is History Today . . . ?* (London: Macmillan, 1988).

Gibbs, Christopher. 'Performances of Grief; Vienna's Response to the Death of Beethoven', *Beethoven and His World*, ed. Scott Burnham and Michael P. Steinberg (Princeton, 2000), pp.227–85.

Gillett, Paula. *Musical Women in England: 'Encroaching on all Man's Privileges' 1870–1914* (New York: St. Martin's Press, 2000).

Gramit, David. 'Constructing a Victorian Schubert: Music, Biography, and Cultural Values', *19th Century Music*, 17 (1993), pp.65–78.
Griest, Guinevere L. *Mudie's Circulating Library and the Victorian Novel* (Bloomington, IN: Indiana University Press, 1970).
Graves, Charles L. *The Life & Letters of Sir George Grove, C.B.* (London, 1903).
Graves, Charles L. *Post-Victorian Music, with Other Studies and Sketches* (London, 1911).
Graves, Charles L. *Hubert Parry. His Life and Works* (London, 1926).
Greenwood, Thomas. *Public Libraries: a History of the Movement, and a Manual for the Organization and Management of Rate-Supported Libraries* (London: Cassell, 4th edn, 1894; rept University Microfilms Ltd, 1971).
Grove, George. ed. E. Blom. *Beethoven, Mendelssohn and Schubert* (London, 1954).
Grove, George. *Geography*, History Primers No. 4, ed. J.R. Green (London, 1877).
Grove, George. *Beethoven's Nine Symphonies: Analytical Essays*, with a preface by Georg Henschel (Boston, 1884).
Grove, George. *Beethoven and his Nine Symphonies* (London and New York, 1896).
Grove, George, ed. *A Dictionary of Music and Musicians*, (*4 vols* [1879, 1880, 1883, 1889] with index; London and New York: Macmillan & Co., 1890).
Grove's Dictionary of Music and Musicians: 2nd edition, ed. J.A. Fuller Maitland (5 vols, London and New York, Macmillan & Co., 1904–10); 3rd edition, ed. H.C. Colles (5 vols, London and New York: Macmillan & Co., 1927); 4th edition, ed. H.C. Colles (5 vols, with supplement, London and New York: Macmillan & Co., 1940); 5th edition, ed. E. Blom (9 vols, London and New York: Macmillan & Co., 1954); Supplement, ed. D. Stevens (London: Macmillan, 1961).
Grove's World. An Exhibition to Mark the Centenary of the Death of Sir George Grove (1820–1900), handlist prepared by Peter Horton (London: Royal College of Music, 2000).
Gunn, Simon. 'The Sublime and the Vulgar: the Hallé Concerts and the Constitution of 'High Culture' in Manchester c.1850–1880', *Journal of Victorian Culture*, 2 (1997), pp.208–28.
Haight, Gordon S. *George Eliot. A Biography* (Oxford: Oxford University Press, 1968).
Hall-Witt, Jennifer L. 'Representing the Audience in the Age of Reform: Critics and the Elite at the Italian Opera in London', in *Music and British Culture, 1785–1914: Essays in Honour of Cyril Ehrlich*, ed. Christina Bashford and Leanne Langley (Oxford: Oxford University Press, 2000), 121–44.
Hallé, Charles. *Life and Letters of Sir Charles Hallé, Being an Autobiography (1819–1860)* with Correspondence and Diaries, ed. C.E and M. Hallé (London, 1896).
Hanslick, Eduard, trans. Henry Pleasants. *Music Criticisms 1846–99* (Harmondsworth: Penguin, 1963).
Hogarth, George. *The Philharmonic Society of London from its Foundation, 1813, to its Fiftieth Year, 1863* (London, 1862).
Houghton, Walter E. ed., *Wellesley Index to Victorian Periodicals, 1824–1900*, (5 vols, Toronto: University of Toronto Press, 1966–89).
Howes, Frank. *The English Musical Renaissance* (London, 1966).
Hueffer, Francis. 'The Chances of English Opera,' *Macmillan's Magazine*, XL, 235 (May 1879), pp.57–65.
Hullah, John. 'Report to the Lords of the Committee of Council on Education, on the Examination in Music of the Students of Training Colleges in Great Britain', *Musical World*, 5 November 1881.
Irving, Howard. *Ancients and Moderns: William Crotch and the Development of Classical Music* (Aldershot: Ashgate, 1999).
Jacobs, Arthur. *Arthur Sullivan* (Oxford: Oxford University Press, 1984; 2nd edn, 1986).

Kinsky, Georg, ed. Halm, Hans. *Das Werk Beethovens. Thematisch-bibliographisches Verzeichnis seiner sämtlischen vollendeten Kompositionen* (Munich, 1955).
Kneschke, Emil. *Das Conservatorium der Musik in Leipzig. Seine Geschichte, seine Lehrer und Zöglinge*, Festgabe zum 25jährigen Jubiläum zum 2. April 1868 (Leipzig, [1872]).
Kreissle, Heinrich von Hellborn. *Franz Schubert* (Vienna, 1965).
Kreissle, Heinrich von Hellborn,trans. A.D Coleridge, *The Life of Schubert* (London, 1869).
Kingsley, F. ed. *Charles Kingsley: His Letters and Memories of His Life* (London, 1877).
Krebiel, H.E. *The Philharmonic Society of New York; A Memorial* (New York, 1892).
Lawrence, Arthur. *Sir Arthur Sullivan – Life Story, Letters and Reminiscences* (London, 1899).
Lehmann, R.C. *Memories of Half a Century, a Record of Friendship* (London, 1908).
Lewis, Ruby M. 'The Educational Functions of the Royal Liverpool Philharmonic Society, 1840–1990' (PhD diss., University of Liverpool, 1998).
Lipman, V.D. 'The Origins of the Palestine Exploration Fund', *Palestine Exploration Quarterly*, 20 (January–June 1988), pp.45–54.
MacKenzie, John S. *The Victorian Vision. Inventing New Britain* (London: Victoria and Albert Museum, 2001).
Mackerness, E.D. *A Social History of English Music* (London, 1964).
Maine, Charles Sumner, 'A Conservatoire of Music for England: Report of Prince Christian's Executive Committee Since its Foundation by the Prince of Wales', *Macmillan's Magazine*, XLI, 242 (November 1879), 145–53.
McVeigh, Simon. 'The Society of British Musicians (1834–1865) and the Campaign for Native Talent', in *Music and British Culture, 1785–1914: Essays in Honour of Cyril Ehrlich*, ed. Christina Bashford and Leanne Langley (Oxford: Oxford University Press, 2000), pp.145–68.
Mitchell, Sally ed. *Victorian Britain. An Encyclopedia* (New York and London: Garland Publishing Inc., 1988).
Mulhauser, F.L., ed., translations ed. J. Turner. *The Poems of Arthur Hugh Clough* (Oxford: Clarendon Press, 2nd edn, 1974).
Musgrave, Michael. *The Musical Life of the Crystal Palace* (Cambridge: Cambridge University Press, 1995).
Musgrave, Michael. 'Leighton and Music', in *Frederic Leighton, Antiquity, Renaissance, Modernity*, ed. T. Barringer and L. Prettejohn, Studies in British Art (New Haven and London: Yale University Press, 1999), pp.295–314.
Musgrave, Michael. 'Costa and Manns' Changing Values in Performance',in *Music and British Culture 1785–1914. Essays in Honour of Cyril Ehrlich*, ed. C. Bashford and L. Langley (Oxford: Oxford University Press, 2000), pp.169–92.
Napier, James. *Life of Robert Napier of West Shandon* (Edinburgh, 1904).
The New Grove Dictionary of Music and Musicians, ed. S. Sadie (20 vols, London: Macmillan, 1980); *The New Grove Dictionary of Music and Musicians II*, ed. S. Sadie (29 vols, London: Macmillan, 2001).
Nottebohm, Gustav. *Thematisches Verzeichniss der im Druck erschienenen Werke von Ludwig van Beethoven* (Leipzig, 2nd edn, 1868; rev. 1968).
Palgrave, Francis Turner. *The Golden Treasury of the Best Songs and Poems in the English Language*, selected and arranged with notes by Francis Turner Palgrave (London, 1861).
Parry, C. Hubert H. 'Sir George Grove, 1894', College Addresses delivered to Pupils of the Royal College of Music, ed. H.C. Colles (London, 1920).
Pritchard, Ada. *Charles Pritchard. Memoirs of his Life* (London, 1897).
Prictor, Megan. 'To Catch the World: Percy Scholes and the English Musical Appreciation Movement, 1918–1939', *Context: a Journal of Music Research*, 15–16 (1998), pp.61–71.
Raven, James. 'From Promotion to Proscription: Arrangements for Reading and Eighteenth-Century Libraries', in James Raven, Helen Small, and Naomi Tadmor,

eds. *The Practice and Representation of Reading in England* (Cambridge: Cambridge University Press, 1996) pp.175–201.
Raven, James, Small, Helen and Tadmor, Naomi, eds. *The Practice and Representation of Reading in England* (Cambridge: Cambridge University Press, 1996).
Richards, Robin. *Two Bridges over Menai* (Cardiff, 1945).
Reicha, Antoine. *Traité de mélodie* (Paris, 1814) and *Cours de composition musicale* (Paris, 1818: trans. London, *c.* 1860).
Reid, Thomas S. *Trinity Church Bermuda: a Sketch of Its History Drawn from Various Sources* (Bermuda, 1886).
Ricks, Christopher, ed., *The Poems of Tennyson*, 3 vols (London: Longman and University of California Press, 1969; 2nd edn, 1987).
Rolfe, W.J. *The Complete Poetical Works of Tennyson* [Cambridge Edition] (Cambridge, MA, 1898).
'Royal College of Music', *Musical Times*, 26, 484 (1 June 1883), pp.309–10.
Russell, Dave. 'Musicians in the English Provincial City: Manchester, c.1860–1914', in *Music and British Culture, 1785–1914: Essays in Honour of Cyril Ehrlich*, ed. Christina Bashford and Leanne Langley (Oxford: Oxford University Press, 2000), pp.233–53.
'Samuel Coleridge-Taylor', *Musical Times*, 50, 793 (March 1909), pp.153–58.
Scholes, Percy A. 'The Annotated Programme', in *The Mirror of Music, 1844–1944: a Century of Musical Life in Britain as Reflected in the Pages of the Musical Times* (*2 vols*, London, 1947), I, pp.216–18.
Scholes, Percy A. 'Annotated Programmes', in *The Oxford Companion to Music* (London, 1938), pp.36–7.
Scholes, Percy A. *The Appreciation of Music by Means of the 'Pianola' and 'Duo-Art'* (London, 1925).
Scholes, Percy A. *The Columbia History of Music through Ear and Eye* (London, 1930–38).
Scott, Rosemary. 'Poetry in the Cornhill Magazine: Thackeray's Influence', *Victorian Periodicals Review*, 32, 3 (Fall 1999), 269–74.
Shaw, George Bernard. 'Grove's Beethoven and his Nine Symphonies', *Saturday Review* (14 November 1896).
Shedlock, J.S. 'Analytical Programmes', *Musical Times*, 38, 655 (1897), pp.593–6.
Sherr, Richard. 'Schubert, Sullivan and Grove', *Musical Times*, 121 (1980), pp.499–500.
Simeone, Nigel. 'The Analytical Programme Note': Exhibition Handlist (Faculty of Music, University of Cambridge, 26–29 September 1986).
'Sir George Grove's Autobiography', *Musical Herald*, 628 (1 July 1900), pp.195–7.
Smith, William. *A Dictionary of the Bible, Concerning its Antiquity, Biography, Geography and Natural History* (3 vols, London, 1860–63).
Smith, William. *A Smaller Dictionary of the Bible* (London, 1866).
Solie, Ruth A. 'Beethoven as Secular Humanist: Ideology and the Ninth Symphony in Nineteenth-Century Criticism', in *Explorations in Music, the Arts, and Ideas; Essays in Honor of Leonard B.Meyer*, ed. Eugene Narmour and Ruth A. Solie (Stuyvesant, NY, 1988), pp.1–42.
Stainer, J. and Barrett, W.A. eds. *A Dictionary of Musical Terms* (London, 1876).
Stanford, Charles Villiers. *Interludes, Records and Reflections* (London, 1922).
Stanford, Charles Villiers. *Pages from an Unwritten Diary* (London, 1914).
Sullivan, Herbert and Flower, Newman. *Sir Arthur Sullivan* (London, 1927; 2nd edn, 1950).
Sutherland, John. *Stanford Companion to Victorian Fiction* (Stanford: Stanford University Press, 1989).
Temperley, Nicholas, ed. *The Lost Chord: Essays on Victorian Music* (Bloomington, IN: Indiana University Press, 1989).

Terry, R.C. ed. *Oxford Reader's Companion to Anthony Trollope*. (Oxford: Oxford University Press, 1999).
Thayer, Alexander Wheelock. *Ludwig van Beethovens Leben,* i–iii ed. and trans. H. Deiters (Berlin, 1866–79;); iv–v ed. H. Riemann (Leipzig, 1907–8); 2nd edn, 1901; 3rd edn, 1917; Eng. orig. ed. H.E. Krehbiel (New York, 1921) rev. E. Forbes as *Thayer's Life of Beethoven* (Princeton, 1964, 2nd edn, 1967).
Thompson, F.M.L. *Chartered Surveyors: the Growth of a Profession* (London, 1968).
Tovey, Donald Francis. *Essays in Musical Analysis: Chamber Music,* ed. Hubert J. Foss (London, 1944).
Tovey, Donald Francis and Parratt. G. *Walter Parratt, Master of the Music* (London, 1941).
Trollope, Anthony. *An Autobiography*, ed. Allen Booth Bradford (Berkeley, LA, 1947).
VanArsdel, Rosemary T. '*Macmillan's Magazine* and the Fair Sex, 1859–1873'. *Victorian Periodicals Review,* 33, 4 (Winter 2000), pp.374–96 [Part 1]; 34, 1 (Spring 2000), pp.2–15 [Part 2].
Vann, J. Don and VanArsdel, Rosemary T., eds. *Victorian Periodicals and Victorian Society* (Toronto: University of Toronto Press, 1994).
Vann, J. Don and VanArsdel, Rosemary T., eds. *Periodicals of Queen Victoria's Empire* (Toronto: University of Toronto Press, 1996).
Weber, William. *Music and the Middle Classes* (London: Croom Helm, 1975).
Weber, William. *The Rise of Musical Classics in 18th Century England. A Study in Canon, Ritual and Ideology* (Oxford, 1992).
Werner, Eric, trans. D. Newlin. *Mendelssohn. A New Image of the Composer and his Age* (New York, 1963).
Wilshere, Jonathan. *William Gardiner of Leicester (1770–1853): Hosiery Manufacturer, Musician and Dilettante* (Leicester: Leicester Research Services, 1970).
Wyndham, H. Saxe. *August Manns and the Saturday Concerts* (London and New York, 1908).
Young, Percy M. *George Grove, 1820–1900. A Biography* (London: Macmillan, 1980).
Young, Percy M. 'Grove, Sir George', *The New Grove Dictionary of Music and Musicians*. ed. S. Sadie, (20 vols, London: Macmillan, 1980), 7, pp.752–5; see also: 'Grove, Sir George', *The New Grove II* (29 vols, London: Macmillan, 2001).

Index

Lightning Source UK Ltd.
Milton Keynes UK
UKHW022148260221
379474UK00003B/323

9 780333 948040